Gnostic Return in Modernity

Gnostic Return in Modernity

CYRIL O'REGAN

STATE UNIVERSITY OF NEW YORK PRESS

Published by
State University of New York Press, Albany

Printed in the United States of America

For information, address State University of New York Press,
90 State Street, Suite 700, Albany, NY 12207

Production by Diane Ganeles
Marketing by Patrick Durocher

Library of Congress Cataloging-in-Publication Data

O'Regan, Cyril, (date)
    Gnostic return in modernity / Cyril O'Regan.
      p. cm.
    Includes bibliographical references and index.
    ISBN 0-7914-5021-X (alk. paper) — ISBN 0-7914-5022-8
(pbk. : alk. paper)
      1. Gnosticism—History.   I. Title.

BT1390.O74 2001
299'.932—dc21   00-049300

10 9 8 7 6 5 4 3 2 1

Dedicated to Ger Meehan

Of the roads that led from your green
room and their soft vanishing borders
only one of which led to me,

all are kissed. I fold a blue page
over a bouquet of absences,
the morning promises of a child
that would dream and not wake.

Some nights I spy those shadows,
directions' excess, distances traveled
back there before morning. I play

the game of cataloguing the selves
that might have been, or the game
plays me with its metaphysical hand.

Each morning I wake to the miracle
of the fabulously familiar.

Contents

Acknowledgments

The creation of this book constitutes no exception to the rule that a text is always a chorus of voices and a work of more than one hand. In this text the voices of three Yale friends, David Kelsey, Wayne Meeks, and Gene Outka resound. Their support of this text and others on the return of Gnosticism in the modern period has been as unconditional as their correction has been insightful and persuasive. In addition, the editorial hand of Gene Outka is on every page. He was assiduous, even heroic, in his efforts to get me to write in something like English prose. I am grateful also to Jim Dittes for his kindness and support while at the department of Religious Studies at Yale, and to Steve Fraade who as chair of the Department of Religious Studies procured for me much-needed time-off in 1997–8. To the cabal of Yale graduate students who read carefully and critically evaluated the first draft of this volume, and who go under the proper names of Andrew Dole, Alicia Jaramillo, Todd Ohara, Stefano Penna, and Madhuri Yadlapati, I offer thanks. I would like to express my thanks also to John Jones—now marketing editor at Crossroad/Herder—for his critical reading of the early fragmentary outline of the present book and the one that immediately follows. My debts in my new home of the Department of Theology at the University of Notre Dame are no less real. The Department of Theology under the able leadership of John Cavadini has provided a welcoming and hospitable environment for reworking, revising, and editing this text and the one that follows it. Sue Meyer did a wonderful job proofing the manuscript and introducing consistency of style. In this not obviously rewarding venture she was ably assisted by Cyril Gorman O.S. B. Michael Lee provided valuable assistance in constructing an index. I am deeply in debt to all three of my readers at SUNY Press. I can safely say that more generous readers could not possibly be found. They were lavish in their praise of what worked in the text, and constructive in their criticism of what was not enlightening. It was humbling, as well as astonishing, to find oneself so well understood. Many of their written recommendations have been integrated into the book, and those which have not haunt the text. But my SUNY readers also exhibit in their own way that the gift keeps giving. Two of the readers, Thomas Altizer and David Walsh, broke the anonymity of their identities and initiated conversations which further fructified this text. Throughout, the support of SUNY Press has been outstanding. Jane Bunker, acquisitions editor at SUNY Press, has combined enthusiasm with patience, support with intelligent interrogation. I have felt, and continue to feel, extraordinarily well-served. Such also is the case with Diane Ganeles. She has made the whole process of proofing (and improving) the text seem totally effortless. Marilyn Semerad took over from Diane at the stage of final pages and has brought the manuscript over the final hiatus between the private and the public. I am both relieved and happy to release this text to its fate.

Introduction

I begin this book with the conviction that all attempts up until now to justify either a Gnostic labeling of modernity or a significant band of modern discourses have failed. At the same time I hold the view that this failure is a contingent fact and not a necessary feature of projects that link various modern discourses with the Gnostic discourses of the Hellenistic period. I attempt nothing less than the kind of relatively comprehensive account of the Gnostic nature of an important band of modern Christian discourses for which the nineteenth-century historian of dogma, Ferdinand Christian Baur (1792–1860), stands out as the best exponent. That it is the nineteenth-century Baur rather than some major twentieth-century thinker who serves as the template may seem odd or even anachronistic, but it is so only on the presumption that twentieth-century thinkers have surpassed Baur in terms of methodological refinement and content knowledge, especially of the period between Luther and Hegel. I submit that neither is the case, and one of the burdens of the text is to provide reasons why this is not so. It is time then, I believe, to do Baur again, or redo him, essentially to bring his Gnostic genealogical project up to twenty-first-century genealogical code.

Baur's conception of his project, as well as his articulation, leaves much to be desired, as both scholars of ancient Gnosticism and those engaged in a genealogy of modern discourses have not hesitated to point out. Within twentieth-century scholarship Baur has been rightly criticized for his lack of method, the poverty of his sources, the arbitrariness of his selection of Gnostic candidates, and the superficiality of his treatment of these Gnostic candidates.[1] Yet he has been insufficiently praised for his profound intuition of the existence of a band of ostensibly Christian discourses

1

in the post-Reformation period, which are neither orthodox nor liberal, but of a genuinely third kind. At the same time, although his treatment of some figures to whom he casually ascribes gnosis is superficial, Baur's general grasp of the discourses of both the ancient and modern periods dwarfs that of most of his twentieth-century critics. Again, there has been a real failure to note that Baur's account of the Gnostic character of a select band of Protestant discourses from Boehme to German Idealism is determinate in the way few other proposals of the return of Gnosticism in the modern age are. In addition, not enough attention has been paid to Baur's hint of a narrative criterion whereby we might judge whether post-Reformation and post-Enlightenment discourses are continuous with Gnosticism of the first centuries. And finally and relatedly, Baur's reflection on the interrelation between the reemergence of gnosis in the modern period and the consequent change in meaning and function of the Trinity has never enjoyed the prominence it deserves.

All of these elements of Baur's program are worth retrieving, although Baur's own program will have to be submitted to extension, development, and emendation. The details of this extension, development, and emendation will be supplied in the main body of the text. The points I wish to make at this juncture are quite general.

First, to do Baur again is to perform functionally the same task at the beginning of the new millenium that he performed in the first half of the nineteenth century. This is the provision of a relatively comprehensive account of Gnostic return in Protestant discourses that are distinct both from the discourses of Protestant orthodoxy and liberal Protestantism. Isolating a third line of Protestant discourses is very important for understanding modern Christian thought because it modifies significantly what has come to be the consensus perspective. Put simply, Protestant thought in the modern period is characterized as a battle between the forces of orthodoxy and liberalism. And it is so characterized whether the story is told from the point of view of the orthodox or the liberal. For instance, Karl Barth's *Protestant Thought in the Nineteenth Century* has this cast.[2] At the same time, Adolf von Harnack tells the story of Christian thought from the Reformation on as one of progressive disentanglement from orthodoxy.[3] Alhough at some root level, Baur too shares significant elements of this picture, in *Die christliche Gnosis* he suggests that this picture represents a simplification:[4] Although the third line of Protestant discourses from Boehme to Hegel revises Christianity as rationalist and romantic forms of Christianity do, the revisions of the standard rendition of Christianity cut more deeply and are premised on a much deeper engagement. This engagement essentially has to do with the Christian narrative, which is neither avoided nor retrieved in part, but retrieved as a whole and radically, even transgressively, revised.

Taking up the challenge of doing Baur again also involves this genealogical project in a complex relation to Hans Frei's *The Eclipse of Biblical Narrative*.[5] One the one hand, I agree with Frei that any account of the story of modern Christian thought, essentially European Protestant thought, will have to frame it in terms of the struggle between orthodoxy and apologetic theology of various stripes. Frei has provided a magisterial account of the different configurations of this struggle: orthodoxy and theological rationalism in the seventeenth and eighteenth centuries, and orthodoxy and more subtle forms of nonrationalist appropriations of Christianity in the nineteenth and twentieth centuries. I especially agree with Frei in his focusing the struggle in what happens to the biblical narrative, which is not only expressive and productive of belief, but also expressive and productive of a particular form of life.[6] The biblical narrative is applied to life as a whole: The narrative absorbs the world.[7] On the other hand, however, I worry about Frei's tendency to group all forms of nonorthodox Christian thought as representing the eclipse of biblical narrative. Despite Frei's meticulous sense for detail, this has the effect of obscuring differences in the mode of revision that cry out for attention. More specifically, I worry about Frei's disinclination to think of modes of Christian thought that retrieve the biblical narrative as a whole only to revise it radically (e.g., Hegel) as distinct from other forms of Christian thought in which retrieval either does not occur (e.g., English deism) or is selective and partial (e.g., Lessing). In particular, this lack of distinction makes it difficult for Frei to understand why the Trinity is important and how it functions in forms of Christian thought in which the biblical narrative is retrieved and radically revised. How it goes with the Trinity is one of the concerns of this book and will be focused in our treatment of Jacob Boehme, Hegel, and Jürgen Moltmann in later volumes.

To recommend Baur here is to recommend a complexification of the story of modern Christian thought. To recommend Baur is also to prohibit accounts in which *Gnosticism* is applied either to liberal or orthodox forms of Protestant thought as such in the modern period. The ascription more usually is made of liberal modes of Protestant thought, as liberal thought is seen to depart from orthodox truth.

While notes of Gnosticism are produced to legitimate *Gnostic* ascription of liberal forms of Christian thought, to a significant extent the ascription functions by analogy: as Gnosticism defines the most egregious departure from normative faith in the ancient period, liberal Protestantism defines the most egregious departure in the modern period. Nevertheless, the case of Thomas Altizer suggests that this may not be a one-way street. Altizer,[8] for instance, maintains that the classical Christian tradition itself shows Gnostic tendencies in its picture of a God removed from the world and that orthodox trinitarian theologies such as those of Barth exacerbate the Gnostic tendency.[9] In this volume I address the way Altizer prosecutes his case and whether his view can be sustained. At this juncture, however, it is important to underscore the limitations of the general prohibition against Gnostic ascription of orthodox or liberal forms of Protestant thought in the modern period. The prohibition is against assigning a Gnostic label to a form of Christian thought precisely because it is orthodox or liberal. It does not prohibit, however, assigning a Gnostic label to a particular form of Christian thought, commonly regarded as belonging to the orthodox or liberal camp, on the grounds that it betrays particular features that identify it as Gnostic.

Second, and as important, to do Baur again is to redo him. Baur's individual insights, as well as his programmatic ambitions, are developed as well as preserved. To redo Baur involves supplying a fully explicit criteriology for *Gnostic* ascription that is not present in Baur. It involves deepening the analysis of discourses that are candidates for *Gnostic* ascription, for even on the most charitable reading, Baur's treatment of his major candidates in the modern period (for example, Jacob Boehme, 1575–1624)[10] is illustrative rather than demonstrative. It also involves extending investigation into literary discourses, which are not covered by Baur's proposal, and into discourses that come after Hegel, whose religio-philosophical discourse is the telos of Baur's narrative. A central facet of my doing Baur again is to tell the story of post-Hegelian Christian discourses that seem to represent prolongations of the third line of post-Reformation discourses espied by Baur. A final aspect of the redoing of Baur involves entertaining rival accounts of the third line of Protestant discourses and demanding that *Gnostic* ascription demonstrate its explanatory superiority over other kinds of ascription, actual or possible, such as *apocalyptic, Neoplatonism,* or *Kabbalah.*

Taking account of the weaknesses of Baur's Gnostic proposal, as revealed by his critics, is also to undo him. Undoing Baur involves questioning his easy assumptions about the continuity of Christian discourse across the gap of modernity, critically examining his view that the narrative that defines Gnosticism is more or less invariant, and raising the issue of entitlement with respect to Baur's developmental or theogonic parsing of Gnostic narrative. It also involves asking questions about whether in Baur's narrative rendition of Gnosticism he sufficiently distinguished it from Neoplatonism and other narrative forms of thought that themselves replace and/or refigure Christian narrative.

Taking account of the redoing and undoing, as well as the doing again, of Baur's account of 'Gnostic return' in modernity, I assign a Baurian label to the project as a whole. It demands more extensive and deeper knowledge of the discourses of modernity and ancient Gnosticism than is evident in Baur, and a methodological approfondisement lacking in Baur, but arguably also in many of his more corrosive critics. Moreover, one cannot presume, as Baur tends to do, that a particular discourse in modernity represents an instance of Gnostic return or be satisfied with adducing prima facie grounds for *Gnostic* ascription. The onus probandi is on the Gnostic genealogist. From a methodological point of view it is best to assume against a particular Christian discourse in the post-Reformation or post-Enlightenment fields being Gnostic. The genealogist is required to demonstrate and not simply illustrate. In addition to more extensive analysis of the discourse that is a Gnostic candidate, demonstration involves engaging rival interpretations and especially interpretations that agree in viewing this discourse as belonging to a third line of Protestant discourses in modernity. Demonstration also requires focusing on the narrative structure of such discourses as basic. It will come as no surprise, therefore, that what in Baur is confined within the covers of a single book, albeit a very big book, is here distributed over many. Although it risks the gigantesque, the Baurian project of Gnostic return in modernity will be prosecuted over seven volumes. After this introductory volume individual volumes will be devoted to the German mystic Jacob Boehme, English and German Romanticism, G. W. F. Hegel, and F. W. J. Schelling, anti-Gnostic discourses of the nineteenth century (e.g., Franz Anton Staudenmaier, Søren Kierkegaard, S. T. Coleridge), and Gnostic (e.g., Paul Tillich, Thomas Altizer, Jürgen Moltmann) and anti-Gnostic discourse (e.g., Hans Urs von Balthasar, Eberhard Jüngel) in twentieth-century theology.

If the ambitions of such a project are daunting, the difficulties of such a project seem positively Sisyphus-like. The current babble of tongues on the topic of Gnostic return in modernity throws off much more heat than light. Indeed, on the evidence available, the task of prosecuting a case for thinking of modernity, or a significant band of its discourses, as being Gnostic seems impossible. A Zeitgeist that privileges historical change and human malleability, in both its Enlightenment and self-reflectively postmodern strains, provides a thoroughly uncongenial environment for any kind of genealogical attribution. Gun-slinging nomination of all kinds of discourses—literary, political, philosophical, and religious—as Gnostic[11] does nothing to lessen this credibility gap. A common frustration comes to a head in the rage of Ioan Culianu, who accuses himself of being naive for ever thinking that Gnosticism had determinate historical or conceptual boundaries: "Not only Gnosis was gnostic, but the catholic authors were gnostic, the neoplatonic too, Reformation was gnostic, Communism was gnostic, Nazism was gnostic, liberalism, existentialism and psychoanalysis were gnostic too, modern biology was gnostic, Blake, Yeats, Kafka, Rilke, Proust, Joyce, Musil, Hesse and Thomas Mann were gnostic. From very authoritative interpreters of Gnosis, I learned further that science is gnostic and superstition is gnostic; power, counter-power, and lack of power are gnostic; left is gnostic and right is gnostic; Hegel is gnostic and Marx is gnostic; Freud is gnostic and Jung is gnostic; all things and their opposite are equally gnostic."[12]

Culianu's jeremiad could be endlessly multiplied, and although it ignores some very insightful work, especially in the area of literary criticism and theory, undoubtedly there is cause for alarm. What is being claimed when a discourse is being called *Gnostic* and how we demonstrate this is often not made clear. The claim of Gnosticism is either made too seriously or not seriously enough. The former is betrayed in the excess of connotation over denotation, the latter by the largely aesthetic-cultural use to which Gnosticism is put: As an interesting marginalized discourse of the past, Gnosticism is the presumed property of equally interesting marginalized discourses of the present. In the face of difficulties that have proved intractable, one can despair, or recur, as I do here, to Kierkegaard's trope of impossibility not simply being higher than actuality and possibility,[13] but alone worthy of embrace. This volume, which introduces the genealogy, represents what the great Marxist thinker Louis Althusser would call an intervention.[14] It intervenes in a context marked by chronic looseness of *Gnostic* ascription,[15] and general lack of methodological rigor by developing a conceptual framework within which Gnostic return in modernity is made intelligible and defensible.

Convinced that whole-cloth descriptions of modernity as Gnostic are insupportable and convinced more specifically that accounts of all modern Christian thought being Gnostic have not come near demonstrating their claim, the intervention has a limited aim: to isolate a band of Christian discourses in modernity that on prima facie grounds seem to be good candidates for *Gnostic* ascription.

The lack of clarity with regard to the meaning of the terms *Gnosticism* and *Gnostic*, the proper range of their application, and the absence of criteria that would entitle the genealogist legitimately to designate a theological, philosophical, or literary discourse in modernity as Gnostic discourage proceeding directly to charting a genealogy. The addition of other kinds of difficulty more or less prohibite it. The objections posed by postmoderns about grand-narratives and historicists about grand-narratives that feature a premodern discourse as the explanation of modern discourses are important and need to be engaged seriously. But objections also come from quarters where the legitimacy of a genealogical account of the discourses of modernity, or an important set of such discourses, is accepted. Indeed, some genealogical accounts of the discourses of modernity pick out the third line of Christian discourses marked by Baur but disagree about the ascription. A variety of alternative labels are suggested, the most important of which are *apocalyptic*, *Neoplatonism*, and *Kabbalah*, for all three tend to focus narrative structure as Baur's own *Gnostic* ascription does. Given that these ascriptions have prima facie no less interpretive and explanatory power than Gnosticism, it is important to rehearse in a preliminary and formal way how Gnosticism might be able to show its explanatory superiority.

A viable account of Gnostic return in the discourses of modernity demands the construction of a conceptual model and the generation of a technical vocabulary whose purpose is to demonstrate the possibility of a Gnostic genealogy. Demonstration is actual, or becomes actual, however, only in and through the detailed analysis of particular discourses in modernity. In theory the construction of a conceptual model could be quickly dispatched and thus serve as a preface to a volume in which the genealogical account at least gets under way. However, two structural impediments exist. First, there is the number and kind of methodological difficulties of which I have been discussing. It seems wrongheaded to assume that such difficulties can be expeditiously resolved. Second, the extent and depth of analysis required to show that any post-Reformation or post-Enlightenment discourse represents a moment of Gnostic return makes it antecedently unlikely that a quick judgment can be brought in. For instance, with respect to Jacob Boehme, whom I consider with Baur to be a highly plausible candidate for designating the alpha point of the genealogy of Gnostic return in modernity, and thus the possible subject of a book in which we have both a discussion of method and an account of the first moment in post-Reformation discourse of Gnostic return, it is not easy to see how anything less than a book-length analysis could suffice. One is obliged to provide a recognizable description of Boehme's extraordinarily complex discourse, place it in a post-Reformation context with multiple other orthodox and heterodox discourses, articulate its narrative base, show the measure of deviance from standard Christian discourse and how it surpasses that of other heterodox discourses, entertain rival interpretations of Boehme (especially those that focus on narrative as apocalyptic, Neoplatonic, and Kabbalistic interpretations all do), and finally demonstrate the superiority of *Gnostic* ascription. I judge, therefore, that from a practical point of view it is best to let the methodological reflections stand on their own as a preface to the genealogical account that is prosecuted over six volumes with our treatment of the German speculative mystic Jacob Boehme opening our account.

The horrors of methodological volumes are too well-known for me not to announce such separation with regret, even as I insist on the hermeneutic circle between the conceptual model constructed here and the actual analysis of movements and individual figures that constitute the third line of Protestant discourses in modernity. A conceptual model is necessarily formal and abstract. Moreover, compensating for its formal and abstract character with examples is possible only in a very minimal way. The problem with examples is that if they are intended as illustrations, they presuppose what they need to prove. The fact that I do intend to show demonstratively in the genealogy that the discourses of Boehme, Hegel, Blake, and Altizer, among others, exemplify Gnostic return makes even more problematic the status of examples in a programmatic text. Nevertheless, for readability and some semblance of anchorage in historical reality, examples are required. Thus, I supply them with the caveat that they can at best have a probative status. As probative, they are essentially anticipatory; that is, the examples of Gnostic return I supply anticipate the redemption of their validity claims in the full-bodied interpretation prosecuted in later texts where the Gnostic character of particular discourses and particular forms of discourse are demonstrated.

Yet, while this book shares in the deficits of volumes on method, it also shares in their general benefits. One benefit of a compendious sorting through of issues that systemically bedevil interpretation in a particular field of inquiry is that the concepts and vocabulary generated can be used to analyze discourses and texts not envisaged in its actual construction. Whereas methodological models are constructed with respect to a determinate content, and even with quite definite results in mind, they are at least in part separable from such content. Another benefit of books on method is that they tend to cross disciplines, as the examples of psychoanalysis, Marxism, and structuralism show. I take it that the conceptual model articulated herein is capable of adoption and adaptation with respect to modern discourses either known in a very superficial way by the author or not known at all. For instance, one could entertain something like a Russian Gnostic lineage that moves from Vladimir Soloviev (1855–1900) through Nicholas Berdyaev (1874–1948) to Sergei Bulgakov (1871–1944).[16] Again, pace the Polish poet Czeslaw Milosz,[17] one might suggest that tracking a Gnostic trajectory in nineteenth- and twentieth-century East European literature is possible. Because of the possibility of adaptability, this programmatic volume is at least incipiently interdisciplinary and arguably helps to underscore the de facto interdisciplinary nature of the genealogical project as a whole. If my account of Gnostic return concerns a third line of Christian discourses in modernity, these discourses are then variously theological, philosophical, and poetic.

As I have indicated, my main concern in prosecuting a genealogy of a third line of Protestant discourses in modernity is to make a contribution to theology. As this volume outlines the basic concepts and vocabulary of a plausible model of Gnostic return in modernity, it makes a contribution to theology. At the same time, I understand this volume on method to make a contribution to religious studies in general in that it indicates the contemporary relevance of scholarship on classical Gnosticism, while showing to the scholar of classical Gnosticism what a responsible genealogical use of Gnosticism might look like in the context of an analysis of a particular line of Christian discourses in modernity. Again, I understand this volume on method to make a contribution to philosophy to the extent to which philosophy concerns itself with the issues of modernity, its various discourses, and the possibility of premodern discursive survivals. A particular feature of the volume is its critical dialogue with the thought of the German cultural philosopher Hans Blumenberg. Finally, I understand this book on method to make a contribution to literary theory and literary criticism: the former to the extent that literary theorists have focused on narrative and on a transgressive modality of interpretation, the latter to the extent that literary critics have puzzled over the relation between Christian (specifically biblical) discourse and English and German Romanticism. Specifically, I conceive this text as speaking with narrative theorists such as Gérard Genette,[18] and with a literary theorist-critic such as Harold Bloom[19] who has produced some of the most intuitively insightful work on the relation between Gnosticism and modern literary discourse. Indeed, without the assistance of both narrative and hermeneutic literary theory, the conceptual framework that I supply in this volume would be empty. Yet to complete the Kant evocation, without the conceptual model provided here, *Gnostic* ascription in literary theory and criticism would be blind.[20]

This methodological volume, therefore, enjoys a certain advantage with respect to the number of potential audiences over its successor genealogical volumes. One could say that some of the genealogical volumes that follow might interest only one audience. For instance, my account in the final genealogical volume of twentieth-century Gnostic and anti-Gnostic theological discourse is most likely to be of interest almost exclusively to theologians. Other volumes, perhaps, will have something to say to two audiences. Whereas I would like to think of the Boehme volume that opens the genealogical account to contribute to literary history since Boehme is taken up in Romanticism, and by Blake in particular, I will not be surprised if this volume finally appeals to the theologian and the philosopher. Similarly, the volume on Romanticism is most likely to appeal primarily, if not exclusively, to those interested in literature and theology and their interrelation. By contrast, this introductory volume has the prospect of the widest array of audiences. It can speak to theologians, colleagues in religious studies, philosophers, literary theorists and critics, and historians who take seriously intellectual history.

At the outset defining the appropriate expectations for this methodological volume, the various interests it subserves, the angle of vision, and the kind of genealogical enterprise it represents is necessary.

In these methodologically self-conscious days in which debates about foundationalism, nonfoundationalism, and antifoundationalism preoccupy, I initially need to clarify the nature of the programmatic discussion. One way of understanding what is and is not going on in this book is to contrast two quite different approaches to method, with interestingly different titles, that is, René Descartes's *Discourse on Method* and Jean-Paul Sartre's *Search for a Method*.[21] In the case of Descartes's second-most famous text, the title itself suggests Descartes's assurance that he has hit a bedrock of certainty from which to proceed to establish reliable knowledge in the face of the twin threats of the obscurantism of tradition and skepticism. By contrast, Sartre's text, which is directed against the foundationalism of Descartes's precursor text, as well as its twentieth-century Husserlian and Marxist variants,[22] thinks that method cannot function apodictically. Over the historical domain, at least, method consists of generalizations that attend a complex interpretation of historical events, structures, and discourses that display continuities and discontinuities, sedimentation and innovation. More important than Sartre's decision in favor of aspects of discontinuity and innovation is his view that method is resolutely a posteriori. It is no accident that *Search for a Method* is the introduction to the tomelike *Critique of Dialectical Reason* and the mammoth work on Flaubert.[23] Similarly, our own text on method is a posteriori. It is inseparable from the interpretation carried out on post-Reformation and post-Enlightenment discourses in the six volumes that constitute the actual genealogy. Only in the order of appearance is this text first. More exactly, it represents a kind of concluding scientific postscript to a genealogical discussion prosecuted in volumes that explore the Gnostic proclivities of Boehme, Romanticism, German Idealism, and twentieth-century theology.

This methodological introduction, and also the genealogical account it anticipates, tries to stand clear of the partisanship and polemical tone that so mars the application of the terms *Gnosticism* and *Gnostic*. And it is catholic in that even when it refuses to embrace certain methodological and substantive positions of those who have applied the terms, it takes up wherever possible what is insightful in these positions into its own methodological and substantive discourse. In the face of Thomas Nagel's proscription against the "view from nowhere" and post-Nietzschian as well as critical theory's suspicions about disinterested discourse, however, it is idle to claim that our discourse represents no point of view and subserves no interest. The point of view is that of a theologian who has affinities with the common tradition and who has been schooled in classical and continental philosophy. A less theologically oriented point of view might conceivably pick out different discourses as exemplifying Gnosticism in modernity than those of Boehme, Blake, Hegel, Schelling, and a variety of modern theologians; one might also analyze any of the chosen discourses differently. One can, for example, imagine a literary historian positing a Gnostic interpretation of a French line of literary discourses stretching from de Sade to Genet, and including Lautrémont and Bataille.[24] One can also imagine—although with considerably more difficulty—a Gnostic interpretation of the dualistic understanding of the self in modern philosophy from Descartes to Husserl.[25] Three points should be made with respect to point of view, however. First, obviously the range of permission with respect to modes of analysis is limited by the claim made in the text that the approach recommended here is superior to other current approaches. A viable alternative point of view similarly would have to avoid the methodological pitfalls evident in the current models. Second, any alternative would still have to think of Gnosticism as related to the biblical traditions (and the doctrinal forms of Christianity it helped elicit) and to have a knowledge not only of the heresiological sources but also of attempts in theological discourse from the eighteenth century on to think of modern discourses as continuous with the Gnosticism of the first centuries.[26] Third, it seems necessary when ascribing *Gnostic* or *Gnosticism* to literary discourses in the modern field to conceive these discourses, however functionally aesthetic, as being in some way religious.

At the same time, this programmatic text and the more substantive genealogical texts that follow are also interested in a way that goes beyond clearing up the ways in which *Gnostic* and *Gnosticism* are used and bringing some conceptual clarity to an area of discussion where confusion and imprecision reign. While I attempt to provide a model of Gnostic return that could be agreed on both by those who celebrate or mourn such return, I take a position on such return with respect to Gnostic return in modernity. That the position is finally, if respectfully, negative, is indicated on the metaphoric surface of my text by the language of *haunting* and *derangement*. Both of these terms have a neutral descriptive core. In the case of haunting, a putatively dead discourse (i.e., Gnosticism) returns later in a form that is the same as and other than the original. In the case of derangement, one discourse (biblical) is deregulated by another and submitted to new rules of organization (essentially a different narrative grammar). Still, totally erasing evaluative overtones is impossible. Second, and at a deeper level, the succeeding volumes at least have something of an Irenaean form. On the one hand, detecting of Gnostic forms of thought is intrinsically tied to breaking their spell,[27] on the other, I suggest an alternative to discourses that evidence Gnostic return that bears a relation to Irenaeus's *regula fidei* or rule of faith.[28] But here I do not speak of an identity, and certainly not an identity if the rule of faith is identified exclusively with the sedimented tradition. The analogy I find between the position evident in this and the following works and that of Irenaeus holds to the extent to which the rule of faith points to a traditioning process open to significant innovation and even stretching. One of the leitmotifs of the genealogy to be pursued in subsequent volumes is the line of demarcation that must be drawn between stretching that remains compatible with Christian grammar, Christian narrative grammar in particular, and stretching that does not. It is important to know the difference. In the former case, one is talking about modes of narrative experimentation that risk heterodoxy, but remain includable instances of a generous orthodoxy. In the latter, one is talking about the swerve from all possible as well as actual forms of Christian grammar. Examples of the former to which we will pay particular attention over the course of our genealogical investigation are the discourses of Milton in the seventeenth century, Coleridge in the nineteenth century, and Balthasar in the twentieth century. Needless to say, we will have our work cut out to make clear what we mean by *Christian narrative grammar*. All I wish to say at the moment is that 'Christian narrative grammar' indicates that multiple interpretations of the biblical narrative are possible, and across history or even within a particular period quite different interpretations can be legitimate.

I am especially interested in the volume on Romanticism to uncouple Milton from Blake, who is the prime Romantic candidate for *Gnostic* ascription. Acknowledging that Milton's epic poetry offers a daring extension of the biblical narrative, and that he seriously modifies Christian and specifically Reformed positions on a number of important points, for example, on the Trinity and Christ, I will argue that he remains faithful to Christian narrative grammar. Indeed, I will show that he provides the paradigm of an imaginative extension of biblical narrative in literature that remains faithful to Christian narrative grammar and that he provides the critical leverage against the tendentious uses to which he was put by Blake and Blake's narrative alternatives. Showing that Milton is both generously orthodox and that he can be turned critically on a poetic discourse like Blake's that is a candidate for Gnostic ascription means for me that Milton is important theologically, even if one were to put in parenthesis his voluminous theological work, although I do not perceive any need to do so.

Similarly, in the penultimate volume I will argue that Coleridge provides the best nineteenth-century example of a form of orthodoxy, experimental both in terms of language and substance, that recapitulates the biblical narrative and resists the kind of Gnostic revision of narrative grammar represented by the later Boehme and the German Idealists. Coleridge has especially compelling things to say about what constitutes a trinitarian discourse that operates within a Christian narrative grammar and what does not. Again, in the final volume, Balthasar, who owes so much to the Romantic and Idealist traditions, will be offered as an example of a Christian thinker whose narrative thought operates within the parameters of Christian narrative grammar while being bold and original at various points. I will pay particular attention to his trinitarian thought as this distinguishes itself from that of Hegel and successors such as Moltmann, who Balthasar believes articulates a tradition of narrative discourse that can be traced back to Gnostic thought of the first centuries. As with Baur, Balthasar seems to have a sense of a modern Gnostic line of discourses that achieves its high point in Hegel. He is, of course, especially interested in what happens in theological discourse after Hegel. Although he continues to complain about the division into theological rationalism and fideism,[29] he is convinced that the tradition Hegel sums up and bequeaths is a particular strain of theological thought of extraordinary allure.[30] Of course, Balthasar is also important for this methodological volume. He makes, for instance, an essential contribution to indicating how one might deny Baur's theogonic assessment of ancient Gnosticism, and yet read it in such a way that there is continuity as well as discontinuity between classical forms of Gnosticism and the explicitly developmental narratives in the third line of Protestant discourses in the modern period.

Related to the interest in promoting a generous orthodoxy implicated in a grammatical reading of the biblical narrative is the interest in defending the metanarrative of Christianity, whether trinitarianly rendered or not, from charges that its discourse is totalitarian and self-legitimating. The kinds of narrative often cited in the postmodernist literature as most culpable, for example, those of German Idealism, are equally often regarded as legitimate interpretations and extensions of biblical narrative. By showing that such narratives are instances of a Gnostic narrative grammar rather than Christian narrative grammar, one is in a position to suggest that renditions of Christian narrative grammar may possibly exemplify the same critical posture toward self-legitimating metanarrative that marks many postmodern discourses (e.g., Theodor Adorno, Jacques Derrida, Jean François Lyotard, Marc C. Taylor). Yet Christian narrative grammar also goes beyond such a critical posture. It has a community function that is undermined by the radical commitment to a *petit récit* that may tend toward idiosyncrasy and incommunicability. It has a commitment to truth, even if this truth cannot be interned in either propositions or the inherited tradition, that is not embraced in the postmodernist environment in which Nietzsche's slights against the possibility of truth prevail. Furthermore, in the final volume I will show that in some postmodernist discourses, for example that of Marc C. Taylor, there exists a commitment to a Gnostic narrative form even in the eulogy of erring as the end of metanarrative.[31] Specifically, I will show that this narrative form at once represents a translation of Altizer's death of God discourse, which together with his more recent apocalyptic forms of thought, is a serious candidate for *Gnostic* ascription and can be illuminated by classical Valentinian narratives.

With its point of view and its interest, this project in Gnostic return can be called a middle-voiced genealogical discourse. Applying Quintillian's and Cicero's distinction in rhetoric between high-, low-, and middle-voice styles of speech to styles of genealogy,[32] I think it accurate to say that the genealogy to be enacted, after this volume shows its possibility, operates neither at the genealogical minimum of a supposedly disinterested history of ideas (low genealogy), nor engages in the practice of reducing discourses to their origins, however identified, whether psychological or sociological (high genealogy). Clearly from what I have already said, low genealogy is not my intention. In any event, a Gnostic trajectory in modern discourses is not available to analysis in the way, for example, the trajectory of philosophical discourses from Descartes, Spinoza, and Leibniz is— although I do not deny that interpretation is required for this movement of discourse also. Nevertheless, Spinoza and Leibniz both know that they represent modifications of Descartes, just as Leibniz understands himself to modify both. But most of the plausible candidates for *Gnostic* ascription in the modern field do not understand themselves in this way, although even here there are exceptions with the figure of Baur's great mentor, Hegel,[33] looming large.

This brings me to the distinction between this genealogy and high genealogy, especially of the post-Nietzschian ilk. One learns from the work of Foucault,[34] for example, that there are different kinds of interest, interests that determine that all discourses with claims to truth are involved in plays of power with specific strategies of legitimation. Moreover, a Foucaultian genealogy rules out attempts to adjudicate truth-claims, because this would perpetuate the illusion that knowledge is anywhere divorced from power. But one can sustain the point that the battle of truth is always at the same time a battle of or for power without reducing truth to power. The battle for meaning between Gnostic and Christian discourses in modernity, what we might call the narrative agon, is a battle for truth, specifically the truth to which narrative gives one access. Again, our middle-voiced genealogy does not partake of the epochalism that is so common in postmodernist discourse, although as the example of the later Derrida perhaps shows, this is not necessarily an ineluctable feature of post-Nietzschian genealogies. Epochalism can be defined as the view that the present age (Lyotard's emphasis) or its immediate predecessor (Foucault) represents a new beginning indicated by a fundamentally new form of discourse. The intention of the genealogical account herein is not to try this vexed question in an explicit manner. I do not systematically sort out either here or in later volumes the relations between modernity and postmodernity. The question is broached only to the extent to which it bears on the possibility of the third line of modern Protestant thought being continued in postmodernist discourses of the post-Nietzschian sort. But as early as the next volume I will contest what I take to be Foucault's drawing a line of demarcation between premodern and modern discourses that denies the possibility of a premodern discourse, and especially a premodern narrative discourse whose ambition it is to map reality, having effect in the modern field.[35]

To sum up our reflections on the kind of genealogy introduced by this volume, this genealogy is neither a genealogy manqué, then, nor a genealogy of a post-Nietzschian ilk. Rather it represents a third option that essentially offers a middle between the low and the high. Like its middle-voice rhetorical analogue, as Quintillian spoke about it in his rhetorical prognostications to be followed by Augustine in *De doctrina christiana*,[36] I expect this middle or between form of genealogy to prove more persuasive than its low or high genealogical alternatives.

Against the backdrop of the outline of point of view, interest, and type of genealogical project, I want to say something more about the contribution of Irenaeus to this programmatic volume and the genealogical project as a whole, as well as address the question to what extent the project can be characterized as Irenaean as well as Baurian. In this volume Irenaeus is regarded as indispensable for our knowledge of Gnostic sources, for his insight into the centrality of narrative in Gnostic texts, for his exploration of Gnostic hermeneutics, and finally for the hints he supplies about the difference between the surface and depth implications of the various classical Gnostic narratives. Nevertheless, whatever the contributions of Irenaeus, they are not such as to displace the primacy of the Baurian characterization. *Baurian* is the most apt general characterization of a project, whose focus is on the third line of Protestant discourse in the modern period and that finds Baur a more useful methodological and substantive point of entry than other kinds of nineteenth- and twentieth-century genealogical proposals. Clearly, as a second-century theologian, Irenaeus is not genealogically apropos in the same way, even if one were to construe his *Against Heresies* to provide in its own way a genealogical account of the emergence of Christian Gnosis from pre-Christian gnosis.[37] Nevertheless, *Irenaean* may be an appropriate secondary characterization of this genealogical project especially when one considers not only evaluation and recommendation but also specific modes of the analysis of narrative and hermeneutics.

I take the evaluative and recommending contributions of Irenaeus into consideration when I acknowledge that, like Irenaeus rather than Baur, I am on the side of the mourners rather than celebrators of Gnostic return, and also when I recommend a Christian narrative grammar in opposition to a Valentinian narrative grammar. I, of course, in siding with Irenaeus, modify him. Mourning need not be hysterical, and the recommendation of a Christian narrative grammar is a recommendation of an orthodoxy generous enough to sustain some elements of heterodoxy. But one also needs to keep in mind Irenaeus's understanding of the narrative criterion of Gnosticism that Baur found so important and the hermeneutical angle that defines it. Unlike Baur, Irenaeus not only suggests that Gnosticism is distinguished by a particular narrative, but that this narrative represents a disfiguration and refiguration of the biblical narrative. Moreover, this disfiguration-refiguration is a function of a hermeneutic program that is broadly transgressive in nature. Irenaeus's understanding of the relation of Gnostic to biblical narrative is central to this text, as is his hermeneutic reflection. These contributions from Irenaeus, together with the evaluative thrust, justify a secondary characterization of this project as Irenaean. At the very least one is called on to acknowledge that this Baurian genealogy has a definite Irenaean twist.

The secondary Irenaean characterization is important to me because I conceive the genealogical project as a whole, and this volume inchoately, to represent an answer to John Milbank's challenging question as to who or what kind of discourse will play Irenaeus to modern Gnosticism.[38] I submit that this genealogy of Gnostic return as a whole represents an answer. Granted, Milbank's explicit framing of his question is more narrow: What contemporary discourse will play Irenaeus to Hegel's Valentinianism? But Milbank's work as a whole suggests that Hegel is the rule rather than the exception. Thus, the question is broader and implicates multiple discourses in modernity. In *The Heterodox Hegel*,[39] I responded, as much as my analytic frame allowed, to the narrower framing of the question of *Irenaeus redivivus*. I brought Valentinianism into the discussion of Hegel's trinitarian metanarrative and suggested that it might prove the best taxonomic candidate for this narrative as a whole. Moreover, I analyzed Hegel's metanarrative discourse with a view to a much larger band of discourses in modernity. Jacob Boehme, for example, was invoked as setting the proximate precedent for both the encompassing and radical nature of Hegel's metanarrative, its metamorphic relation to the biblical narrative as embraced by the Lutheran community, and its trinitarian landscaping.[40] Herein, however, I still feel obliged to return to Hegel and make the Irenaean quality of the interpretation more explicit. This becomes really possible only with the construction of a model that is able determinately to designate a modern discourse as Gnostic. In addition, the discussion of Hegel that is prosecuted in volume 3 is framed by detailed discussions of figures in the third line of modern Protestant discourses that both precede and succeed him. If Hegel is not simply one example among others, given the effective history of Hegelian discourse in modern Christian thought, nevertheless, he is an example of a Valentinian narrative grammar that fundamentally exceeds him.

I am not suggesting that this is the only Irenaean style genealogy that has been prosecuted. I do believe, however, that the genealogy that will be executed is the most methodologically surefooted, the most determinate, and the most comprehensive to date. Certainly, the work of Milbank and Balthasar indicate a self-conscious application of an Irenaean label that seems to be supported by the tendency to characterize discourses in the Baurian line as Gnostic—although forms of modern discourse outside this line are also characterized as Gnostic.[41] And as in my own case, they are especially emphatic about the candidacy of Hegelian discourse for *Gnostic* ascription. I am in debt to both. My debt to Balthasar in particular is enormous. He will be a presence throughout the genealogical project as a whole, although he will come in for explicit discussion only in the final volume. Here is not the place to provide a complete checklist of what I owe to him. In the main body of this programmatic volume, I comment on some of his contributions with respect to the envisagement of classical Gnosticism that might assist in mapping continuities between modern theogonic discourses and the narrative discourses of classical Gnosticism. I should mention one general feature of Balthasar's work that influences the entire genealogical project. This is Balthasar's taking literary discourses seriously from a theological point of view and his sense that theological discourses such as those of Boehme and Hegel have aesthetic properties. This means, on the one hand, that literary as well as theological discourses are in principle open to *Gnostic* ascription, and on the other, that a feature of the Gnostic nature of theological discourses in the third line of Protestant thought is their aesthetic quality. I will capitalize on Balthasar's use of aesthetics as a mediation among genres of discourse throughout the project. For example, I will argue in the next volume that Boehme's Gnostic theological discourse has an aesthetic dimension; conversely, I will argue in the succeeding volume on Romanticism that the poetic discourse of Blake has to be taken absolutely seriously from a theological point of view since it blatantly offers a Valentinian alternative to the biblical narrative.

Two essentially complementary parts to this text serve as an introduction to a multivolume genealogy. Taking its lead from Baur, part 1 defends the general possibility of talking about Gnostic return in modernity. This involves cleaning the Augean stables of much contemporary genealogical use. It involves promoting a narrative criterion of identification. It also involves vindicating this genealogical project against historicist objection and suggesting the superiority of a *Gnostic* or *Valentinian* ascription over rival narratively focused ascriptions such as *apocalyptic, Neoplatonism*, and *Kabbalah*. Admittedly, my discussion in part 1 operates to some extent in terms of conceptual need. In the order of presentation, concepts such as Valentinian narrative grammar, as well as subordinate and satellite concepts, are generated to take care of specific difficulties. This means that such concepts tend to be elucidated only to the extent required to meet these difficulties. Additional aspects of the concepts generated in part I are brought out in part II.

Part II adduces grounds for believing that a Gnostic or Valentinian narrative grammar is a reality, and comparing and contrasting this grammar with Christian narrative grammar, which in the modern period it interrupts and revises. Showing the reality of Valentinian narrative grammar enables one to think of narrative discourses of the third line of Protestant discourses in modernity as instances of such a grammar without needing to be identical in every respect to the classical genres or paradigms of Valentinianism. The basic rule is that grammar exceeds its classical paradigms. Of course, elucidating the classical paradigms is necessary, and I focus on three paradigms, two from Nag Hammadi and one from the heresiological reports provided by Irenaeus in *Against Heresies*. The systematic features of the modern examples of Valentinian narrative grammar that make them different from classical Valentinian paradigms are outlined. At the same time, I argue that differences with respect to whether the encompassing narrative is developmental, whether the divine is pathetic or apathetic, and the value of cosmos, time, and history are consistent with both the classical genres of Valentinian narrative and narratives in the Baurian line belonging to the same narrative grammar. I also note the differences in epistemological incidence between modern narrative discourses in the third line of Protestant thought and the classical Gnostic or Valentinian paradigms. In addition, I reflect on the ways in which the presence of narrative discourses such as apocalyptic, Neoplatonism, and Kabbalah in the third line of Protestant discourses contribute directly to specifying their difference from the classical Valentinian paradigms while indirectly contributing to their basic Valentinianism.

Part II further broadens the narrative reflection of part I by considering how the narrative deployment of binary oppositions such as dark and light, blindness and seeing, inexpressibility and expressibility, death and life, heavy and light, and so forth contribute to making modern Valentinian narratives different from classical paradigms with respect to a developmental interpretation of the narrative of divine fall and return, with respect to the view that this narrative of fall and return involves a commitment to divine pathos, and finally with respect to the capability of supporting a truly affirmative view of the world and history. A further way in which part II develops part I is that we cease to rely on the authority of Baur to identify Gnostic return with Protestant discourses and try to justify a connection that is far from being intuitively obvious. The converse side of the argument is also presented, specifically that, as the conditions for Gnostic return are present in post-Reformation and post-Enlightenment forms of Protestant thought, they are absent in Catholic thought.

PART I

~

Baurian Model of Gnostic Return
and Its Challenges

In part I, I wish to challenge and be challenged by the impossibility of Gnostic genealogy by offering nothing less than a sketch of its possibility. I do so by offering a model of Gnostic return, which adopts as its basic skeleton the genealogical model of the great Protestant historian and theologian of the nineteenth century, Ferdinand Christian Baur, and which then submits it to serious extension, even radical reconstruction. I judge that Baur still offers the most promising starting point toward constructing a viable model of Gnostic return, but that without significant extension and reconstruction Baur's proposal too is inadequate to the genealogical task. Thus the model I construct is Baurian in an almost inverted-comma sense. In chapter 1, I proceed to recommend Baur's reflection on "ancient gnosis."[1] I recommend especially his isolation of a third line of Protestant discourses in addition to the orthodox and enlightenment varieties, and his employment of a narrative criterion in attempting to define a band of discourses that stretches from Boehme through Romanticism and German Idealism. I discuss the limitations that require me to correct some of Baur's basic tendencies and sketch the basic forms of extension and reconstruction. Beginning with Baur's understanding of ancient and modern forms of Gnosticism, I offer as the major avenue of reconstruction a grammatical reading of narrative that accounts for discontinuity as well as continuity between Gnostic, and specifically Valentinian, narratives in the Hellenistic field and complex narrative discourses in modernity. Whereas Valentinian narrative grammar is my key concept, I introduce several supplemental concepts, the most important of which is *rule-governed deformation of classical Valentinian genres*. The concept of Valentinian narrative grammar and the supplemental concepts are, however, further developed in chapter 2 and in part II.

Yet, without testing, a grammatically reconstructed Baurian model of Gnostic return still looks arguably too fictive or aesthetic, a possibility that is not yet a real possibility. My tests are two: first, a testing outside the courtroom of the historicist Zeitgeist by a reflective antigenealogical discourse that actually engages Baur-like genealogies and second, a testing by rival non-Gnostic genealogical models of the explanatory power of the Gnostic hypothesis. Testing necessarily has this order. For only if the reconstructed Baurian Gnostic return model avoids fatal wounding by an antigenealogical discourse and shows itself able to respond to some of its concerns, does it make sense to engage the Baurian Gnostic return model with non-Gnostic genealogical rivals such as apocalyptic, Neoplatonism, and Kabbalah. Chapter 2 then moves from showing the formal possibility of a Gnostic genealogy to its material possibility, defined by its ability to indicate superior explanatory power over its genealogical rivals. Indeed, in this chapter I accept that non-Valentinian strands of narrative discourse such as apocalyptic, Neoplatonism, and Kabbalah may be present along with the Valentinian in the third line of Christian discourses in modernity picked out by Baur. Yet I suggest that the Valentinian is primary and effectively can enlist the non-Valentinian narrative strands. I underscore this in two essentially complementary ways. The first avails of a topological model and construes Valentinian narrative to constitute the narrative base in the third line of Protestant discourses with the other narrative strands constituting the superstructure. The other model—and ultimately the more adequate one—is grammatical and/or linguistic and construes these modern complex narratives speaking a Valentinian language whatever the presence of non-Valentinian narrative strands. In part II, I develop the argument of the primacy of Valentinian narrative in the complex modern narratives of the third line of Protestant discourses, bring out more clearly the complementarity of the two models, and spell out the enlisting of the non-Valentinian narrative strands by a Valentinian grammar and how this enlisting actually contributes to the modernity of the third line of Protestant discourses.

CHAPTER 1

❧

Redeeming and Reconstructing
Baur's Model of Gnostic Return

Placing Western culture as a whole, or certain of its discourses, as an after to a before seems an irradicable feature of interpretive behavior, as if the *what*, or the *who* implied in the *what*, cannot be determined, even imagined, without speaking of the effects of discourses whose pastness encourage the sense of conceptual securability in the way the discourses in process of an evanescent present do not. Naming, it appears, demands the resources of the plot. Yet what is thus irradicable has been submitted to tireless critique. In a postmodern culture of suspicion, all such emplotments of wherefrom are deemed plots in the pejorative sense, that is, conspiracies of consolation in a situation indelibly marked by ambiguity and perplexity. And in the rebuff to naming the present by means of the vocabulary of the past, whether in the light of the present's contingency or uniqueness, or in the light of the diagnosis of the ideological claim of a presence to which knowledge can be adequate in principle, the unborn future is also protected, for emplotment with its wherefrom is ordered toward a whereunto that is predictable because in a sense it is already known. At one level, it must be confessed that the suspicion of plot is undefeatable. No clean bill of health can be given any plotline and not simply for the reason that many authoritative plotlines have revealed themselves as superficial when they have not been exposed as coercive rather than persuasive. Genealogical accounts have more than occasionally offered themselves as being beyond debate, thereby suggesting that genealogy as such represents a descent into ideology and an authoritarian form of discourse.

Yet plot too seems undefeatable. The discourses of demonizers of plots such as Jacques Derrida, Jean François Lyotard, and Mark C. Taylor, in their different ways, eloquently, but unwittingly,

23

testify to this.[2] The chaos or chaosmos supported by hyperbolic valorizations of contingency are full of plots;[3] our principled inability to situate ourselves is justified in terms of precise genealogies why this is and must be so; and our condition, discursive and otherwise, seems to have a massive consistency, even if this consistency is that of erring, to use Taylor's word. If wayless, we are certainly not tractless: what Heidegger calls *Wegmarken*, literally "way-markers," are everywhere.[4] Certainly we seem to have little difficulty marking where we have come from and where we are, and we have a determinate idea about change in direction. The persistence of plot suggests something beyond accident. Yet even if all one could do was appeal to naked survival, it is uncertain that survival is not the proxy for truth or that Darwinism is not the manifold of alethic claims. And, of course, many antigenealogical discourses themselves suggest some discomfort regarding their disavowals. They may make pained confession or simply acknowledge that continuity is a posited element even of antigenealogical discourses. Thus continuity is something to be abjured in one's own performances in the name of the unsayable discontinuity that is the truth, or continuity is embraced reluctantly as a serious fiction, complementary to the other truer historiographical fiction of absolute discontinuity. Here is not the place to test the relative merits of genealogical and antigenealogical discourse in the variety of its forms. Although in a later chapter I present the agon between a genealogical and a sophisticated antigenealogical discourse, all I wish to suggest for the moment is that genealogical discourse, at least in an epistemically humble form, can survive antigenealogical critique and thus gain a measure of vindication.

In a project that will unfold over a number of volumes I wish to deal with *Gnosticism* and *Gnostic* as items of genealogical discourse, as ways of relating discourses of modernity to discourses of the past with the interest of naming important discursive structures of the contemporary world. I do not suggest that these are the most common and decisive ones. Specifically, I wish to illustrate the work these genealogical counters do with respect to certain discourses of modernity, aesthetic (Romanticism), philosophical (German Idealism and its development), as well as expressly religious (Jacob Boehme, Thomas Altizer, Paul Tillich, Jürgen Moltmann), which suggest that they have at once revived and revised Christianity and by so doing made it culturally pertinent as well as intellectually and morally defensible. An inescapable aspect of this illustration, however, is determining what role these genealogical counters *can* play in assessment: determining their conceptual parameters is a condition of the possibility of legitimate employment.

In attributing Gnosticism to specific fields of discourse in modernity or summing up the work of an individual author or a particular text as Gnostic, one needs to know what is being claimed about these discourses. Indeed, given the vagueness of much taxonomic use, one needs to know whether anything is being claimed, whether the words *Gnostic* or *Gnosticism* simply function as a longhand for a particular state of mind regarding the world, most often an agitation with respect to its polymorphous out-of-jointness. Certainly, quite often the terms have more rhetorical than propositional force. They are likewise heavily polemical, although I grant that the rhetoric can function positively by indicating an elective affinity to discourses marginalized by the mainline traditions of religious and philosophical discourse or suggesting an aesthetic dismissal of the banality of public traditions. Large swatches of relatively heterogenous modern discourses, some rationalistic or mystical, others contemplative or practical in orientation, others again which consider knowledge to be method or which consider method as absolute knowledge are denounced. These discourses can be subjected to pathological examination in which the hatred of social, communal, and ethical reality is evinced and in which the overweening will to power expressed in the portentious claim to have the key to reality's secrets is revealed. Eric Voegelin is, arguably, the thinker most responsible for the polemical and pathological use of the term *Gnostic* with respect to modern discourses.[5] Not denying the sometimes high level of insight and sound judgment with respect to a number of major modern thinkers, the careless attribution of Gnosticism risks making Gnosticism an element of a demonological discourse.[6] Lamentation is declamation's other side: *Gnosticism* and *Gnostic* are ciphers of decline at best, violation at worst, with classical and/or Christian culture as their favored object. Although judgments about the overextension of application, and its demonological character, risk being too harsh, such interpretive use suggests more nearly the discourse of prophecy than philosophical analysis. Certainly the overplus of tone over meaning of which Kant complained and that Derrida, recently repeating Kant,[7] insists should be resisted, is something that urgently calls for attention.

Needed, then, is a nonrhetorical, or at least nonhyperbolic genealogical deployment of Gnosticism and Gnostic that makes clear the cognitive dimensions of the claim while indicating why the claim should matter. A good place to start is Baur's *Die christliche Gnosis,*

written in 1835, because it still represents the benchmark of genealogical employment of Gnosticism and Gnostic. This very early
work of Baur's, written under the influence of Hegel, is by no means
Baur's last word on Gnosis or Gnosticism. The great historian of
dogma in his later work will retreat significantly from the brave new
world of a speculative genealogy and significantly revise his assessment of the Gnosis of the first centuries.[8] Yet in terms of history of effects in general intellectual culture, although not necessarily in
theology, it is his early reflections that have continued to matter.
Much twentieth-century genealogical deployment of Gnostic or Gnosticism points back directly or indirectly to *Die christliche Gnosis*, and
in terms of comprehensiveness of proposal, determinacy of criteria,
and general explanatory power, Baur's epochal text sets a standard
that most twentieth-century accounts of the Gnostic physiognomy of
modern discourses palpably fail to meet. This is not to suggest that
Baur's thesis is adequate in the form presented in *Die christliche
Gnosis*. Without supplementation, correction, and fundamental methodological rehabilitation, Baur's position seems unviable at key
points. What I suggest here, therefore, is not so much that we capture
a Baur *in actu* as a Baur *in posse*, not the actual model of Baur but a
model of genealogical use that has Baur at its base.

   In *Die christliche Gnosis* Baur is not unaware that his thesis of
the return of "ancient Gnosis" in modernity is provocative, and
provocative on both philosophical and theological fronts. On the
philosophical front, Baur is effectively contesting the Enlightenment
thesis of the *absolute* novelty of modernity, which is supported by the
view that its characteristic discursive structures do not repeat premodern forms of discourse or present their contents. For Baur, a
major trend in modern thought, which receives its apogee in Hegel,
displays manifest signs of repetition across the gap of rupture between the premodern and the modern. Furthermore, one can think
of ancient Gnosis as providing a template for a speculative philosophy of religion that points to the intimate relation between religion
and philosophy that is denied by skeptical forms of rationalism and
forms of Christianity that are fideistic or biblicist in orientation. On
the theological front—the front of most concern to Baur—he contests
a reading of the theological situation that makes the only cogent
choice that between a newly minted rationalism and an ancient and
moribund orthodoxy. A third option is represented by the speculative
strand of Christianity in the post-Reformation tradition, which not
only has a vitality lacking in more traditional forms of Christianity
but also represents the return of ancient forms of thought marginal-

ized by emergent orthodoxy. If the Reformation is the condition of the possibility of this speculative strand of Christianity because of its pneumatic emphasis, it is the theosophic mystic Jacob Boehme who sets in motion a particular stream of Christian discourse that is further developed in Romanticism and German Idealism. Whether some of the inclusions (such as Friedrich Schleiermacher) rightly belong in this trajectory matters less for the moment than the caliber of the discourses that are included.[9]

In any event Baur's diagnosis of heterodox repetition cannot avoid the metaphorics of haunting. The metaphorics are double: a dead gnosis inhabits the Christian bodies of Protestant thought and paradoxically is responsible for any vitality they display; ancient gnosis spawns multiple doppelgängers in the modern field occupied by rationalism and orthodoxy. This metaphorics, which must necessarily be regarded as mythological by rationalism, is shared by Baur's Roman Catholic contemporaries, Johann Adam Möhler (1796–1838) and Franz Anton Staudenmaier (1800–1856). They, however, contest Baur's evaluation at every turn. To the degree to which ancient Gnosis returns, Möhler sees no friendly ghost but a sign of the demonic and judges Protestantism to be not a scene of health but a scene of endless multiplication of the self-centered, incurving spirit.[10] And Staudenmaier,[11] who focuses on the details of Baur's return hypothesis in a way that does not engage Möhler, specifically on the post-Reformation trajectory from Boehme to Hegel, calls for a kind of Irenaean exorcism.

In what turns out to be both a philosophical and theological provocation, Baur perceives himself to be working on the authority of his master Hegel with respect to both the form and content of his thesis.[12] The return of ancient Gnosis is cast in the language of development (*Entwicklung*), which with its teleological connotation recalls the Hegelian philosophy of history. The language of development at once disguises and realizes the metaphorics of haunting. On the one hand, the metaphorics is disguised to the extent that development suggests unilinear progress in the order of appearance of discourses. On the other, the metaphorics of haunting is ultimately conceptually realized in that development is thought to be dramatic: negated ancient thought reemerges in new philosophical and religious forms after a nonspeculative Catholic interregnum that represents its overcoming, or as it turns out, merely its repression. And these new forms of speculative thought surpass the ancient forms insofar as they realize dimensions of discourse that were not fully explicit in ancient forms of gnosis.

It is true that on the level of content Hegel does not elaborate a thesis that explicitly links his own discourse to ancient Gnosis by way of Lutheran pneumatism in which Jacob Boehme is a major figure. Nevertheless, such an extrapolation can be made on the basis of Hegel's extraordinary positive judgments in *Lectures on the History of Philosophy* on Gnostic and Neoplatonic metanarratives and on the thought of Boehme[13] where all evaluation is referenced to the realization of the thrust of discourse in the Hegelian system. My interest in recalling the Hegelian background of Baur's thesis is more than historical. From a systematic point of view one of the desiderata with regard to redeeming Gnosticism and Gnostic in genealogical discourse is to contest the teleological pattern of Hegelian discourse, whose purpose is to overcome contingency and to provide a narrative intelligibility that reaches all the way to logical necessity. Only by conceding the antiteleological point to an anti-Hegelian historicist such as Hans Blumenberg is a defensible genealogical discourse possible at all.[14] I discuss this at length in chapter 2.

As indicated, the superiority of Baur's model over its Gnostic genealogical rivals rests on its comprehensiveness, the determinacy of criteria for identifying modern discourses as Gnostic and its explanatory power. We begin with the issue of comprehensiveness. The scope of Baur's genealogical use of Gnostic is significantly larger than much twentieth-century use. With respect to the return of ancient Gnosis, one is not talking about a particular text or author, or even a particular religious, aesthetic, and philosophical movement, but of a broad discursive trajectory in modernity that displays attention-getting features. Yet if the scope is significantly large, it is not exhaustive. Specifically, the scope of genealogical use is not coextensive with modernity as such. In identifying as Gnostic a band of post-Reformation discourse, which has its alpha in Luther, its omega in Hegel, and an important mediating link in Boehme, Baur is determinate in attribution in a way Voegelin, for example, is not. In Voegelin the term *Gnostic* covers a dizzying array of religious, political, philosophical, and psychological discourses that amounts to an indictment of the whole of modernity. The whole postclassical tradition in political thought from Machiavelli and Locke to the present day is excoriated as *Gnostic*, as are Descartes, Romanticism, Idealism, phenomenology, Heidegger, existentialism, psychoanalysis, and religious movements such as Puritanism.[15] A comprehensive Gnostic genealogy steers between the Scylla of a focus on a particular discourse at a particular moment in modernity and the Charybdis of identifying as Gnostic the entire range of discourses generated in the modern period.

A first and general condition of *Gnostic* ascription is that the discourses are theological in the broad sense. Discourses, therefore, which are intrinsically atheological or explicitly atheistic, are not exemplary candidates for *Gnostic* ascription; they are not even viable candidates. This is not to say that there is not a critical element vis-à-vis the definition of modernity in *Die christliche Gnosis*. Not only does Christianity have available alternatives to confessional orthodoxies, but whatever the essential constitution of modernity—and Baur does not contest its methodological foundationalist leanings, its this-worldly proclivities, and its tendency toward univocal discourse—full description has to allow for the presence of narrative discourses that are not formally methodological, nor reductively this-worldly, nor purely nonsymbolic. What the relationship is between these discourses and the discursive field in general, and whether these discourses play any legitimating role with respect to the overall tendency of modernity, are issues that Baur does not decide, although Hegel has left relatively cogent answers. Put most simply, Hegel's particular metanarrative discourse, which he acknowledges has antecedents in ancient Gnosticism and Boehme,[16] represents the realization of modernity on the level of discourse, and functions to legitimate it. In fact, Hegel's reading has come to function as a template for all metanarrative discourse in modernity, whose authoritarian and ideological intentions have to be exposed.[17]

A second feature, marking Baur's genealogical model, is the relatively determinate criterion for identifying a Christian discourse in the modern field as Gnostic. In *Die christliche Gnosis* (arguably following August Neander[18] and undoubtedly influenced by Hegel's synoptic reflection on Hellenistic thought), in one fundamental drift at least, Baur tends to identify ancient Gnosis with ontological story in general, a specific ontological story in particular.[19] Thus Gnostic return has to do with the repetition in modern Christian discourses of a narrative focused on the vicissitudes of (divine) reality's fall from perfection, its agonic middle, and its recollection into perfection. In identifying Gnostic return in this way, Baur offers one of the two major paradigms of Gnostic genealogical assessment not only for the nineteenth century but also for the twentieth century. A central line of his contemporary Staudenmaier is that his assessment of the perdurance of Gnosticism in modern Christian thought operates in terms of this paradigm. Similarly, Balthasar finds himself with Staudenmaier in fundamental agreement with Baur's judgment that Hegel represents the completion of a post-Reformation line of narrative discourses that justify a Gnostic attribution.[20] Perhaps most tellingly, because of Hans Jonas's profound knowledge of the literature of Gnosticism and, surprisingly, in light of the fact that much of his work operates in terms of another paradigm, some of Jonas's later essays also articulate this paradigm.[21]

If Baur, at his most disciplined in *Die christliche Gnosis*, offers essentially a narrative paradigm from which to generate and justify use of Gnostic with respect to modern discourse, which we support, the experiential or existential paradigm of genealogical assessment, which is its main rival, is rejected. This paradigm has by and large dominated in the twentieth century. Harold Bloom, C. G. Jung, Eric Voegelin, and the early Hans Jonas are just a few of the more important thinkers whose reflections operate in terms of this paradigm, although, obviously, interests, strategies of interpretation, and assessment differ. In all of these authors Gnosticism is identified with a particular mind-set, fundamentally one of displacement and alienation from reality that, nonetheless, is a condition of one's specialness. Bloom's texts, for instance, display an interest in exploring (1) the Gnostic mindset in its pure phenomenological form, (2) Gnosticism's transgressive hermeneutic paradigm that challenges all authoritative texts right down to *the* text, the Bible, and (3) Gnosticism's various historical instantiations within literature and modern religions.[22] Jung is interested in the Gnostic mind-set to the extent that its symbols have a boldness and clarity lacking in many traditional religious accounts, but above all because these symbols reveal feminine and negative archetypes, exiled in history by monotheism, which point toward what needs to be integrated in the psyche, and in some cases reveal the processes of integration.[23] Voegelin is interested in the mind-set, which in his view is primarily one of revolt against order and the will to power,[24] to the degree to which this mind-set is illustrated in the thought of modern high culture and especially in political theory. On the level of interpretive strategy, if Bloom sometimes reads mind-set off literary symbols, most often he adopts the more indirect route of excavating Gnostic assumptions from the modalities of interpretation in and through which Gnostic texts dismantle the authority of prior texts and by implication the biblical text as the primordial authoritative text. The interpretive strategy of Jung is more straightforward with the symbols of ancient religious texts indicating the presence of archetypes, elsewhere confirmed in the analysis of dreams. Although Voegelin does not totally avoid the analysis of symbols or the nature of intepretation, he tends to focus on the explicitly declared programmatic ambitions of major discourses, an important example of which is Hegel's famous declaration in the Preface to *Phenomenology* that "the science of experience" is the movement toward a state of absolute knowledge or wisdom that transcends philosophy, conceived as the love of wisdom.[25]

But the experiential-existential paradigm also has nineteenth-century roots. It is found, for example, in the Catholic Tübingen School. For Möhler, Gnosticism, as with all heresy, is indicative of a state of mind that is egotistical and aggrandizing and that puts excessive emphasis on freedom.[26] This is true also for Staudenmaier, who at once operates in terms of the Baurian paradigm and against it. In his *Zum religiösen Frieden der Zukunft*, which is a text that anticipates Voegelin's concern with the social consequences of Gnostic thought and perhaps to some extent John Milbank's *Theology and Social Theory*, the Gnostic mind-set is chaotic, essentially antinomian, and finally demonic. That this state of mind turns out to be pathological is important and relatively unimportant. It is important historically in that the Catholic Tübingen School initiates a particular evaluative trajectory, which, one could argue, receives its crescendo in Voegelin. It is unimportant, or at least less important methodologically and systematically, in that evaluation of a state of mind, whether negative (Voegelin, Balthasar, Milbank), positive (Bloom, Jung), or ambivalent (Jonas) is secondary relative to identifying Gnosticism with a state of mind.

Within the second interpretive paradigm, there are in turn essentially two streams of interpretation with decidedly different evidentiary requirements. At one end stand Möhler and Voegelin, who tend to ascribe Gnostic states of mind on the basis of a perceived sense of a discourse's swerve from the normative traditions;[27] at the other end are Jung, Jonas, and Bloom, who think of states of mind as analytic results from the complicated process of interpretation of symbols and their relations in which states of mind are embodied. Clearly, the first kind of Gnostic state of mind ascription escapes testability. But difficulties also exist with respect to the second stream of interpretation. Not only are specific symbols often interpreted differently, and different relations with other symbols highlighted, but also the same or similar symbols can belong to different fields or matrices of symbols so that without some means to define the field or matrix within which symbols or local networks of symbols operate, determining whether individual symbols (such as exile) or local networks of symbols (such as death and life, sleep and wakefulness) indicate the presence of a dualistically exaggerated Christian discourse, a Platonic, Neoplatonic, or Gnostic discourse is difficult. Thus, while important and useful as a supplement, symbolic analysis presupposes a broader and deeper discrimen of symbolic matrix that establishes the horizon of symbols and their interpretation. *Die christliche Gnosis* responds to this need by identifying this matrix with a dramatic narrative ontology or ontotheology, which has a high index of testability. This lack of a testable evidential criterion, therefore, bedevils the experiential or existential paradigm of Gnostic attribution in both its forms.

The third and most important factor with regard to the superiority of Baur's hypothesis over its Gnostic genealogical rivals lies in its explanatory power. Of course, explanatory power depends on the first two criteria of comprehensiveness of genealogical scope and determinacy of criterion of assessment. It has three more specific aspects: (1) the interpretive fertility of Baur's Gnostic genealogy from a historical point of view, (2) potential extendibility of discursive terrains covered by the genealogical terms *Gnosticism* and *Gnostic*; and (3) the ability of Baur's genealogical model to demonstrate its explanatory power in competition with alternative, non-Gnostic genealogical hypotheses that cover essentially the same discursive terrain. Even Baur himself suggests the possibility of a non-Gnostic genealogical account of narrative ontotheologies from Boehme to Hegel. I cover each of these three aspects in turn.

(1) Baur's genealogical Gnostic hypothesis has proved interpretively fertile in that it has been recalled, explicitly or implicitly, in whole or in part, by a number of important nineteenth- and twentieth-century thinkers interested in the complex shifts in basic attitude and discursive forms of modern culture and concerned specifically with the state of confessional Christian discourses, forced to share discursive space not only with rationalistic, fideistic forms of Christian discourse but also with simulations of the biblical narrative and/or its first-order theological translation. Staudenmaier repeats more than one Baurian genealogy in his prolific output in the 1840s, but in one drift at least *Zum religiösen Frieden der Zukunft* (1845–1851) recalls the Gnostic genealogy of *Die christliche Gnosis*. Gnosticism returns in and through Lutheran pantheism (e.g., Boehme) and has its crescendo in German Idealism.

Balthasar also recalls the complete plotline of Baur's Gnostic genealogical thesis. In his early multivolume work *Apokalypse der deutschen Seele*, Balthasar ascribes as Gnostic a fundamental tendency in German Romanticism and Idealism.[28] Other aspects of

Baur's scheme are filled out in his great trilogy. In *Glory of the Lord*, the first part of the trilogy, while heroizing Irenaeus's authentically theological aesthetic,[29] Balthasar links Boehme with the aesthetic theological project of German Romanticism and Idealism in which the divine mysteries are grasped independently of Christ and articulated by means of organic, teleological categories.[30] At the very least, a strong analogy is implied between Gnosticism on the one hand, and Boehme and German Idealism on the other, since as the antitype of the theological aesthetics of Irenaeus, Gnosticism is a singularly intense version of an aesthetic theology that includes Boehme and German Idealism as representatives. In *Theo-Drama*, the second part of the trilogy, Balthasar associates mythological thought in general and Gnostic mythological thought in particular with German Idealism, but the grounds for association go deeper than and are more determinate than those found in *Apokalypse*, where the emphasis on knowledge (*gnōsis*) rather than faith (*pistis*) appears to be regarded as a relatively sufficient reason for *Gnostic* ascription. Balthasar suggests that what unites the myth that Irenaeus resists and the religious thought of German Idealism is a dramatic narrative ontology or ontotheology, whose function is to provide an explanation for evil and a justification of the divine.[31]

As figured in Hegel in particular, the divine, as trinitarian, is not given, but becomes. Specifically, it becomes through the economy of creation, incarnation, redemption, and sanctification, in which the pathos of the cross has an essential place. In line with Staudenmaier's extended critique of Hegel in the nineteenth century, for Balthasar this is to confound ontotheological story with the necessity of speaking about the divine in a narrative fashion, to think of this story as fundamentally self-legitimating and uncontestable, rather than a narrative being verified in community confession and practice. It is also to install deipassionism as essential to a vision of the divine. And from Balthasar's perspective, once again against the background of his nineteenth-century Tübingen precursor, Staudenmaier, this is to reinstate Gnosticism or more specifically Valentinianism. For Valentinianism of the second century elaborates not the narrative of faith but incontestable myth as logos, which myth requires no community, or more specifically practical, sources of verification.

Explicit recalls of important sections of Baur's genealogical trajectory are fairly common throughout scholarship. Working from within Gnostic studies, both Gilles Quispel and Hans Jonas have noted the affinities between Gnosticism and German Idealism.[32]

In a powerful essay, "Delimitation of the Gnostic Phenomenon—
Typological and Historical," undergoing something of a methodological *metanoia*, Jonas argues that the relationship is constituted in the
final analysis not so much by particular states of mind or networks of
symbols but rather by a narrative ontotheology, since the real subject
of becoming is directly the divine and, perhaps, indirectly, the more-
than-human self. Not only have I made the connection between
Boehme and Hegel, with Gnosticism functioning as a background category, but David Walsh and John Milbank have also made the connection.[33] Even if with both of these authors, after the pattern of
Voegelin, we see a tendency to focus on social and political discourses,[34] there are definite gestures in a Baurian direction. If Walsh
interests himself in the corresponding symbolisms of Boehme and
Hegel, it is nonetheless clear that aside from the claim to absolute
knowledge, the attribution of Gnosticism is predicated on the repetition of a narrative ontology that is characteristic of ancient Hellenistic modes of thought. Although the link of Boehme and his tradition
to Hegel and the post-Hegelian tradition does not enjoy the same
status for Milbank, nevertheless in *Theology and Social Theory*, Milbank suggests that the connection of Hegel with Boehme clarifies the
ascription of gnosis and, moreover, that the content of ascription is
once again a narrative ontology or, better, a narrative ontotheology.

(2) I have said enough, perhaps, about the fertility of Baur's
model of Gnostic return. It is time to say something about a second
aspect of the explanatory power of the Baurian model, that is, the
extensibility of its modern trajectory. The discursive terrain covered
by Baur's thesis admits to being extended in three directions. First,
one can ask whether figures, broadly speaking in the Protestant tradition but outside Baur's own German cultural tradition, display the
kind of narrative ontology that would justify ascriptive use of *Gnosticism* or *Gnostic*. A second important extension concerns that of
genre. In *Die christliche Gnosis*, Baur privileges theological and
philosophical forms of discourse. Although Baur has good reasons to
limit discursively attribution in this way, including finitude, interest, perceived competence, and theological pertinence of a direct
sort, the exclusion of the genre of literature arguably underesti-
mates this discursive genre's importance in modernity, removes the
possibility of seeing that it may come to function as a replacement
discourse to Christianity, and denies purchase on the aesthetic vision that inflects the discourses of Schleiermacher (626–668),
Schelling (611–626), and Hegel (668–735) who are regarded as instances of Gnostic return in modernity.[35]

Balthasar, who follows Baur with respect to both the paradigm of ascriptive use of *Gnostic* and his basic genealogical plotline, improves on Baur here. Balthasar makes both cultural-historic and systematic points. He posits as a matter of fact that the discourses of Romantic culture are mutually inflecting but that one important direction of influence is from the aesthetic to the theological and philosophical. Religious thinkers such as Schleiermacher and Hegel must be seen against the background not only of Herder but also against the background of Schiller and Hölderlin.[36] At the same time, Balthasar more systematically suggests (a) that aesthetic discourses may be privileged vehicles of religious response, for bad as well as good, even if in genuine aesthetic discourses there is always a fundamental quotient of illumination, and (b) that theological and philosophical discourses in the modern field may be intrinsically aesthetic in their vision of reality as a self-organizing, self-constituting whole that is affectively and noetically satisfying. With respect to the second systematic point, Balthasar has Staudenmaier as his precursor, and especially the latter's still important text on Hegel, *Darstellung und Kritik des Hegelschen Systems* (1844), which struggled mightily against Hegel's aesthetic holism. Such holism was a singularly attractive feature in the wake of the atomization of theology that is both cause and effect of the rationalistic reduction of faith and the fideistic exclusion of the content of faith.[37] Moreover, the second kind of extension, the extension of genre, can overlap with the first kind of extension, that is, extension outside Baur's cultural field, by making the poetic discourses of English Romanticism—themselves frequently the subject of Gnostic attribution—candidates for inclusion in an expanded Baurian model.[38]

The third and most obvious extension of Baur's model is temporal. While *Die christliche Gnosis* has a tendency to echo Hegel's own teleological assessment of his system, in principle, if not necessarily in fact, as the dominant intellectual influence in Germany of his generation, Hegel is simply the latest in a line of Protestant thinkers who offer variations on Gnostic return. Although the Baur of *Die christliche Gnosis* is somewhat reluctant to see it,[39] after the death of Hegel there could be others, even if these others would have to be classed as Hegel epigones. More realistically, discursive improvisations on the variations of Gnostic return could be offered by figures such as Boehme, Schelling, and Hegel. Given their deep affinities with Boehme and Schelling, and their sense of the necessity of a narrative ontotheology with the suffering of the cross at the center, Nicholas Berdyaev,[40] and to a lesser extent Vladimir Soloviev and

Sergei Bulgakov, are prime candidates for analysis, given their complex weave of myth, Idealism and the Eastern orthodox tradition. They present different kinds of complication than those found in the Western Christian tradition. The latter will receive the bulk of our attention in subsequent volumes. Our twentieth-century focus will fall mainly on theologians such as Altizer, whose extra-confessional theology from his early death of God theology to his more recent celebrations of apocalyptic shows remarkable consistency, Tillich, who provides the classical Protestant mediational theology of the twentieth century; and Moltmann, whose trinitarian political theology seems more nearly to stretch confessional theology than break it. These theologians, and theologians associated with them, come under examination for essentially two reasons. First, their texts display, overtly or covertly, a dramatic narrative ontotheology. Second, we find evidence of actual influence by one or more of the emblematic variations of Gnostic return in modernity diagnosed by Baur. For example, in the case of Altizer it is preeminently Hegel, but lately Boehme and Schelling; in the case of Tillich, it is the later Schelling with echoes of Boehme; and in the case of Moltmann, it is again primarily Hegel, but Hegel inflected by Schellingian and Boehmian elements.

Arguing for *Gnostic* ascription in these cases is understandably difficult. The cultural location of each bears at best an analogy to pre-1835 Germany and, of course, the cultural situation of each of these theologians is hardly identical. In addition, each presents unique obstacles. Altizer, who covers much of the terrain of Baur's Gnostic genealogy, refuses *Gnostic* ascription to these discourses and, placing his own discourse in this lineage, defines it as just the opposite of Gnosticism. In the case of Tillich, not only is the Schellingian reprise attended by a demythologizing urge that marries Enlightenment apologetic with Kierkegaard's existential analysis, but Schelling's philosophy of freedom is thought to be a bulwark against nontheistic cooptions of Christianity. This position is one which German theologians entertained almost from the first appearance of Schelling's post-Idealist work, not excluding Staudenmaier, and is also very much alive in contemporary theology, as evidenced by the work of Walter Kasper and Wolfhart Pannenberg.[41] Moltmann also provides numerous obstacles. The biblical intention of his work cannot be ignored, nor can his eschatological configuration of history, which owes much to Joachim of Fiore.[42] Although I carry out no extended analysis of these theological figures in this introductory volume, I hope by demarcating here the deep narrative structure that is in fundamental respects Valentinian that I can go on to show how it is constitutive of all three theological twentieth-century figures.

(3) I come now to the third factor relevant to the explanatory power of Baur's Gnostic genealogical model, that is, its ability to demonstrate its explanatory superiority with respect to a field of narrative ontological or ontotheological discourse in modernity over alternative non-Gnostic genealogical rivals. Again, only the series of volumes in their entirety can pass for such a demonstration. One is not in a position to outline the basic shape of Gnosticism's superior explanatory ratio until the Baurian model has been further adjusted and corrected. I sketch in the next chapter a somewhat formal account of the explanatory superiority of Baur's Gnostic genealogical model, and specifically its ability to assimilate its non-Gnostic rivals. This sketch is filled out significantly in part II, especially in chapters 4 and 5, when the discussion of assimilation or enlisting, as I refer to it, proceeds on the basis of the excavation of a Valentinian narrative grammar from classical Valentinian narratives. All I offer at this stage is an inventory of the important non-Gnostic genealogical rivals attended by a brief description of each.

Three kinds of non-Gnostic genealogies cover the discursive field of Baur in both its unextended and extended versions. That is, three rival accounts exist for the third line of Christian discourses fundamentally constituted by an encompassioning narrative of dramatic divine self-constitution. These rival models of return can be labeled apocalyptic, Neoplatonism, or Kabbalah.

To begin with the apocalyptic genealogy, we find numerous instances of apocalyptic interpretation of various figures (e.g., Boehme, Blake, Shelley, Hegel, Moltmann), and various discursive regions of Baur's genealogy (e.g., German Idealism). But we find fewer instances of genealogies that cover the full scope of Baur's genealogy, in principle allowing for cultural, generic, and temporal extension. Where we do, they seem to fall into two types. The first is genuinely non-Gnostic because it does not expressly exclude or deny a Gnostic genealogy. The second is anti-Gnostic in that it expressly contests *Gnostic* ascription of the Baurian chain of narrative discourses. The first type is associated with Henri de Lubac,[43] although suggestions of this genealogy are also found in Staudenmaier and Voegelin and his followers,[44] who support the Gnostic hypothesis. The second is associated with Altizer. Within the coordinates of the first type, the Reformation in general with Boehme at its apex and subsequently German Romanticism and Idealism and

their successor discourses, are regarded as representing a repristi-
nation of the apocalyptic theology of Joachim of Fiore. Within the
second, whatever the prima facie link between classical Gnosticism
and a chain of narrative discourses in which Boehme, Blake, Hegel,
and Schelling feature, the pronounced this-worldliness of these discourses and their commitment to time and history mark them as
belonging to another genealogical dispensation. Altizer feels com-
pelled to identify them with (or as) apocalyptic. Both apocalyptic
types overlap with Baur's actual trajectory of narrative ontological
discourse while extending it culturally, generically, and temporally.
De Lubac includes post-Idealist discourses[45] and plausibly would include Moltmann, given Moltmann's self-consciously apocalyptic and
specifically Joachimite commitment. Altizer includes English
Romanticism and its precursor (e.g., Milton) and successor 'poetic'
discourses (e.g., Joyce) as well as his own kenotic theology that constitutes, in his view, a postmodern radicalization of the modernity of
Romantic and Idealist discourses.

The second serious non-Gnostic genealogical rival is that of Neoplatonism. Influential Neoplatonic readings of German Idealism
have been offered this century by Werner Beierwaltes and others,[46]
but the practice dates back to nineteenth-century interpreters such
as Friedrich Creuzer, who felt entitled to think of German Idealism
as representing the revival of the Neoplatonism of Plotinus and Proclus, a determination that had some basis in the works of Hegel and
Schelling and one not particularly resisted by them.[47] Similarly, if
matters are otherwise with regard to German Romanticism, Neoplatonic readings of the major figures of English Romanticism are
relatively commonplace. Coleridge, Wordsworth, and Shelley have
all been read in this way, and Blake in particular has been submitted to powerful analyses that argue that not only is the dominant
symbolism of Blake's poems Neoplatonic but so also is their basic
metaphysical frame.[48]

Neoplatonic readings of the entire Baurian line of narrative discourses, in both its unextended or extended forms, however, are once
again fairly rare. As with the apocalyptic genealogy, however, the
Neoplatonic genealogy also has two emblematic renditions, both of
which are articulated in the nineteenth century. Ironically, the first
is provided by Baur himself, and the second, almost as ironically, by
Staudenmaier. In the case of Baur, the Neoplatonic genealogy is first
simply an implicate of the lack of unique reference for the signifer
"ancient Gnosis," which includes various forms of Platonism with
Valentinian and other Hellenistic discourses. One can just as legiti-

mately speak of Platonic or Neoplatonic as Valentinian return in Boehme and beyond, given the lack of determinacy of Gnosis. What is implied in *Die christliche Gnosis* is made more explicit in Baur's great work on the Trinity,[49] where Neoplatonism not only provides the proximate context for the interpretation of the Trinity in the patristic period, but dynamic modulations of Neoplatonism are suggested to be constitutive of the trinitarian conceptuality central to the modern dramatic narrative ontotheologies cited as instances of Gnostic return in *Die christliche Gnosis*. Staudenmaier follows Baur in tracing a Platonic or Neoplatonic trajectory that has German Idealism in general, and Hegel in particular, as its apogee. Following his *Darstellung und Kritik des Hegelschen Systems*, in his important *Die Philosophie des Christentums*,[50] Hegel and the Idealist Schelling are taken to complete a Neoplatonic trajectory that extends from Plotinus and Proclus via medieval and Renaissance Neoplatonism with Bruno being especially important. Moreover, the privileged Christian location in modernity is Lutheran Protestantism (671–743), in which a figure such as Boehme stands out for his speculative bravery (726–740). For Staudenmaier, if *Neoplatonism* is relatively interchangeable with *pantheism*, as the generic term of opprobrium, he also makes clear that the pantheism that is of interest is a dynamic, narrative, and finally, theogonic variety (234, 809).

The Kabbalah, or better its Christian cooption in modernity, represents the third non-Gnostic genealogical rival to the Gnostic Baurian genealogy. It is also, arguably, the least prominent of the non-Gnostic genealogical rivals for, on the one hand, it tends to get paired with Gnosticism without differentiation, as is sometimes the case in Balthasar and Milbank,[51] and on the other, with the possible exception of Bloom,[52] it lacks powerful proponents of the kind found in the other two non-Gnostic genealogical schemes. Individual figures and determinate regions of Baur's field of narrative ontotheological discourse, viewed in both its unextended and extended dimensions, however, have been characterized in this way. Hegel offers a surprisingly appreciative account of the Kabbalah in his *Lectures on the History of Philosophy*, and his description of it offers analogues to his own dramatic narrative ontotheology.[53] Ernst Benz has focused attention on the Kabbalistic line that runs from Boehme to Schelling through Friedrich Oetinger.[54] Balthasar has made gestures toward the importance of Kabbalah in the Romantic-Idealist field,[55] an importance underscored by Herder's borrowings from the Kabbalah as he proposes a dynamic organicist alternative to a static Christian theism.[56] And

Harold Bloom suggests that the Kabbalah might very well be a more adequate taxon than Gnosticism for English Romanticism and especially William Blake if the Kabbalah's view of the world is taken into account together with its mode of interpretation of the biblical text. Moreover, theologians such as Altizer and Moltmann,[57] who self-consciously think of the Baurian field of narrative ontotheological discourse as one of their major inheritances, either suggest that Kabbalah is a relatively adequate taxon or draw attention to the way (or ways) in which the Kabbalah can help correct skews within the Christian tradition, especially those that exaggerate divine transcendence, emphasizing the incommensurability of the divine sphere with the cosmos and that operate with a conviction of the basic ontological meanness of human being that supports a rhetoric of heteronomy and fear.

I return to these three rival genealogies in chapter 2, when I illustrate in a provisional way the superior explanatory power of Baur's Gnostic genealogy. What I now turn to are the steps that necessarily must be taken to rehabilitate the Baurian model so that it can successfully engage its genealogical rivals. At a minimum, four steps need to be taken.

As a first desideratum, Baur's Gnostic genealogical model, as elaborated in his classical text, must be de-Hegelianized. Specifically, the imperious teleological code by which ontological discourses in modernity are interpreted as repetitions and realizations of ancient Gnosis ought to be curbed. While Baur can call on the dramatic, (dis)ruptive element implied in a dialectical modality of development and can take for granted the Hegelian view that modernity as a whole is not a repetition, but spins on its own axis, the teleological code brings with it a number of dangers to which a philosopher of culture and history such as Hans Blumenberg has been especially sensitive. First, the danger exists that the discontinuity between the modern field of narrative discourse and that of ancient Gnosticism is insufficiently acknowledged. Baur, if not necessarily his successors Balthasar and Jonas, here seems to fall below the level of Voegelin, who insists on this point.[58] Second, and relatedly, the danger exists of ignoring telling differences in narrative ontological commitment: narrative ontologies or ontotheologies in modernity appear to be explicitly progressive and developmental in a way that those of classical Gnosticism are not. And third, the danger exists of inadequately attending to the contingency of history: history happens or is made and is not the effect of the cunning of intrahistorical reason with its cogent teleological aim.

A second step of correction lies in achieving a higher index of determinacy with respect to Gnostic ascription than that attained by Baur himself and many of his successors. When it ascribes Gnostic to discourses that unfold narrative ontotheologies, as we have seen already, the Baurian genealogy has a determinacy advantage over what we might call its Möhlerian competition, where the emphasis falls on experience.[59] Möhler, of course, is not the most significant advocate of the experiential paradigm, but he has the advantage from a typological point of view of being a contemporary of Baur's, indeed a Catholic Tübingen colleague who took exception to Baur's hallowing of the post-Reformation Protestant tradition. In competition with relatively powerful genealogical rivals, however, it becomes clear that even this level of determinacy is inadequate. Getting in the way of a fully adequate *Gnostic* ascription are (a) the tendency in Baur and his tradition to plot the same modern narrative ontotheological discourses in a multitude of genealogies of which Gnosticism is only one and (b) relatedly, the lack of specificity regarding the referent of Gnosticism in the ancient world.

With respect to (a), like Voegelin, who primarily operates in terms of the Möhlerian experiential paradigm,[60] Baur and some of his successors clearly see a particular Protestant strain of narrative ontotheologies as repetitions-realizations of a number of traditions. As shown earlier, Baur thinks that these modern narrative ontotheologies repeat and realize Neoplatonism and Gnosticism. Staudenmaier adds apocalyptic,[61] and Balthasar adds the Kabbalah. Multiple genealogical ascription, where no attempt is made to adjudicate between ascriptions or order them, obviously affects the degree to which modern narrative ontologies can be illuminated. To the degree that the ascriptions are determinate, the more equivocal will appear the description of the Baurian band of modern discourses. Contrariwise, if more than one ascription is regarded as legitimate, then the less the ascriptions themselves have determinate boundaries.

With regard to (b), greater determinacy with regard to the referent ancient Gnosis is evidently in order. As used by Baur, it functions as an umbrella term for heterogeneous discourses that include Hermeticism, Neopythagoreanism, Marcionism, Manichaeism, as well as Valentinianism. And the early Jonas at least displays a similar tendency to use *gnosis* as an umbrella term, with Gnostic religion covering Hermeticism, Marcionism, Manichaeism, as well as the non-Valentinian and Valentinian species referred to by Irenaeus and exemplified in the cache of Nag Hammadi. Demanded then is a restriction of Gnosticism to a determinate religious phenomenon, defined by particular texts, which articulate quite specific narrative ontotheologies. Specifically, Gnosticism finds its focus in Valentinianism that, from a methodological point of view, must be regarded as finding its determining expression in the texts of Nag Hammadi. Such determinacy with regard to *Gnostic* ascription, however, does not rule out complex historical and systematic relations between Valentinianism and other non-Gnostic taxa put to genealogical use.

Third, it is necessary to deny that Baur is entitled to his presumptive reading of Valentinian narrative ontotheology as theogonic. In addition to insistent avowals in classical Valentinian texts of the unsurpassable perfection of the divine before narrative adventure, the massive structural contrasts between unfallen and fallen states of reality leads to the plausible conclusion that the implied ontology or ontotheology is static rather than dynamic, and most certainly not progressive and developmental. Nevertheless, a denial of the necessity of a theogonic reading is not a denial of its possibility. As Balthasar and Jonas have both argued,[62] the surface semantics of Gnostic narrative discourse should not be fetishized, and in effect a split occurs between the surface and depth narrative intentions and ontological commitments in Valentinian texts with the latter being dynamic and developmental in a way the former is not. By observing the phenomenon of splitting or doubling in Valentinian discourse, both Balthasar and Baur bring out a feature of Gnosticism alluded to by Baur's master Hegel,[63] and they provide a necessary step in the argument for significant continuity between ancient and modern narrative discourses.

Fourth and lastly, if good reasons exist for examining Baur's presumption of theogonic continuity between Valentinian Gnosticism and modern heterodox forms of thought, even more compelling reasons exist for avoiding the presumption of an *Urnarrative* that either accompanies or undergirds theogonic assertion. The postulate of a Gnostic or Valentinian *Urnarrative* has at least two invidious consequences, the first affecting relations between classical Valentinian texts, the second affecting relations between classical Valentinian texts and Romantic and Idealist texts, as well as their precursors and successor texts. In the context of classical Valentinian texts themselves the construct of a Gnostic *Urnarrative* is in grave danger of functioning as a prescription that ignores the patent surface plurality of Valentinian narratives with regard to personae, attitude, and nuance in ontotheological position. Because the textual surface may be just that, the interpreter is not entitled to presume the semantic split between surface and depth in each and every case. Nor may the interpreter simply assume that in the event of verifying such a split, the textual surface is neatly resolvable into a relatively simple narrative ontotheology of which it is the allegory. In the context of the relation between classical Valentinianism and Boehmian, and between classical Valentinian forms and Romantic and Idealist forms of thought, the construct of *Urnarrative* is perhaps even more invidious. For the *Urnarrative* view to work, the interpreter has to negate plurality in the Romantic and Idealist fields and repress narrative differences between these discourses and those that emerge in the Hellenistic field. Implied also is a repression of the reality of historical change indicated by the discontinuity in discourse.

Against this background of reinscribing historical discontinuity and contingency, I want to insist on taxonomic determinacy, announce the need to prove that theogony is a legitimate (if nonobvious) reading of Valentinian narrative ontotheologies, and promote a plurality of Valentinian narrative ontologies. To pursue these aims, I turn to a notion that has proved helpful elsewhere in philosophy and theology, that is, the notion of *grammar*.[64] Specifically, I wish to propose the construct of Valentinian narrative grammar as offering the theoretical means for a justification of Baur's profound intuition of repetition and development of Gnostic narrative ontotheology by taking account of the four desiderata of rehabilitation. Now, as grammar allows plural lexical instantiations, indeed lexical instantiations with substantial amounts of difference, Valentinian narrative grammar points to an underlying set of rules of formation of Valentinian narrative open to plural instantiation and difference. While we find the exemplary instances or paradigms of this narrative grammar in the second- and third-century texts of historical Valentinianism, nothing rules out the possibility that later systems, including Romantic and Idealist systems, and their precursor and successor discourses, might not be discovered to be substantially determined by the same rules of narrative formation. Grammatical continuity between early and late would permit in principle a substantial degree of difference, as well as sameness, between narrative ontotheological discourses in the modern field and the Valentinian narratives of the Hellenistic period.

The construct of Valentinian narrative grammar allows, therefore, for serious discontinuity as well as continuity over time. But grammars can be generous or restricted. If one is to steer this construct toward the pole of generosity and underwrite more than trivial discontinuity, then grammar may need a conceptual supplement. The supplemental concept I propose is a variant of *rule-governed deformation of classical narrative genres*, which I borrow from Ricoeur's *Time and Narrative*.[65] Ricoeur uses the concept in the context of discussion about the possibility-impossibility, advisability-inadvisability of a total destruction, or at least deconstruction, of narrative in postmodernity. In accepting that massive differences exist between modernist and classical literary discourses, Ricoeur argues that the modernist novel continues to be literature only to the extent to which it recalls—even if it represses—systemic features of classical genres or styles of narrative rendition, above all plot structure. Whatever the level of change of modernist novels from classical forms of plot or, put somewhat differently, whatever the level of deformation wrought by modernist novels with respect to classical narrative genres, there are both de facto and de jure limits to change and/or deformation. For instance, Ricoeur does not believe that modernism constitutes a successful denarratization or dechronologizing of literature. Plot is rendered less visible, but still remains ineluctable. And Ricoeur thinks this failure is built into the nature of the literary enterprise as such. If modernism were to succeed in what sometimes is its express aim, it would do so at the price of ceasing to be literature. But Ricoeur's account is not nostalgic. Deviation from the classical narrative genres or paradigms is a good thing; it is the way in which over time narrative form avoids sclerosis. Or positively put, deviation or deformation is the way in which novelty is produced.

The first and primitive sense in which Ricoeur uses rule-governed deformation of classical narrative genres is that change, deviation, or deformation has limits. This means that deformation itself is covered by the rules of formation, and in the final analysis remain subordinate to them. For the most part Ricoeur is satisfied with this first sense, leaving it to the literary historian to articulate the ways and means by which plot (and character) are challenged without being erased. Despite the division of labor, the elucidation of the rules of deformation is clearly important to seeing the continuity in discontinuity and the discontinuity in continuity of narrative form and provides a second and more maximal sense of rule-governed deformation of classical narrative genres.

Rule-governed deformation of classical Valentinian narrative genres is my variant of Ricoeur's important concept forged in *Time and Narrative*. As with Ricoeur's concept, it is intended to point to continuity in discontinuity, and discontinuity in continuity, the former when it insists on the limits to the deformation of classical Valentinian genres, the latter when it emphasizes the deviation from, or actual deformation of, classical Valentinian genres by narrative discourses in the Baurian field, from Boehme to Altizer. As with Ricoeur's concept, rule-governed deformation of classical Valentinian genres has more minimal and more maximal senses. The more minimal sense is that there are limits to the deformation wrought by the modern narrative ontotheologies on the classical Valentinian paradigms, where these limits are essentially set by the rules of narrative formation, what I call rules of narrative grammar. This has the very important consequence that whereas pragmatically rule-governed deformation of classical Valentinian narrative genres can function as a coordinate concept to Valentinian narrative grammar, theoretically it is a subordinate concept. It is theoretically a subordinate concept given that deformation occurs only to the extent to which a narrative discourse, as a language or grammar, permits, even encourages, different narrative formations over time. The onus, of course, is to demonstrate that Valentinianism has or is such a narrative grammar. This is one of the major burdens of part II.

This brings me to the second and more maximal sense of rule-governed deformation of classical Valentinian narrative genres. I observed earlier that Ricoeur also implies the analogate of this second sense in *Time and Narrative*, while for the most part parsing rule-governed deformation in the more minimal way. Unlike Ricoeur, I focus in general as much on the maximal as the minimal sense of rule-governed deformation in this text and in the genealogical articulation that follows. Specifically, I elucidate the systemic kinds of deformation that are enacted on the classical Valentinian genres by modern narrative genres, which still, however, obey the same general rules of narrative formation. Although I begin at the end of chapter 2, chapter 4 carries the bulk of the interpretive burden. In chapter 4 I justify Baur's insight that the theogonic and pathetic character, even world-affirming character, of the third line of post-Reformation Christian discourses does not disqualify them from Gnostic or Valentinian attribution. I do so by showing that theogonic, pathetic, and world-affirming figuration are some of the systemic deformations wrought by modern narrative ontotheologies—which themselves obey the basic rules of Valentinian narrative formation—on the classical Valentinian genres or paradigms.

Summary

In this chapter I made a fundamental decision regarding the most promising line of inquiry into the possibility of constructing a Gnostic genealogy of discourses in modernity. I judged that the early Baur of *Die christliche Gnosis*, and to an extent also Staudenmaier and Balthasar, offer a more sound methodological entree in their focus on narrative than nineteenth- and twentieth-century proponents of Gnostic return, who focus on experience. Although numerous twentieth-century thinkers focus on either narrative structure or experience, parsing the fundamental opposition of paradigm by the opposition of two nineteenth-century German theologians, Baur and Möhler, who were colleagues at Tübingen, I affirmed the value of the Baurian paradigm over the Möhlerian. I acknowledged, however, that both paradigms find a precedent in heresiological discourse, above all in the discourse of Irenaeus. Irenaeus provides us with both classical examples of narrative structure and motif—the myths of the *gnostikoi*—and attempts to analyze the motives of the purveyors of myths and the kinds of selves that create them.[66] To the extent to which I wish to claim that, in some analogical sense, the general character of the Baurian model of Gnostic return I am in the process of constructing is Irenaean, I am forced to decide between two equally essential drifts in Irenaeus. That the preference for a narrative focus in genealogical construction does not automatically guarantee a more irenic disposition is shown by the example of Staudenmaier, who could not be more vituperative with regard to Hegel,[67] whom he regards as the supreme instance of Valentinianism in the modern period. Nevertheless, narrative focus, arguably, promotes a measure of irenicism, if only because a narrative criterion is in principle more analytic. Diagnosing states of mind, which is a feature of the Möhlerian paradigm, tends to encourage (e.g., Voegelin), although it does not demand, pathological description as the examples of Bloom and Jung clearly show.

Despite the merit of its narrative focus, Baur's Gnostic genealogy of the third line of post-Reformation discourses has to be extended culturally, generically, and temporally. Specifically, a Baurian Gnostic genealogy has to cover more than German Protestant thought, although this continues to be a major part of the story. A Baurian genealogy must include nontheological and nonphilosophical discourses that refigure Christian narrative in a unique way. Thus, it must include not simply Romantic theoretical reflection or its echo in a religious thinker such as Schleiermacher, but also must include Romantic poetry itself in its predilection to totalizing narrative as an object of analysis. Of course, we are also obliged to ask whether Hegel and Schelling, as good Gnostics, have any nineteenth- or twentieth-century successors. That I answer in the affirmative provides the raison d'être of this entire genealogical project.

But Baur is not simply extended, he is also corrected. Again, there is more than one form of correction. In Baur Gnosis, as applied to discourses in the Hellenistic world, suffers from a lack of referential determinacy. Because Gnosis includes most of the speculative narrative discourses of the Hellenistic period, defining it more narrowly is necessary. This is done by stipulating that it is defined by Valentinianism whose textual bases are Nag Hammadi with supporting material from the heresiologists, especially Irenaeus. Again, and relatedly, the tendency in Baur toward ambiguous genealogies and multiple genealogical construction must be corrected. To imply that one can speak indifferently of the third line of modern Protestant discourses as Valentinian or Neoplatonic undermines genealogy itself, which demands determinacy. With this in mind, I sketched in a very preliminary way the kinds of genealogical rivals that a *Gnostic* or *Valentinian* ascription of the third line of Protestant thought must face and defeat by showing greater explanatory power. I leave until the next chapter some plausible account as to how a Baurian view of Gnostic return shows such greater explanatory power. The third and most basic line of correction takes the form of forsaking Baur's tendency to think of Gnostic return as the repetition of an invariable narrative structure. The most important concept introduced for this revisionary purpose is that of Gnostic narrative grammar or Valentinian narrative grammar. A Gnostic or Valentinian narrative grammar is sufficient to guarantee the kind of continuity between modern Christian narratives to the side of both orthodoxy and the Enlightenment and classical Valentinian narratives. Rule-governed deformation of classical Valentinian narrative genres is an important supplemental concept introduced to underscore the systemic differences between the modern forms of Valentinian narrative grammar and the classical paradigms of this narrative grammar. While pragmatically coordinate with Valentinian narrative grammar, rule-governed deformation of classical Valentinian narrative genres is theoretically subordinate to it.

CHAPTER 2

~

Baurian Gnostic Genealogical Model
and Its Contestation

Arguing that the Baurian narrative paradigm offered the best
prospect for a *Gnostic* ascription of Romantic and Idealist discourses, as well as their precursor and successor discourses, I
demonstrated in chapter 1 the necessity of not only extending the
model of *Die christliche Gnosis*, but also rehabilitating it in such a
way that we not repeat the Hegelian disrespect for historical contingency, that we not ignore the specificity of the premodern and
modern ages, that we not assume the theogonic characterization of
Gnostic narrative, and that we avoid the conviction of a Gnostic
Urnarrative. Chapter 1 culminated in a grammatical reformulation
of Baur. Although the level of the discussion is quite formal, I provided some general indications with regard to this grammatically
reconstructed Baurian Gnostic model's prospective genealogical
power. In this chapter the burgeoning grammatical model is exposed to two serious challenges, the first a historiographical account of modern discourses that embodies the fundamental
historicist objection to any and all genealogical schemes without
shirking the responsibility to account for perceived continuities
between premodern and modern discourses, and the second, the
challenge offered by the three rival non-Gnostic genealogies of apocalyptic, Neoplatonism, and Kabbalah.

As I open with the historicist challenge of Blumenberg, it is important to acknowledge that I am not taking on more stringent, and
more strident, versions of historicism, which would suggest that any
narration of history, whether of society as a whole or its discourses,
is fictive in a pejorative sense. While refutation of historicism is important, I will not take on this responsibility. Instead, I broadly
situate myself within the charting of responsible historiography

prosecuted in *Time and Narrative* in which events, discursive or otherwise, demand incredibly detailed description if their integrity is to be respected, without this meaning that they cannot be charted in broader stories that can be relatively adequate (but which cannot make a claim of absolute adequacy).[68]

2.1. Historicist Challenge: Hans Blumenberg and Epochal Shift

As grammatical continuity allows for significant variation in discourse, rule-governed deformation allows for patterned ways of breaking with classical genres over time and, in effect, for the constitution of new genres of discourse. In principle, therefore, any narrative grammar, and thus a Valentiniann narrative grammar, allows for narrative variation to the point of wide departure from deeply sedimented narrative forms. Consequently, Valentiniann narrative grammar is not unfriendly to all aspects of historicist account. With the emphasis on rule-governed deformation of Valentinian narrative genres, it may well be friendly in fact to certain aspects. Nevertheless, this friendliness remains abstract, unless modernity in general, and specifically Romanticism and Idealism (and their discursive presuppositions and consequences), are granted an integrity of their own such that they are taken to constitute the determinate context for a specific set of deformations enacted on classical Valentinian narratives forms. To ensure that this is so, I submit the as yet inchoate grammatical conceptuality to the challenge that Hans Blumenberg's work presents, where the case for discontinuity between the modern age and the age or ages that preceded it is made with an unrivaled power and authority. The challenge is in essence threefold. First, it asks whether the kind of discontinuity permitted by the grammatical revision of the Baurian model is exposed as insufficient by historicism, or more specifically, a historicist account of the modern age. Second, it asks whether even in the context of relativized continuities one can fruitfully speak of Gnostic and/or Neoplatonic return in modernity. Third, it asks whether it is possible to continue to assert a strong relationship between Christianity and Idealism and Romanticism—as well as its precursor and successor discourses—in which one is recommending that the secularization model of relation be dropped, and at the same time, considering the possibility that Romantic and Idealist forms of discourse continue, in however a fragmented a fashion, premodern discourses other than Christianity, for example, Neoplatonism and Gnosticism.

In the magisterial *The Legitimacy of the Modern Age*, Blumenberg is anxious to dispute any view of modernity that does not affirm its fundamental discontinuity with what preceded it. Modernity is, indeed, as modernity's epochal understanding would have it, founded on a break (e.g., 9, 116, 119), a *caesura* (464–465). Affirmation of the reality of this break takes conceptual priority not only over the issue of whether the break is punctiform or a differential of transitions (469), but also over the issues of epochal markers or ineluctable presuppositions. If ultimately intended to make a contribution to historiography in general, proximately the intent of *The Legitimacy of the Modern Age* is to expose the explanatory pretensions of a specific genealogical account of modernity. The specific genealogical account that engages Blumenberg's attention is the view that the modern age represents the secularization of Christianity (4–5, 15, 18–19, 24, 27 ff. inter alia). While Blumenberg's proximate opponent is Karl Löwith, his real dispute is with Idealist philosophy of history and Romanticism's fictional construal of origins that provide Löwith and other proponents of the secularization thesis with their intellectual warrant. At bedrock level, both Idealism and Romanticism articulate a substantialist model of history that functions to justify its speaking of the modern age and its discourse as the metamorphosis or pseudomorphosis of what preceded it (9, 18, 27, 59, 113–114). But it is precisely such a substantialist model with its implication of continuity that is disqualified by the recognition of *break* and *caesura*. Blumenberg's resolute historicism, then, is fundamentally suspicious of any view of modernity as representing essentially a return to the past. However resolute his historicism, when Blumenberg sets about his positive constructive task, it quickly becomes evident that his form of historicism is nonradical.[69] Blumenberg accepts that the historiographic task is impossible without positing a minimum of continuity. *Reoccupation* is the concept deployed by *The Legitimacy of the Modern Age* to achieve this continuity minimum. Because *reoccupation* not only is meant to rhyme with the antisubstantialist thrust of his magisterial text, but also to carry the burden of an alternative (49, 57, 65, 77), Blumenberg rules out thematic continuity with any premodern discourse, but especially with Christianity. *Reoccupation* means quite literally "taking the place of," however much an antecedent language is invoked. For example, historical progressivism does not represent a form of Christian eschatology, as the secularization thesis would have it, but rather its functional replacement. Blumenberg sums up an important line of reflection in the following passage:

> Thus the formation of the idea of progress and its taking the place of the historical totality that was bounded by Creation and Judgment are two distinct events. The idea of 'reoccupation' says nothing about the derivation of the newly installed element, only about the dedication it receives at its installation. If one wishes to speak here of an alienation or expropriation, a reinterpretation or overinterpretation, then its object was not the theological substance of eschatology in its late, medieval forms; rather what was laid hold of was the independently generated idea of progress. (49)

Nor does materialism represent an exegesis or even eisegesis of the doctrine of the incarnation (115). Materialism is a functional replacement for an immanence theologically represented in the premodern period by the doctrine of the incarnation. The world as a whole will reoccupy the place of the incarnate Logos.

In my judgment Blumenberg sustains his critique of the secularization thesis in significant part and makes a good case for an anti-substantialist alternative. The real issue, as I see it, is whether he has sustained the more general case for the absence of any thematic continuity between premodern and modern discourses.[70] On examination his position here is problematic. First, for all his allowance for transition, Blumenberg often talks of the gap dividing modernity from what precedes it in univocal terms: The hiatus is both a constant and too broad and deep for anything to cross over. The two points are linked, for an admission that the gap is itself a variable allows the theoretical possibility of some discursive or ideational element making it across a gap no less real because it is not uniformly wide and deep across culture. Second, it leaves unclear the status of a number of pre-Enlightenment figures, such as Bruno (549–596) and Boehme[71] (seemingly important to Blumenberg) as well as their relation to one another. Is Giordano Bruno premodern or modern, and if the latter, to what extent is his discourse involved in reoccupation? Moreover, what about Jacob Boehme, who lives somewhat later than Bruno? Is he premodern or modern? What is his relation to the more self-consciously modern Bruno? Third, if only sparingly in *The Legitimacy of the Modern Age*, Blumenberg suggests the possibility of the continuation of modes of thought that represent an eisegesis of Christianity. Provocatively, the two candidates are Gnosticism and Neoplatonism (126–128, 290–292). The point to be made here, however, is less that Blumenberg is not absolutely consistent than that he seems to suggest a difference in continuity potential across the epochal break between standard Christian modes of thought and their eisegesis in and by other discursive frameworks. This distinction, or its trace, may, of course, be nothing more than another indication that the most urgent drive in Blumenberg's text is the contestation of the secularization thesis. In any event, despite his express intentions, Blumenberg can be read as leaving an opening for the possibility of some measure of thematic continuity, although any thematic continuity will be subject to interference by systemic pulls that belong to this side of the epochal threshold. The reminder of this interference is salutary, for minimally, factors in modernity torque any discourse that makes its way across the epochal threshold. If the epochal shift brings to the fore human autonomy in a way unmatched before, it also foregrounds knowledge, yet a knowledge no longer constituted by authority and its traditionary wisdom. Method and curiosity are the new forms of knowledge, and they are reciprocal: method is the ambition for the whole of knowledge as system, and method is regulated by *curiositas*. Yet if system is the inspiration of curiosity and the goal of method, it is undone by the infinite desire for knowledge that is self-replicating and unable to achieve satisfaction. At his most positivistic, Blumenberg asserts the absolute character of these general features of modernity and suggests their irresistible power to alter totally discursive forms that may happen to migrate into the modern manifold. Of course, this is to say that these migrated discursive forms are no longer alive but merely the outer integuments for a new spirit and a new set of meanings. We have seen, however, that *The Legitimacy of the Modern Age* seems to step back a little from this too-clean picture, especially when it concerns discourses other than Christianity.

We come now to the second of our two issues, namely, that if there is warrant for some kind of thematic continuity across the epochal threshold, does it make sense to speak of Gnostic and/or Neoplatonic revival, or one over the other? Of course, at one level it is not clear that Blumenberg can ask this complex question, given the consistent lack of distinction in *The Legitimacy of the Modern Age* between Gnosticism and Neoplatonism (128, 286, 294). Aiding this lack of distinction is a massively dualistic interpretation of Neoplatonism, which seems to substitute Plutarch and Numenius for Plotinus and Proclus, to suffer complete amnesia regarding Plotinus's paradigmatic act of differentiation in *Enneads* 1, 8 and 2, 9, and to defend a strange view of the historical relation between Gnosticism and Neoplatonism in which the former reoccupies the latter.[72]

For Blumenberg, Gnosticism reoccupies Neoplatonism by substitut-
ing the transcendent God of salvation for the theological Idea and
the demiurge for a demonized matter. Blumenberg, who seems to ignore Plotinus's act of differentiation between both discourses seems
at the same time to be dependent on him for his explanation of the
relationship between Platonism and Gnosticism with the emphasis
falling on the latter as belated. But this is to take Plotinus to be
making a historical more nearly than a normative claim and to gen-
eralize illegitimately from a particular region of Hellenistic discourses, completely ignoring the intentional relationship of Gnostic
discourses to Hebrew and Christian scriptures. In any event, Gnostic and Neoplatonic invocation is frequently attended by the most
blatant of historicist markers whose purpose is to establish thematic
discontinuity between the modern and the premodern. Blumenberg,
for instance, is persuaded that the cases of Cusanus and Bruno
demonstrate that Neoplatonism can functionally assist explicitly
modern or essentially post-Christian ways of construing the cosmos
and the self. Yet he brings no clarity to the question whether this
means that these figures cannot properly be regarded as premodern.
Nor does he shed light on their relationship to classical Neoplatonic
discourse that they both surpass and retain.

If anything, one can only be less sanguine regarding the credentials of Gnosticism, particularly because Gnosticism is supposed
to perdure beyond the Hellenistic period. Blumenberg does talk of
"the revival of Gnosticism," but as the following passage indicates,
this turns out to be something of a tease if thematic continuity is
expected.

> The thesis that I intend to argue here begins by agreeing that there
> is a connection between the modern age and Gnosticism, but inter-
> prets it in the reverse sense: The modern age is the second over-
> coming of Gnosticism. A presupposition of this thesis is that the
> first overcoming of Gnosticism, at the beginning of the Middle Ages,
> was unsuccessful. A further implication is that the medieval period,
> as a meaningful structure spanning centuries, had its beginning in
> the conflict with late-antique and early-Christian Gnosticism and
> that the unity of its systematic intention can be understood as de-
> riving from the task of subduing its Gnostic opponent. (p. 128)

It is nominalism, defined as *practical Gnosticism*, that represents
the second overcoming of ancient Gnosticism (154), and this practical form bears only the most indirect relationship to classical Gnosticism. As practical Gnosticism, nominalism is in fact the result of

the classical tradition's failure to provide an adequate replacement for the speculative narratives of classical Gnosticism. Here, obviously, Blumenberg remains faithful to his historicism and his focus on the operation of reoccupation. If no thematic continuity between classical Gnosticism and the renewed Gnosticism of nominalism can be posited (and however much the renewed Gnosticism anticipates the modern, it remains a premodern discourse), a fortiori no thematic continuity can be posited between classical Gnosticism and the discourses of modernity. And thus, we can entertain no haunting of the discourses of modernity by Gnostic survivals.

This historicism, however, appears to be qualified in both indirect and direct ways. An indirect qualification occurs when Blumenberg suggests that both Augustine and nominalism repeat the dualism, anticosmism, and soteriological selectivity of classical Gnosticism (134–136).[73] This suggests more than reoccupation: something like a material repetition and continuity is being asserted, such that one could easily imagine grafting Jonas's reflection on the Gnosticism of Pascal's experience of the absence of the divine in the cosmos,[74] and his terror before a God who saves and redeems. At the same time, Blumenberg seems to qualify directly his injunction against thematic repetition by making the Jonas-like point (289) that Gnosticism can be read against its surface implications and be seen to point to a radical narratization, even historicization, of divinity.[75] Blumenberg also suggests that in the figure of *Sophia*, Valentinian Gnosticism validates (in a way classical Christianity does not) the *curiositas* (291) that becomes an indelible marker of modernity. Although Blumenberg discounts thematic continuity between Christianity and modern modes of thought, he seems, unaccountably, to have less difficulty suggesting continuities in content between distorted forms of Christianity and the ethos and discourse of modernity. Blumenberg's difficulty here does not confirm our grammatically emended Baurian model. Indeed, to the extent to which he suggests repetition of content, Blumenberg appears to follow the early Jonas, whom we observed operates in terms of the Möhlerian-experiential rather than Baurian-narrative Gnostic genealogical paradigm. To expose the traces of thematic continuity in Blumenberg's would-be reoccupations does, however, weaken a fundamental objection that *The Legitimacy of the Modern Age* makes to genealogical schemes in general, and this weakening obviously strengthens the case for the rehabilitated Baurian model I am proposing.

The Legitimacy of the Modern Age presents a third challenge. Even if we can sustain a minimum of thematic continuity across epochs over Blumenbergian objections, we still face Blumenberg's challenge that Idealism's and Romanticism's very fictionalizing relationship to Christianity itself constitutes a problem that has to be dealt with in any interpretive account of Gnostic elongation into modernity. Contrary to Romanticism's and Idealism's somewhat cozy self-interpretation, their relationship to Christianity is intentional rather than organic. Across the hiatus of the Enlightenment, Christianity is not so much retrieved as invoked as a provocation for usurpation and displacement (105). Romanticism and Idealism, then, are neither extensions nor improvements of Christianity, dogmatic, biblical, or otherwise, but replacement discourses that cannot set the Enlightenment aside. Blumenberg's point is a hugely important one and contests much of the critical literature on Romanticism and Idealism that too easily accepts Romantic and Idealist self-interpretation. Blumenberg tends to think of the relation of Romanticism and Idealism to Christianity as agonistic, as paradigmatically aggressive. Interestingly, however, Blumenberg fails to provide an example from the Romantic-Idealist field announced as the scene of intentional relation. No Schiller or Schlegel, Blake or Shelley, Hegel or Schelling is mentioned. Instead, Nietzsche is the prototype, the figure, his violent usurpation of "I am that I am" of Yahweh.

The choice of Nietzsche marks a shift in the text from a historical to a rhetorical mode. We are enjoined to read Nietzsche as the truth of the Romantic and Idealist response to Christianity. A determination of the baseline level of Romantic-Idealist usurpation of Christianity would have been more theoretically and historically valuable. Furthermore, a more concentrated search within Romantic and Idealist ranks might well have uncovered degrees of aggressiveness in reading but also at a limit an example of aggressive usurpation matching that of Nietzsche. Such a search would uncover misreadings of a different scope deploying different strategies of subversion. Certainly, Blake suggests himself as a candidate for the former, whereas Hegel suggests himself for the latter. Blake expressly announces in his famous *Marriage of Heaven and Hell* that he is going to read scripture in an infernal sense,[76] and certainly the great prophetic poems such as *Milton* and *Jerusalem* give us good reason to believe that Blake systematically enacts just such a transgressive reading of scripture, its narrative from Genesis to apocalypse in particular. And if Hegel does not secularize Christianity, as Löwith so influentially suggests,[77] cannot he be read more easily, as I argued in *The Heterodox Hegel*, as a comprehensive and subtle usurper of Christianity rather than a purely Enlightenment thinker? Again, what is the status of Boehme, who, when he is read in connection with Goethe's maxim of *Nemo contra Deum nisi Deus ipse*, points to an act of insurgency against Christianity rather than its continuation?[78] This insurgency, in fact, precisely represents Blumenberg's interpretation of Schelling.[79]

The Blumenbergian challenge brings real theoretical and historical gains. On the most general level, responding to Blumenbergian historicism helps the revised Baurian model rid itself of any ahistorical latencies and residues, and the concept of *reoccupation* helps to chasten the kind and amount of continuity that our grammatical model can historically and theoretically posit with any degree of plausibility. On the more specific level, Blumenberg's discussion of Gnostic and Neoplatonic elements in modernity bring him sufficiently close to our investigation to make it worthwhile not only to present his view as a foil, but also to assess in a preliminary way the validity of the reasons offered to support the case of merely functional continuity across the epochal divide. On perhaps an even more specific level again, Blumenberg's view that neither Idealism nor Romanticism can jump over the Enlightenment attenuation of the authority of Christianity, that other discourses assume authority (yet are baptized in the name of the replaced Christian discourse), and that usurpation is accompanied by tendentious interpretation of biblical and Christian givens, represent contributions that no attempt to put the Baurian model on an adequate theoretical footing can choose to ignore. It is in the light of the pressures provided by *The Legitimacy of the Modern Age* that I propose the christening of the usurpative hermeneutic practice vis-à-vis the biblical text, and the narrative that it renders or at least shapes its reading,[80] as *metalepsis*.

Voegelin helpfully reminds us[81] that, as used by Aristotle, *metalepsis* means "participation." Now, this element of "connection with" or "participation in" ought to be regarded as ineluctable, even if under the influence of literary theory and especially Harold Bloom,[82] one thinks of metalepsis as a revisionary ratio, the way in which a later discourse both neutralizes an earlier discourse and siphons off its authority. Metalepsis indicates retrieval (but only across the gap of difference), and what is retrieved is both disfigured and reconfigured. It is possible, maybe even necessary, to describe the relation between Idealist and Romantic discourses and the discourse of Christianity as tropic in this way. Definitionally, however, thinking of metalepsis occurring at a single strength would be a mistake. Yet Blumenberg tends to suggest this when he offers violent retrieval-substitution and massive disfiguration-reconfiguration as the paradigm for metalepsis. From the vantage point of a more differential mode of analysis demanded for historical and theoretical reasons, Blumenberg describes the extreme limit of metalepsis. Less violent substitutions, that is, less vicious torquing of central aspects of Christianity—the Christian narrative in particular—are possible. One Idealist or one Romantic may instance an extreme animus toward Christianity, for example the Fichte of *Attempt at a Critique of All Revelation* (1793)[83] and the Blake of the *Book of Urizen*, another may not, for example, the Hegel of the *Phenomenology of Spirit* and the Coleridge of the famous speculation on imagination in *Biographia Literaria* (chap. 13). Moreover, the range of disfiguration-reconfiguration may differ: it may cover the whole of the Christian mythos or focus on particular aspects such as the Christian view of creation and the doctrine of the fall. Moreover, aggressiveness in metaleptic relation to Christianity need not necessarily correspond to range. A Romantic discourse may violently usurp Christian discourse, yet its range of disfiguration-reconfiguration be limited. For instance, in our volume on Romanticism we show that for all his violence against conventional Christianity, Shelley does not challenge key elements of the Christian narrative such as the goodness of creation, freedom of will, and the possibility of human transformation. Pre- and post-Idealist usurpations may involve disfiguration-reconfiguration of the entire Christian mythos without metalepsis functioning at such an extreme level that there is no accommodation to the usurped discourse. Jacob Boehme and the Schelling of the *Essay on Human Freedom* (1809), *The Ages of the World* (1815), and the somewhat later *Philosophy of Revelation* (1840) are two examples of thinkers who articulate narrative ontotheologies that disfigure-refigure the biblical narrative[84] but not without some concession to the narrative that is transformed. For instance, interested as he is in divine becoming, Boehme wishes to suggest that material and temporal creation are not necessary ingredients for divine self-constitution.[85] Similarly, Schelling, who explicitly asserts his theogonic agenda, nevertheless feels called upon to suggest that creation is gift.[86] One can stipulate, then, that the strength or weakness of metaleptic ratio is a function of level of aggressiveness plus range. At the top-most rank of strength are those discourses that combine the maximum of aggressiveness with the maximum range of disfiguration-reconfiguration of the Christian narrative. At the bottom, obviously, are those whose aggressiveness is muted and whose range is small.

While metalepsis helps us assimilate and go beyond Blumenberg's usurpative reading of Romantic and Idealist reoccupation, more important it helps to complete our grammatical mode of analysis. For one could hypothesize that at a certain level of disfiguration-refiguration, or in somewhat hyperbolic shorthand, at a certain level of derangement, the Christian mythos is so swerved that it indicates proximally a new narrative formation, and ultimately a new narrative grammar. On the face of it, this contradicts what our rehabilitated Baurian model seems to suggest, that is, something like continuity of an esoteric tradition that is not finally Christian in substance and commitment. But the contradiction is only apparent. For if I suggest that Romantic and Idealist discourses, and their precursor and successor discourses, belong to another tradition—that of Valentinian Gnosticism—then this particular tradition has two important characteristics: First, Valentinian Gnosticism is a tradition of texts without being a tradition of scripture in the strict sense, where scriptural assignation depends not only on texts having authority and community use but also on a given number of texts being regarded as constitutive of the community tradition and incapable of being added to, displaced, or fundamentally emended.[87] Gnostic texts, by contrast with the emergent Christian understanding of the canon, are both examples of and promoters of aesthetic play and free variation, precisely the sort of thing that makes Irenaeus believe that classical Valentinianism fails to conform to the most rudimentary demands of a religion of the book. Second, it is a tradition that is not something in itself, but a tradition of metaleptic relation to biblical discourse.[88] In short, Valentinian Gnosticism is a tradition of a particular narrative grammar that involves altering biblical narrative grammar. Thus, Valentinian narrative grammar is always at the same time a transformational narrative grammar.

The Legitimacy of the Modern Age constitutes a fundamental testing of the rehabilitated Baurian genealogical model, for the very possibility of a grammatical model of continuity is tried by a powerful historicist model that accounts for continuity as well as discontinuity between ancient and modern discourses. In this testing, the Baurian model remained standing—in that it was difficult for Blumenberg always to execute successfully his intention to remove all traces of thematic continuity. Moreover, Blumenberg offers insightful comments on Gnosticism that turn out to have constructive potential, even if they are not fully satisfactory from a systematic point of view. By contrast, Blumenberg's *Work on Myth*, which has been a covert presence throughout our discussion of

Blumenberg's best-known text, more obviously represents a field of opportunities for articulating the rehabilitated version of Baurian genealogy. For here not only does Blumenberg have important things to say about classical Gnosticism, which will be exploited in the next chapter, but he also has interesting things to say about important figures and episodes in Baur's narrative, specifically Boehme, Schelling, and Hegel, and their relations to each other and to ancient discourses.

In offering a functionalist account of myth, specifically that myth is a discursive means intended to keep a threatening reality at bay, or in Blumenberg's language, a means to alleviate the absolutism of reality (13–145), Blumenberg does not break fundamentally from the historicism of *The Legitimacy of the Modern Age*, where continuity is understood as functional rather than thematic. Not in the slightest trying to be provocative, Blumenberg thinks that myths and stories "are told in order to 'kill' [*vertreiben*] something. In the most harmless, but not least important case: to kill time. In another and more serious case: to kill fear" (34).

A specific task of *Work on Myth* is to explain the perdurance of myth in an age of reason, characterized by methodological and foundationalist pretensions. For according to Blumenberg, such perdurance in Western high culture is a fact. At a basic level the question of perdurance concerns organic myths, that is, myths that seem to have natural staying power and adaptability over the centuries (e.g., the myth of Prometheus). Ingredient in Blumenberg's story, however, is the question of whether, or rather when, organic myths are replaced in modernity, first by the self-conscious art myths of Romanticism (208, 213), and then by the final myths of German Idealism in which total myth is not so much excised as rendered conceptually transparent (209, 266–269, 291). An important leitmotif appears to be the analogy between these inorganic or transorganic myths and Gnostic myth as self-conscious, aesthetic, and intrinsically hermeneutical, that is, defined by the stance it takes with respect to Christian myth or narrative. In attempting to keep the relation between myth in the Romantic-Idealist field and Gnosticism strictly that of analogy, Blumenberg marks the theogonic intent of myth in the Romantic-Idealist field (269, 290–291) as distinguishing it from Gnostic myth (122–123), even as he observes that theogony in Jonas constitutes a modified Gnostic myth (290–291). Blumenberg's inconsistency here at once raises an important problem ignored by Baur, although not in the rehabilitated Baurian model and suggests a solution. The problem is the lack of match between narrative ontotheologies in the modern field and those of classical Gnosticism, given that the latter are not theogonic, or at least not so in any obvious way. The suggested solution is that even theogony need not imply a complete breach between classical Gnostic or Valentinian narratives and narrative ontotheologies in modern Protestant thought. This solution is redeemed within the coordinates of the Baurian frame by appeal to Balthasar and Jonas, who suggest that the depth narrative logic of classical Gnostic texts differs from its surface narrative logic, and that this depth logic, more hospitable to theogonic interpretation, establishes links between the narratives of Hellenistic Gnosticism and the narrative ontologies of Romanticism and Idealism and their precursor and successor discourses.

Work on Myth represents a development of *Legitimacy* in that it is more acutely aware of the inextricably hermeneutic nature of Gnostic myth. Specifically, Gnostic myth is the result of a fundamental assault on biblical narrative, an assault marked by aggression and satire (18), which fundamentally changes the meaning of key elements of the Christian story: first-order elements such as creation (130), and second-order elements such as trinity (260), and by implication the entire canonic narrative. Blumenberg, then, reminds us of a point suggested by an extant Valentinian fragment concerning the creativity of Adam vis-à-vis the angels or planetary rulers, noted by Bloom.[89] This creativity is taken account of by Irenaeus in *Against Heresies* in his figure of *metharmottein*,[90] which Baur tended to repress. Any operative analogy between Gnostic myth and the aesthetic myths of modernity will necessarily repair to the feature of disfiguration-refiguration of narrative, or what we have referred to already as metalepsis. Metalepsis is not simply one aspect among others in Gnosticism: its interpretive relation to another narrative discourse, biblical narrative in the first instance, but also second-order interpretations that introduce trinitarian discourse, is constitutive of its identity. In thinking of metalepsis once again as operating at simply one strength, that is, maximal strength, Blumenberg repeats an exaggeration of *The Legitimacy of the Modern Age* that effectively closes off distinctions between Valentinianism and Neoplatonism.

Another repetition in *Work on Myth* is also of moment. In *The Legitimacy of the Modern Age*, Marcion is regarded as more than a legitimate specimen of Gnosticism; he represents its exemplary instance (129–130). This problematic view, which Blumenberg in all likelihood owes to the early Jonas,[91] is attended by a lack of clarification about what divides and unites Marcionism and

Valentinianism.[92] Similarly, in *Work on Myth*, Blumenberg once again makes a plea for Marcion being regarded as a Gnostic (194–195, 199) and makes no attempt to define Marcionism's relation-difference to Valentinianism (199–201). It is important to see what is at stake here. Certainly, Blumenberg exaggerates the metaleptic strength of Marcion and fails to appreciate sufficiently the metaleptic strength of Valentinianism. By doing so, Marcion unhelpfully becomes the analogate for Romantic and Idealist art myths with their hermeneutic relation to biblical and canonic narrative, thereby disguising the full extent of the disfiguration-refiguration of biblical and canonic Christian narrative operative in these mythic and transmythic discourses. For in Marcion the truncation of the biblical text is not based on a lack of respect for tradition, but its reification, and the dualistic separation of creation from redemption is not attended by the kind of fascination with the why and wherefore of an evil creation that is typical of Valentinianism and modern myths of Romanticism and Idealism or their precursor and successor discourses. Only a Marcionite reading of Gnosticism in general, and the erasure of Valentinianism, could issue in the judgment that as a discourse Gnosticism is not fundamentally interested in theodicy. Even if Marcion, then, could be claimed to disfigure completely the biblical narrative, he does not completely reconfigure it. But this is what happens in German Idealism, and, arguably, in Romanticism at its limits.

But the distinction is important for another reason also. Precisely as operating at a very different metaleptic strength to Valentinianism, Marcionism is released to become a possible taxon for discourses in modernity that seem to challenge biblical narrative in a serious but, in the strict sense, nonradical way. For example, it might well be the case that most of the discourses of German and English Romanticism are more nearly Marcionite than Valentinian and that Valentinian typification can be justified as the exception rather than the rule. For instance, I will argue in a later volume that the poetic discourses of Novalis and Hölderlin on the German side and the early Coleridge and Shelley on the English are Marcionite rather than Valentinian. While there is much critique of the sovereign divine of biblical depiction, whose rule is capricious and whose laws are instruments of slavery, ultimately the focus is on the redemptive side of the Christian narrative. One can say that while the problematic behavior of the demiurgic divine and the unfolding of human redemption are related in a dramatic narrative sense, they are not related in the almost logical narrative sense of Gnosticism of before and after, understood as ground and consequent. Crucially absent also is the obsessive concern with accounting for the problematic features of the demiurge that are so central in the texts of Gnosticism. It is precisely this different narrative aptitude and his concern with giving an etiological account of divine fault that differentiates Blake from all other Romantics. In poems such as *The Book of Urizen* and *Milton*, redemption is read against the background of the malice of the creator. But these poems do not simply condemn the creator, they inquire into his origin in the depths of the divine from which fault emerges. In this respect Blake could be said to represent the limit of Romanticism in the sense of *limen* or threshold, which places Blake at once inside and outside Romanticism.

It might well be the case that, as an ascription, *Marcionism* covers a greater terrain of discourse than Valentinianism. In addition to its possible taxonomic value with respect to Romanticism, it may serve, for example, as a plausible taxon for Kantian and post-Kantian theology. It may do so to the extent that both tend to repress the otherness and sovereignty of God, and think of the redeemer as the good unwrathful God who functions without positive or prescriptive laws. Kant's *Religion within the Limits of Reason Alone* is involved in this repression,[93] and in this he is followed by Ritschl and liberal Protestant theology. Harnack's *What Is Christianity?* clearly reflects the judgment articulated in his great history of dogma about the central importance and fundamental rightness of Marcion.[94] The category of Marcionism also may more perspicuously illuminate the work of Schleiermacher than Baur's ascription of *Gnosis*,[95] which fails to make the requisite distinctions between Schleiermacher and German Idealism. It should be granted, however, that if it is impossible to justify *Gnostic* ascription of Schleiermacher, it is not necessarily easy to justify *Marcionite* ascription of Schleiermacher's work as a whole. This is especially so in Schleiermacher's *The Christian Faith*,[96] which phenomenologically redeems a doctrine of creation in its pointing to the sense of absolute dependence on a divine whence as foundational for Christian faith. Yet this sense of dependence is so ordered to the experience of redemption that the sovereignty features of the divine are put in parenthesis. The issue of the Marcionite tendency of Schleiermacher, and its limits, will come in for discussion in my volume on Hegel's Valentinian commitment when, in opposition to Baur of *Die christliche Gnosis*, I contrast rather than link Hegel with Schleiermacher.

The crucially important point here is that a principled distinction exists between these two kinds of discourse. Where the tendency in Marcionism is to contract Christian discourse by emphasizing the redemptive aspect of biblical narrative, to discourage speculation into the mysteries of creation and evil, and to promote a practical form of communal life, the tendency in Valentinianism is to expand the narrative, to make claims to have an exhaustive knowledge of the deep things of God, the mysteries of creation and evil in particular, and to place a supreme value on knowing, specifically knowing the new metanarrative, which reconfigures and thereby reinterprets the biblical and canonic narrative. Indeed at one point in *The Legitimacy of the Modern Age* (130), Blumenberg seems to make this very distinction. Marcionism is not full-blown Gnosticism, that is, full-blown Valentinianism that, from his point of view, is total myth, total narration. What prevents Marcionism from becoming total myth is its emphasis on love (*charis*). This dictates that there is not a significant preoccupation with the divine as creator and lawgiver and with the status of creation and its juridical rule. While negative comments can be made with respect to both—though there are also balancing positives—they are not systematic, and thus the demonic creator-lawgiver and radically evil creation do not become the focus of Marcion's story. In the context of the emphasis on *charis*, which narratively is reflected in a preoccupation with redemption, claiming that Marcionism does not elaborate a theodicy makes sense. But even granting Blumenberg the controversial point that Marcionism is a kind of proto-Gnosticism, claiming that the total myth situation of Valentinianism does not alter the theodicy quotient makes no sense, for total myth functions to leave no gap in explanation.[97]

Against the backdrop of his own softening of his embargo against thematic repetition, Blumenberg suggests the possibility that Gnostic modes of discourse broadly conceived have a measure of genealogical potential. Although Blumenberg suggests continuities between Romanticism and Idealism and Gnosticism, not surprising given his historicist-functionalist leanings, he leaves this genealogical potential relatively underdetermined. In addition, Gnosticism is thought to include both Valentinianism and Marcionism. Surprisingly, Marcionism is the banner Gnostic discourse and thus quintessential metaleptic Christian discourse. Whatever the legitimacy of Blumenberg's reasoning here, neither judgment is without precedent. Indeed, they are not without precedent in quarters that would find Blumenberg's functionist historiographical model much too stingy. Specifically, Blumenberg's indistinction between Valentinianism and Marcionism is in line with Baur's *Die christliche Gnosis* and to a significant extent even the early Jonas. At the same time, his relative prioritization of Marcionism over Valentinianism finds an echo in Balthasar who suggests in a fully assertoric way a Gnostic return thesis.[98]

Both Blumenberg's inclusion of Valentinianism and Marcionism under the categorial umbrella of *Gnosticism* and his prioritization of Marcionism from a genealogical point of view play a constructive role in our own Baurian genealogical program. The former forces one not simply to stipulate a distinction, but to produce criteria for this distinction that genealogically can be set in play. The latter forces one to recognize that Marcionism may well provide a better label than Valentinianism for the general drift of much of modern Protestant thought without the interpreter having to concede the priority of Valentinianism with respect to Protestant thought of the third line.

2.2. Agon between Gnostic Baurian and Non-Gnostic Genealogies

The possibility of genealogical discourse has been shown by meeting Blumenberg's historicist challenge, although admittedly the variety of historicism advocated by Blumenberg while thoroughgoing was not absolutely radical. More specifically, the possibility of Baurian genealogical discourse was shown by meeting the challenge presented by Blumenberg's functional model of continuity between Gnostic and modern narrative ontological discourses. There is, however, an additional challenge to be met, which is presented by the three rival non-Gnostic genealogies sketchily outlined in chapter 1. Here we wish to register in a somewhat more detailed way the kinds of challenge presented by apocalyptic, Neoplatonic, and Kabbalistic genealogies to the Baurian model. I want also to indicate in a provisional and formal way the ability of the rehabilitated Baurian model to respond to these challenges by taking account of the phenomena that these genealogical models isolate as central. In so doing, I hope to put into genealogical play a number of concepts to go along with Valentiniann narrative grammar, rule-governed deformation of classical Valentinian narrative genres, and metalepsis, the three major constructs generated thus far.

We begin with the apocalyptic genealogy, and more specifically with Altizer's anti-Gnostic version, since this version offers reasons why *apocalyptic* is preferable to *Gnostic* and other terms of ascription when we consider that band of modern narrative on-totheological discourses that the Baurian model privileges. As we shall see shortly, the reasons Altizer supplies seem not to support his apocalyptic genealogy but rather their Baurian contrary. To conclude that the Baurian Gnostic model is more satisfactory than Altizer's apocalyptic one does not imply its superiority over the non-Gnostic apocalyptic genealogy of de Lubac, which is considerably less idiosyncratic than that of Altizer. Yet given areas of overlap between the two apocalyptic models, I suggest that the superiority of the Baurian genealogical model in its engagement with the apocalyptic version of Altizer in fact suggests its superiority over the version proposed by de Lubac.

Before opening my presentation and critique of Altizer's apocalyptic genealogy, I want to underscore both the general importance of Altizer's genealogical reflections and their specific relevance to my own genealogical project. Altizer is unusual in stressing the theological importance of narrative or narrativity versions of Christianity in the post-Reformation and post-Enlightenment periods and problematizing their contribution to modernity. He is one of a small number of religious thinkers who have pointed to Jacob Boehme as a seminal speculative theologian. He is almost unique in the theology guild in promoting the theological importance of William Blake. Baur-like in his tracing of a line of dynamic narrative thought from Boehme through Hegel and Schelling, he is Baurian in my extended sense in that he broadens this line to include Romantic poetic production and draws attention to how this line extends beyond Hegel, Schelling, and the Romantics into the twentieth century. More, even if his apocalyptic labeling of this distinctive line of narrative ontotheological discourses, which like Baur he identifies as fundamentally Protestant, is untenable, it provides an ascriptive clue. For in denying the propriety of *apocalyptic* ascription to this line of narrative ontotheologies, we might want to suggest that (1) that Gnosticism in general or, specifically, Valentinianism, can itself be regarded as a genre of apocalypse, and (2) that a Valentinian genre of apocalypse is not simply other than apocalyptic, but represents among other things its incorporation or sublation, if I may be forgiven that dreaded Hegelian technical term.

In texts such as *The Genesis of God* (*GG*) and *Genesis and Apocalypse* (*GA*),[99] Altizer celebrates the reemergence of apocalyptic in the modern period after its repression in mainline Christianity. Summing up a position that he has argued with ever-greater clarity from the time of his book on Blake,[100] Altizer asserts that it is only "in the world of late modernity that a historical discovery of original Christian apocalypticism occurred, this was also a world that was born with the advent of a uniquely modern apocalyptic vision" (*GA*, 10). While distinguishing repression by Christian mainline tradition of apocalyptic from Gnosticism's own exclusion of apocalyptic is difficult,[101] Altizer offers both marks and criteria for distinguishing between *apocalyptic* and *Gnostic* as plausible ascriptors for the narrative ontological discourses of Boehme, Blake, Hegel, Schelling, and his own work. Marks of distinction include the systemic this-worldliness and friendliness to time and history found in these modern narrative ontotheological discourses palpably absent in Gnosticism (*GA*, 41–42, 81). Criteria of distinction include (1) differences in the construal of creation, (2) differences in the perception of narrative as a whole and the nature of narrative relations, (3) differences in the presence and meaning of eschatology. Here I focus on criteria of distinction because the marks provided by Altizer are at best too indeterminate to justify the self-conscious counterascription of apocalyptic. At worst, they do not square very well with classical apocalyptic, where the cosmos, as Blumenberg rightly points out,[102] is suspended in a kind of worldlessness, and time and history are relativized as well as imbued with significance. I admit that the features Altizer picks out succeed in offering criteria to demarcate these modern narrative ontotheological discourses from most premodern discourses, and especially those of orthodox Christian stripe. Still, I hope to show that this does not necessarily rule out Valentinian ascription. Indeed, I suggest that all of these features are possibilities of Valentinian narrative grammar, and that at the same time they represent rule-governed deformation of classical Valentinian genres or paradigms.

1. Differences in the construal of creation. Altizer argues that a major difference between classical Gnosticism and the modern narrative thinkers he admires lies in their respective construal of creation (e.g., Boehme, Blake, Schelling, Hegel). Altizer is certain that classical Gnosticism implies that creation is evil: "Ancient Gnosticism could mythically name the dichotomy of the Creator, but it could do so only by knowing the Creator as the alien God who is totally dissociated from Godhead or pure Spirit, so that then that creation is a fall from the absolutely inactual and purely primordial Spirit" (*GG*, 98).[103] By contrast with classical Gnostic thought, for all four narrative thinkers he praises—but perhaps especially Blake—the material, psychic, even sexual order can be embraced as good.[104] This distinction is relativized, however, when Altizer admits that in

all four thinkers creation is itself viewed as fall (*GG*, 80, 97–98),[105] rather than fall referring to an already good creation—as is the case in Genesis and throughout the biblical canon. In a sense, then, the metaphysical and imaginative ratios of the cosmos are at odds: Metaphysically, and perhaps aboriginally, the cosmos is evil; imaginatively, and, arguably, eschatologically, the cosmos is good because it is able to be redeemed. By thinking of the cosmos as metaphysically evil, these four narrative thinkers at a fundamental level reprise a classical Gnostic trope. Thus, if a difference exists between these thinkers and classical Gnosticism, it lies in the tension in the former between the metaphysical and the imaginative construal of the cosmos, rather than in a straightforward account of the essential goodness of the cosmos. Altizer in fact is suggesting that creation is comprehended by the figure of felix culpa in which the creation as fall plays a role toward the elevation and actualization of the divine (*GG*, 80, 95, 131–132). But this is an unusual usage of felix culpa. In the canonic tradition, *fall* never refers to creation but to the fall of human being. This fall affords an opportunity for the just and good God to make visible the gratuity of divine love, which he does in the redemption.[106] Altizer does not seem to notice that it is by reference to precisely such figures as Boehme and Hegel that Baur thought himself entitled to make a Gnostic attribution. What Altizer suggests by way of the warrant these thinkers provide for moving from metaphysical negation to imaginative affirmation, brings us to Altizer's second and pivotal criterion of discrimination.

2. Differences in the perception of narrative as a whole and the nature of narrative relations. For Altizer, since an evil creation is teleologically linked to crucifixion and resurrection (*GG*, 68–69, 80–81, 102, 108), its evil nature is always implicitly overcome or redeemed. He sees this as true for thinkers in the Boehmian line, above all Blake and Hegel. The chain of narrative intimacies warrant, therefore, the reversal of evaluative sign. It provides something like a second-order justification for a creation that cannot be justified on the first-order metaphysical level. A similar difference marks the modern view of the relation between the transcendent Godhead and the creator God. The latter can no more avoid evil than he can avoid creation (*GG*, 80–81). In the Boehme-Schelling milieu (*GG*, 15, 41–42, 118, 138–139), the transcendent divine surpasses itself in creation, just as creation becomes linked to redemption through crucifixion. Essentially, then, these teleologically ordered narrative ontotheologies are theogonic discourses: the divine becomes authentically divine in the movement from transcendence to

immanence with the cross at the center. For Altizer, the originary symbol for this process of divine development across narrative episodes is kenosis.[107] Crucifixion-redemption continues a process of divine self-emptying, there already in the would-be transcendent and alien God. Yet this emptying does not deplete the divine but rather has the paradoxical property of making the divine concrete and actual (to borrow the terms of Hegel). Emptying, therefore, is a form of filling: *Kenōsis* is a form of *plērōsis*. That this is the only possible interpretation of Altizerian kenosis is clear from the following passage where the resurrection inaugurates the completion of the divine narrative circuit: "That [the resurrection] is the apocalyptic triumph of a final self-emptying and self-negation, a kenosis which is the kenosis of the pleroma of the Godhead of God, and thus a kenosis which is the fullness in emptiness of the Kingdom of God" (*GA*, 87, also 88, and *GG*, 100). It is kenosis, therefore, as the genesis of the divine that Altizer takes to be central in his understanding of apocalyptic (*GG*, 106, 161).

Persuaded that the theogonic and kenotic character of these modern narrative discourses differ toto coelo from premodern orthodoxy and Gnosticism, and impressed by the agonic center of the narrative, Altizer tends to assert rather than argue for *apocalyptic* ascription. At a fundamental level, however, *apocalyptic* is an extremely bad taxonomic candidate for theogonic discourses. While classical apocalyptic does figure a supremely involved divine, it offers no reason to suppose that the divine either becomes in the struggles between good and evil in history, or that the cross is a fundamental ingredient in divine self-development. Indeed, apocalyptic discourse can offer consolation to the elect, precisely because one can trust in a sovereign divine beyond becoming, who nonetheless involves itself salvifically in and with the world. Thus, in classical apocalyptic driving a wedge between the transcendent and engaged divine is difficult. Altizer's own purpose in doing so—he wants to deny the viability and validity of the former by suggesting that the transcendent divine is overcome and realized in the creative and redemptive divine—does not alter the difficulty.

Of course, it is open to Altizer to draw back somewhat and suggest that *apocalyptic* is a relatively adequate ascriptor for these discourses, since one must allow for relevant differences that are a function of transformation from the premodern to the modern world. Formally, of course, I do not deny this because I uphold a version of the transformation view. On a material level, however, it is antecedently unlikely that classical apocalyptic is stretchable into a theogonic discourse without constituting a *metabasis eis allo genos*. For a divine that would need to empty into the world is not the divine of classical apocalyptic. It certainly is not the divine of Revelation. Nor is a divine that suffers an ontological split between goodness and justice a divine that is recognizable from apocalyptic texts. The merciful God is precisely the Lord of history who is righteous and wrathful judge. This brings us back to the dismissed candidacy of Gnosticism. I think that after Jonas and Balthasar in the Baurian tradition, it can be shown that classical Gnosticism, and particularly classical Valentinian Gnosticism, committed itself, although nonobviously, to a theogonic construal of the divine. But, then, given the constitutive importance of theogony in all of the modern narrative ontotheological discourses, mentioned by Altizer, not excluding his own radically kenotic narrative ontotheology, a *Gnostic* or *Valentinian* ascription becomes more plausible. Indeed, if Jonas and Balthasar are right, the narrative movement between protological *plērōma* and eschatological *plērōma* in Valentinian texts could turn out to be incremental rather than circular, thus a process of filling or *plērōsis*, but filling only through the loss and depletion of the aboriginally given perfection of the transcendent divine, whose ontological status turns out to be questionable. The next chapter offers evidence in classical Valentinian texts to support precisely such an interpretation.

   3. Differences in the presence and meaning of eschatology. The third feature that distinguishes this modern band of ontological narrative discourses from classical Valentinianism as well as classical Christianity is their radical eschatological thrust. In these discourses, plenary value is placed on the realization of the kingdom of God.[108] Yet for the most part the end is considered more nearly as the realization of time and history rather than as their negation. This seems to deal a serious blow to apocalyptic ascription. Altizer's eschatological option is obviously in negotiation with classical apocalyptic while indebted to the Joachimite pneumatic tradition.[109] Yet it fails to reproduce either exactly. If in one of its emphases classical apocalyptic thinks of the end as the realization of time and history, in another, the end represents its abolition. And while it is certainly true that Joachim, in his reflections on Revelation, thinks of the end of time and history as their realization, he too has in place a contrastive relation between time and eternity. Even more important, the end is the realization of the divine plan, the divine *oikonomia*.[110] It in no way connotes the narrative realization of the divine in and through time and history. But this realization appears to be precisely what Altizer suggests with respect to the eschaton in these

narrative ontotheological discourses. This suggestion is, of course, entirely consistent with the theogonic figuration of these narrative ontotheological discourses that Altizer contends is basic. But if basic, then eschatology must be reconceived as a function of a process of divine becoming that finds its completion in the pleromatic realization of time. Such reconceiving remains at odds with the paradigmatic eschatology of the Bible and with eschatologically focused theologies of salvation history, even those that are anchored in biblical apocalyptic texts, above all Revelation.

Demonstrating a weakness in Altizer's argument in favor of an *apocalyptic* ascription of the eschatological thrust of important dynamic ontotheologies in the post-Reformation and post-Enlightenment periods does not demonstrate the truth of my own *Valentinian* ascription. I acknowledge that the kind of endorsement of time and history, typical of these dynamic narrative ontotheologies, is not found explicitly in classical Valentinian texts. But if the "lying against time" of which Bloom speaks is a prototypical feature of Valentinian texts and is not repeated in these modern narrative ontotheologies, envisaging endorsement of time and history as a possible element of Valentinian narrative grammar is still feasible. This possibility derives from a thrust toward divine perfection that must necessarily appropriate time and history, as well as agony, as part of Valentinian narrative economy. Such a possibility seems more likely in Valentinianism than in apocalyptic. While this point, however counterintuitive, can be sustained on the basis of an analysis of classical Valentinian texts, I still want to emphasize the way in which these narrative discourses on this side of the hiatus that divides the modern from the premodern world depart from classical Valentinian paradigms. Gnostic narrative grammar permits then such a valorization of time and history without however absolutely calling for it. Nevertheless, I want to speak of narrative discourses in the Baurian line as representing rule-governed deformation of classical Valentinian narrative genres, which intimate a validation of time and history only against the grain of official rejection.

One can think of these modern narrative discourses as bringing two genres of apocalypse or revelation discourse into an intimate relation: that is, Valentinianism, which has a narrative ontotheology as the object of revelation and knowledge, and classical apocalyptic, with its focus on the dynamic engagement of the divine, christological agonistics, and its profound eschatological sense of history. But if theogony represents the ultimate horizon for these modern narrative discourses and if Baur and his successors can be proved right in their theogonic diagnosis of Valentinianism, then *Valentinian apocalypse* represents the manifold for *apocalyptic inscription*. Inscription covers both first- and second-level forms of apocalyptic discourse. That is, it covers biblical apocalyptic discourses and discourses that represent something like a straightforward reprise or application of biblical apocalyptic, but also more reflective orders of discourse such as Joachim de Fiore's theology of history that represents an interpretation of biblical apocalyptic rather than a straightforward reprise or application. I discuss the distinction of level within the apocalyptic genre of discourse in chapter 4.

Obviously a metaphor, *inscription* is intended to suggest that first- or second-level apocalyptic is written into or incised upon another apocalypse form that is hegemonic with respect to it in a number of ways. The first and most important way is that of narrative. As the object rather than the subject of inscription, apocalyptic obeys the rules of narrative formation that permit rather than prohibit a theogonic construal. In brief, Valentinian apocalypse permits this construal and apocalyptic does not. Again the inscribing apocalypse form sets terms for the adequacy of vision that are not apocalyptic's own. In the host environment the reality in excess of apocalyptic's iconic vision is brought into the zone of access. Finally, the process of interpretation of first-level apocalyptic, evident, for example, in the second-level apocalyptic of Joachim, where interpretation remains essentially open, is in the new apocalypse environment put under the pressure of closure, so that total explanation becomes actual.

Apocalyptic inscription involves as its correlative concept, *apocalyptic distention*. Similarly metaphorical, *distention* has as its root the Latin *distentio*, important in classical Neoplatonism,[111] and central to Augustine's treatment of human temporality in the *Confessions* (Bk. 11). Referring primarily to the narrative dimension, *apocalyptic distention* refers to the phenomenon of the inscribed apocalyptic form extending the narrative of the receiving apocalypse form along the lowest of its narrative levels, that is, the level of the cosmos, time, and history. But distention does more than simply extend the horizontal axis: it brings about important changes in the evaluation of cosmos, time, and history in the receiving apocalypse form. The fundamental negativity of assessment is revised but not obliterated by the effect of horizontalization. Moreover, on a christological front, apocalyptic distention tends to remove any docetic residuals from the Christ figure, dictated by the host apocalypse form, while making this figure central. Secondarily, however, as in the case of its correlative concept, *apocalyptic distention* refers to qualification of the dominant mode of vision and interpretation of the inscribing apocalypse form. If I am correct, the dominant mode of vision of the inscribing Valentinian apocalypse form is that of complete adequacy, and the dominant mode of interpretation one that is able to translate every and all symbol without remainder into univocal concepts. If the inscribed apocalypse form qualifies the inscribing apocalypse form, then one could expect not only much greater horizontal extension of narrative, which indicates an appreciation of time and history, but some modification with respect to the claims for knowledge and interpretive completeness. Nevertheless, however great the effect of distention on the receiving apocalypse form, where the phenomenon of apocalyptic inscription is in operation—and I hope to show its operation in Boehme and his successors, Blake, Schelling, and Moltmann among others—distention is contained. Distention does not become or make for a "disaster" in Blanchot's language.[112] That is, the inscribing apocalypse form is not scattered or undone, but rather still remains the reference point for narrative, vision, and interpretation.

In the distinction I drew in *The Heterodox Hegel* between two genres of apocalypse, I was already pointing to this analytic pair.[113] There I acknowledged the presence in Hegelian discourse of Joachimite eschatology, a form of discourse we now are identifying as a second-level form of apocalyptic. I pointed out that there were many ways in which Hegel's articulation of the revelatory divine did not correspond to this apocalypse form, and I suggested more nearly a Boehmian frame in which theogony was central. Our task being that of conceiving, therefore, the relation between two modes of revelation discourse, I argued that Joachim's apocalyptic form of discourse is not only trumped by, but included within, a discourse that accounts for divine self-development. While history is an important milieu for divine self-development, it does not exhaust it. Eschatological or apocalyptic discourse is secondary at a fundamental level while exerting massive influence on the encompassing apocalypse frame of divine becoming that surpasses it. Thus, Hegel's trinitarian metanarrative shows evidence of both apocalyptic inscription and distention, although the challenge to the inscribing theogonic form may be more apparent at the level of narrative than that of knowledge and hermeneutics. I will discuss the differences between the various aspects of apocalyptic distention to effect the inscribing apocalypse form and, more generally, the ability of the conceptual pair of apocalyptic inscription and apocalyptic distention to do work with respect to Hegel in a new volume on Hegel that will appear under the title *God's Story: Hegel's Valentinian Curriculum.*

Perhaps another example or two would help to explicate this pair of concepts—although again I remind the reader of their essentially probative character. Blake and Boehme provide two of the clearest examples with Boehme being particularly important (because he is in the background of Blake's as well as Hegel's revelatory discourses). First of all, in the case of both Blake and Boehme, the apocalyptic discourse inscribed is more nearly that of first-level than second-level apocalyptic, although second-level apocalyptic is not absent from either with Joachim being important for Boehme.[114] In Blake's *Milton* and in Boehme's *Aurora* and *Mysterium Magnum*,[115] one can see that time and history are important, even as the primary interest is in the becoming of a divine that is superior to the righteous and wrathful God of biblical apocalyptic. One also sees in both cases that the pain and suffering so central to the Christ figure of Revelation becomes an element of the economy of divine becoming, the movement in which the divine moves from less to more, and finally, the unsurpassably most: that than which none greater can be thought. Central elements of biblical apocalyptic are thus contained by a larger apocalypse frame, yet modify it significantly. Unlike Hegel, however, there is the sense that claims made on behalf of a fully adequate vision and a fully completable hermeneutic program—which are claims implied by the inscribing apocalypse frame—have to be qualified by the relative adequacy of the mode of vision realizable in biblical apocalyptic and the uncompletability of interpretation that is a function of the irreducibility of symbol, its excess over thought.[116]

Undoubtedly, we could do with further illustration of this analytic pair. As I explained at the outset, however, a relative poverty in illustration cannot be helped within the coordinates of a methodological discourse. But I do wish to underscore the importance of this analytic pair as it is deployed over the whole Baurian trajectory in succeeding volumes starting with the volumes on Boehme, Hegel, and Romanticism. For with this pair one is in a position to (1) account for relations between apocalyptic elements and nonapocalyptic elements in complex narrative discourses of the post-Reformation and post-Enlightenment periods, and (2) account for why discourses with blatant theogonic thrust might be mistaken for examples of apocalyptic. This might be one way to understand, and to some extent excuse, Altizer's reading of apocalyptic in Boehme, Blake, and Hegel. This pair of concepts is explored in the next two chapters.

Chapter 4 puts forward as a negative condition of the possibility of apocalyptic inscription the inherent friendliness in the Hellenistic field of Valentinian and apocalyptic modes of revelation. Chapter 5 speaks to the positive conditions of the possibility of apocalyptic inscription in the third line of Protestant thought in which if there are instances of Valentinian narrative grammar, they will represent rule-governed deformation of classical Valentinian genres.

But to return to Altizer, I have shown my disagreement with Altizer's *apocalyptic* ascription of a line of Protestant discourses that maps almost exactly what I have been calling the Baurian line of narrative ontotheologies and argued the case for a *Gnostic*, or more specifically *Valentinian*, ascription. This *Auseinandersetzung* with Altizer provides a real test regarding relative taxonomic and genealogical adequacy. Nevertheless, promoting the advantages of *Valentinian* ascription not only is not incompatible with Altizer's insight that in important respects these modern narrative ontotheologies betray apocalyptic figuration of both first- and second-level types, but in fact it demands its incorporation into any final account. This I have done by considering narrative discourses in the Baurian field as special forms of apocalypse discourse—although justification of this cannot even begin until we have examined classical Valentinian texts—and by speaking of the assimilation and sublation of biblical apocalyptic by a nonbiblical apocalypse form. Again, my dispute with Altizer over criteria for specifying the peculiarity of the narrative ontotheology does not prevent me from recognizing the value of his three criteria for apocalyptic, that is, ontotheological felix culpa, radical kenosis, and an eschatological thrust that contributes to divine identity, for my own proposal of the Valentinian identity of these discourses. In part II of the text, it will be more apparent than here that I use Altizer's criteria to identify a mode of nonbiblical apocalypse that assimilates and sublates first- and second-level forms of biblical apocalyptic.

As indicated earlier, Altizer does not provide the only apocalyptic designator of a line of modern narrative discourses that subvert in a fundamental way the biblical narrative. His account is simply the most explicitly contentious in so far as it denies *Gnostic* or *Valentinian* ascription, focusing the issues of the relation between different forms of apocalypse and the criteria for calling or refusing to call narrative discourses in the Baurian line *apocalyptic*. There are also noncontentious apocalyptic contenders. There are thinkers who advocate an apocalyptic reading of discourses within the Baurian line without explicitly rejecting a Gnostic or Valentinian reading, indeed, without any real engagement with a rival genealogy. Henri de Lubac offers an apocalyptic reading that I briefly consider before moving on to the other two main genealogical rivals, Neoplatonism and Kabbalah.

Henri de Lubac's apocalyptic genealogy is less vulnerable to Gnostic trumping for two reasons. First, it does not engage alternative genealogies, and thus does not assert genealogical primacy. And second, the notes of apocalyptic, or more explicitly of the second-level interpretive form found in Joachim, are thoroughly uneccentric. If the narratives of Boehme, Hegel, and Schelling, among others, have a profound degree of eschatological thrust that recalls Joachim, de Lubac does not speak to the complex interpretation of creation and the theogonic drive of narrative that characterizes Altizer's interpretation. Nevertheless, if Altizer is right in thinking the first two features of these modern narratives are fundamental, especially the second—and, as I hope to show in subsequent volumes, there is good reason to suppose he is—then it is possible to think of the Gnostic genealogy as having the ability to assimilate de Lubac's apocalyptic model by thinking of eschatology as being inscribed within a larger theogonic narrative frame. Thus, *apocalyptic inscription* and its correlative concept, *apocalyptic distension*, enable one to do justice to the superb eschatological thrust of these discourses without necessarily specifying the genre of apocalypse as apocalyptic. The genre of apocalypse logically could be otherwise than apocalyptic, and our suggestion is that it is Valentinian. Arguably, this reading of the matter would also square Balthasar's commitment to an apocalyptic reading of discourses in the modern field, specifically his avowal of de Lubac's reading in *La postérité spirituelle de Joachim de Flore*,[117] and his Valentinian reading of important ontotheological narratives in modern thought.[118] For certain narrative ontotheological discourses would genuinely admit of a double description or even double ascription (e.g., Boehme, Hegel, and Schelling). But one description or ascription would be penultimate (i.e., apocalyptic) because it focuses on conspicuous narrative features of a discourse, the other, ultimate "i.e., Valentinianism," because it is the host narrative frame that sets the terms for the narrative form or forms that are inscribed in it.

I have said enough about the challenge presented to our Gnostic or Valentinian genealogy offered by the two types of apocalyptic genealogy, although for intrinsic as well as extrinsic reasons I have privileged Altizer's more contentious account. Neoplatonism, whose genealogical profile is no less powerful because less blatant than apocalyptic, offers a second powerful challenge to the Gnostic Baurian genealogy. As we saw in chapter 1, Baur and Staudenmaier thought Neoplatonism to be as adequate an ascription for modern narrative ontotheologies as Gnosticism. Although Blumenberg is leery of the genealogical enterprise as such, he manages to exacerbate Baur's and Staudenmaier's lack of consistent distinction between Gnosticism and Neoplatonism when he suggests in *The Legitimacy of the Modern Age* formal, and perhaps more than formal, correspondences between classical Neoplatonic discourses and discourses in the Baurian manifold, such as the discourses of Boehme, Hegel, and Schelling. Interestingly, however, in *Work on Myth* Blumenberg proposes a fundamental distinction between Neoplatonism and Gnosticism with the genealogical advantage going to the former rather than the latter. The distinction is that between a narrative ontotheology, whose circular pattern constitutes a *restitutio in melius*, an excess of end over beginning, and a narrative pattern in which the beginning is simply restored in and by the end and the between overcome (76–81, 361, 365).[119] The importance of the distinction is obvious: Neoplatonism is granted considerably more illuminating power regarding modern narrative ontotheologies when its various forms are regarded as narratively developmental in a way that the ontotheologies of Gnosticism are not. As we saw in our discussion of apocalyptic, the developmental nature of narrative ontotheology, or its theogonic character, was the single most important element in deciding that apocalyptic could not sustain a full-blown genealogical claim. Moreover, for Blumenberg, Neoplatonism is at no dramatic disadvantage with respect to Gnosticism when it comes to characterizing the cosmos: no less than in Gnosticism, the cosmos is demonized. Ontotheological alienation, then, is an essential feature of theogonic development. On analysis, however, both of Blumenberg's assumptions turn out to be unsupportable. Indeed, as with the challenge presented by the apocalyptic model, failures here point, at least negatively, to the superior genealogical capacity of the Baurian Gnostic model.

Neoplatonism in Blumenberg's discourse is generally vague. He recognizes it as a classical non-Christian Hellenistic discourse, a Christian appropriation of some significance, and a Trojan horse with respect to the Christian world of assumption in the Renaissance (Cusanus and Bruno). None of these attributions is especially problematic in the abstract, but one would appreciate some effort to distinguish between distinct historical instances of Neoplatonism and supply a clue whether Neoplatonism has a normative instance. Here Blumenberg does not oblige. So it is at once important to historicize Neoplatonic discourse and establish its baseline. I begin with the latter. The baseline of Neoplatonism can be thought of as defined by the global ontotheological narrative of a *proodos-epistrophē* kind, rendered in the classical texts of Plotinus and Proclus. This circumscription excludes Hermeticism and Porphyrian theurgic Neoplatonism from functioning as the baseline. Importantly, it also excludes the texts and narratives of Middle Platonists such as Numenius and Plutarch,[120] whose dualism is excessive when measured by the classical standards that Plotinus and Proclus provide. In a sense, therefore, after Baur and Jonas and against Blumenberg, it makes sense to build into our definition of Neoplatonism the *Enneads*'s classic act of resistance to a gnosticizing interpretation of Plato (2.9), in which demiurgic activity and the resulting cosmos are demonized. Built in also is a second and related element of Plotinian rebuke. This element, as Bloom in particular underscores,[121] concerns not so much the results of a particular interpretation as the style of interpretation in which the sacredness of the Platonic tradition is profaned by a willful and arbitrary misreading (2.9.6).[122] To the degree to which in its historical filiation Neoplatonism remains more or less faithful to its classical form, it will repeat these constitutive anti-Gnostic features.

Although they might have been more emphatic, neither Baur nor Staudenmaier, the two major promoters of Neoplatonic genealogy, ignore these two features of Neoplatonism that saddle it with a significant amount of genealogical disability. Nevertheless, the above-mentioned narrative criterion proposed by Blumenberg to distinguish Neoplatonism from Gnosticism seems to more than offset these potentially significant genealogical handicaps. The possibility of a theogonic interpretation of the exit-return narrative of Neoplatonism ensures that it matches up with Romantic and Idealist myths of the divine in a way that the putative circular narrative ontotheologies of Gnosticism cannot. The problem with Blumenberg's theogonic reading of Neoplatonism, however, is not that he offers a reading that is counterintuitive—a theogonic reading of Valentinianism is similarly counterintuitive—but rather that he does not offer reasons for this reading. Specifically, he fails to exploit the potentially important resource of the figure of Ulysses,[123] for if he could show that the model of exit and return to the One had itself a Ulyssean pattern, rather than this simply being the pattern of the exiled and home-seeking soul, then he would have successfully argued for a developmental reading. And crucially he is silent on the interpretive obstacles to the developmental case for Neoplatonic narrative ontotheology. The greatest obstacle, obviously, is the general consensus that if any religious-philosophical discourse provides us with an example of a circular narrative discourse, Neoplatonism is that discourse. Blumenberg's insights into Neoplatonism are profound. For instance, he may ultimately be right in thinking that Neoplatonism is more nearly defined by the dynamic of manifestation and the move into plurality than by the apophatic regime of a unity that is beyond being (*epekeina tēs ousias*). Nevertheless, the dynamic of manifestation does not in itself justify a developmental reading. The main impediment to such a reading lies in classical Neoplatonism's vision of the One as unitive source, which diffuses itself for no other reason than perfection's tendency to communicate itself, or in terms of the classic Timaean trope, the tendency of the divine (*to theion*) not to be jealous.[124] The One is sufficiency without the shadow of deficiency. The very sufficiency of the One, as source, demands a circular pattern, for the original One, or the One as origin, cannot be improved on. To suggest otherwise is to insinuate that the perfection of the One is not primal, a position that is not sustainable within Neoplatonism's metaphysical horizon. Thus, one has to deny to classical Neoplatonism the narrative taxonomic advantage, suggested by Blumenberg, and similarly deny such advantage to any premodern version of Neoplatonism that is relatively continuous with classical Neoplatonism. Thus, this advantage has to be denied to Bruno also, who is regarded as relatively continuous with classical Neoplatonism and for whom Blumenberg reserves special prerogatives. The particular way in which diffusion serves as a block against a developmental ontotheology suggests that development is predicated on a mechanism for the abolition of deficiency inscribed or inscribable in the original perfection. In the next chapter I argue for the presence of just such a mechanism in the classical texts of Valentinian Gnosticism.

Although not determined by it, premodern Neoplatonism is constrained by its classical instance. Prior to the modern age the multiverse forms of Neoplatonism almost invariably define themselves in interaction with particular religious traditions (e.g., Jewish, Muslim, and Christian). In the case of Christianity, Neoplatonic narrative ontotheological structures are intended to (re)describe and nonexhaustively explain the Christian narrative, although in the complicated history of interaction we find continual tension between the interpreting narrative discourse and the discourse of Christian faith that calls for comment, criticism, and moves of correction reaching all the way to excision. This tension is often focused in the clash between emanation and creation (e.g., Pseudo-Dionysius, Eriugena), but sometimes the tension is expressed in the relative value of the unmanifesting and manifesting divine (e.g., Eckhart) and at others in christology, where the historicity and unsurpassibility of Christ is challenged by a modality of thought that stresses paradigm and repeatability. While there are exceptions, later forms of Neoplatonism generally repeat those features that mark off the classical Neoplatonism of Plotinus and Proclus from Gnosticism: if the cosmos is dissimilar to divine perfection, it is not antithetical; the hermeneutical stance adopted vis-à-vis the Christian narrative, as well as its own metaphysical tradition of exit-return, is generally respectful; and we find no suggestion that in the narrative of manifestation the divine undergoes development.

Two Christian Neoplatonic trajectories are especially important here because they have been genealogically enlisted in naming either the whole modern narrative ontotheological terrain covered by Baur's Gnostic hypothesis or significant regions of figures. The first has its presuppositions in Pseudo-Dionysius, but its narrative crescendo in Scotus Eriugena, whose *De divisione Dei* offers an unsurpassed account and vindication of theophany.[125] The second has its origin in Nicholas of Cusa, whose radical gestures toward immanence are realized by Bruno.[126] Staudenmaier gets closest to entertaining the Dionysian-Eriuginian strain as a relatively adequate genealogical construct for the speculative Protestant narrative discourses privileged by Baur.[127] In Beierwaltes and his students, testing the genealogical case of classical Neoplatonism for German Idealism has been accompanied by explorations concerning the genealogical merits of the Dionysian-Eriuginian line.[128] Furthermore, if Beierwaltes has not absolutely ignored the figure of Cusanus and his effective history, it is the particular merit of Blumenberg to have drawn attention to the special affinity between Bruno and Cusa and the influence of his brand of Neoplatonism in German Idealism, albeit with the caveat that the freestanding novelty of modernity does not permit this brand of Neoplatonism, any more than any other, to function genealogically in the full and proper sense.

Now while the differentiation of Neoplatonism into distinct types complicates the genealogical agon, it is necessary for two reasons. First, one cannot make an appeal to Valentinian narrative grammar and reduce the genealogical opposition to the procrustean bed of its classical instance. Second, one cannot rule out beforehand the possibility that one of the distinct types of Neoplatonism may be more genealogically powerful than the others with respect to modern narrative ontotheologies of the Baurian field, or more perspicuously illuminate particular features of these ontotheologies. With respect to the first point, one widens the variety of prototypical instances across the premodern development of Neoplatonism within Christian culture with a view to seeing whether hints of demonization of cosmos, metaleptic interpretive posture, and theogonic construal of the narrative of manifestation are evident. If no significant traces of this ensemble are to be found in any of these varieties, this begins to suggest at least a fundamental narrative grammar incapacity vis-à-vis modern narrative ontotheologies that seem to betray all of these features. It is important to show not only what kind of genealogical work Neoplatonism can do generically, but also what work each of the varieties of Neoplatonism can do.

Against the backdrop of what we have seen to be the productive result of the agon between *apocalyptic* and *Gnostic* ascription of narrative ontotheologies in the Baurian line, we come to the question of the prospect of Neoplatonism having some degree of secondary or supplemental genealogical power in the event of failing to sustain a genealogical position of the first order. This supplemental power may come in three forms: (1) Neoplatonism best describes particular features of modern narrative ontotheologies in the Baurian line, (e.g., apparent commitment to the diffusion metaphor regarding manifestation, and the salient deployment of the language of providence when dealing with the problems of finitude and evil); (2) Neoplatonism accounts just as well for tensions apparent in modern narrative ontotheologies between the radical mystery that is the basis of ontotheological narrative, linguistically evoked by *apophasis*, and the ontotheological narrative of manifestation itself; and (3) Neoplatonism can be seen to destabilize, in a way similar to classical Valentinianism but over a more extensive historical period, important aspects of the Christian narrative, especially the sense of the Trinity as consisting of relations between three equally divine persons.

I discuss these aspects of Neoplatonism's supplemental genealogical power in chapter 5, although I advise against any expectation that Neoplatonism's supplemental explanatory power will be demonstrated. Short of actual execution of the genealogy in and through sustained readings of intellectual movements in Christianity and of specific figures who make significant contributions toward a revised Christianity, the notion of Neoplatonism having supplementary taxonomic and genealogical power remains hypothetical. But something of what I want to claim now with respect to the third line of Protestant thought I have already broached in *The Heterodox Hegel*. There I showed that if Neoplatonism does not provide a fully adequate label for Hegel's narrative discourse, it is recalled in such significant ways that it must be registered in any final account.[129] Leaving in parenthesis what specific forms of Neoplatonism are recalled, one has to endorse in some measure the view of Beierwaltes and his followers concerning the importance of Neoplatonism for an understanding of German Idealist thought. Neoplatonism makes a contribution to Hegel's view that the drive to manifestation is an ineluctable property of divine. Indeed, Hegel sides with the Neoplatonists over what he takes to be the Gnostic position on this point.[130] God is intrinsically nonenvious. Relatedly, Hegel's metanarrative discourse operates with a very Neoplatonic view of divine providence that insists on the legitimacy and essential exonerability of divine reality despite the palpable presence of evil.[131] Again, the radical commitment to manifestation seems to undermine the possibility of a hypostatic or personal interpretation of the Trinity, whether the Trinity is narrowly conceived as the differentiated divine infinite outside the network of relation to finitude or as the divine infinite that is constituted in and through its relation to the finite.[132]

I recall Hegel here only because he is typical of what we find in the Baurian line that stretches from Boehme to Altizer. In the next volume, I will show how Boehme provides just as clear a case for positing a Neoplatonic taxonomic supplement. His embeddedness in the tradition of German mystical theology dictates that Neoplatonism is an inevitable element of his complex narrative discourse and has effects that are similar to its effects on Hegel's narrative discourse. Indeed, as in many other respects, Boehme anticipates Hegel here. The three features that we see present in Hegel are also present in Boehme. Boehme insists on the ineluctable drive toward manifestation as characterizing the divine from the very beginning. It is this drive that leaves behind the silence and hiddenness that is the background of divine manifestation, and that guarantees that there is no personal identity of the divine short of the termination of the narrative of manifestation. And again, it is the teleological terminus of the narrative that underwrites the providential character of the entire process of manifestation. One essential way in which Boehme differs from Hegel, however, is in his greater insistence on the background of hiddenness and apophasis, a point on which he is followed by both Schelling and Tillich, as we hope to show in later volumes. This distinction, however, I will want to argue, is an intramural or specifically intra-Valentinian distinction.

To speak of the possibility of genealogical supplementarity is in no way to reintroduce multiple genealogical ascription, for supplementarity implies that one genealogical ascription, in this instance, Valentinian Gnosticism, can be regarded as determinative in the last instance. But as we saw in the case of apocalyptic, the appeal to Neoplatonic narrative forms may be necessary to account for particular features of these modern narrative ontotheological discourses that stretch Valentinian grammar by departing in significant ways from classical Valentinian genres or paradigms. This suggests something like a *narrative stratigraphy*. In each of the complex narrative discourses in the Baurian line, one can imagine a base Valentinian narrative form open to modification by means of a variety of discourses that includes Neoplatonism and apocalyptic and, as we shall see momentarily, possibly also the Kabbalah. It is important, however, to underscore the openness of the Valentinian base for modification, for such openness is essential to Valentinian grammatical potency, without which one would be left dividing the taxonomic and genealogical spoils between different premodern narrative discourses with one or other narrative discourse having quantitatively, rather than qualitatively, more taxonomic and genealogical power.

The topological model is, of course, only approximate. It provides a picture of how classical Valentinianism is modified by other narrative discourses in complex Christian narratives in modernity with a view to indicating both the continuity and discontinuity between these discourses and the Valentinianism of the Hellenistic period. The model is also heuristic, for we are not actually suggesting that classical Valentinian genres perdure whole cloth throughout modernity to be modified by these other discourses. We are rather saying that these other narrative discourses function in an environment in which, in interaction with remnants of classical Valentinian narratives, they aid in the production of new forms of Valentinianism. The aid they provide can be mapped as a series of transformations enacted on a classical Valentinian base, none of whose actual paradigms prove wholly viable in the modern age. With its approximate and heuristic nature, the topological model clearly needs to be supplemented by some nontopological constructs. Here Louis Althusser's construct of *overdetermination* can provide some assistance.[133] One can think of modern narrative ontotheologies within the Baurian frame as a center of a number of discursive and narrative forces, but with Valentinian narrative being determinative in the final analysis. And Valentinianism is determinative in the final analysis, not because it is the most powerful regional force, but because its force is involved with all other forces and essentially regulates them.

Even with this qualification, there is only so much work that the topological model can do. Ultimately, only a linguistic or grammatical model of narrative ontotheological discourse is adequate, for only in this case can one talk about continuities between narrative species, both synchronically and diachronically, and account for differences. Well-formed sentences of Valentinian narrative grammar need not look the same; indeed, they can look quite different. I wish in fact to underscore difference. One important aspect of difference is the presence in the complex narratives of the third line of Protestant discourses in the modern period of narrative strands that do not have their origin in ancient Gnosticism. Even accepting that Neoplatonic, apocalyptic, and Kabbalistic narrative discourses are not idle in the complex narrative discourses of figures such as Blake and Schelling, and Hegel and Altizer, this would not rule out that these complex discourses are instances of Valentinian narrative grammar, while at the same time examples of rule-governed deformation of classical Valentinian genres. But even here we may have to be careful. In the next chapter I point to the fact that even the classical genres of Valentinianism show openness to apocalyptic and Neoplatonism, and in the following chapter I argue for the intrinsic hospitality of Valentinian narrative grammar for these narrative discourses.

This brings us to the third genealogical contender that the Gnostic or Valentinian genealogy must face, namely, the Kabbalah. Chapter 1 showed that Kabbalah amassed a surprising amount of mention as a taxon of narrative ontotheologies in the extended Baurian field. Crucially important, however, is some further specification of the Kabbalah. For it seems odd at best, perverse at worst, to entertain a Kabbalistic interpretation of modern narrative ontotheologies within the overall discursive horizon of Christianity if the *Kabbalah* functions as a term for a speculative discourse that expands rather than contests the Hebrew textual canon and continues to have a relation to Torah and to the life of Jewish prayer and devotion. But this is essentially the point: as a genealogical counter with respect to Christian narrative discourses in the Baurian field, the Kabbalah functions as a Christian and speculative *Ersatz*. Moreover, the Kabbalah is not only uprooted from Jewish and transplanted onto Christian soil. Given the highly pneumatic nature of the Christian narrative discourses in the Baurian field, which operate at the very least on the Marcionite assumptions of the fundamental disconnect between the God of Christianity and the God of Hebrew scriptures and Jewish law, to the extent to which the Kabbalah has a presence that encourages a Kabbalistic genealogy, it can only be as an anti-Jewish discourse. This is, professedly, to think of no form of Christian Kabbalah as particularly innocent with respect to Judaism and to adopt a stance much closer to Moshe Idel's view of the relation between Christian Kabbalah to its Jewish ancestry than that of Gershom Scholem.[134] I want to suggest that in the post-Renaissance and post-Reformation field of narrative, and especially in the Baurian field, the anti-Judaism dimension of the appropriation of the Kabbalah—I am not prepared to say anti-Semitic factor—is exacerbated.

Independent of the genealogical issue, the discursive parricide in which the Kabbalah is deployed against its Jewish origins is a historical phenomenon of great importance. Nonetheless, in terms of genealogy, the credentials of the Kabbalah, or what we are calling the Kabbalistic *Ersatz*, are far from insignificant. Not only is the Kabbalah often explicitly recalled in these discourses, and its presence just as often signaled, but Kabbalah also accounts for constitutive elements of the narrative ontotheologies of the Baurian field that depart from mainline Christian versions, which are not accountable in any straightforward way by Gnosticism or Valentinianism. For example, we find fully appropriated the doubleness of the created order, its metaphysically evil character yet its teleological value, the developmental drive of the divine, and the displacement from the unknowable divine unto human being or Adam. And clearly the Kabbalah can be made to serve Valentinian purposes. Not inherently a metaleptic discourse with respect to Hebrew scripture, abstracted from its Jewish roots, it can and does become so in the complex speculative narratives of the Baurian line.

I have argued in a somewhat lengthy article on Hegel that the German philosopher appropriates the Kabbalah to a surprising extent.[135] Hegel effectively baptizes the Kabbalah, only then to have it circulate within his own discourse and play a role in his revision of the Christian narrative, including its trinitarian book ends. In the next volume I will argue the same point with respect to Boehme, who is the figure in Baur's third line whose discourse shows the greatest Kabbalistic saturation. And in a succeeding volume on Romanticism, I will argue that an epic poem such as Blake's *Jerusalem*, which I submit provides an instance of Valentiniann narrative grammar, not only recalls much of the theatrical and iconic machinery of apocalyptic and constitutive features of Neoplatonic narrative, but also a number of important Kabbalistic tropes, above all that of *Adam Kadmon*. Finally, in the concluding volume to the genealogy, I will discuss how the Kabbalah is introduced into Molt-mann's, as well as Altizer's, discourse—much as it is in Hegel—in the interest of a revision of the standard Christian construal of the God-world relation.

As it points to elements of revision in the narrative ontotheolo-gies of the Baurian field with respect to standard renditions of the Christian narrative, the Kabbalah is, arguably, less a productive metaleptic discourse than a reproductive one.[136] And this suggests that the Kabbalah finds its ground in an aboriginal metaleptic dis-course of Valentinianism that distorts every and all aspects of the biblical and Christian narratives (e.g., creation, christology, trinity), even to the point of making Christianity a theogonic discourse. Moreover, it suggests that even the displacement from the transcen-dent divine onto Adam featured in the Kabbalah finds its original form in Valentinian discourse.

Now if the suggestion here is that this aboriginal metaleptic dis-course is Gnosticism, specifically Valentinianism, this does not imply a historical judgment about the relation of Kabbalah to Gnosticism that has exercised historians of Jewish religious thought. Specifi-cally, it does not decide the issue of the origin of chariot or Merkabah mysticism or adjudicate whether a Gnostic origin or influence is plausible.[137] Nor does it try to assess what the relations are between chariot mysticism of the sixth and seventh centuries and the specu-lative thought of classical Kabbalah that dates from the twelfth and thirteenth centuries. Rather it suggests that, with regard to the nar-rative ontotheologies that constitute the third line of Protestant dis-course, the Kabbalah functions best as a genealogical supplement to Gnosticism or Valentinianism. In this respect, therefore, the Kab-balah is in a similar position to apocalyptic and Neoplatonism: It il-luminates certain features of modern narrative ontotheologies more perspicuously than the classical Valentinian narrative genres or par-adigms; it sometimes illuminates certain features of narratives in the Baurian line better than the rival non-Valentinian narrative paradigms; and finally in tandem with the other non-Valentinian narrative paradigms it sheds light on bands of features not ac-counted for directly by the classical Valentinian paradigms. Thus, the Kabbalah, or the Kabbalistic *Ersatz*, indicates genealogical overdetermination. Yet, as suggested implicitly in the case of apoca-lyptic, and explicitly in the case of Neoplatonism, it is Valentinian-ism that is taxonomically and genealogically determinative in the last instance and in a qualitative rather than quantitative way. For in what appears to be the narrative stratigraphy of ontotheological narrative discourses in the Baurian field, the Valentinian serves as the base. Not only do the narrative paradigms of classical Valentinianism find significant repetition, but departures from or deformations of these paradigms, which open up the prospect for other genealogical explanations, are traceable back to elements of subversion hinted at in these paradigms, but never fully enacted. These elements include revising the estimate of the cosmos as fundamentally evil, rethinking the predominant circular narrative pattern in light of the movement from perfection to perfection, and, in the light of the dynamic developmental pattern, rethinking the relation between pathos and the divine.

Although a narrative discourse that is interpretively more derivative than Neoplatonism with which it has complex historical relations,[138] the Kabbalah is, arguably, topologically closer to Gnosticism to the extent to which it thinks of evil as substantial and aggressive rather than privative, the divine in terms of process and development despite starting with a divine that is statically and negatively determined, and points to something other than ontological generosity as being at the base of a movement of manifestation. Something like this point is suggested by Bloom,[139] who in a profound intuition suggests that the Kabbalah plays the role of intermediating between Valentinian and Neoplatonic styles of interpretation in Romantic poetics. It is possible to think of the Kabbalah not only as a hermeneutic of intermediation, but also as a narrative discourse that mediates between a Valentinian infrastructure and Neoplatonic superstructure, thus essentially a discourse of intercalation for the complex narrative ontotheologies in the Baurian field.

Nevertheless, as I have said more than once, the topological model is approximate and as much, if not more, heuristic than categorial. Consequently, speculations such as the relative proximity of secondary narrative discourses to the primary narrative discourses in the complex narrative ontotheologies of the Baurian line have at best a relative adequacy. Only the grammatical or linguistic model is finally explanatory. The topological model, however, enables the interpreter to envisage, somewhat less abstractly than would be the case with the grammatical model alone, how the primacy of Valentinianism in narrative ontotheologies in the Baurian line is effected, even as these non-Valentinian narrative discourses assist in making modern Valentinian forms different in important ways from classical

Valentinian genres or paradigms. I will try to demonstrate in the analysis of the important discourses in the Baurian line that all three of the taxonomic and genealogical rivals to Valentinianism are enlisted by Valentinianism, while they in turn modify it. In addition, I argue that all three narrative discourses contribute to the difference between the Valentinianism of narrative ontotheologies in the Baurian line and the classical Valentinian paradigms. Or in other words, I show how these narrative discourses contribute to the constitution of modern narrative ontothelogies in the Baurian line being rule-governed deformation of classical Valentinian genres. I am, however, far from finished with my elucidation of genealogical supplementarity in this programmatic text. In part II, and especially in chapter 5, I expand further on this in the context of specifying the modernity of narrative discourses in the Baurian line and their specifically Protestant cast.

Summary

In this chapter I submitted the burgeoning Baurian model to two serious challenges: first, to the historicist challenge represented by the genealogist, *malgré lui*, Hans Blumenberg, and, second, to the challenge represented by rival genealogical accounts of the third line of Christian discourses in modernity. I determined that the Baurian model of Gnostic return survived both challenges. Moreover, I showed how these challenges play a positive role in constructing a viable Gnostic or Valentinian genealogy. Engaging Blumenberg deepened our objection to any view that would suggest uninterrupted continuity of discourse, narrative or otherwise, across history. It entailed specifically a modification of Baur's *Urnarrative* interpretation of Gnosis. At the same time, engaging Blumenberg encouraged sharpening the distinction between Valentinianism and Neoplatonism, and drawing a line of demarcation between Marcionism and Valentinianism both with respect to narrative structure and metaleptic ratio. Both distinctions are crucial from a genealogical point of view. The former is crucial if we are to avoid the kind of ambiguity that characterizes Baur's genealogical account of a line of speculative Christian (that is, Protestant) thought in modernity that he wishes to recommend. The latter is crucial if we are to distinguish between the broader patterns of transformation of biblical narrative and/or its first-order interpretation in the modern age that seem more appropriately labeled as

Marcionite and the narrower patterns of transformation, which we associate with the comprehensive disfiguration-refiguration of the biblical narrative, typical of complex narratives of the third line of Protestant discourse. Only narrative discourses in this third line are, properly speaking, Valentinian, even if they turn out to be deviant with respect to classical Valentinian genres. The counter-genealogical challenge posed by the supporters of apocalyptic, Neoplatonic, and Kabbalistic characterization of discourses in the third line of Protestant discourses also turned out to be productive with respect to developing an adequate Gnostic or Valentinian genealogical model. For I suggest more than that it is antecedently unlikely that any of these genealogical rivals provides a more adequate label for narrative discourses that reach from Boehme to Altizer, and perhaps even beyond to Mark C. Taylor and certain varieties of deconstruction. I suggested nothing less than that apocalyptic, Neoplatonic, and Kabbalistic discourses are capable in the context of complex modern narrative of being enlisted to subserve a Valentinian narrative agenda. Obviously, given such enlisting, the mode of Valentinianism will necessarily look different than that found in classical Valentinian genres or paradigms. At the same time, given the presence of these narrative forms in the complex narrative discourses of the Baurian field, we did not rule out that, either singly or together, these ascriptions could function in a secondary way for individual discourses or indeed the entire band of narrative discourses that constitute what we are calling the Baurian line.

This chapter has added conceptual depth to the constructs of Valentinian narrative grammar, rule-governed deformation of classical Valentinian genres, and metalepsis. To this end it has also generated further elements of technical vocabulary such as *apocalyptic inscription* and *apocalyptic distention* and *narrative stratigraphy* that can be put into play in the actual execution of genealogy. *Apocalyptic inscription* and *apocalyptic distention*, of course, refer to the specific mode by which *apocalyptic* is enlisted by the governing Valentinian visionary narrative discourse and which it reflexively affects. In principle, the enlisting of apocalyptic enjoys no privilege over the enlisting of Neoplatonism and Kabbalah by a discourse whose narrative grammar is Valentinian. Denial of principled privilege to apocalyptic over Neoplatonism'and Kabbalah does not rule out, however, something like a de facto privilege. While one of the key theses of part II is that for every discourse in the Baurian line the primary Gnostic or Valentinian ascription is supplemented by all three ascriptions, this does not preclude dominant-recessive relations among the supplements. Specifically, it does not rule out that apocalyptic may be dominant in a number of discourses in the Baurian line such as, for instance, the mythopoetic discourse of Blake and the apparently evangelical discourse of Moltmann.

~

PART II

Toward Valentinian Narrative Grammar

On the basis of criteria such as categorial determinacy, fertility and influence, and explanatory power, part 1 proposed a retrieval of Baur's Gnostic return. I determined that, appearances to the contrary, it was superior to the other models of Gnostic return currently in circulation. The retrieval was critical, however, in that I judged that, as articulated in *Die christliche Gnosis*, Baur's model was inadequate and could be deployed only after considerable extension and serious correction. At the center of such correction was resistance to Baur's tendency to assume the existence of a dynamic and dramatic Gnostic *Urnarrative* common to the Hellenistic and the modern Protestant field, and the argument that a grammatical account of Valentinian narrative better protects the discontinuity as well as continuity between ancient and modern narrative ontotheologies that swerve from the biblical narrative. My grammatically revised Baurian proposal was, however, formal, its modality that of the possible rather than the actual. Transcending such formality and making the model actual demands reversing direction. Specifically, it involves examining classical Valentinian discourses themselves to ascertain whether these discourses are defined by a narrative grammar, and then only subsequently and consequently going on to argue that narratives in the Baurian line can be read legitimately as exemplars of this narrative grammar.

This demands in the first instance a return to the sources of Valentinianism, which in the wake of Nag Hammadi are on an entirely different level than they were in Baur's own day. Here we cannot take shortcuts. In the absence of agreement about the validity and value of a grammatical conception, we must argue for such a conception, not assume it. This necessarily involves a detailed reading of classical Valentinian texts by which we attend to their diversity as well as unity. It is by taking diversity in classical Valentinian discourses as seriously as unity, to the point in fact of imagining even greater diversity, that one is able to generate a Valentinian narrative grammar. We cannot overstate the genealogical importance of a successful prosecution of a case for Valentinian grammar. Such grammar could not only account for the diversity and unity of a band of discourses in the Hellenistic field, but it could also account for later discourses beyond the Hellenistic field, since there is no principled reason why Valentinian grammar should be exhausted by its Hellenistic instances or paradigms. At the same time the individual Valentinian discourses within the Hellenistic field that are examined are not mere rungs on the analytic ladder to be thrown away once they have served the purpose of pointing toward a narrative grammar. Individual classical Valentinian discourses are not disposable in this way. Beyond their general argumentative function, they continue to be relevant as genres or paradigms of Valentinian narrative grammar and even continue to enjoy a certain privilege because they articulate the sedimented tradition of Valentinianism. And these paradigms invite individual comparison with forms of thought in the Baurian field regarded as candidates for ascription of *Gnostic return*. Of course, on both pragmatic and systematic grounds it is necessary to be selective with respect to Valentinian sources. The three Valentinian discourses that come in for detailed examination are discourses of the most encompassing narrative scope that focus on the origin and end of evil and bear a metaleptic relation to the biblical narrative of a good god who creates, redeems, and sanctifies the world.

In the analyses of individual texts I underscore the systematically metaleptic relation of Valentinianism to Christian belief and narrative. In an astonishing variety of ways a biblical narrative will be disfigured and reconfigured, analytically broken down and then synthesized in new narrative structures, according to different rules of formation than those operative in more orthodox circles. Crucially, disfiguration-refiguration of the biblical narrative is comprehensive and radical. It is comprehensive in that every single aspect of the biblical narrative from creation to apocalypse is distorted and basic commitments reversed. And it is radical in that this comprehensive rereading or misreading of the biblical narrative is understood not to belong to the order of faith but to that of knowledge, moreover a knowledge that saves. In addressing how this metaleptic operation is carried out, I highlight the way in which the binary oppositions of light and dark, seeing and not seeing, fullness and emptiness, silence and speech, lightness and weight, life and death, fertility and sterility, and positive and negative aspects of the feminine play roles in the narrative economy of classical Valentinian discourses. I also highlight the register of the narrative, specifically whether the narrative suggests an extramental state of affairs or series of events, or whether the narrative renders a state of affairs or series of events of a more than human psyche.

Not only as a source, but as an interpreter, or exemplar of a style of interpretation, Irenaeus is an important figure in the second part of this programmatic text. Narrative disfiguration-refiguration or *metalepsis* is an original Irenaean contribution and at once indicates his superiority to Baur, at least the Baur of *Die christliche Gnosis*, and functions as an important categorial element in our rehabilitation of Baur. Moreover, Irenaeus is not simply the connoisseur of metalepsis, he is the commentator-critic of Gnosticism in general, Valentinianism in particular, who understands that the proliferation of narrative construction or fabrication is not simply a matter of fact but a matter of fundamental principle. Thus more than any other interpreter, Irenaeus encourages the move to a grammatical rendition of Valentinian narrative, indeed a move to the concept of a Valentinian narrative grammar as a transformational grammar.

Reflection on Irenaeus as offering a particular style of interpretation is best separated from an analysis of classical Valentinian texts that occupies the opening chapter of part 2 (chap. 3), and in which Irenaeus plays the role of source—although by no means the only or the most important source. Similarly, although the topic is necessarily broached in the exegesis of classical Valentinian discourses, it is important to make thematic the relation-difference between Valentinian and other narrative discourses that also historically inform Christianity and are players in the configuration of its narrative or narratives. Keeping in mind the discussion in part 1 (chap. 2) of rival taxonomies for the narrative discourses in the Baurian field, I comment on what distinguishes Valentinian from Neoplatonic and apocalyptic narratives in the Hellenistic field, especially in the context of Valentinianism showing a certain hospitality to these discourses. I suggest that the porousness of Valentinianism with regard to these narrative discourses does not damage its narrative integrity. In fact the openness of Valentinianism to other narrative discourses gives it explanatory advantages with respect to narrative ontotheologies of the Baurian field in which literary and substantive elements of all three discourses are found. This is especially the case when one can espy the operation of a powerful metalepsis of Christian narrative, untypical of the behavior of Neoplatonism and apocalyptic in the Christian field.

Chapter 4, then, takes an explicitly grammatical turn in which the transformational nature of Valentinian narrative and Valentinianism's ability to enlist other narrative discourses are major foci of concern. Although I try for the most part to avoid explicit genealogical discussion, this chapter points both indirectly and directly to genealogical application. Given the genealogical ponderings of part 1, it would be disingenuous to deny that the articulation of a Valentinian narrative grammar is pointed toward the possibility of such a grammar being reactivated this side of the Reformation and the Enlightenment. While neither the concept of Valentinian narrative grammar, nor its articulation, is directly dependent on Irenaeus, I do wish to acknowledge his contribution to a grammatical understanding of Valentinianism. Accordingly, I devote a substantial portion of the first section discussing his manifold contributions. This articulation also makes sense of the evaluative thrust of the entire genealogical enterprise in which I am engaged. In the first section of chapter 4, I make a somewhat more complicated genealogical gesture when I argue that the Christian narrative, which is the subject of Valentinian metalepsis, has itself to be regarded as a grammar rather than an invariant form. Here Irenaeus has to be corrected, since his gesture toward a grammatical conception of Valentinianism is accompanied by a gesture toward an invariant Christian narrative. Moreover, this grammatical revision shows that what is at stake in every act of metalepsis of the Christian narrative is not only a particular form of narrative, but narrative grammar. The fight, therefore, in the modern field between narrative ontotheologies in the Baurian line and more orthodox renditions of the Christian narrative, as between Irenaeus and Tertullian and the various Gnostic specimens they are combating, is nothing less than a *grammaromachia*. In my elucidation of this agon of narrative grammars I argue that (1) Christian narrative grammar is every bit as generous as Valentinian narrative grammar and allows a similar amount of variation,[1] and (2) serious deviance from majority views on the level of individual units of the narrative, for example, the construal of the divine, creation, Christ, and so on, should not be considered as rendering a discourse heterodox in the strong sense. The latter is very important from a genealogical point of view because I do not want to limit the opposition to Valentinian narrative grammar to exemplars of the most unaccommodating orthodoxy.

Chapter 5 is explicitly genealogical. It argues categorically that discourses in the Baurian line exemplify a Valentinian narrative grammar. At the same time it acknowledges the epochal character of these discourses; that is, that these discourses are marked by social and historical conditions, specific to modernity and its threshold. In the context of a programmatic and methodologically oriented discussion, the epochal point can only be made quite formally. What this amounts to becomes evident in subsequent treatments of the major movements of post-Reformation, Romantic, Idealist, and post-Idealist narrative discourses. It is the epochality of these discourses that prevents these discourses from being pure ahistorical repetitions of classical Valentinian paradigms and from contributing to the collapse of grammar or syntagma into paradigm that not only a historicist, but any theorist with a sense of history, rightly fears. If dechronicization is supported by a blind spot with respect to the specificity of conditions of discourses, the collapse of grammar into paradigm is encouraged by the assumption that Valentinian narrative grammar is ungenerous, that it allows for few variations and permits very little difference in narrative formation and narrative register. I embrace neither position here, and contest the second directly. I hope to persuade that the variety of classical paradigms and the major differences between them, outlined in chapter 3, suggest a Valentinian narrative grammar of considerable fertility.

Although the discourses in the Baurian field recapitulate, sometimes in extraordinary ways, the classical Valentinian paradigms, they nevertheless deviate significantly from them. I gestured to this in part I. The gesture can now in part at least be redeemed. It is redeemed also by changing the mode of discourse from the hypothetical to the categorical in the concept of rule-governed deformation of classical Valentinian genres. Valentinian narrative grammar exceeds the classical paradigms and permits deviance. It is, however, by reference to these classical paradigms that one measures deviance. At the same time, the patterned ways of deviance from, or deformation of, the classical paradigms or genres that one recognizes in narrative ontotheologies in the Baurian line can be extrapolated from the more radical but recessed tendencies evident in the classical Valentinian genres. Here, by contrast with part I, one is entitled to assert with categorical force that narratives in the Baurian field deform classical Valentinian paradigms by radicalizing and amplifying the developmental and teleological gestures in these narratives. This defining deformation is in turn specified by radicalization in the relation of pathos to the divine, the trope of ontotheological felix culpa, and a view of *kenōsis* that is better interpreted as filling rather than emptying.

In this chapter, I also redeem my speculative reflection in part 1 that narrative ontotheologies in the Baurian field show a tendency to subvert standard trinitarian mappings of the biblical narrative, and above all show the tendency to subvert the distinction between the immanent and economic Trinity. Proximally responsible for such subversion is the theogonic thrust of the dramatic narratives in the Baurian field. But ultimately, such a subversion is an effect of grammar. It is an effect of Valentinian grammar in the first instance in that it can be shown that these theogonic narratives are innovative paradigms of Valentinian narrative grammar, and in the second instance in that the phenomenon of triadic simplification and synopsis of a nontriadic narrative, which was a recessed feature of classical Valentinian narratives, sets the condition for such deformation by essentially hijacking traditional trinitarian language for a theogonic purpose.

Two additional features of chapter 5 deserve mention. First, it is here that I attempt to cash in genealogically the phenomenon of narrative enlisting that is extrapolated as a grammatical feature of Valentinianism (chap. 4.2). Harkening back to the discussion in part I, however, I add the Kabbalah to apocalyptic and Neoplatonism. In this chapter, I show negatively how Valentinian narrative integrity is maintained in the narrative ontotheologies of the Baurian line, and positively the way in which Valentinian narrative regulates these other narrative discourses and makes them subserve its own narrative economy. The reverse of this regulation also comes in for attention. I provide some indications how these enlisted narrative discourses reflexively modify the enlisting Valentinian narrative. Second, I question the easy identification of Baurian line of ontotheological narrative and the third line of Protestant thought. It is one thing to take seriously Baur's identification—repeated by his Catholic critics—it is another thing to treat it as a fundamental assumption. Let us take the most proximate case: Is Catholicism excluded in fact and/or in principle from the Baurian manifold? Excluding Catholicism in fact seems difficult. In the Romantic field Novalis's rendition of Christian narrative is idiosyncratic enough to merit investigation. Moreover, Franz von Baader's (1765–1841) huge debt to Schelling and Anton Günther's (1783–1863) equally huge debt to Hegel opens up the Gnostic return door. Even more interestingly, Balthasar's own enormous debt to Hegel has led more than one commentator to surmise that Balthasar too belongs in the Valentinian line.[2] Can Balthasar, who ironically plays a significant role in our diagnosis of modern Valentinianism, be exonerated from such a charge? Fully justifying identification of Baurian line of narrative ontotheologies with the third line of Protestant thought involves treating these test cases. Such a treatment, however, belongs properly to the execution of the genealogy itself in the subsequent volumes. All I can say here is that I believe that I can show that none of these reactivate or rearticulate Valentinian narrative grammar. In this programmatic volume the focus is on the issue of principle. In chapter 5, I specifically look at broad ideational features that serve as the background assumptions for reading the biblical narrative and determine which set of features belongs to Protestantism and which to Catholicism. I argue that only in Protestantism the set of assumptions is such as to encourage the kind of radical deformation of Christian narrative that justifies speaking of Gnostic return.

CHAPTER 3

~

Classical Valentinian Narratives:
Variety and Unity

Current Gnostic return theories suffer from many defects. One of the most basic and vitiating of these is the lack of anchoring in classical Gnostic or Valentinian texts. Without such anchoring, however, there is insufficient categorical determinacy in the use of the terms Gnostic and Valentinian, and only dim prospects for redeeming a genealogical case that rests upon justifying some significant form of continuity between discourses of the Hellenistic and discourses of the post-Reformation and post-Enlightenment fields. Relatively extensive discussion of classical Valentinian texts may at first appear to defer irresponsibly genealogical discussion, while at the same time their sheer variety obstructs the reasonable prospect of uniting discourses from the premodern with the modern field under a common ascription. I argue on the contrary that (1) only detailed analyses of Valentinian texts reveal those elements that lessen the apparent discontinuity between classical Valentinian texts and texts in the Baurian line, and (2) that the very variety of classical Valentinian forms argues for the presence of a Valentinian narrative grammar, which alone can account for the unity between the narratives of two different epochs.

Any responsible dealing with Valentinian Gnosticism must take account of the revolution in the text situation constituted by the Nag Hammadi discovery and with it the correlative limitations of the pre–Nag Hammadi horizon of interpretation, based as it was on secondhand reports. Although the understanding of Gnosticism in the early part of the twentieth century benefited considerably from the newfound status of *Religionsgeschichte* and reached new heights in the early Jonas's retrieval, which joined the finesse of a literary critic with Heidegger's powerful apparatus of existential categories, nevertheless, specific information on Valentinianism remained relatively unchanged from the time of Baur. It still consisted of heresiological reports, the first among equals being Irenaeus's *Against Heresies*. That a reading of Valentinianism had to be neither tendentious nor consist in mere reports is shown by Baur's *Die christliche Gnosis*. He extrapolates nonobvious implications of Valentinianism with insight and originality on the basis of Irenaeus's presentation. The problem with Baur's reading, and those before him, such as Neander and Hegel,[3] and those after him, such as Balthasar, is the problem of entitlement in a situation in which secondhand reports such as *Against Heresies* lack sources of corroboration. In its anthology of writings of different genres and distinct orientation, Nag Hammadi has fundamentally altered the interpretive possibilities and perhaps for the first time permits interpretations that can make claims to relative descriptive and explanatory adequacy. Initially the excitement about the treasure trove of primary texts, in concert with the perception of the interested nature of heresiological description, led to a marginalization of Irenaeus. In a correcting move in which the hermeneutic of suspicion has been transcended in the direction of a hermeneutic of critical appropriation, Irenaeus has essentially been reinstated. The operative interpretive model has come to be one of complementarity. From the one side, Irenaeus provides both indispensable historical information while setting determinate constraints on the interpretation of Nag Hammadi texts. From the other side, the texts of Nag Hammadi provide data that can support and amplify Irenaeus's readings of Valentinianism, although, of course, they do not necessarily call for his kind of evaluative judgment. As I clearly state in my introduction, while I am anxious to be as irenic as possible, my basic evaluative stance is Irenaean.

In the current situation of complementarity there is some general agreement—although hardly amounting to absolute consensus—on four major issues: (1) Valentinianism relates in some way or ways to non-Christian forms of Gnosticism, now identified as Sethian;[4] (2) Valentinianism bears not only an iconoclastic, but also metaleptic, relation to the biblical text; (3) Valentinianism has a narrative or metanarrative disposition; and (4) the unity of Valentinian texts and/or narratives is to be demonstrated, not assumed. If the first three elements, at least, are identifiably Irenaean, they appear to be corroborated in the texts from Nag Hammadi. Overlaps with regard to basic symbols, attitude toward creation and cosmos, the reading of Hebrew scriptures, the understanding of salvation,

and above all overlap with regard to total narrative pattern between
the *Tripartite Tractate*, and even the *Gospel of Truth*, and Sethian
texts such as *The Apocryphon of John* and *The Origin of the World*,
seem to validate a typological version of Irenaeus's claim in *Against
Heresies* that Valentinianism represents the domestication of non-
Christian *gnōsis*.[5] Similarly, the above- mentioned Valentinian texts
also appear to support Irenaeus's judgment that Valentinian interpretive practice is characterized less by outright rejection of Christian scriptures than by revisionist interpretation in which the
authority of scripture is relativized and contrary positions taken on
the nature of the divine, the value of creation, the interpretation of
the fall of human being, Christ and his redemptive mission, and finally the nature of salvation. These texts also seem to encourage a
large-frame view in which narrative comes once again to the fore.
The focus on narrative forges a link between contemporary commentators and a commentator such as Baur,[6] even as these modern
commentators are conscious, in a way that Baur and some of his
successors were not, of the difference between narrative as discourse, that is, a form of language, and narrative as story, that is, reality as such having the shape of a plot.[7] One can affirm without
contradiction, for example, that a Valentinian text is a narrative discourse that has as its object either a static reality or at least a nondevelopmental one. And *pace* Baur, I adopt the position that the
surface logic of Valentinian texts does not support a developmental
or story reading. I do, however, propose that there is a developmental or story undertow in the texts that allows for further explication.
Here I call upon Jonas's and Balthasar's suggestion that a distinction exists between the surface and depth semantics of Valentinian
narrative.[8] With respect to the fourth element of general agreement,
some tension may very well exist between the contemporary modus
operandi of treating Valentinian texts as distinct entities and the
tendency in Irenaeus to assert the existence of a Gnostic *Urnarrative*. It should be said, however, that Irenaeus is a witness for the
prosecution and actually undermines the legitimacy of the *Urnarrative* view by supplying thick descriptions of the various Gnostic narratives that do not show themselves to be reducible to a simple unity
and by focusing on the creativity evident in Valentinian literary production. I discucss Irenaeus's positive contribution in chapter 4.

My analysis of Valentinianism in this section presupposes the interpretive horizon of complementarity. As instances of the plurality of
Valentinian narratives, I exegete Ptolemy's Valentinian Gnostic system, the *Gospel of Truth*, and the *Tripartite Tractate*, in that order.

Among relevant differences I note are distinct takes on the representation of the sphere of divine perfection and its breakup, the visioning of the identity of creator and the status of the cosmos, and the understanding of Christ as savior figure. More structural differences in the texts such as the mythological or nonmythological register of the texts and their commitment or lack of commitment to the circular narrative pattern, which Blumenberg thinks typical of Valentinianism, also come in for discussion. Only on the basis of the elucidation of differences is any attempt made to suggest a measure of unity. The suggestion of unity between Valentinian texts coheres around the perception of similarities in the relation between these texts and non-Christian forms of Gnosticism, in the interpretive relations between these texts and Christian scripture, and similarities in narrative episodes and overall narrative structure. One specific form of unity especially worthy of note is a common tension between surface and depth narrative commitments. It is important to point out, however, that talk of unity in this chapter is more nearly descriptive rather than explanatory. Chapter 4 takes on the burden of moving beyond generalization to grammatical theory in the proper sense.

3.1. Ptolemy's Valentinian Gnostic System[9]

Although *Ptolemy's Valentinian Gnostic System (PSY)* makes continual appeal to Christian symbols such as Only Begotten, Christ, Holy Spirit, Jesus, and so forth, the dominant tendency, evincing fairly massive correspondence to forms of non-Christian gnosis now independently verifiable in the Nag Hammadi Library,[10] gives at least prima facie plausibility to Irenaeus's etiological account in *Against Heresies*. According to this account, Valentinian Gnosticism represents the Christian adaptation of a system of symbol and myth, which, if it emerged in the same field as Christianity, is not identical with it.[11] Consider these examples: the technical use of words such as *pleroma* and *aeon* to indicate the realm of divine fullness and hypostatic manifestation respectively; the centrality of the Sophia myth to describe an aeonic fall from the pleroma; the theme of the arrogant *archōn*, who is responsible for psychic and material reality, yet is unaware of his lack of control over pneumatic being.[12] While Irenaeus may omit some of the finer points of Ptolemy's account, the account provided in *Against Heresies* is nevertheless quite full and describes a narrative whose alpha and omega is identified with the sphere of divine plenitude or the pleroma, a sphere perfectly stable and harmonious. Here the main body of the narrative focuses on the introduction of flaw within the pleroma, the extrusion of the offending aeon, the generation of the demiurge who is responsible for the construction of the material universe and psychic and material man, the appearance of the Savior Jesus, and the eschaton.

As Irenaeus presents it, the ultimate foundation of all reality, specifically divine reality, is the Forefather (*Propatēr*) or Depth (*Bythos*) (1.1). The Forefather is a crucial figure in a weave of kataphatic and apophatic discourse. As the reality behind any movement on the level of divine perfection, the Forefather is at once eternal, still, ungenerated, uncontainable, and invisible (ibid). Yet when Ptolemy wishes to represent the divine alpha as truly originary and foundational, it is not the Forefather alone who is posited, but the Forefather in conjunction with Silence (*Sigē*). And conjunction is the right word, for Ptolemy understands this primordial dyad as a male-female pair, and indeed subsequent pairs (or syzygies of male and female) in sexual and specifically procreative terms. In the generation of Mind (*Nous*) or Only Begotten (*Monogenēs*) the Forefather is said to have deposited his seed in silence (1.1). Mind or Only Begotten seems to have special prerogatives in the aeonic system that differentiates and structures the pleroma. Full knowledge of the Forefather is asserted only of Mind or the Only Begotten. Indeed it could be said that Mind or Only Begotten *is* the knowledge of the Forefather, for it is not at all clear that Ptolemy wishes to predicate knowledge as such of the Depth. In any event,[13] Mind or Only Begotten marks a break with the ineffable mysteriousness of the ultimate foundation and/or depth of reality.

The five succeeding aeons that constitute the primary pleromatic field (i.e., the Ogdoad) are Truth, Logos and Life, and Man and Church. As a sign of discursive rupture from the Johannine Christianity with which Ptolemy shows a special familiarity,[14] it should be noted that whereas in the Fourth Gospel *only-begotten*, *truth*, *logos*, and *life* are names referring to a single reality, in Ptolemy they refer to distinct entities. In addition to the primary aeonic field of the pleroma, for Ptolemy both secondary and tertiary fields exist, the former consisting of ten, the latter of twelve aeons, respectively. Thus, the sum of aeons is thirty, with Sophia being the last of the aeons. Irenaeus does not dwell explicitly on the fact of Sophia being the last of the aeons or on the ambiguity in the Ptolemaean treatment of the pleroma that comes to the surface in the positing of Sophia as main actor in the generation of fault, whose cosmogonic and anthropogonic consequences so provoke hostility. On the one

hand, given that all the aeons belong to the pleromatic field, no principled distinction of an ontological and gnoseological kind exists between aeons outside the originary dyad; on the other hand, in
addition to the suggestion of the privileged status of Mind or Only
Begotten, a tendency exists to prioritize anterior over posterior
aeons and suggest qualitative distinctions among three distinct
aeonic zones of the pleroma. As the last aeon of the third field, and
thus the last aeon of the pleroma as such, Sophia appears to be
structurally fragile in a way in which aeons of the first aeonic field of
the pleroma are not. That it is Sophia and not another aeon who pre-
cipitates the crisis of flaw is not in any unqualified sense an accident, despite Ptolemy's obvious interest in absolving the divine as
such from blame with respect to the introduction of fault and ultimately the material world and its horrors.

In the Ptolemaean account the destruction of the perfection and
stability of the pleroma is self-consciously attributed to the auda-
cious attempt by Sophia to comprehend the mystery of the Forefather. Such comprehension is a prerogative properly belonging only
to Mind or Only Begotten. Nevertheless, we are not dealing with an
Eve-like etiological account of evil projected into the divine sphere.[15]
Searching into the mystery seems to be positively encouraged by the
Forefather. At this point *PSY* seems to be sending mixed messages
that undermine its theodicy interest. If the Forefather is the lure of
searching, surely it is the Forefather who is ultimately responsible
for Sophia's fall! As rendered by Irenaeus, it is possible to see how
PSY attempts to avoid this conclusion by insisting on the built-in
limitations to knowledge implied in the Forefather's enticement, indeed incitement to knowledge.

Sophia is culpable less because she sought the mystery than because she sought to fathom and exhaust the mystery. Knowledge is
encouraged, but apparently not of the full sort that Mind or Only Begotten possesses. That such metaphysical restrictions exist with regard to knowledge is mythologically depicted as the event in which
Limit (*Stauros*), also referred to as Cross, Redeemer, or Emancipa-
tor, serves as the check to Sophia's will to unrestricted knowledge.
Religiously, Limit or Stauros functions at once as judge and merciful
savior, for in being balked by Limit, Sophia realizes the inappropri-
ateness of her will to knowledge (defined as desire) and repents, and
thus allows the mystery to remain undisclosed. Nonetheless, as the
introducer of disturbance and flaw in the pleroma, Sophia in the
form of desire (1.2.2.–1.2.4), or in personalized terms *Achamoth* or
Physis, must be extruded from the pleroma. Still Sophia in her

higher tendencies is reestablished in her proper relation to the Fore-father and the pleroma as a whole. The thoroughgoing systematic nature of Ptolemaean reflection is in evidence when in the next phase of the narrative two aeons of decidedly Christian vintage (i.e., Christ and the Holy Spirit) are said to be emitted by Only Begotten. The express purpose of such emission is twofold: On the one hand, there is some need to bolster integration in the pleroma, presump-tively not fully achieved by higher Sophia's rehabilitation (1.4.1); on the other, there is a need to reveal to the aeons the secret of aeonic generation and the knowledge (*epignōsis*) of the Forefather. In any event, the result of the soteriological ministration is the establish-ment of harmonious unity between the aeons and the rendering ex-plicit of the doxological aspect to knowledge (1.2.6).

From the harmonious unity of the full aeonic system of the pleroma comes Jesus. Jesus, who is also called *Logos, Savior,* or *Christ*, is strictly speaking identical to none of these, since each of these names refers in fact to a distinct aeon or soteriological actor. That the names *Jesus, Christ, Logos*, and so on have distinct aeonic reference represents a transparent revision of the attitude of the New Testament writers for whom these names function as appella-tives of the same being, Jesus of Nazareth. Yet, having made a dis-tinction between the referents of these names and their particular soteriological domain of activity, Ptolemy wishes to underscore the analogy between their respective situations and activities. For in-stance, even in her fallen form as Achamoth, Sophia is not left with-out assistance. Ptolemy has Christ and Holy Spirit play exactly the role Stauros does in the pleroma,[16] namely setting legitimate re-strictions to Achamoth's desire for light while promoting her conver-sion from her erstwhile passion. In fact, Ptolemy discusses the soteriological activity of Christ and Holy Spirit under the sign of the cross whereas at an earlier juncture of the narrative Christ and the Holy Spirit function as synonyms for *Limit* or *Stauros*.

It is Achamoth, as fallen Sophia, or more specifically Achamoth in her state of conversion, which constitutes the prime matter from which comes the demiurge and the cosmos. And it is the latter and not Achamoth to whom is ascribed direct cosmogonic (1.5.2) and an-thropogonic function (1.5.5). As in such extra-Christian Gnostic texts as *The Hypostasis of the Archons* and *The Apocryphon of John*, the attitude toward the demiurge, who is assimilated to the Old Testa-ment God, is negative (1.5.4). *PSY* shares with the earlier-mentioned representatives of non-Valentinian Gnosticism the motif of the arro-gant archon who has a deluded idea of his power and its extent. This power in fact extends only over hylic and psychic reality, the demi-urge making illegitimate claims on a pneumatic reality to which he is not equal. Yet one should note that *PSY* does not break out into open hostility to the creator God. That this is the settled position of the Ptolemaean school of Valentinianism is evidenced by Ptolemy's refusal in the *Letter to Flora* to demonize the creator. While Irenaeus does not offer us in *Against Heresies* (1.1.8) an account of demiurgic hubris in attempting the creation of pneumatic being, such an attempt and its failure must be presupposed if Ptolemy is going to insist on the privileged soteriological possibilities of the pneumatic. In addition, the fall of pneumatic being must also be supposed if salvation is to make any sense.

Irenaeus does not provide us with sufficient detail in his account so that one gets a full-bodied sense of the exigencies of existence that call for salvation. Still the symbol of the Prince of the World in the *Letter to Flora* suggests that the governing experience is that of disorder and evil in the cosmos and human existence. As in the New Testament texts the savior is Jesus, whose ontological status as in other Valentinian accounts is summarized in the symbol the fruit of the pleroma. In a proposal that gravitates toward the condition of being a self-consuming artifact, Ptolemy insists (*Against Heresies*, 1.6.1) on Jesus inclusive assumption of *all* reality on grounds that anticipate the grand soteriological anti-Gnostic principle of Alexandrian and Cappadocian Christology of the fourth century. At the same time Jesus adopts matter or flesh in only an "as if" fashion. The docetic thrust of Ptolemy's Christology is exacerbated when the historicity of the passion is seen to affect Jesus only in his assumed psychic substance, leaving Jesus pneumatic core uninvolved. As loudly as any Platonist in the second century, Ptolemy is involved in affirming the apathetic axiom that what is divine cannot suffer, that is, that the divine transcends suffering, as it transcends mutability.[17] The suffering of the psychic Jesus has no salvific role with respect to the pneumatics, who share in the passionlessness of the pleroma and who are destined at death (or in the eschaton) to go to their rightful place. But neither is it the case that Jesus passion subserves an atoning function with respect to the psychics. Rather the main function the passion serves is the symbolic-educative one whereby the passion of Achamoth is disclosed.

Salvation is referenced to two categories of human being and denied to a third (i.e., the hylics), who in the eschaton, accompanied by apocalyptic signs (e.g., fire), are annihilated. As a leading codifier of the Western Valentinian School, Ptolemy extends salvation to the psychics, those of the Middle, as well as the pneumatics, but tries to qualify the modality of salvation in such a way that the superiority of the pneumatics is still maintained. Only the pneumatics are so constituted as to enter the pleroma as such. In *Against Heresies* (1.1–1.8) Ptolemy's view of how salvation comes to the pneumatic is not specified. Yet on the basis of what Irenaeus says elsewhere in the text, assuming that the way is through gnosis is not unreasonable. This assumption also finds support in Ptolemy's *Letter to Flora*, where ethical practice is expressly denied as the soteriological vehicle of/for pneumatics. Of course *knowledge* or *gnosis* is a technical term and does not mean self-contemplation, but rather knowledge of a complex narrative that answers the urgent question of existence, acknowledges flaw and fault, the dread of the cosmos, and manages at the same time to exculpate the divine from being incriminated in evil.

Ptolemy's system is essentially constituted as an ontotheological narrative of six stages.[18] (1) In the beginning there is only the pure undisturbed divine realm called the *pleroma*. While the pleroma illustrates a *stasis* and stability contrary to the *kinēsis* of time and history and the mutability of the cosmos, dynamism is nevertheless exhibited in the generation of a complex aeonic system. At the basis of the aeonic system as a whole, and totally beyond any movement whatsoever, is the Forefather and/or the dyad of Forefather and Silence. (2) The perfection of the pleroma is ruptured by Sophia, who wishes to know the mystery of the Forefather and the aeonic system. The fallen form of Sophia, Achamoth, or Physis engenders a demiurgic offspring. (3) The demiurge creates the cosmos and material and psychical human being. (4) The demiurge finds himself incapable of creating pneumatic being, whose origin is in the pleroma. Pneumatic being falls, however, and is in need of salvation. (5) Salvation comes in the form of the appearance of the Savior figure Jesus, who is, however, a revealer, not an atoner. Christ is a necessary but not sufficient condition for salvation. (6) Salvation as such comes about through imitative good works in the case of the psychics and by gnosis in the case of the pneumatics, who comprehend not only the symbolic role of the Christ but also the whole narrative.

This sixfold narrative overall has a triadic rhythm, moving from the high of perfection, through the low of loss, back to the high of perfection. If the triadic rhythm of the narrative is isomorphic with that of Christianity, nevertheless, everything is materially different. In *PSY* triadic rhythm is a function of a complex narrative that in each of its episodes disfigures the corresponding episode in the Christian narrative, or any relatively first-order interpretation of it.[19] Thus the entire Christian narrative is submitted to a systematic process of disfiguration. But *PSY* does not simply disfigure the Christian narrative: Each of the episodes of the Christian narrative, indeed, the entire narrative chain, is absorbed into and refigured by a metanarrative of absolutely encompassing extent in which the subject of discourse has changed from God's sovereign acts of creation, preservation, and salvation vis-à-vis the world and humanity to the vicissitudes that the divine undergoes as it deals with its own apostasy. It is this double-sided operation of disfiguration-refiguration that constitutes metalepsis in the full and proper sense. Or otherwise put, it constitutes *strong metalepsis*. In *Against Heresies* Irenaeus confirms that such an operation is constitutive of Gnostic hermeneutic practice and provides the constitutive label in Greek of *metharmottein* (1.8, 1.11.1, 1.20.2). Irenaeus clearly understands not only that *metharmottein* is a process of radical alteration, but also that the alteration primarily affects narrative. In this respect, however, his spatial image of Gnostic alteration of the biblical or Christian mosaic, whereby it rearranges the portrait of the king into that of a dog,[20] fails to render adequately the dynamic and temporal elements of narrative.

If *PSY* is simply one Valentinian narrative among others, historically as well as systematically it is also the stereotype. Of course, the historical prominence of this particular narrative is in large part a function of accident, the lack of primary Valentinian texts and its survival in the heresiological discourse of Irenaeus. But systematic as well as purely historical reasons exist for its function as stereotype. The almost catechetical form of the narrative, its didactic precision with respect to the constitution of the pleroma, the fall of Sophia, and further unraveling in creation make this text seem scholastic by comparison with the other Valentinian texts I discuss. And then there is the flatness of the discourse, its lack of voice and inflection that leaves no telltale lexical signs of tension between what is explicitly said and what is implicitly said. Yet if our exegesis of the text has been accurate, scholasticism and voicelessness notwithstanding, tensions do appear in the text, suggesting that the fundamental intuition of Jonas and Balthasar about a split between surface and depth commitments in Valentinian texts is valid even here. Three tensions are particularly important: (1) the tension between inexpressivity and expressivity; (2) the tension between positive and negative evaluations of knowledge; and (3) the tension between the accidental and nonaccidental nature of rupture of and fall from the pleroma.

The tension between inexpressivity and expressivity is double, both general and particular. On the most general level the tension is between the Depth and Silence and the rest of the pleromatic field. On the more particular level the tension is focused in the relation between Depth and Silence and Mind or Only Begotten. The double aspect of tension was apparent already to nineteenth-century scholars such as Neander, a recognition on which both Hegel and Baur capitalize.[21] The tension between inexpressivity and expressivity has several registers: zoological,[22] ontological, epistemological, and even linguistic. Considered in the last two ways, the tension is that between the relative value of the infinite unconsciousness of the Forefather and the self-consciousness of Mind or Only Begotten, and that between inexpressibility of the depth of reality and its expressibility focused especially in Mind or Only Begotten. The second tension centers around the contrastive relation of Mind and Sophia as figures of knowledge. On the surface the relation is clear: Mind embodies a nontransgressive form of knowledge, just as Sophia embodies the opposite. But matters turn out not to be so simple. First, Mind does not transgress, because strictly speaking no limits are set. Second, Sophia's curiosity is not sui generis, but rather is encouraged by the Forefather. Transgression is, then, elicited. This, indeed, raises the issue of the relative value of different forms of knowledge, an infinite exhaustive form of knowledge and a finite, nonexhaustive form of knowledge. One could say that at a depth dimension the aporetics of representation, the issue of whether representation of the infinite is infinite or finite, influences the narrative.[23] The third tension, discussed at some length already, is between the putative accidentality and irrationality of Sophia's curiosity and her threshold ontological situation, or one might say meontological situation. For on the margin of the pleroma, even before her fall, Sophia is touched by the nothingness that will befall her. To her tenuous ontological situation can be added her tenuous epistemic situation, for knowledge of the infinite is willed by the infinite, and Sophia's will to know is not in any unambiguous sense free.

If anything, these tensions become more pronounced in the other texts that are to be exegeted. But a number of things are already clear. The surface narrative affirming stasis and the transcendence of knowledge and linguisticality has as its undertow kinesis, movement toward consciousness and speech, which, if not radical, is real. Whether such tensions are ingredients in non-Christian or Sethian Gnosticism is a question that need not exercise us here. Blumenberg may very well be correct in his assumption that all Gnostic forms of thought exhibit these tensions, for stasis, unconsciousness, and silence are denied in the very act of narration itself.[24] Moreover, to the degree to which kinesis, consciousness, and speech have to be granted status, however reluctantly, the model of pure narrative circularity officially sanctioned by *PSY* is put under pressure. For a pleroma that would be a consequent of movement, consciousness, and speech would no longer be identical to the pleroma of origin.

3.2. The Gospel of Truth

In the Nag Hammadi Library (I, *3* and XII, *2*) is a text that gains its title from its incipit, *The Gospel of Truth*. Some scholars believe that this text corresponds to one of the same name that Irenaeus mentions: the work of the historical Valentinus completed in the mid-second century C.E.[25] The text has exercised something of a spell not only because it is a text of considerable aesthetic value, significant philosophical refinement, and self-conscious ambiguity, but also because it subverts those expectations of Valentinian Gnosticism one would have thought reasonable once acquainted with Irenaeus's account of Ptolemy's system. The text is primarily religio-philosophical rather than mythological-dogmatic in character.[26] It shows a genuine respect for New Testament scriptures.[27] It does not obviously support the ontological dualism characteristic of Ptolemy's system and typical of non-Valentinian Gnostic texts.[28] And it uses words such as *pleroma* and *aeon* in ways that fail to correspond to their technical usage in Ptolemy's system.[29] Nevertheless, despite the text's colossal surprising of expectation, it is the case that the *Gospel* deals with some of the consummate concerns of Gnosticism, i.e., the origin and nature of evil and/or the material world and material existence, the role of a primordial revelation event as a condition for salvation for nonmaterially defined human existence, and the soteriological event itself understood as appropriation of the central message of revelation. More resolutely perhaps than any other Valentinian text, the *Gospel* discloses the existential matrix that prompts the archaeological account of the emergence of evil as well as the soteriological account of its dissolution. The existential situation of human beings irreducible to matter and the physical is that of being in error (24), forgetfulness (24), drunkenness (22–23), and ignorance (21.30–31; 27.21–22). Thus constituted, human existence has the reality status of a phantom (28.28). Nowhere in Gnostic literature is the existential situation of human being painted in such graphic and lurid colors as the so-called nightmare parable (28.28–30.12). Human history is a fiasco of vengefulness, pride, will-to-power, and violence and murder. And yet the text, qua Gospel, offers itself as good news, for it speaks of genuinely real existence as awakening from this nightmare. Awakening, however, involves more than mere self-contemplation.[30] It demands an irrupting, interruptive event in which the true nature of the self and its world is disclosed. Yet in a way unmatched in other Valentinian Gnostic texts, the epistemological aspect is brought to the fore. Salvation is understood fundamentally to involve a perspectival shift in which one discovers who one is, and the whence and whither of one's existence. In the *Gospel* the philosophical frame for interpreting this shift is decidedly Platonic.[31] Especially conspicuous are the Platonic pairs error-truth, ignorance-knowledge, forgetfulness-remembrance.

Neither the existential thrust of the *Gospel*, nor its Platonic vocabulary, in principle rule out the presence of mythological tropes. Yet some scholars have argued that the philosophical-existential character of the text excises the mythological, making this text fundamentally different from *PSY*.[32] This philosophical-existential character even suggests revision of the notion of what constitutes Valentinian Gnosticism, perhaps even Gnosticism in general. Certainly, such an interpretation is reinforced by the fact that: (1) technical Gnostic terms such as *pleroma* and *aeon* are not consistently used in ways that permit unambiguous identification with either a divine realm of fullness or the personified forces that structure the divine fullness; (2) if the *Gospel* describes a drama, it is a drama palpably without actors such as Sophia or a demiurge. In a related move scholars stress the consistently *monistic* tendency of this particular text.[33] The divine, to whom is ascribed the personal label of *Father* rather than the impersonal label of *Forefather*, it is insisted time and again, is one and unitary and not a dyad as in *PSY*. The fact that words such as *silence* and *thought*, which in *PSY* would denote hypostases, are in the *Gospel* mere predicates of the Father, exemplifies this monistic bias. Other reinforcing notes of monism include the direct relation between the Father and spiritually illuminated human being, and the epistemological rather than ontological registering of the separation of the Father and human being in its nonsalvific state. The positive result of both of the above-mentioned readings is that it prevents the *Gospel* from being reduced to a preconceived Gnostic stereotype. Yet concluding that the *Gospel* has broken entirely with Gnostic myth and the pattern of Valentinian assimilation rendered in *PSY* would, perhaps, be going too far. Gnostic myth is at least present as a trace, even as the *Gospel* takes a kind of critical distance from Gnostic myth.[34] Certainly, the distance does not stop this text from functioning metaleptically with regard to the Christian narrative.

In the *Gospel* the *archē* of all reality is the Father whose transcendence is gestured in a host of kataphatic and apophatic symbols. The Father is the root (31.28, 32.38), one (17.6), incomprehensible and inconceivable (17.7), invisible (20.20), unsearchable (37.25). Antithetical to the economy of the Father is the functioning of error or *Planē*. This philosophical word signals a departure from a mythological form of discourse, and throughout the text rather than being invested with declarative cosmogonic or anthropogonic function, error more consistently describes the existential situation of beings who have exiled themselves from the Father. But clearly this is not the full story. Very early on in the text (17.10–20), as well as somewhat later (26.9–27), the depiction of error suggests precisely the cosmogonic function that in *PSY*, as well as other non-Valentinian Gnostic texts, is played by Sophia. In a narrative episode, which recalls the fall of Sophia in *PSY*, the author of the text speaks in a highly personal way of anguish and terror (17.10), of fog (17.12), and even of the constitution of matter (17.15). Later talk of error being upset seems to recall the moment of repentance, which occurs when Sophia's mistake is disclosed (16.19 ff). In a strict sense, pointing to error as the etiological factor in introducing fault remains semantically ambiguous throughout. It is suggested, on the one hand, that fault is directly engendered by beings who have their base in divine reality; on the other hand, that fault is engendered by a divine hypostasis within which these individual beings, and the community of such beings, inhere. In any event, the important point is that we cannot excise altogether a mythological-cosmogonic accent.

Moreover, if error is a mythological actor as well as metaphysical principle, some evidence in the text exists that the different etiological contributions of Sophia and the demiurge are contracted into the activity of error. For instance, in 17.18 the text speaks of error setting about making its own creature, which recalls the demiurgic intention to create man as well as Sophia's desire to create alone.

Then the *Gospel* represents a contraction of Ptolemy's three stages (2–4) into one (2) while the text modifies the tendency toward pleromatic proliferation by identifying the pleroma with the Father or the unity of the Father. Still the author of the text recognizes the Son as the Mind of the Father and/or the Father's Name, acknowledges the reality of the Holy Spirit (26.56, 27.4, 30.17), and posits the intimacy of Son and Spirit with the Father. This intimacy, while ontologically underwritten, is however emphasized more on the plane of the economy of salvation than on that of divine immanence.

Struck by the difference between the *Gospel* and *PSY*, several scholars of Valentinianism have suggested that one of the ways in which the *Gospel* totally surprises expectation is that it advances a doctrine of *creatio ex nihilo*.[35] Passages crucial to the ex nihilo argument such as 27.27–28, in which error is said to be empty, having nothing inside, and 28.14–15 in which spaces (i.e., beings) come into existence from what does not exist, indicate that the author is not advocating any pure version of the theory. Ultimately, however, the *creatio ex nihilo* reading cannot be sustained. Two observations suffice to rule out this possibility: (1) although it is true that, as with other Gnostic texts, the *Gospel* consistently attempts to disimplicate the divine in the emergence of evil by speaking of the nonreality of that which is premised on perspectival fault, nevertheless, a real cosmogonic and anthropogonic element is recognized; and (2) written by a good Platonist, the text never denies the existential reality of evil and, moreover, whatever the nonreality of error, it cannot be correlated with nothing simpliciter, that is, Parmenidean *ouk ōn*. Rather its philosophical correlative is relative nothing, the *mē ōn* of Plato in the *Sophist* (248e–251), where the term is assigned to the world of becoming, appearance, and opinion. Thus, if we are not dealing with a pure mythological account in which creation has a material source in the fallen form of Sophia, nor with a Platonic prime matter theory,[36] neither are we dealing with a *creatio ex nihilo* vintage that would most likely satisfy the theological scruple of an Irenaeus. In fact, the symbol of nothing, which cannot totally erase a mythological backdrop, functions to disguise the devolution of evil from an antitype constituted within/by the divine. In other words, whatever the differences between the *Gospel* and *PSY* with regard to philosophical sophistication, the creation theologoumenon of the *Gospel* corresponds to the *creatio ex Deo* type of that text.

Christological focus is more pronounced in the *Gospel* than in any other Valentinian text. Genuine respect seems to be accorded the Gospel narrative of Jesus (18.10–18.26), including the cross

(18.26, also 20.11–15). Also, unlike what is found in *PSY*, the figure of Jesus is without distinction called the Christ (18.17) and is associated with Savior (16.39), the Word as fruit of the pleroma (23.25–56, 27.7), and Son (37.8 ff). Thus, in contradistinction to Valentinian scholasticism, soteriological agency is not distributed into distinct spheres with different agents for these spheres, but is compacted in Jesus Christ. And, contrary to the expectancies provoked by *PSY*, exegesis of Jesus passion and death in the *Gospel* does not support in any obvious way a docetic interpretation.[37] Yet, even if we grant the nondocetic nature of the text's Christology, we cannot safely conclude that the christological event is in and of itself redemptive. Pheme Perkin's suggestion that Gnosticism systematically denies transformative power of an ontological sort to Christ's passion and death is as true here as it is in other Gnostic texts.[38] Jesus Christ is primarily a revealer of gnosis (18.17–20, 21.22), and it is qua revealer, and not qua atoner-redeemer, as in Irenaeus, that Jesus Christ has soteriological significance.

The nondocetic Christology is connected in the closest possible way with the *Gospel*'s profound theology of the name, in which the Son is the Name of the Father. As the Name of the Father, the Son is the Father's kenosis to such an extent that in principle it can mediate and transform the error that is both material existence and perspectival fault. As the Son or Name of the Father, Jesus is the articulation of estrangement and its overcoming, a process in which the names participate or imitate. Of the names following the Name, the Valentinian fragment F truly applies: "From the beginning you have been immortal, and you are children of eternal life. And you wanted death to be allocated to yourselves that you might spend it and use it up [*analiskein*], and that death might die in you and through you. For when you nullify [*lyein*] the world and are not yourselves annihilated [*katalyein*], you are lord over creation and corruption."[39] As suggested, if revelation of/from Jesus Christ is a necessary condition of salvation, the sufficient condition of salvation is the actual enlightenment of those to whom the revelatory discourse is addressed. Negatively, *enlightenment* or *gnosis* means transcendence of ignorance, error, and passion; positively, it means union with the Father, union possibly mediated by the Son who is the Name of the unnameable Father, and possibly also mediated by the Holy Spirit.[40] In a way unmatched by other Gnostic texts and, arguably, even the orthodox Christian texts of Clement and Origen, the *Gospel* suggests an intimate connection between seeing and participation in the divine, between *visio mystica* and *unio mystica*.[41] The mystical thrust in the *Gospel* is radical, and it appears that at least in an anticipatory way the Gnostic can enjoy the draft of participation that is sometimes asserted to be the prerogative of the Gnostic only in the postmortem state.[42]

A salient departure from Ptolemy is that nowhere in the *Gospel* do we find the scholasticlike ontological differentiation of human existence into three distinct groups (i.e., pneumatics, psychics, and hylics). From this one should not assume that pneumatic, psychic, and hylic do not function as categories in the *Gospel*, for clearly they do. What the *Gospel* appears to deny is that these categories have developed ontological reference outside the context of the narrative of the Father's grace and mercy. In the *Gospel* we are dealing with a transcendent divine who in no way corresponds to the idle God that is Ptolemy's Forefather. The Father elects or predestines some beings (34) to salvation, and it seems to be the case that, as in *PSY*, psychics as well as pneumatics can be saved, where a psychic is defined as one who comes in contact with matter, yet who has some transcendence with respect to it. Here the author of the text is expressing the position typical of Western Valentinian Gnosticism, which was more inclusive than its Eastern Valentinian counterpart.

Relative to the Valentinian stereotype of *PSY*, the *Gospel* is clearly a deviant text. I have tried to outline both the specific as well as the larger patterns that are constitutive of the text's identity and uniqueness. I have tried also to record the limits of deviancy. Deviancy is limited by the very fact that the *Gospel* is involved in a systematic demythologizing relation with respect to non-Valentinian Gnostic myth and a Valentinianism that has appropriated this myth in a noncritical fashion. At least four facets of demythologization are operative in the text that admit of being arranged in pairs. The first pair is that of hypostatic simplification and narrative contraction. To the examples of simplification that have been cited, one could add the simplification of the Savior figure, who acquires something like a single identity. And with regard to narrative contraction, in addition to compacting fall, cosmogonic, and anthropogonic function in error, one could think of salvific function being collapsed into the Son who is the Name of the Father. The second pair consists of a fundamental anthropological shift reflecting itself in the relation between the gnostic and hypostasis,[43] and a shift in the noetics of space and time, that is, the way in which transcendence-immanence is metaphorized either in an up-down or in-out fashion or in before-after or detemporalized-now fashion. The second pair presupposes the first. Hypostatic trimming and the corresponding emphasis on the self's aeonic status and agency shifts the explicit focus of the text onto the self in situation, between the possibility of ignorance and knowledge, blindness and insight. For this refocused self, transcendence is not "up there," not even "then" or "once upon a time"; transcendence is "here-inside" and always "now."

Resistant if residual presence of myth in the *Gospel* makes it clear that the demythologizing modality corresponds more to Ricoeur's demythicization than to demythologization in a destructive sense. So myth is never excised and continues to elicit interpretation. This demythologization issue has become central in the wake of David Dawson's powerful challenge that by means of the kinds of operations I have described, and by dint of its epistemological-existential register, the *Gospel* has effectively left Gnostic myth behind, indeed, left narrative behind altogether in the construction of a powerfully original apocalypse of the mind.[44] But as indicated, although more than any other Valentinian text the *Gospel* represents Valentinian metanarrative in its more formal triadic rhythm, this formal pattern interprets but does not substitute for the complex narrative, whose stereotypical form is provided by *PSY*. Traces at least of all the episodes of the Gnostic myth, as rendered by Ptolemy, remain a presence in the *Gospel*. The link with narrative, therefore, is not broken. This means that the overcoming of Gnostic narrative and the undoing of plot altogether is a gesture of the *Gospel*, perhaps *the* gesture, but one not fully redeemed by the text itself.

Demythologization of the type represented by the *Gospel* then depends on the covert presence of a myth that disengages and surpasses the regnant forms of Gospel that eventually made it into the scriptural canon. That is, demythologization presupposes the metalepsis of biblical narrative that is typical of Gnostic texts in general, and typical of *PSY* as a stereotypical Valentinian instance. In principle any metalepsis of biblical narrative involves a challenge to the unsurpassable authority of biblical texts, their essential unrepeatability and irreplaceability. Metalepsis at a fundamental level descriptures. This occurs even more perhaps in the *Gospel*, which exercises a critical freedom with respect to the very narrative that disfigures and refigures the biblical narrative. The biblical text is an object of reflection, where no community rules of interpretation apply, so that even the countertradition of metaleptic interpretation provides at best a parameter for free improvisation. Arguably the Valentinian fragments (C, D) provide a clue to the interpretive ambitions that determine the text. Here in order are the two fragments.

> And even as we overcame the angels in the presence of that modeled form because it uttered sounds superior to what its modeling justified, owing to the agent who invisibly deposited into it a seed of higher essence and who spoke freely: so too in the races of worldly people, human artifacts become objects of awe for their creators—for example, statues and paintings and everything that (human) hands make as representing a god. For Adam, as modeled as representing a human being, made them stand in awe of the preexistent human being: for precisely the latter stood in him. And they were stricken with terror and quickly concealed their work.[45]

> However much a portrait is inferior to an actual face, just so is the world worse than the living realm. Now, what is the cause of the (effectiveness of the) portrait? It is the majesty of the face that has furnished to the painter a prototype so that the portrait might be honored by his name. For the form was not reproduced with perfect fidelity, yet the name completed the lack within the act of modeling. And also god invisible cooperates with what has been modeled to lend it credence.[46]

For interpretation to be licit, it must be more than mimetic; it must in fact be a form of bold speech (*parrēsia*) that destabilizes the common patterns and disturbs convention. But interpretation is more than countermimetic; it compensates for the lack (*hysterēsis*) in mimesis in and through what amounts to a supermimesis in which it comes in contact with reality as it is.[47] The pleonastic locution Gospel of Truth signifies precisely the supermimetic intention. Of course, the deposing of the authority of biblical narrative and its replacement by a Gospel with claims to truth raises the issue of the scriptural status of the *Gospel*. At one level, deposing the authority of biblical narrative and biblical texts, whose authority lies in community and community-ruled interpretation, is to engage in an act of descripturing. Not only is the canon not closed, closure finds no sanction in the incitement to interpretive liberty and boldness. At another level it involves deconstituting the difference between scripture and literature, making scripture literary and, because of the claim to authority in supermimesis, making literature scriptural.

By way of concluding analysis of the *Gospel* I want to comment on the way in which the text highlights and offers distinct perspectives on tensions that are recessed in *PSY*. First, more explicitly than *PSY*, the general tension between inexpressivity and expressivity is parsed in epistemological and linguistic terms. The tension is crystallized in the relation between the Father and Son. The Father is the invisible, incomprehensible, un-self-conscious ground of reality; the Son is the visibility, comprehension, or consciousness of the Father. And if the hypostasis Silence is not associated with the Father, the Father is clearly silence since the Son is the Name, the Son is speech.[48] Yet if the tension is reenacted, the covert kataphatic bias is clear. First, the fact that *Father* replaces *Forefather* means that the father is always root and always the Father of the Son. Moreover, the *Gospel* speaks in kenotic terms of the relation, whereby the Father empties himself into the Son. Despite the presence of a fairly elaborate apophatic apparatus, the movement thus is systemically toward self-consciousness and speech represented by the Son. The *Gospel* also repeats the tension, observed in PSY, between different modalities of self-consciousness, the self-consciousness of the Son as the Name of the Father and the sons and names of the enlightened. Limits are to be observed by the latter that do not seem to apply to the former, even if the former is invoked as the standard by which the latter are judged in their curiosity. If the *Gospel* could not be more eloquent in depicting the consequences of this searching into the Father who is protected by a reserve of mystery, figured in the trope of Withheld Completeness (18.13), nevertheless, the *Gospel* seems to suggest divine incitement in its appeal to the Platonic trope of the nonenviousness of the divine (18.38). This suggests, after the manner of *PSY*, some anxiety about the conditions of representation, whether an infinite representation is possible (Son) or whether representation must necessarily be transgressive because it is necessarily finite.

3.3. The Tripartite Tractate

Regarded as a later Valentinian Gnostic text involved in self-conscious apologetic appeal to Christian and Neoplatonic audiences alike, the *Tractate* lacks some of the elements one might expect to find in a Valentinian narrative and possesses others not found at all in *PSY* and that are, at best, only incipient in the *Gospel*. Philosophically informed like the *Gospel*, the *Tractate* nevertheless lacks its existential thrust and its systemic ambiguity. In the *Tractate* we are dealing with a text of Gnostic myth, involved in a metaleptic relation to biblical narrative, yet whose narrative form reveals revisionary features vis-à-vis the Valentinian stereotype of *PSY*.

Like *PSY*, the *Tractate* articulates a pleromatic system in the sense of a configuration of the divine sphere. Yet, as with the *Gospel*, the pleromatic system is founded upon a unitary transcendent principle (51.12, 53.23–40, 55.36), which, as with the *Gospel*, is referred to as the Father. If the transcendent divine is described kataphatically as father, one, unity, God, root, good (53.6), its mysteriousness is protected by a litany of apophatic ciphers (i.e., invisible, immutable, unchangeable, unvariable, incomprehensible, unknowable, inscrutable, unbegotten) (56). In articulating his understanding of the pleromatic system the writer of the *Tractate* seems to meld features of both *PSY* and the *Gospel*. As in *PSY* the transcendent divine is at the basis of a system of hypostases that structure the pleroma. But whereas in *PSY* *hypostasis* and *aeon* are more or less synonymous, in the *Tractate* they are not. The use of *aeon* in the *Tractate* more nearly corresponds to that of the *Gospel* in that aeons, said to rest in the Father, are existences in their divine aspect. Using Stoic vocabulary,[49] the *Tractate* speaks of aeons as spermatic existences (60–61), which, as with the hypostases from which they are distinguished, have their ontological ground in the Father.

Agreeing with *PSY* that divine hypostases can be posited, the *Tractate* makes a heroic effort to trim their number. A triad of hypostases, obviously modeled on the Christian Trinity, is posited, consisting of Father, Son, and Church. I comment on the replacement of the Holy Spirit by Church presently, but first a few words ought to be said about the *Tractate*'s important theology of the Son. In nontechnical vocabulary, which suggests an environment of Christian Platonism or Platonic Christianity,[50] the Son is referred to as the form of the formless, the face of the invisible, the mind of those who exist (66). That linguistic concessions are being made to emerging Christian orthodoxy is evident in the text's insistence that the Son is at one and the same time "the first-born Son" (57.18) and "the only Son" (57.21). In the text the Coptic words translate *Prototokos* and *Monogenes*, the former an epithet ascribed to the seventh aeon in *PSY* (*Against Heresies*, 1.12.3), the latter used of *Nous*, the third hypostasis in the same Valentinian system (*Against Heresies*, 1.2.2, 1.2.1).[51] Perhaps the most interesting reflection on the Son revolves around his status as self-consciousness (55.3–4) and mind (66). While this language is relatively standard in emerging Christian orthodoxy, the *Tractate*'s designation of the Son as the projection (*probolē*) (56.25) of the Father shows more decided Neoplatonic leanings,[52] and the suggested relation of Son and Father recalls the relation of Nous and the One. Nonetheless, the text is more Christian than Neoplatonic in its insistence on the equality of the Son with the Father, even if the language in and through which equality is expressed is imprecise. The *Tractate* speaks, for instance, of the Son as dependent upon the Father but also as unbegotten (58.19).[53]

The third hypostasis, unequivocally belonging to the pleromatic field, is Church. Its relatively privileged place in the pleromatic field contrasts with the relatively unprivileged place it occupies in *PSY* (1.1.1) as the eighth aeon. This validation of Church is accompanied by a demythologizing move in which the generation of Church is seen as proceeding in some mysterious way through the Father and Son and not through the pairing of male-female hypostases. The mythological model of biological generation, it seems, is deemed inappropriate to the divine. Perhaps the most interesting description of Church in the *Tractate* is that of aeon of aeons (58.33). While various points throughout the text insisted that the aeons are in the Father (60) and in the Son (67), this seems to be especially true of Church, which, as I have suggested, may reasonably be regarded as the author's substitution for Holy Spirit.

Unlike the *Gospel*, the trinitarianism of the *Tractate* shows a clear discernment of the distinction between a merely economic appraisal of the Christian Trinity and an appraisal of the Trinity *in se*. The apologetic attempt to be consistently trinitarian breaks down, however, when the issue becomes that of the emergence of fault in the pleroma whose most glaring symptom is the cosmos. To disimplicate any member of the Trinity, and at the same time to account for the emergence of fault and cosmogony, the *Tractate* posits a fourth hypostasis called *Logos* (75 ff). Thus, whereas Logos in *PSY* is one of the aeon-hypostases (fifth) of the Ogdoad, and in the *Gospel* is one of the names of the Son, who is also identified with Jesus Christ, in the *Tractate* Logos plays fundamentally the same role Sophia plays in *PSY*. Through the inquisitiveness of the Logos to know the transcendent divine, fault or fracture is introduced. And this fault in turn determines the generation of an extrapleromatic system. The immediate result of the curiosity of Logos is similar to the result of Sophia's unrestricted desire for knowledge (i.e., division, forgetfulness, and ignorance) (78). Moreover, just as a consequence of the fault introduced by Sophia is her own division into a higher Sophia, which is able to rejoin the pleroma, and a lower Sophia (i.e., Achamoth or Physis), which is not,[54] so also with the Logos, part of which is elevated into the pleroma, part of which becomes confused and emasculated (78).

Although fallen Logos ultimately does cede hegemony over the material and psychical cosmos to a chief archon or ruler, the general thrust of the *Tractate* makes the Logos at once assume the responsibility of the introduction of fault and cosmogony. The twinning of both events is more typical of the *Gospel* than *PSY*, as is the author's more metaphysical than physical depiction of the realities brought into being. In speaking, after the manner of the *Gospel*, of these realities as shadows (78, 80), as without root (79.15), and as nothing (79.04), the Platonic commitment of the text shines through. Once again, no more than the *Gospel* is the *Tractate* involved in denying the reality of matter. In calling material and physical reality *nothing* the text has to be understood as appealing to its relative nothing rather than absolute nothing sense, or technically put, *mē ōn* rather than *ouk ōn*. The real genius of the *Tractate*'s account of the introduction of fault and cosmogony, however, lies neither in its substitution of Logos for Sophia, nor in its sophisticated philosophical vocabulary. It lies rather in its revisionist, teleological reading of the introduction of fault and cosmogony, which in non-Valentinian Gnostic texts and even in *PSY* are interpreted as unequivocally evil. The defense of the fall of Logos is startling: "It is not fitting to criticize the movement which is the Logos, but it is fitting that we should say about the movement of the Logos, that it is the cause of a system, which has been destined to come about" (77.5–15). Fault and cosmogony here are put in a positive light not by reneging on negative description of the basis of the universe (still more chaos than cosmos in the Greek sense [80–81]) but by removing the accidental index of fall and cosmogony by situating them in a providential context.

In making his revisionary proposal, which may perhaps be intended to assuage Christian and Platonic discomfort regarding total negation of the physical material universe, the author of the *Tractate* has at his disposal the Valentinian motif of the Withheld Completeness. We have seen how this motif functions in the *Gospel* (18.38) and *PSY* as a background etiological factor in the emergence of an extrapleromatic reality. In both cases the motif connotes at once the principled impossibility of fully adequate comprehension of the transcendent divine (whether Father or Forefather) by hypostases and/or aeons and the transcendent divine's encouragement of such search. The consummate expression of this motif in the *Tractate* is perhaps the following: "Though the Father revealed himself eternally, he did not wish that they should know him, since he grants that he be conceived in such a way as to be sought for, while keeping to himself his unsearchable primordial being" (71.14–19). It is not denied that a hypostasis-actor is proximally responsible for cosmogony. More conspicuously than in the *Gospel* or *PSY* the *Tractate* implicates the divine. In addition, the rationale for the divine play of tease in withholding and encouraging searching into the mystery of the divine is in the *Tractate* more perspicuously rendered. The text suggests that the attempt by Logos to grasp the Godhead is consistent with the transcendent divine's intention that aeonic existences have knowledge and existence for themselves (61). Thus, significantly, transgression is divinely authorized, if not authored, in the name of autonomy. Reinforcing the divine's extrapleromatic intention, if not conceptually underwriting it, is the appeal to the Platonic trope of the nonenviousness of a divine, which recalls a similar move in the *Gospel* (18.38). In the *Tractate*, then, the fall of Logos, which is the basis of cosmogony, is seen as a felix culpa. Indeed, relative to non-Valentinian texts, and arguably even other Valentinian construals, the *Tractate* is prepared to attenuate the fall element that is a structural feature of the movement from pleromatic to extrapleromatic existence, and diminish the fault quotient accruing to the aeon or hypostasis who proximally ruptures perfection.

The *Tractate* does acknowledge, as all Gnostic accounts do, the tragedy of primordial fault and fall. Yet it wishes to *write over* the tragic aspect of this primordial occurrence. It does this by inserting tragedy into a teleological horizon whereby there is something like a net gain. By using language such as *write over* I intend to suggest that the *Tractate* accepts, as other Valentinian texts do, the ineluctably negative nature of fault and fall, and the evil of the resulting cosmos, but submits this negative evaluation of fall and result to a second-order positive reinterpretation. The second-order reinterpretation, however, does not simply null the negative. Rather it twists it to a positive direction. Such positive twisting or torsion strengthens the theodicy capability of the text by insinuating that the debacle of extrapleromatic existence can and will turn out to be positive in the long run. And this strengthening is a sine qua non when the foundational role of the transcendent divine in the generation of extrapleromatic existence comes to the fore in the way it does in the *Tractate*.

As in *PSY* cosmogony is intrinsically related to the repentance of the fallen aeon-hypostasis. Now, whereas the repentance of

Logos is a condition for the appearance of material and psychic being, Logos is not proximally responsible for such being, but rather an inferior demiurgic power is (100.19–105.19). Logos remains, however, proximally responsible for the emergence of pneumatic being, although only on condition of the appearance of a Savior figure. As is typical in Valentinian accounts, the Savior in the *Tractate* is described as "the fruit of the pleroma" (85.33), that is, the product of the pleroma as a whole. In the *Tractate* the Savior is also called *Son*, who is not to be confused with the Son of the trinitarian or quaternarian structured pleroma. Undoubtedly, homonymity is here a function of the fact that the Savior in the extrapleromatic system plays a role similar to the Son on the intrapleromatic level, that is, as revealer of the knowledge of the Father. Within the context of extrapleromatic constitution, the *Tractate* explores in some detail the specifically anthropogonic aspect. As in many other Gnostic accounts such investigation keeps clearly in view the Genesis creation accounts.[55] The *Tractate* is especially anxious to insist, via a reading of the second creation account, that there exists an element in human being irreducible to demiurgic activity, that is, the element of pneuma. This power belongs to the higher order, and as in other Gnostic accounts, Valentinian or otherwise, is associated with the repentant form of the hypostasis aeon who officially brings lack into being, in most cases Sophia, in the *Gospel* Planē, and here Logos. With the reading or rereading of the Genesis anthropogonic myth(s) is associated a reading or rereading of the Genesis account of the fall. The *Tractate* is much less radical and certainly much less fanciful than the non-Valentinian Gnosticism laid bare in so-called Sethian texts in the Nag Hammadi Library.

In fact, as in standard Christian-Platonic reading, the fall is understood as implying human being's exile from a paradisiacal state of deathlessness and knowledge and emergence into a state of death and ignorance. Unlike non-Valentinian accounts the serpent is not viewed positively but negatively, not as a revealer of gnosis but as a deceiver who tempts and inaugurates a diminished human estate. Specifically, unlike texts such as *The Hypostasis of the Archons* (89.32–90.10) and *The Origin of the World* (118.24–119.7), eating from the tree of the knowledge of good and evil, provoked by the serpent, constitutes the degradation of the pneumatic to the psychic level rather than an unveiling of spirit. Nevertheless, the *Tractate* has a complicated view of the aboriginal state that justifies using knowledge in only an inverted-comma sense. On the basis of the benefits the *Tractate* ascribes to the fall, knowledge within the prelapsarian state cannot be regarded as perfect or at least as fully developed. The disenfranchisement of the paradisiacal state is understood as an opportunity for appropriation of full selfhood, as the disenchanting of the knowledge of the aboriginal state reveals that paradisiacal knowledge was restricted because of its contexting in a psychic manifold, and thus was more nearly innocence than knowledge in the full and proper sense.

The genius of the *Tractate* relative to other Gnostic accounts, including even other Valentinian accounts, is that fall initiates development, and the alienation and death, which are consequent to fall, function pedagogically to enlighten human being with regard to their true destiny. Once again, as with the fall that is at the basis of the cosmos, the fall of pneumatics is reinterpreted as a *felix culpa*. Although negative evaluation of fall and consequence is not erased, the absoluteness of the negative is withdrawn by seeing fall in a teleological context in which the issue is ultimately an increase in pneumatic power and luminosity. From a second-order and thus reinterpretive point of view, *Endzeit* can be read as offering, at least potentially, an increment over *Urzeit*.

Whatever the possibility of reading the ordinances of time and history in the *Tractate* in a more positive light than is usual in Gnostic accounts, the appearance of the Savior figure in the unfolding story or pedagogy of human being is not marked by a determined emphasis upon its historicity. An index of this is the general avoidance of *Jesus* as a title for this Savior figure.[56] Nevertheless, a significant number of the more surprising christological notes of the *Gospel* are recapitulated: the incarnation seems to be granted genuine reality status, and suffering and even the death can be attributed to the Savior figure (114.3–118.14).[57] What is not claimed, however, is that the passion and death of the Savior figure exercises any direct soteriological agency with respect to human being. At best, suffering and death are paradigmatic for a specific category of human beings, that is, the psychics who are of special interest to this Western Valentinian text, and symbolic for the pneumatics of the suffering of the Logos. A particular mark of distinction of the *Tractate*'s treatment of Christology is the articulation of the symbol of kenosis (114.32–34).[58] The author is familiar with Philippians 2.6–11 and is able to suggest that in the extrapleromatic sphere even the Savior or Redeemer participates in deficiency and thus is in need of redemption. Redemption of the Savior is achieved only in the reentry of the Savior into the pleroma. The constitutive deficiency of all

being in the extrapleromatic sphere has the interesting effect of ho-
mologizing the kenosis of the Savior with every and all entry into
lack. This obtains especially for the kenosis of a tragic type at the
basis of cosmogony. The *Tractate*'s reflection on kenosis definitely
bears a resemblance to that of the *Gospel* in that the ability to enter
into the domain of unlikeness and otherness is valued, although the
price of such entry is taking on the reality, or rather nonreality, of
otherness from which one must be cured.

The anthropology of the *Tractate* differs in important respects
from that in both the *Gospel* and *PSY* in thinking of hylic, psychic,
and pneumatic existence as potentialities that are actualized, or fail
to be actualized, in response to the revelation of the Savior.
Whereas in *PSY* behavior seems to follow nature, in the *Tractate*
nature seems to follow behavior.[59] And whereas in the *Gospel* behavior is in accord with election, in the *Tractate* responsibility does
not appear to be ruled out. The author of the *Tractate* seems to be
granting something to both Platonic and Christian audiences: to a
Platonic audience he appears to grant that each human soul ex-
hibits a tripartite structure of pneuma-psyché-hylé, thus pneumatic
existence is not rigidly confined within a particular exclusive class.
To a Christian audience the author seems to offer the concession
that free response is an infrastructural condition determining one's
ultimate dominant class assignation, whether pneumatic, psychic,
or hylic.

As a representative of Western Valentinian Gnosticism, the
Tractate concedes that those of psychic disposition or determination
can attain salvation. At the same time, however, the *Tractate* insists
on the distinction between the pneumatics and the psychics, or between those elected and those called (123.25–124.25).[60] This specifies itself in a corporate context as the distinction between Man of
the Church (122.25) and perfect man (125.4), or between the visible
institutional church with its ethical and sacramental rules and an
invisible church, which in principal transcends these vehicles. Sote-
riologically speaking, however, the psychic is no less privileged than
the pneumatic. For unlike the *Gospel* and *PSY*, the *Tractate* does not
distinguish between a higher and lower order of salvation. Specifically, it does not allot to the pneumatics the higher order of salvation
in the divine milieu itself, and grant to the psychics a modality of
salvation less in dignity, and in Valentinian noetics of space depicted
as belonging to the interstitial territory between pleroma and the
cosmos (i.e., the Middle).[61] According to the *Tractate* all those to be
saved, whether psychic, or pneumatic, enter the pleroma in the

eschaton. One advantage enjoyed, however, by the pneumatics is that proleptically they already participate in the pleroma. Here the *Tractate* recalls the mystical aspect of the *Gospel* in which gnosis entails an *unio mystica* whereby the pneumatic transcends the conditions of time and history and deficiency in general in the now, not the then, of the future.

It is time to summarize the *Tractate* and pick out its most salient general features. Crucial to any understanding of the *Tractate* is its elaboration of an ontotheological narrative that explicitly recalls the six-stage narrative of *PSY*. The narrative, which is the content of a revelation, proceeds as follows: (1) pleroma, (2) faultfall, 3) cosmogony and anthropogeny, (4) fall of pneumatics, (5) appearance of the Savior figure, and (6) eschaton and integration of savable being in pleroma. And as with *PSY* this sixfold narrative has a synoptic triadic rhythm. If it recapitulates the self-same narrative structure of *PSY*, however, the *Tractate* departs from Western Valentinian scholasticism in myriad ways. Its less mythological style is just one salient point of departure. It differs from Western Valentinian scholasticism in its determined effort to keep hypostatic proliferation in check and attempt a trinitarian interpretation of the divine. Again, its substitution of Logos for Sophia declares a departure, as does its attenuation of the tragic element involved in divine and human fall. Other important departures include its nondocetic Christology, its less nature-oriented anthropology, and in its greater inclusiveness regarding the higher modality of salvation (i.e., admittance into the pleroma). Contrariwise, in its more philosophical orientation, in its distinguishing between divine hypostases and aeons as prototypes or spermatic existences, and in its notion of election, its realist Christology, the *Tractate* more nearly resembles the *Gospel*.

In some of its departures from *PSY* in particular, the *Tractate* clearly intends to put a conspicuously Christian face on its metanarrative. Undeniably, however, its relation to Christian narrative remains strongly metaleptic. No important element of the Christian narrative remains unaffected. *Church* becomes a hypostasis at the intradivine level in a way that makes no sense to a theologian such as Irenaeus, who tries to keep the biblical picture in view. The divine act of self-negation and fall is a surd in a biblical system that holds that God's perfection is absolutely stable, though often expressed differentially. Creation from a demiurgic expression of the fallen divine and the farce of demiurgic creation of spiritual human being represent revisionist interpretations of the two creation stories of Genesis. Stipulating that the suffering and death of the Savior has paradigmatic and symbolic rather than saving capability seems to contract the claims on Christ's behalf made in the New Testament. The relative privilege of knowledge over good behavior also represents a departure, even if one allows for the tension between faith and works that theologians have read from Paul. The disfiguring of each of the episodes of the Christian narrative implies the disfiguring of the whole, and this disfiguring operation has its complement in a refiguration in which each of the elements acquires a different meaning and renders a different story. No less than *PSY*, then, the *Tractate* illustrates the operation of *metharmottein*, Irenaeus's technical term for what I call *strong metalepsis*.

Arguably the constitutive distinguishing mark of the *Tractate* as a Valentinian text is the way in which it systematically rereads episodes of tragedy such that the net result of tragedy is positive rather than negative, a gain rather than a loss. In the exegesis I noted two striking examples of reading in which the felix culpa trope was in operation. One of these, the rereading of the tragedy of human being's fall and exile, has a correlative in the field of Platonic Christianity (e.g., Gregory of Nyssa),[62] whereas the other, the rereading of the tragic fall of the divine, has no correlative in the mainline Christian environment, Platonic or otherwise. Two aspects of this redescription are analytically separable: (1) rupture, which, as providentially guided, is always implicitly sutured, (2) fall, which, again, as providentially guided, turns out to be gain rather than loss, a fall downward, which submitted to the positive torsion, engendered by teleological context of tragedy, is transformed into something like a fall upward. Of course, this means that in some important respects the tragic narrative of the divine is sublated into a divine comedy.

The rereading of tragedy and its elements is a singularly important move in Valentinian Gnosticism and of profound movement for a truly adequate view of Valentinian Gnosticism. Indeed, one could contend that the *Tractate* reinterprets not only standard renditions of Valentinian narrative episodes, but the essential thrust of Valentinian narrative as a whole. Of course one might plausibly argue that the increment in the quality of existence that is the ultimate result of rupture and fall has no effect on the divine in either its extended horizon as pleroma, or more narrowly as the transcendent divine at the basis of the pleroma, yet such a position is difficult to sustain in face of the evidence that: (1) aeons play a role (as hypostases do) in determining the pleroma, and indeed their unity may constitute the hypostasis Church, and (2) the intentionality of the transcendent divine for more differentiated existence and knowledge of the divine is only gained in and through extrapleromatic adventure. Granted the formal symmetry between the pleroma of alpha and the pleroma of omega, there does appear to be a surplus in the pleroma of omega over alpha, which is a consequence of the pedagogy of aeonic existence in the narrative interregnum of the extrapleromatic field. The lack of material identity between the pleroma of alpha and the pleroma of omega to the advantage of the latter suggests that a narrative pattern is not purely circular. In other words the circular pattern must assimilate an irreducible element of linearity. Thus, the *Tractate* ruptures the would-be narrative pattern of a *reditus in integrum* type. Looked at formally, the narrative of the *Tractate*, qua discourse, seems to have reality as story or narrativity as its object. Facilitating this hugely significant gesture is the proleptic anticipation of plurality to which the divine perfection is open from the beginning. Given the value that is placed on the organization of a plurality, this means that the finale of the narrative endorses the anticipation and honors the means to achieve the end. Thus, unlike *PSY* and the *Gospel*, one sees in the narrative discourse of *Tractate* the explicit operation of anticipation (*prolepsis*) and recollection (*analepsis*).[63]

The *Tractate* definitely seems to validate Jonas's judgment of the essential split and tension between the static surface and kinetic depth commitments of Valentinianism and its deeply ironic espousal of development,[64] while providing a measure of vindication for Baur, and before him Neander and Hegel, who already saw traces of precisely this kind of Valentinian self-subversion in *PSY*.[65] And, indeed, if on the one hand the *Tractate* can rightly be regarded as deviant with respect to *PSY*'s commitment to absolute symmetry and thus equality between the originary and concluding pleroma, on the other hand the *Tractate* can be regarded as a radicalization of its constitutive tensions, that is, the tensions between inexpressivity and expressivity, between infinite and finite forms of consciousness, between the accidental and more than accidental nature of fall, with greater weight being shifted onto the second term of each of these binary oppositions.

One hugely important corollary of the *Tractate*'s suggestion of lack of parity between the pleroma of narrative alpha and the pleroma of narrative omega is the insinuation of a measure of lack in the pleroma of alpha. This lack is obviously not the same as the lack of the extradivine or extrapleromatic world, but a lack that hides in, or perhaps is parasitic with respect to, the putative fullness, stability, and stasis of the pleroma of alpha. Nevertheless, one could argue that this lack, which sometimes is expressed (and repressed) by means of the Neoplatonic trope of the nonenviousness of the Father, is the condition of the lack that (ir)rationally irrupts and as externalized is the ultimate basis of physical and psychical reality. Clearly, if this is the case, then the *Tractate* is involved in a subtle but decisive departure from a determinate Valentinian position. Yet if our reading of *PSY* is accurate, this departure represents at the same time a radicalization of a Valentinian given.

One way of getting at and highlighting this departure is by examining the range of meaning of *pleroma* in the second and third centuries. Here I merely canvas Christian texts and omit from consideration Platonic or Neoplatonic uses. At least two distinct uses of *pleroma* are found in the New Testament. Texts such as Colossians 2.9 and Ephesians 1.23 mean by *pleroma* nothing less than divine fullness. Obviously, this was the meaning that Valentinian Gnostics favored in both their technical and nontechnical deployment of the term.[66] The other meaning of the term stresses the action rather than state. In Matthew 2.3 *pleroma*, still retaining its metaphorical density, means "filling a hole," and in Romans 13.10 *pleroma* means "that which fills." The Matthean view and the Pauline view, as expressed in Romans, more or less correspond. Although examples of both uses can be excerpted from Valentinian Gnostic accounts, it is the first use that is sanctioned and codified. Its importance is at once existential and narrative: existential insofar as the notion of a divine realm as aboriginally home and a home to be regained provides consolation and hope, and narrative insofar as the *pleroma* is the axial construct in a narrative elaboration in which it played the role of alpha and omega. The *Tractate* sanctions on a technical level the meaning of *pleroma* as filling that which needs to be filled, whether hole, deficiency, lack, or gap without reneging on the primary sense of divine fullness.[67]

Moreover, the *Tractate* here goes beyond the *Gospel*, which in a nontechnical way sanctioned the more active sense of pleroma. Whereas in the *Gospel pleroma* connotes the filling up of deficiency in the extradivine milieu from resources belonging to the divine alpha, understood as unsurpassably perfect, in the case of the *Tractate* "filling up" so nearly defines *pleroma* that "filling up" touches not merely the outright deficiency and lack of the extradivine milieu but any imperfection, however infinitesimal. That a measure of imperfection haunts the pleroma of alpha is indicated in this: The pleroma of omega asserts a desirable increment of knowledge and existence. The originary pleroma is less than the greatest that can be thought or imagined. We see this from the retrospective vantage point of the pleromatic completion of ontotheological narrative. What the pleroma is engaged in is nothing less than filling in the hole or gap implied in the pleroma of alpha, although the text gives no official notice of hole or gap. The filling of all holes or gaps is the eschatological event wherein pleroma legitimately and really, rather than illegitimately and by courtesy, answers to the definition of divine fullness. But this realized perfection, the eschatological pleroma as it were, cannot be sundered from the activity of perfecting, that is, *plerosis*, which is an abiding operation throughout the entire ontotheological narrative, guaranteeing the transfiguration of would-be accident into providential expression, would-be tragedy into divine comedy, rupture into implicit suture, fault into felix culpa, fall downward into something like a fall upward.

The radical nature of the *Tractate*, therefore, cannot be gainsaid. Yet it is important to see how it is restricted in a text that operates in terms of Valentinian conventions, even if it does not remain absolutely loyal to them. One graphic way of illustrating the restriction is by attending to the deployment of symbolic oppositions that structure the text, for these oppositions provide opportunities for supporting, amplifying, and deepening the narrativity or theogony undermining of Valentinian narrative. That the *Tractate* remains between Valentinian convention and innovation is illustrated by the way in which narratively coded symbolic oppositions, what I call *narrative codes*, present in the other two texts, are repeated without much overt adjustment for the operation of prolepsis and analepsis, and the disturbance of the parity between the pleroma of alpha and omega that the dispensationalism of the text introduces. As in the other two Valentinian discourses, the ocular code is patent and is registered in the text in terms of the binary oppositions between seeing and not seeing and between light and darkness. The contrasts are structural, that is, the seeing and light of the pleroma of alpha and omega have the same exclusionary relation to the blindness and darkness of the nonpleromatic hiatus. Fully appropriating its own more radical narrative thrust would involve concluding that the seeing and the light of the pleroma of omega would have a different relation to blindness and darkness. For the latter would serve as conditions of the former, and thus of the superiority of the modes of seeing and light of the pleroma of omega over those of the pleroma of alpha. Similar points can be made with respect to the code of weight and the code of nothing, or the binary contrasts between, on the one hand the heaviness of the extrapleromatic realm and the etheriality or lightness of spirit, and on the other between the nothing of the extrapleromatic realm and the unsurpassable reality of the pleromatic sphere (79, 102). It is true that the *Tractate* exerts pressure by its narrativity *Tendenz* to destructuralize the oppositions, and to think of the relation between the heaviness and nothingness of the extrapleromatic realm and the lightness and reality of the pleroma of omega not simply as that of preceding and succeeding episodes in a narrative, but as having the relation of ground to consequent. Nevertheless, the *Tractate* still retains a commitment to a structural interpretation of binary oppositions.

The *Tractate*'s deployment of three other narrative codes important to *PSY* and the *Gospel* is consistent with what we have seen with respect to the first three. Although variously rendered, the code of speech is obviously an important one in the three Valentinian texts. It is registered complexly insofar as a relation obtains between silence and speech at the intrapleromatic level, and between silence and speech as a relation between the extrapleromatic and pleromatic level. Only in the second case is the relation that of contradiction, that is, the relation between silence as a refusal of speech and communication and revelatory speech and communication. Again on the express level, the contrast remains structural. No difference is posited in the relation between the speech, or Name or naming within the pleroma of omega and the nonspeech and miscommunication of the extrapleromatic sphere that precedes it, and that of the speech and communication of the pleroma of alpha and the nonspeech that succeeds it. Appropriation of the underlying narrativity drive need not have taken this course; that is, the speech and communicability of the pleroma of omega might have been read as dependent on the nonspeech and noncommunication of the extrapleromatic, which dependence, paradoxically, would be a condition of the superiority of this mode of speech and communicability over that mode operative at the level of the prefallen pleroma.

Matters stay intact with the organic code, moreover, which is expressed in Valentinian texts by a variety of constrasts—fertility-infertility, generation-abortion, seed-seedlessness, but perhaps above all life-death. Life is ascribable to the pleroma and is a property of any being who participates in it. The extrapleromatic realm is the realm of death. The victory of life over death signaled in Christ and its recapitulation in the pneumatic does not however suggest any difference in the relation between life and death in the postlapsarian state. Officially the relation is indifferent to narrative place and remains exclusionary. One might say the relation remains inorganic despite the *Tractate*'s dispensationalism; that is, death is not made a condition of life or greater life.

The final code that should be mentioned is the code of gender. The contrast here is not that of the masculine (spirit) and the feminine (matter), as much as that between the feminine constrained and the feminine unconstrained. Unconstrained femininity is abyss, darkness, and a kind of illegitimate fertility, curiosity, error, and desire. Such femaleness is consistently excoriated and is nonintegratable into the pleroma, either preeschatologically or eschatologically. It is female as other, indeed, the totally other. But again, the *Tractate* does not appropriate its deepest drift, which is to suggest that femaleness, even of this kind, is spermatically encoded in the pleroma, and thus femaleness is a means to move from glory to glory.

In all six of the cases discussed the narratively coded oppositions fail to support the underlying narrativity drift. The split between the surface and depth is real and indicates that not even the *Tractate* legitimates a full-blown theogonic ascription in the sense proposed by Baur. If theogony is a presence, it is presence as gesture and trace. For a Valentinian discourse such as the *Tractate* to realize its theogonic potential, the split between surface and depth would have to be abolished. One of the signs of this abolition would be the way the narratively coded oppositions would support and amplify the narrativity drift. Without getting overly genealogical, this is a possibility only outside the classical Valentinian field.

At this juncture posing the question of unity between accounts of these three Gnostic texts is necessary because without some degree of unity it is well-nigh impossible to validate any interpretive discourse that includes the locution *Valentinian Gnosticism*. Because the three accounts manifestly differ, we cannot presuppose such unity. While all three accounts have an ontotheological narrative at their center, they diverge with regard to narrative structure itself, the interpretation of fundamentally corresponding narrative episodes, or both. Nevertheless, I claim here that a fundamental measure of unity underlies the three accounts, and that the unity is narratively determined.

By way of arguing toward unity, specifically narrative unity, I offer the following observations. Although they variously configure the divine realm, all three accounts propose the fullness of the divine as both the alpha and omega of a drama in which the aboriginal integrity of the divine is lost and regained. In addition, whatever the differences in construing the nature of the divine fullness or pleroma, all three accounts concur in depicting the pleroma as the field of divine expressiveness and manifestation, which renders present a mysterious transcendent-divine that is evoked in apophatic as well as named by kataphatic ciphers. Again, while the move may be registered in distinct dominant keys (i.e., ontological or epistemological), all three accounts of the metastasis from pleromatic to extrapleromatic existence figure a theogonic account of evil (i.e., evil has its source in the divine) while engaging in a concerted effort to exculpate the divine as such in the origin of evil. Whereas theodicy exculpation may often seem contrived, tortuous, or both, the theocentric vision of Valentinianism is forced to explore an origin anterior to human being consonant with divine perfection and power but also goodness. The upshot is the positing of a source in and from the divine that reveals itself as nondivine. Moreover, in all three accounts, whoever the protagonist, Sophia, Planē, or Logos, the emergence of evil is associated with the creation of the material and psychic world.

In addition, in none of the three accounts is a *creatio ex nihilo* view of creation upheld, notwithstanding explicit gestures in this direction in two of the accounts. Creation devolves from the fallen, disfigured aspect of the pleroma that is the fruit of misrecognition and failure to acknowledge limits. In none of the accounts, however, is it the case that the extrapleromatic or *kenomatic* order is reducible without remainder to matter or matter and psyche. Whether viewed as coextensive with cosmogony or as a distinct narrative episode in its own right, in the generation of human being and its cosmic existence the accounts suggest the mediated presence of the divine in the extrapleromatic environment. All three accounts also agree that in human being the divine or pneumatic element may be dysfunctional, and a divine being, either explicitly or implicitly associated with Jesus Christ, enters the extrapleromatic world to recall human beings to their true destiny. In all cases it is the pneumatics who occupy the soteriological foreground, however, salvation is not denied the psychics who constitute the inferior, one might say, visible church. Again, although different theological interpretations of Jesus Christ exist, all three accounts focus in some way on the New Testament passion narrative. Moreover, the reading is so realistic that it becomes impossible to affirm without reservation Irenaeus's docetic stereotype, even if the passion and death of Jesus Christ has more emblematic and paradigmatic than full-blown soteriological significance. Finally, all three accounts reveal in their depiction of narrative closure or *synclasis* a wished-for symmetry between narrative alpha and omega, such that ontotheological narrative essentially shapes a circle. The following schematization shows the diversity and unity of the three Valentinian accounts.

Narrative	PSY	Gospel	Tractate
I. 1. Pler–mc	complex, 30 hyp	simple, Father, Son	trinity, quaternary
–bc	dyadic, natural procreation model	monadic, eternal generation	monadic, eternal generation
–nq	not conspicuous,	not conspicuous,	conspicuous,
–prol	not explicit	not explicit	explicit
II. 2. Fault–origin	attempt to know transcendent	ditto	ditto
actor	Sophia	Planē	Logos
rationale	happenstance,	ditto	teleological design
consequence	evil as fallen é of pler—Physis —engendering of demiurge	evil as separation from pler	evil as fallen é of pler engendering of demiurge
judgment	negative unqualified	negative unqualified	negative qualified
3. cos + anth	separate but	inseparable but	separate but
creation	extension of emergence of evil	extension of emergence of evil	extension of emergence of evil
4. FPN–origin	forgetfulness, self-will	ditto	ditto
rationale	happenstance	ditto	teleological design
judgment	negative	negative	negative, positive twist felix culpa
III. 5. Savior–type	Teacher of Gnosis	ditto	ditto
Xology–type Passion	docetic	non-docetic	non-docetic
reference	suffering of fallen é of pler-Sophia	ambiguously this worldly and other-worldly	suffering of fallen é of pler-Logos
function	paradigmatic for psys and symbolic of suffering of fallen hypostasis	paradigmatic for psys (maybe pns) possibly symbolic	paradigmatic for psys and symbolic for pns of suffering of fallen hypostasis

Narrative	PSY	Gospel	Tractate
6. Eschaton	return of pns to pler, psys to Middle	ditto ditto	return of pns and psys to pler
realized eschcrology	no	yes	suggestion
nc	Recaps pler of alpha	ditto	possible excess over pler of alpha
Analepsis	not explicit	not explicit	explicit
Register	mythological-ontological	philosophical-mythological-epistemological	ontological
evidence of presence of demythologization	insignificant	significant	significant

Key to abbreviations. Pler= pleroma; mc= mode of configuration; bc= basis of configuration; nq= narrative quality; cos= cosmogony; anth= anthropogony; prol= prolepsis; hyp= hypostasis; FPN= fall of pneumatic being; nc = narrative closure; psys= psychics; pns= pneumatics; é=element.

Summary

This chapter has provided an account of classical Valentinian texts—which would be recognized as relatively adequate by scholars of Gnosticism—that draws attention to the narrative structure that is central to each. It elaborated in extenso each of these narratives, attended to the six narrative episodes that articulate each, commented on the narrative codes that support the movement from perfection to perfection through the interregnum of fault and alienation, and pointed to the systemic metaleptic relation of each narrative to biblical narrative. It has commented at least on the hospitality of classical Valentinian discourse toward other discourses, especially platonism and Neoplatonism. At the same time, it has underscored real differences between these narratives, both at the level of substantive proposal and the way in which the narrative is registered, whether dominantly mythological-ontological or epistemological-existential.

The underscoring of plurality is especially important. Ruled out, for example, is the reduction of Valentinianism to an *Urnarrative*. As chapter 2 demonstrated, several other objections are to be dealt with when constructing a genealogical account of Gnostic return, but the *Urnarrative* objection is particularly serious. For what trust can be placed in a Valentinian genealogical account that does not take seriously the narrative complexity of the original Valentinian situation? Is it not likely that the reduction to *Urnarrative* in the classical Valentinian field will carry over into the genealogical account and encourage the repression of differences between the classical metaleptic and the modern metaleptic Christian narratives? To affirm the plurality of Valentinian narrative forms is not to eschew unity. The diagram that ended the chapter clearly indicates unity as well as plurality. The beginning of chapter 4 reflects on the grammatical nature of this unity and speaks explicitly of *Valentinian narrative grammar*. This concept will enable us also to see continuity between the Christian narratives of a metaleptic sort in modernity and the classical Valentinian narratives examined in this chapter.

To prevent the exposé of plurality of narrative forms simply serving the argumentative purpose of indicating the presence of a grammar, I brought out the individuality of the major narrative options within classical Valentinianism on the basis of a thick rendering of three narrative discourses. The emphasis on the individuality of the classical forms suggests that if one were to conceive the possibility of new forms of Valentinian narrative in modernity, seeing these forms negotiate with the *PSY*, the *Gospel*, and the *Tractate* that bear the weight of the classical tradition is important. I am especially interested in the ways in which the so-called new forms of Valentinian narrative both recapitulate and deviate from the classical forms that continue to set a baseline for Valentinianism, even if Valentinianism's grammatical potency exceeds that realized in its classical forms.

One of the most interesting conclusions of our analysis of classical Valentinian texts is that, although none of the Valentinian narratives are theogonic in an explicit sense, some evidence exists, especially in the *Tractate*, that at the depth level the apparent commitments to narrative circularity, the view of an aboriginally given perfection, and the extrinsicality of passion with respect to the divine are all being challenged. Certainly, some tension is apparent between explicit and implicit commitments, which opens up the prospect of affirming some measure of continuity as well as discontinuity between modern metaleptic Christian narratives and those of classical Valentinianism.

$\sim$

Valentinian Narrative Grammar:
Irenaean Gestures and the Phenomenon
of Valentinian Enlisting

This chapter mediates between chapter 3 in which, through an analysis of the classical Valentinian discourses, something like a Valentinian narrative grammar is hinted at, and chapter 5 in which the concept of Valentinian narrative grammar is genealogically deployed. This chapter underscores the point that the concept of Valentinian narrative grammar represents one way beyond the impasse of *Urnarrative* on the one hand, and an emphasis on plurality that would deny manifest unities on the other. The concept of Valentinian narrative grammar is friendly to plurality and diversity because, as with all grammars, Valentinian narrative grammar allows not only multiple but quite different instances. Valentinian narrative grammar is the sum of the rules of formation of a narrative, which bears a metaleptic relation to biblical narrative, that moves from a state of divine perfection to its reconstitution through fall and alienation. In their variety, *PSY*, the *Gospel*, and the *Tractate* are evidence for such a grammar, as well as being its exemplary classical instances or paradigms. Obviously, I need to say more about Valentinian narrative grammar because although it may well have been gestured to in chapter 3, it was not made thematic.

When I spoke to the results in the summary of the last chapter I did not mention the most important extrapolation that seemed to be called for by our discussion of the unity and plurality of classical Valentinian discourses; that is, that as the relations and differences between Valentinian narratives are caught in crude capsule form in the diagram, these relations and differences outline a Valentinian narrative grammar, exemplified but not exhausted by the *PSY*, the *Gospel*, and the *Tractate*. As indicated in and by the second numbers on the left of the diagram, Valentinian narrative grammar has as its content a six-stage inclusive narrative of divine perfection, loss, and recovery. Specifically, Valentinian narrative grammar concerns an invariant sequence of episodes, each episode of which transgressively interprets an episode of the biblical narrative, at least as the biblical narrative is read or constructed in communities committed to the authority of canon.[68] These episodes are in order: (1) a realm of pure and undisturbed divine perfection, presumptively immune from change and narrative adventure; (2) introduction of fault into the realm of divine perfection and fall from the divine that is the fall *of* the divine and the emergence of the creative capacity that parodies the creator God of Genesis; (3) creation of the cosmos and nonspiritual human being that depends directly or indirectly on the fallen divine; (4) the fall of pneumatic being in excess of the psychic and material specimens that are the limit of the creativity or discreativity of the fallen divine; (5) the appearance of a redeemer figure who is associated with Jesus; and (6) the salvation of more than the perfect, the realization of a human perfection, associated with knowledge, and the full-scale reconstitution of divine perfection.

As illustrated by the three Valentinian narratives analyzed, considerable variation is permitted both on the general narrative level and on the level of individual narrative episodes. The summary to chapter 3 provides broad indications to the kind of variation permitted at the general narrative level, so here I can be brief. As it operates within the Hellenistic field, Valentinian narrative grammar permits a triadic synopsis of the six-stage narrative, or a triadic substitution for the six-stage narrative. It permits nonteleological and teleological versions of the narrative, thus nonerotic and nonagonistic exemplars as well as erotic and agonistic exemplars. Furthermore, it allows narrative versions that evidence a measure of distance from mythological production and those that do not. And relatedly, Valentinian narrative grammar allows for both epistemic and ontological registers of the basic six-stage narrative.

Considerable variation is also endorsed at the level of individual narrative episodes, and I address each in turn. With respect to the depiction of the aboriginal divine perfection (1), posited in classical Valentinian narratives, constants include the view that divine perfection is in some important respect a differentiated totality, a divine milieu rather than divine simplicity, and that this realm of perfection is ontologically, noetically, and existentially superior to the order of creator-creation defined by the biblical text, which constitutionally suffers from deficiency, ignorance, and passion. But extraordinary variation is permitted depiction of the reality at the root of the realm of divine perfection, as well as what I referred to in my diagram as the mode or base of configuration respectively of this realm of divine perfection. First, depiction of the ultimate basis of divine perfection can be registered in apophatic or kataphatic language, or any combination thereof, the degree of kataphasis or apophasis depending in large part on whether the basis is perceived as oriented toward expressivity and manifestation. Second, considerable variation in the mode of configuration or differentiation of divine perfection is permitted. Aside from the necessity that divine perfection be configured or differentiated, this configuration can be relatively profuse or economic, and in the latter case trinitarian or quaternarian. Third, considerable latitude is also allowed the base of configuration, by which I mean the way in which the differentiated realm of perfection is generated or articulated. The two options favored in the classical Valentinian texts are monadic and dyadic, but one could imagine at least a triadic option. Fourth, and finally, reading a grammar from classical Valentinian texts suggests considerable variation with respect to narrative quality and especially with respect to the operation of prolepsis. That is, Valentinian narrative grammar allows depictions of perfection that involve no orientation toward the nonperfect and no anticipation of another and richer kind of divine perfection and those that definitely involve such orientation and anticipation.

As extrapolated from the classical Valentinian narratives, constants with respect to the faulting of divine perfection (2) in Valentinian narrative grammar include a first-order evaluation of the faulting as a catastrophe that accounts for deficiency, ignorance, and passion, or ontological, noetic, and existential evil respectively. At the same time, Valentinian narrative grammar permits considerable variation with respect to the depiction of the faulting of perfection. The names of the actors responsible for the introduction of fault, as well as their gender, are both variable. Also variable is the degree of personification involved and whether faulting as a whole, and not simply its consequence, is registered in terms of knowledge. Variation is also permitted regarding the logic, or lack thereof, of the introduction of fault. If it is not a possibility of Valentinian narrative grammar to regard the introduction of fault as anything other than a catastrophe, importantly different perspectives on catastrophe are permitted. Faulting can be figured as purely accidental and tragic, and thus something that the divine only suffers, or as having a rationale that makes fault and the fall of the divine a felix culpa, and thus retrospectively at least endowing the divine as a whole with a measure of agency. In addition, there can be variability with respect to what I referred to as the consequence of fault, specifically whether a demiurge is engendered who becomes the proximate origin of the order of creation or whether the fallen divine is more directly responsible for the catastrophe of the world.

As extrapolated from our study of classical Valentinian texts, constants in the depiction of the generation of physical and psychical reality (3) include a characterization of these spheres of existence as ultimately devolving from the realm of divine perfection while representing its antithesis in terms of reality, knowledge, and existence. Variable, however, is whether the creation of the cosmos and non-spiritual human being is seen as one indivisible act or as two discrete acts and whether the negative judgment with respect to creation is unqualified or qualified in a felix culpa manner. Similarly, as extrapolated from classical Valentinian texts, Valentinian narrative grammar's depiction of pneumatic human being and its fall (4) has constant and variable features. Constant features are that pneumatic being is superior to the cosmos and its psychical and physical constituents, although susceptible to a forgetfulness that brings him down to the level of the cosmos and its rule(r). At the same time, spiritual human being is superior to all forms of the fallen divine, especially if the divine is figured as the creator-lawgiver of Hebrew scriptures. But variation is allowed with respect to figuration of the fall, specifically whether fall is sheer accident or whether there is a measure of teleology, and relatedly whether judgment is unqualifiedly negative or whether modified from a higher order point of view that takes the teleological note into account.

And finally, taking narrative episodes (5) and (6) together, that is, the interpretation of Jesus as savior figure and what and who is saved, as extrapolated from our analysis of classical Valentinian texts, Valentinian narrative grammar evinces both constants and variable features. If a constant in Valentinian depiction is that Jesus or Jesus Christ can have no saving significance for others, variables include whether incarnation and suffering are conceived docetically or not, and the symbolic nature of suffering, specifically the extent to which it refers to the suffering of a fallen aspect of divine perfection. Again, if constants in Valentinian soteriological depiction include the view that more than the pneumatics may be saved at least eschatologically, and the view that knowledge or gnosis itself constitutes salvation, variables include whether a pneumatic is constituted by nature, grace, or even free will and whether the event of gnosis itself relativizes eschatology. An important variation permitted in Valentinian narrative grammar is whether in the eschatological all-in-all that brings closure to the six-stage narrative the selfsame perfection lost in the fall is recovered, or whether a mode of divine perfection in excess of originary divine perfection and recollective of the entire narrative movement comes into being (*analepsis*). Finally, variation is allowed as to how conspicuous a role the preeschatological event of gnosis plays with respect to the reintegration of divine wholeness.

I suggest, then, nothing less than that the unity and plurality in classical Valentinian discourses suggests the presence of a Valentinian narrative grammar of which *PSY*, the *Gospel*, and the *Tractate* represent the paradigmatic instances. But precisely as a grammar, Valentinian narrative grammar exceeds its paradigmatic instances. At least two entailments are relevant with respect to the Hellenistic field in which Valentinian texts or narratives are produced. First, Valentinian texts such as the *Treatise on the Resurrection*, *The Gospel of Philip*, and *Apocalypse of Adam*, which are less expansive in their narrative reach than the Valentinian texts analyzed herein, do not constitute counterfactuals in the Hellenistic field. This is to put the point negatively. The point can also be put positively. Valentinian texts in Nag Hammadi, which are less expansive in their narrative reach, are regulated by Valentinian narrative grammar, which we extrapolated from an analysis of Valentinian texts with maximum narrative reach. Second, ex hypothesi, were other Valentinian texts of the Hellenistic period to come to light, however different these texts would be from those in Nag Hammadi, their narratives would be regulated by the Valentinian narrative grammar that we have generated.

With respect to my grammatical reading of Valentinian narratives, I do not find myself without precursors. I particularly want to do justice to Irenaeus's reading of Valentinianism that, despite a denunciatory rhetoric that distracts from a powerful narrative analysis and a tendency toward an *Urnarrative* understanding, succeeds in underscoring the variable as well as constant features of Valentinian narratives. Honoring Irenaeus also involves capitalizing grammatically on his hint that the disfiguration-refiguration of biblical narrative is double: At one level, the Valentinian challenge is constituted simply by the six-stage narrative that disfigures and refigures biblical narrative. At another level, the narrative challenge consists of the six-stage narrative construed dynamically as the story of the becoming of the perfection of the divine. In this chapter, however, Irenaeus also becomes important for another reason. If Irenaeus actively encourages a grammatical reading of Valentinianism in his detection of the deformation wrought on the biblical narrative, he actively

discourages a grammatical reading of biblical narrative in his refutation, where he elaborates the substance of Christian faith. The structural impediment here is Irenaeus's view of faith as a deposit, which
not only anachronistically suggests that faith always was, despite the
fact that it is getting clarified and developed precisely in opposition to
Gnostic interpretations of scripture, but also that such faith, essentially constituted by the biblical narrative, is invariant. I engage in
what might be called a grammatical recoding of Irenaeus's view of
Christian faith. The grammatical recoding has two bases. The first
is essentially that of symmetry: If both Valentinianism and orthodox
Christianity are defined in terms of their narrative—and, of course,
the forms of life that respond and correspond to the narrative—there
is no legitimate reason to construe one narrative commitment (i.e.,
Valentinianism) in terms of the optics of grammar and not the other
(i.e., standard Christian renditions of the biblical narrative). The second is more or less a logical point. If Valentinianism is construed as
an infraction against appropriate interpretation of the biblical narrative, the implication is that not only does each Valentinian paradigm
constitute a metalepsis of a particular community rendition of the
biblical narrative, but by implication of all possible renditions. Or
simply put, any particular Valentinian infraction is an infraction
against biblical narrative grammar.

The first section of this chapter consists, therefore, in detailing
Irenaeus's contribution to the construct of a Valentinian narrative
grammar as a grammar of transformation and correcting his tendency toward an *Urnarrative* view, not absent in his reflections on
Gnosticism but particularly prominent in the case of biblical narrative. This amounts to a refiguring of Irenaeus, which in turn has the
happy consequence of making Irenaeus genealogically pertinent
with regard to the thesis of Gnostic return in a way that an unre-
vised Irenaeus might not be. This chapter, then, delivers on a
promise made in the introduction that, although the construction of
a model of Gnostic return would proceed under the banner of Baur,
Irenaeus would at least play a supplementary role.

Although the grammatical generalization and deepening of
what is at stake between Valentinian and Christian narrative is the
central concern of the chapter, the topic of the relation between
Valentinian and other narrative discourses in the Hellenistic field is
not too far behind. This is the second and complementary focus of
the chapter, and is the subject of the second section. Nothing less
than a thematic treatment is called for, given that interpretation of
classical Valentinian genres revealed significant hospitality to Pla-

tonic and Neoplatonic narrative discourses. I argue that this hospitality seems to operate in classical Valentinian discourses without
compromise to Valentinian narrative integrity, so that one can speak
legitimately of Valentinianism enlisting other narrative discourses
including apocalyptic. Thus, enlisting itself can be understood to be
a grammatical feature of Valentinian narrative formation. Our discussion of enlisting here harks back not only to chapter 3, but also to
the more genealogical discussion in part 1, which suggested the possibility that discourses in the Baurian line could still be regarded as
Valentinian despite the presence of other narrative discourses.
Thinking of enlisting as a grammatical feature of Valentinian narrative makes a more categorical declaration of the reality of this
phenomenon in the Baurian line of narratives possible. This assertion is one of the key objects of the next chapter.

4.1. The Contributions of Irenaeus: Developing the Grammatical Hints

The narrative grammar reading of Valentinianism is first and last
my responsibility. It does not proceed on the basis of an appeal to the
authority of any particular interpreter, or set of interpreters, but
stands or falls on its ability to persuade that a narrative grammar
can be extrapolated from a reading of classical Valentinian texts. At
the same time, I have not refused, and will continue to avoid refusing, the assistance of any commentator or critic of Valentinianism
whom I believe helps to illuminate the phenomenon of Valentinianism either in whole or in part. Here I am speaking of contributions
or of voices other than that of Baur, who provides my point of entry
into the question of Gnostic return and provokes my grammatical reformulation of his genealogical hypothesis. My own interpretive
voice is thus unabashedly plurivocal. This is neither to say, nor
imply, that all voices are either the same or equal. Irenaeus is a powerful voice that resists being one among others. As recently as the
last chapter I pointed to Irenaeus's importance as well as question-
ability. The reason why both attitudes are appropriate is that
Irenaeus himself speaks in more than one voice. Certainly, one voice
is that of the opportunistic condemner in which the myths or stories
of Valentinianism can never be denounced often enough nor dismissed too roughly. In *Against Heresies* Valentinians are "falsifiers"
and "liars" (1.Preface, 2.Preface), "creators of fictions" (1.8.1,
3.12.12), "deceitful" (2.3.1), "presumptuous" and "vain" (1.Preface.1),

"depraved" (3.2), "riddled with intellectual pride" and "perverse" (2.1.1), "ridiculous trusters of personal experience" (2.32), and "antinomian" (4.1–5). The code is that of pathology, and Irenaeus is prepared to make it explicit. Valentinians are responsible for bringing about disease (3.2). They are sick and in need of a cure, the two parts of the therapy of which consist in Irenaeus's rough refutation of their pseudo-Christian proposal and his provision of a "grammar of motive," to evoke Kenneth Burke's famous phrase. This is the paradigmatic heresiological voice that provides the code for abuse of positions deemed to be other than orthodox for the best part of the next two millennia. It is also, as I indicated in part 1, the voice echoed by Möhler in the nineteenth century and echoed in very high decibels by Voegelin in the twentieth century. Irenaeus, however, speaks also in another and different voice. This is the analytic voice that recounts the Valentinian stories and proceeds to explicate the ways in which they entail a deformation of scripture and the salvation-history story that scripture renders.

On the basis of part 1, where I sketched the methodological difficulties of an existential-pathological analysis of Gnosticism in general, Valentinianism in particular, let me say unequivocally that the polemical voice of Irenaeus finds no echo here. This is a voice that must remain past. This does not mean, however, that the interpreter gives up on evaluation, but rather that evaluation is tied to the description of the ways in which Valentinian narratives bleeds the authority of scripture and systematically deforms the biblical narrative. Otherwise put: evaluation is a function of analysis. The second voice of Irenaeus, therefore, represents an interpretive opportunity rather than an interpretive liability. This second voice in fact provides nothing less than a template for a critical reading of Valentinian texts that fairly presents their narratives, deftly outlines their challenge both to Christian beliefs and the forms of life tied up with these beliefs, and that is adept at extrapolating the nonobvious implications of Valentinian narratives, and thus nonobvious dimensions of their challenge to Christianity. This second voice of Irenaeus is echoed strongly in the evaluative voice that inflects my articulation of the Baurian model of Gnostic return.

This articulation, as I have said repeatedly, is an articulation of Valentinian narrative grammar. Needed I believe is a sketch of the contribution Irenaeus makes toward a narrative grammar conception of Valentinianism and its critical evaluation. It is not sufficient to observe Irenaeus's clear sense of the plurality and diversity of Valentinian narratives, although without some such sense a narrative grammar reading of Valentinianism is impossible. Of central importance are Irenaeus's reading of Valentinian narratives as metaleptically related to biblical narrative and his sense that the biblical narrative is challenged not only in different but also complex ways by Valentinian narratives whose depth narrative tendencies are in tension with their surface tendencies. In addition to addressing this core contribution, I also comment on Irenaeus's insight about how Valentinian narratives gain authority despite—although, perhaps, ultimately because of—their literary readings of biblical narrative, whose plot is recounted in a book, indeed the book that brings an end to authoritative discourse and fabulation.

It is important, however, to underscore not only the proleptic nature of Irenaeus's contribution to a narrative grammar proposal, but also its nonsystematic character. Irenaeus does not, nor could he be expected to, put together all the pieces of the narrative grammar puzzle. It borders on miraculous that Irenaeus achieved analytically as much as he did. Nevertheless, it is impossible not to enter caveats. For example, however much Irenaeus's analysis of Valentinianism promotes a narrative grammar interpretation, his interpretation of the biblical narrative suggests the opposite. The law of inverse proportion seems to apply when Irenaeus insists on biblical narrative being a deposit of the church, and articulates the rule of faith that is intend to legitimate the past, or freeze the present as the past, rather than set guidelines for theological innovation and experimentation. Here I am especially interested in opening up the rule of faith to a grammatical interpretation that underpins the diversity in the reading of the biblical narrative. I will not attempt independently to justify this grammatical reading, a task that would be at least as arduous as the one that I am currently undertaking with respect to Valentinianism. Obviously, general arguments adduced in favor of a grammatical interpretation of Valentinianism are also applicable to mainline Christianity, as is the work of theologians who have tacitly or focally invoked the concept of narrative grammar. But in significant part my point is a point of logic: If Valentinian narratives, both classical and modern, illustrate a narrative grammar, and each illustration bears a metaleptic relation to biblical narrative, then the attack against a particular form of the biblical narrative is an attack against its grammar of which it represents a historically specific illustration.

I begin my analysis of Irenaeus's contribution toward a narrative grammar view of Valentinianism with Irenaeus's insight into the literary character of Valentinian texts. As Irenaeus reads it in

Against Heresies, the purely literary quality of Valentinianism, as Gnosticism's ultimate expression, is determined essentially by three characteristics: (1) relative impenetrability or lack of penetrability, (2) creativity of an individual sort, (3) discursive paradoxes of an aporetic kind. For him, the presence of these features disqualifies Valentinian texts from serious consideration as scripture. I briefly elucidate each of these characteristics and show how each runs counter to what one would expect if one thinks within a biblical paradigm.

1. Relative impenetrability or lack of penetrability. By contrast with the putative simplicity, pellucidity, and fixed nature of the Bible as canon, for instance, Valentinian texts, Irenaeus judges, are complex in their organization, obscure in their expression, and evidence a commitment to continued production that rules out of court the closure to textual production necessary for scripture to be scripture, and to have the kind of authority scripture has, or ought to have. For these reasons, the self-consciously difficult Valentinian texts encourage as well as justify a distinction between esoteric and exoteric forms of Christianity (1.10), and by so doing essentially make community impossible.

2. Creativity of an individual sort. Again in contrast to the putative general Christian commitment to the community reception of the biblical text where the subject matter of salvation is rendered with appropriate sobriety and where the commitment to truth and realistic depiction is apparent, Valentinian texts put the emphasis on individual production (1.10), render the subject matter of salvation with inappropriate frivolity (2.14), proceed solely on a basis of a commitment to plausibility that pleases rather than edifies (1.Preface), and eschews realism for a basic idealism or nominalism in representation. A few words should be spent on each of the elements that parse Valentinian commitment to individual creativity and provoke comparison with modern and postmodern writers, both those who are explicitly religious and those who are not.

For Irenaeus, Valentinian textual production is a scene of wild improvisation, of virtuoso performance whose aim is to top rival performances that mushroom all around.[69] Put in the language of pathology that Irenaeus calls on—to be followed not only by the heresiological tradition but by the majority of commentators ever since—Valentinians are suffering the disease of authorship. Of course, given the spiritual nature of this authorship and the interdefinability of spirit and divinity, at the very least this authorship is not reductively human. For Irenaeus this authorship not only maligns the creativity

of the creator the world, but displaces and surpasses the creativity of
the Spirit who is the essential author of the biblical text (3.1, 3.8,
3.24). While the creativity of the latter is tied to language explicitly in
ways that the former is not, creativity in both cases is at once the expression of Word and the act of shaping. The creative fiat is the Word
of the Father, while God the Father shapes and sculpts reality. And
if the Spirit is the author of the biblical text, it is precisely as a shaper
and arranger of both its language and the story that the Spirit ex-
posits. For Irenaeus too, the frivolity of Valentinian production contrasts unfavorably with the genuine seriousness of the biblically
depicted drama of divine and human interaction, whose bookends are
creation and apocalypse. If the frivolity coexists with an obsessive
concentration on the fall of the divine and the generation of evil, for
all that its proximate literary genre is that of comedy (2.14). Valentinianism is a discourse of personae and masks, of naming in which
the referents have no fixed identities.

Irenaeus's contention that plausibility rather than truth is the
real game of Valentinian production underscores the radically
interrogative basis of Valentinian texts that effectively forswears
conclusion (2.27). Moreover, the interrogative basis means that
Valentinianism, whatever its express claims, deals in hypotheses
rather than truth, or hypotheses *as* truth. In addition, the hypothetical tendency is related to the lack of realistic depiction in which entities with determinate extralinguistic identity and reality regulate
language and naming. Although it is not easy to see on the basis of
PSY alone just how much warrant Irenaeus has for the view that
Valentinianism plies a new game of truth with a new mode of depiction, on the basis of our analysis of the *Gospel*,[70] which Irenaeus may
or may not have read, his concerns are not out of place. The authority of texts seems to be predicated on the persuasiveness of naming.

3. Discursive paradoxes of an aproretic kind. The problem of
the ideal and/or transcendental character of naming in Valentinianism is associated in *Against Heresies* with a third characteristic
of Valentinian discourses, that is, their aporetic character. There
are essentially two aporias. The first in large part explicates the
idealism of Valentinian naming. On the one hand, names do not
necessarily point to extralinguistic realities with determinate identities that both call naming forth and justify it; on the other hand,
names carve out distinct spheres of reference. For instance, by contrast with John's Gospel in *PSY*, *Word, Son, Only Begotten, Christ*,
and *Jesus* refer to different realities, if not necessarily, according
to Irenaeus, realities with truly determinate identities. At a deep

level the issue between Irenaeus and the Valentinians is a philosophy of language, specifically, whether each word is a name with a straightforward referential function. A second and related aporia might be called the iconic aporia. Generalizing from *PSY*, *Against Heresies* concludes that in Valentinianism in general the Unknown God is revealed as unrevealed. Yet far from functioning as a block to investigation, the unnameability or unrepresentability of the divine functions as a prod for representation that issues in extraordinarily detailed mappings or picturings of divine perfection. Thus the unrepresentable divine, or what might be called the an-iconic divine, grounds and justifies an excess of iconism.[71] The iconic aporia is just the opposite of the paradox of biblical representation. The God of the Bible is the God who reveals himself as creator, redeemer, sanctifier/illuminator. God is thus inherently representable rather than unrepresentable. But God is representable only as he represents himself to an intelligence that, if made in the image of God, is finite and created. Thus the paradox is that no human appropriation of representation is fully adequate despite the reliable speech of scripture. God remains mysterious precisely as the known God, a proposition loudly asserted by Balthasar in his critique of what he takes to be modern forms of Gnosticism.[72]

Crucially, however, these three characteristics that define the literary and/or aesthetic character of Valentinian discourses define the Valentinian as a fabulist, a weaver of tales, of narrative fictions, which for all that make claims to truth and estimate their authority to be superior to that of the biblical text. But, of course, it is not the case that a Valentinian fabulation is simply placed alongside the biblical text and the story of God's acts it recounts. Valentinian fabulation depends intrinsically upon the Bible as discourse and story. Its originality is primarily interpretive: It concocts, imagines in a void, impossibly peoples its discourses, only on the basis of the biblical narrative. This brings us to the constitutive feature of Irenaeus's interpretive lens that can and must be salvaged, that is, what we have called *metalepsis*.

A Sketch of Metalepsis

In *Against Heresies* Irenaeus is convinced that Valentinianism represents an idiosyncratic hermeneutic of scripture and the salvation-history scheme that it supports and in turn is supported by. However persuasive Valentinianism is, Irenaeus judges that it represents a swerve from the truth (2.Preface). Irenaeus is particularly unhappy with the Valentinian penchant for elaborate allegorization of scripture, a practice, which he insists depends upon a focus on the obscure and ambiguous passages of scripture (2. 27). Neither the integrity nor solidity of biblical depiction is respected in the allegorization that goes along with Valentinian imaginative free-play. Fragmentation and etherization of scripture are the result.

Valentinian allegorization, however, is not just one other modality of allegorization alongside others in the Hellenistic discursive field.[73] It is not simply careless and far-fetched, it is blatantly transgressive. In a crucial passage in Book 1, which I highlighted in part 1, Irenaeus characterizes Valentinian interpretive practice as consisting of a rearrangement of scripture, specifically its order or taxis. The interpretive figure is *metharmottein* (I.8). As Irenaeus moves from the detection of Book 1 to the refutation of Book 2 and following, it becomes clear that the rearrangement of the biblical text is at the same time a rearrangement—recontextualization—of God's acts. That the real casualty in Gnostic rearrangement is less the lexical elements of scripture than the story of God's salvific engagement with world and human being is both hinted at and obscured when Irenaeus points to Valentinianism's counteraesthetic. "Their manner of acting is just as if one, when a beautiful image of the King has been constructed by some skillful artist out of precious jewels, should then take the likeness of this man all to pieces, should rearrange the gems, and so fit them together as to make them into the form of a dog or of a fox . . ." (1.8.1, p. 326). The image of the mosaic reveals that what is at stake is nothing less than the concept of God as King, who can be identified as God the Father and creator or Christ. It tends to disguise, however, the narrative dynamism responsible for the figuration of the biblical God, that is, the narrative of salvation history articulated in the jointure of Hebrew scriptures and New Testament texts. In *Against Heresies* the rearranging of *metharmottein* clearly supposes disarranging or deranging the order of scripture and, as later parts of the text make clearer, supposes deranging the story that the Bible as a whole relates.

Thus, Irenaeus's image of *metharmottein* at the very least, points to my own concept of metalepsis, which is defined as the disfiguration-refiguration of the biblical narrative, or relatively first-order interpretations of it. Indeed, Irenaeus should get the lion's share of the credit for this concept because Irenaeus makes clear in a way that most contemporary scholars of Valentinianism and genealogists of Valentinianism such as Baur, Voegelin, and Bloom among others, do not, that Valentinianism is defined not only by a transgressive hermeneutic of scripture and an ironic relation to the God who is rendered in the text, but by a disfiguration-refiguration of the salvation history that renders the biblical God. By contrast with Irenaeus, the Baur of *Die christliche Gnosis*, who understands well that narrative formation is key to the interpretation of Gnosticism, never comments on the parasitic nature of Gnostic narrative formation. Similarly, Irenaeus is superior to both Bloom and Voegelin. As one might expect of a great literary critic, Bloom has a particular gift for picking out the hermeneutic as well as literary features that might bind Valentinian discourses and modern Romantic and post-Romantic texts. Bloom, however, does not point to narrative as central to either. And while almost no one has grasped as acutely the transgressive modality of Valentinian hermeneutics, he seems to be sufficiently distracted by Gnostic pastiche and irony that he does not notice that narrative of salvation history is the object of attack in which it is disfigured and refigured. As indicated in part 1, Voegelin makes little of the narrative dimension of Valentinianism,[74] and thus can make nothing of the relation between Valentinian and biblical narrative discourses. In this very important sense, he is perhaps the thinker who is the farthest removed from Irenaeus. But clearly only in this sense. Irenaeus's narrative ruminations in *Against Heresies* are, arguably, the most fertile aspect of his thought. But as I suggested in part 1, another strain is found in Irenaeus that Voegelin and others before him, including Möhler, can capitalize on. This is the essentially the analysis of the authors of Valentinian discourses, specifically an analysis of the spiritual health of the Valentinian. Predictably, analysis yields or exemplifies the conviction of the essentially pathological state of the Gnostic or Valentinian.

In any event, Irenaeus makes abundantly clear in the refutation part of *Against Heresies* that disfiguration-refiguration is total. Not a single important feature of the salvation-history narrative is left intact and is not reconfigured in such a way that its meaning is totally changed. It inverts or subverts the biblical idea of the perfect, omnipotent, good, and just creator God of the Bible by suggesting that there is an unknown God (2.13.3; 3.11; 3.24.2) or a complexly articulated or differentiated divine realm of perfection that lies beyond Him that is superior in the order of being, knowledge, existence, and value. Valentinianism, however, not only disqualifies the creator from the attribution of perfection, but compromises the perfection of divinity in general by making the perfection anterior to the creator subject to lapse and degradation. Of course, Irenaeus also recognizes that Valentinianism goes much further in its negative assessment of the biblical God than simply denying that he is perfect. The biblical God who creates is nothing less than an abortion, or at least the offspring of an abortion. And for the Valentinians the rule or law of the biblical God condemns him. Irenaeus understands that scripture has difficult and hard passages, but fails to see why the biblical God is condemned by law so automatically (4.8, 4.12) and why justice is absolutely incompatible with goodness (3.12.13; 3.25).

The negative estimation of the creator, as detailed graphically in *PSY*, has obvious negative consequences for an evaluation of the created order. The value of the created order is changed from a presumptive plus to a minus, and its status as image turned to that of counterimage. Again, Valentinian degradation of the created order, and specifically of a created or shaped humanity, goes hand in hand with a presumptuous elevation of the status of true humanity. True humanity, defined in terms of spirit and knowledge, is superior to the creator and his creation. The biblical axiom of the incommensurability of God and humanity, both in terms of nature and knowledge (2.25.3, 2.28), is not only compromised, it is shattered by a reversal. Valentinianism also distorts the biblical presentation of the incarnation and passion of Jesus Christ. It distorts it first by questioning the reality of suffering (1.9, but also 3.10, 3.12). Second, it jeopardizes the historicity of the incarnation and suffering. Third, and arguably decisively—since Irenaeus's reading here holds up even in the wake of Nag Hammadi—Valentinianism undermines the saving significance of Christ and refuses to understand the passion and death as the mystery of atonement (3.12, 3.22, 4.8.2). And last, Valentinianism makes a biblically unjustifiable distinction between esoteric and exoteric Christianity, not only in the epistemic but also in the ontological order, and radically questions Christian belief in embodied postmortem existence that is an implicate of Christian belief in Christ's resurrection, which of course is denied.

But it is not only that disfiguration-refiguration of the biblical narrative is comprehensive, it is radical in its explanatory aim of articulating the why of fall and its overcoming (1.10.2, 2.8.5). Despite his interest in tracing all varieties of heresies, and not simply Valentinianism, back to Simon Magus, Irenaeus at the very least insinuates a distinction between Marcionism and Valentinianism, the developed and explicit form of which was introduced in the discussion of Blumenberg and Baur in part 1. The insinuation is made in Book 3 in a discussion of relation that starts out in a very unpromising way. First, Marcion and Valentinus joined together in their common reading of the God of Hebrew scriptures as evil. Then, Irenaeus proceeds to make a shallow distinction that distracts, indeed detracts, from the truly deep one. Irenaeus points out that Marcion's view is less radical than that of Valentinus (3.12.12) in the sense that Marcion is simply less negative than Valentinus, who represents the *ne plus ultra* of negativity.

In his suggestion of the criterion of distinction, however, the deep point is made. The key criterion is that of origin. The obsession with origins shows that Valentinianism differs toto coelo in terms of its explanatory ambitions. Marcion stops at saying that there is a just God, or God of the world, distinct from the good God, or God of redemption. Unlike Valentinianism he is not interested in accounting for why this is so. The narrative does not go back behind this primal pair into the realm of perfection and its vicissitudes. The God of justice is the liminal other of the God of redemption that focally concerns Marcion. This God is to be avoided rather than explained. Ireneaus's grasp of the distinction is momentary and possibly inchoate. He protests on a number of occasions the textual mutilation of the canon by Marcion (1.2.7, 3.12.12). He even does so in 3.12 where he focuses on the contrast between Valentinianism and Marcion. He does not make, however, the obvious connection that textual mutilation is related to an essential contraction in the narrative of divine acts to redemption. Nor does he seem to realize that this narrative contraction involves the surrender of the ambition to total explanation. He reports, however, that just the opposite is the case in and with Valentinianism. Valentinianism's textual expansion goes hand in hand with the generation of metaleptic narratives of an absolutely encompassing kind that bear the burden of an explanation at once comprehensive and unchallengeable.

In an important sense, therefore, on the scales of textual production, narrative span, and explanatory ambitions, ironically, both Marcionism and Valentinianism are each closer to biblical Christianity than to each other. Irenaeus begins to make an important distinction between Marcionism and Valentinianism that is ignored, or at the very least downplayed, in the subsequent heresiological tradition and that, as demonstrated in part 1, modern scholars of the caliber of Baur and Blumenberg continue to ignore. It is imperative to go back and complete a distinction that is at least inchoate in Irenaeus, if not for the sake of retrospective fairness, then in the interest of a genealogy of modern discourses that depends heavily on categorial determinacy. Biblical renditions of Christianity may find themselves stressed by many narrative configurations in the modern period, but which label we provide it makes a real difference. Indeed, the power of resistance depends on the power of taxonomy because resistance necessarily takes different forms in each case.[75]

The metalepsis of biblical narrative is then total. Not a single important element of the biblical narrative of creation, redemption, and sanctification escapes disfiguring-refiguring. In the refutation part of the text Irenaeus leaves us in no doubt concerning the no-exception rule. The analysis continues to expose the deformations that the description of Valentinianism in Book 1 presents without comment. Active throughout the refutation part of *Against Heresies*, however, is a reading of Valentinianism that explores and exploits the depth implications of metaleptic Valentinian narrative or narratives. I suggest that after Balthasar, Irenaeus's exploitation here implies that he has grasped, at least in a rudimentary way, the existence of a tension between the surface and depth narrative commitments in Valentinianism. I return in due course to the need to develop Irenaeus on this point. More important for the moment is a fuller account of how the logic of argumentation in the refutation section brings out elements recessed in the presentation of Valentinianism in the detection of Book 1.

When Irenaeus describes Valentinianism in Book 1 of *Against Heresies*, he provides no notice that the various, even contradictory ontotheological narratives are anything other than static in their basic ontological implications. There is drama, but no development, since Valentinian narratives seem to move from divine perfection through its loss to a recovery of the self same divine perfection. The narrative model therefore is circular, a view repeated consistently in scholarship on Valentinianism, even when Irenaeus's very presentation of Valentinianism—and not simply his evaluation—is treated skeptically.[76] This is also the view repeated by a genealogist of the caliber of Blumenberg when he makes his unfavorable contrast between Valentinianism and Neoplatonism.[77] If there is dynamism in Valentinianism, it exists only on the level of fabulation, the invention of characters, the complexification of plot, the multiplication of events that bring the plot toward resolution and defer it. In addition, Irenaeus also underscores in Book 1 the Valentinian allergy regarding the suffering of the divine, which is rendered on his view in its refusal to accept the reality of the suffering of Christ (1.9). This seems absolutely to preclude making suffering essential to divinity or making suffering constitutive of the narrative economy of the divine. Also within the purely descriptive horizon of Book 1, despite the explanatory interests of Valentinianism, Irenaeus underscores the accidental or purely contingent nature of the fall from/of divine perfection The transgressive act of Sophia in *PSY*, for instance, is fundamentally a surd; it comes from nowhere and can be provided with no rationale.

When Irenaeus moves from detraction to refutation it becomes evident that what he has written in Book 1 is preliminary. In fact, it turns out that he is not prepared to assert categorically that static ontological implication, allergy to divine pathos, and contingency of fall are defining features of Valentinianism. From Book 2 on Irenaeus undertakes an analysis of Valentinianism that draws out the implications that, as far as he is aware, are not explicitly acknowledged by Valentinians. Thus from Book 2 on, operative in Irenaeus's analysis is a distinction between Valentinianism's surface and depth narrative commitments. The point is important hermeneutically in that what is most challenging about Valentinianism may not necessarily be revealed simply by following the surface line of Valentinian stories. A deeper and more latent narrative threat may exist, although Irenaeus does not make this distinction a matter of principle. Moreover, had he done so, he would have been faced with the thorny questions of entitlement. For with *PSY* as his exemplar, although it is possible to upset a reading that would valorize static ontological commitment, emend the embargo against divine passibility, and render necessary the contingency of fall, such a reading is hardly compelling. Arguably, it is not even particularly plausible. Only from the retrospective vantage point of a later Valentinian text, such as the *Tractate*, does this gap in Valentinian texts between surface and narrative depth commitments, of which we ourselves have made much in our own interpretation of Valentinian texts, become evident and plausible. Having at our disposal a Valentinian text such as the *Tractate* allows us to amplify and justify what functions in Irenaeus more or less on an intuitive level.

In his interpretation in Book 2, Irenaeus seriously qualifies his assessment of Valentinianism as committed to a static ontology, inexpugnable divine impassibility, and dramatic contingency. In his revision Irenaeus is not equally deep in his analysis, nor is he systematic. Arguably, Irenaeus is at his weakest in his assessment that Valentinianism subverts its own commitment to the archeological perfection of the divine. Without saying that the whole drama is constitutive of the identity of the merely implicitly divine subject— something that Baur, after Hegel, will tend to assert—Irenaeus does think that in essential respects Valentinian narratives are theogonies (2.14.1). Irenaeus does not develop the point and to the extent to which he does it goes in the direction of a comic depiction of Valentinian storytelling with its proliferation of personae and masks. Had Irenaeus, for instance, made the connection between Valentinianism and Hesiod, or Valentinianism and Orphic theogony, rather than between Valentinianism and Aristophanes, theogony would have functioned more as a concept proper than as a mere conceptual hint.

Irenaeus is stronger in his qualification of the other two descriptive features of Valentinianism. Whatever the allergy of Valentinianism to divine passibility, nevertheless, it commits itself to it. It commits itself when it speaks of the fallen aeon as suffering, for the fallen aeon is still the divine (2.16–17). Moreover, by dint of one aeon of the pleroma suffering, the whole pleroma is implicated, since one has to suppose a fundamental unity of divine substance (2.16).

Irenaeus's discussion of the passion of the aeon on the outermost frontier of perfection serves as a bridge for his withdrawal of his view of the purely contingent nature of the emergence of deficiency in the divine. Irenaeus suggests that if Sophia were really perfect, she could not have fallen. She can only have fallen because a measure of deficiency was present before the fall that paradoxically introduces it. Far from being accidental, the fall, therefore, was necessary—a point to which the author of the *Tractate* will later admit, as mentioned in chapter 3. By implication, then, there exists here, as in the case of divine (im)passibility, at least a tension, and possibly even a contradiction between apparent and real narrative commitments. Irenaeus grasps that the necessity of the fall is also the necessity of creation (2.Preface, 2.1.4, 3.8.3), a position, of course, that he does his utmost to resist (2.1.4, 3.8.3, 4.11, 4.14). This necessity he reads as ontological rather than merely logical, specifically as ontologically compulsive in that need is at its basis (4.11, 4.14). Need points to the imperfection in the so-called perfection of the divine before the emergence of the creator. Moreover it points to the drive to overcome imperfection, however latent, and realize or experience the satisfaction of perfection. Aware that in Plato's texts, and especially the *Symposium*, need is the fundamental aspect of eros, for Irenaeus, the movement outside the pleromatic order is driven by the desire for satisfaction that is multidimensional and has noetic, existential, and axiological as well as specifically ontological aspects. This means that contrary to its express pronouncements, Valentinianism makes the creator and creation necessary to the perfection of the divine that is now a perfection realized only in and through its losing of it.

The erotic reading of perfection, no less than the positing of an archeological perfection distinct from God the creator, is not necessarily good news for those who wish to remain in the biblical universe of assumption. For Irenaeus, John's Gospel fundamentally interprets the relation between God and world, just as John's Gospel also provides the lens in and through which to read Genesis. God is a God of pure love, of agape, a God who gives existence and life, who communicates his presence to human beings before and after the fall (3.25), and who gives his Son who vicariously atones for our sins and reestablishes our right relation with God our Father.[78]

Admittedly, Irenaeus's appraisal of the kind of challenge Valentinian metaleptic narrative presents to those who would be guided by the biblical narrative of salvation history can be read in many ways. Any reading must take in to account the rhetoric of controversy whose prime interest is in making the opposing religious scheme look as bad as possible. The rhetoric is multifaceted. It involves not only ad hominem modes of attack, extrapolations with respect to ethical conduct, but also arguments that bring out implications in Valentinian positions at odds with its express avowals.[79] In addition to Valentinianism not having a stable vocabulary, a limited cast of characters, and unity of plot, in addition to the problems its literary style sets for Christians who are nonliterary, although perhaps not unaesthetic,[80] Valentinianism self-destructs in that it turns out to hold positions that are precisely the contrary to what it deems itself to hold. The argumentative deficit, if not debacle, adds to the steadily mounting case of incoherence. At the argumentative center of this hoisting of Valentinianism on its petard are contradictions in the three pivotal items that we have discussed, that is, contradictions with respect to the view of divine perfection, divine (im)passibility, and contingency of divine fall.

There are different possible ways of viewing the contradictions that Irenaeus reveals. One way of looking at what is going on in the refutation is that Irenaeus is playing the role of philosophical critic of the vain mythologies of Valentinianism and that an essential element of this role is pointing out the logical implications of Valentinian narratives to which only the unintelligent would be blind. Clearly, the text warrants this reading, since Irenaeus in *Against Heresies* is as much a defender of a critical reason that acknowledges its own limitations[81] as he is of revelation. Another way, however, of reading his interpretive focus is to see that Irenaeus regards Valentinian narratives as attacking the biblical narrative not from one side but from two sides. The frontal attack is presented by the underinterpreted narrative in which the perfection of a divine realm beyond the creator is entertained, in which there is squeamishness with regard to any contact of the divine with suffering (hyperbolic sense of divine apathy) and in which there is an attempt to exonerate the divine from evil by asserting the accidental nature of the fall that brings about the disaster of the creator and creation. The even more dangerous attack from the rear is a Valentinianism in which the archeological perfection of the divine is compromised, in which divine passibility is radical (hyperbolic sense of divine passibility), and divine fall and creation are necessary.

One does not have to choose, however, among these readings of how Irenaeus says what is not said in the detection and unsays what is implied. The readings are compatible with each other. Moreover, they involve each other. To make the logical point is to make the narrative point and vice versa. I prioritize the hermeneutic narrative point because this aspect of Irenaeus's complex analysis is taxonomically rich with respect to an analysis of Valentinianism and that is genealogically fertile if only in the long run. Irenaeus's intuitive grasp of the doubling in Valentinian narratives can be elevated into a hermeneutic principle if this doubling can be demonstrated to be displayed in Valentinian texts that Irenaeus did not exegete. This I believe I have succeeded in doing in my last chapter. And, of course, demonstrating this doubling shows how open Valentinianism is to explicit theogonic, erotic, and agonistic configuration.

This phenomenon of doubling makes Irenaeus more our contemporary than scholars of Gnosticism who point univocally to the circularity of Valentinian narratives, their commitment to divine impassibility, and the accidental or tragic nature of fall. For the same reason, this phenomenon of doubling makes Irenaeus more our contemporary than Baur, who equally univocally validates the noncircularity of Valentinian narrative and underscores its commitment to divine pathos and the necessity of fall. Neither reading is stereoscopic. Consequently, neither reading is adequate to the complexity of classical Valentinian narratives that endorses one set of commitments only to undermine them. Moreover, both univocal positions represent genealogical dead ends. The former makes it impossible to think how any continuity could be asserted between these narratives ruled by Hellenistic assumptions and narrative discourses in modernity, and more specifically between classical Valentinian narratives and the developmental and agonistic narratives of the Baurian field. The latter makes it impossible to think of how discontinuity could be asserted between classical Valentinian narratives, miraculously free of static assumption, and the developmental and agonistic narratives of the Baurian field, for the latter would be essentially repetitions in the most literal sense of Valentinian narratives of the earliest centuries.

To summarize this discussions of Irenaeus's contributions toward a narrative and grammatical understanding of Valentinianism, we find that Irenaeus has an acute sense of the diversity and variety of Valentinian narratives that must be taken into account in any conceptualizing of the phenomenon of Valentinianism. At the same time he has a deep appreciation of the fundamentally literary quality of Valentinian production that has a paradoxical, perhaps even aporetic, quality: profligacy and open-endedness of discursive production rules out the possibility of scripture, which depends both on a limited number of texts and that the number of texts that are regulative or authoritative are closed. At the same time, however, these texts arrogate to themselves the kind of authority that is commonly given only to texts as scripture. Thus Valentinian texts make scripture impossible and essentially claim a scripturelike prerogative on behalf of their texts. Irenaeus has more than an elementary grasp of the encompassing nature of Valentinian narrative in contrast with Marcionism, which like it offers a fundamental challenge to a form of Christianity that affirms Hebrew scriptures and the agential God that they depict. Similarly, he has a sense of the difference in their explanatory ambitions, total in the case of Valentinianism, regional in the case of Marcionism.

Central to Irenaeus's contribution is his view that Valentinian narratives represent a metalepsis of the biblical narrative. In what amounts to a six-staged narrative articulation of a movement from divine perfection through loss to its recovery, Valentinian narratives encompass the biblical narrative and completely disfigure and refigure it. Moreover, Valentinian narratives disfigure and refigure the biblical narrative with the self-conscious aim of complete explanatory adequacy that insults revelation as much as it flatters human intelligence. And finally, Irenaeus sees, at least through a glass darkly, that metalepsis is double: The biblical narrative is disfigured and refigured twice by Valentinian narratives, once by the surface narrative that describes a movement from the divine perfection through loss to the recovery of the selfsame divine perfection, and again by the depth narrative that authorizes an erotic view of divine perfection, a form of deipassionism, and necessity rather than contingency in divine fall. Helping, as he does, to confirm and expand on our articulation of Valentinian narrative grammar, Irenaeus also assists considerably in our prosecution of a Valentinian genealogical case. This is especially so with regard to his insight that in Valentinian narratives the ultimate challenge is presented by the erotic, agonistic, and necessitarian drive that is a real and effective presence.

However, some elements of Irenaeus's analysis of Valentinian-ism, and not simply his rhetoric of denunciation, are not especially helpful to our narrative grammar case and consequently must be ignored or corrected. Despite his proper emphasis on diversity and variety, Irenaeus does tend to suggest a Gnostic *Urnarrative*, indif-ferent between Valentinian and non-Christian (or pre-Christian) forms, but also indifferent between Valentinianism and Marcionism. By pointing to a pre-Christian form of gnosis, and ultimately to the discourse of Simon Magus as origin, Irenaeus offers an etiological ac-count whose function, if not intent, is to contain the threat to biblical narrative. The plurality of Valentinian narratives, together with other Gnostic and non-Gnostic options, seem to produce a kind of vertigo that makes resistance difficult. In the interest of resistance, narrative polysemy tends to be reduced to narrative monesemy. Nevertheless, the interpreter does not need to call on the full re-sources of a hermeneutic of charity to agree that a real tendency to-ward something other than an *Urnarrative* view exists in Irenaeus, indeed, a tendency toward a narrative grammar view in which dif-ferences between Valentinian narratives are respected, which in turn allows for a sense of the diversity and variety of Valentinian metalepsis of biblical narrative.

Irenaean Blind Spot and Its Grammatical Correction

I have not yet mentioned, however, the constitutive flaw of Ire-naeus's view, what amounts to its blind spot. When articulating the positive Christian option, which consists of the unity of Old Testa-ment and New Testament interpreted as rendering a unified nar-rative of the workings of Father, Son, and Spirit in creation and history,[82] *Against Heresies* makes little or no admission of the kind of diversity of construal that would ground a grammatical under-standing of biblical narrative. This is hugely important from a ge-nealogical point of view because not only does it deny biblical forms of Christianity the kind of fertility granted to Valentinianism, it preempts a traditioning process that necessarily involves argu-ment. As I have indicated more than once, the sheer variety of in-terpretations of biblical narrative within mainline Christian communities over history have prompted some theologians to sug-gest the operation of something like a biblical narrative grammar. These theologians differ among themselves as to whom can safely be regarded as offering an exemplary instance of this grammar. If there is general agreement on classical cases such as Irenaeus,

Augustine, Aquinas, Luther, and Calvin, there is some disagreement about modern theologians such as Schleiermacher and Tillich. In addition, there are different emphases with respect to the relation between structure and paradigm, and structure and history.[83] But here I no more adjudicate between the different sense of grammar in operation than I attempt to argue from ground-zero for a grammar of biblical narrative or a grammar of biblical narrative interpretation. Instead, I simply stipulate that logically if a band of post-Reformation and post-Enlightenment narrative ontotheologies are taken to be historically specific forms of Valentinian narrative grammar, then these bear a metaleptic relation to equally historically specific forms of biblical narrative grammar.

It is important that I put on record that my complaint against Irenaeus is in service of a refigured or figural Irenaeus in which the blind spot is overcome. Despite Irenaeus's tendency in *Against Heresies* to counter what he perceives to be a hypertrophy of unstable narrative plurality by a hypertrophy of stable biblical narrative unity,[84] I suggest that there are at least hints in his own articulation of tradition and the rule of faith whose development leads to a major revision of his express statements on these matters.

For scholars of ancient Christianity whose sympathies lie with the Gnostics or Valentinians rather than the emerging church with its institutional organization and definite belief system, Irenaeus's assertions at numerous points throughout *Against Heresies* about the constant unity of biblical faith (e.g., 1.10, 1.22, 2.9, 3.1–5 inter alia) is chimerical at best and authoritarian at worst.[85] But even Irenaeus's defenders—and I am one of them—would have to concede at least in part that his proposal is overdetermined by his perception of the exuberant production and motility of Valentinian narrative. Similarly, the most loyal of Irenaeus's supporters would have to agree that Irenaeus seems to be naive about the historicity of his situation and fails to appreciate appropriately the extent of his own theological creativity. Oddly, the Spirit deflects attention away from such creativity. The Spirit guarantees the unity of canon and the shared interpretation throughout the generations of the Christian community. Certainly, in *Against Heresies* the Spirit does not seem to provide any special theological charism. Yet there is a way in which the rule of faith need not have the fixed and static aspect that Irenaeus seems to give it on occasion. Indeed, there is a way in which the rule of faith points, I would suggest, to a biblical narrative grammar that is the correlative of Valentinian narrative grammar.

At the most general level Irenaeus understands the rule of faith to consist of the summary theological conclusions of the Christian community's reading of the Hebrew Bible, the Gospels, and the letters of Paul over what he takes to be an extended period of time and the principles of reading scripture, where such principles exclude as well as include particular readings.[86] Something of a hermeneutic circle seems to exist between the summary theological conclusions and the principles of reading with reading oriented toward summary theological conclusions, and theological conclusions functioning as the presuppositions for principles of reading if not *as* the principles of reading the unity of Hebrew Bible and those texts that describe and inscribe the new dispensation. In addition, the rule of faith seems at once to presuppose something like a canon of Old Testament and New Testament texts and contributes to its formation by picking out the textual universe that confirms its summary theological conclusions.

The doubleness of the rule of faith and the hermeneutic relation between summary theological conclusion and principles of reading scripture represent the core and the constant aspects of the rule of faith. But the rule is not without secondary aspects. Nor is it invariant in the range of its summary theological conclusions or principles of reading. A secondary aspect of the rule of faith, what might be best called a meta-aspect, is its encouraging of a sober, literal style of interpretation of the Hebrew Bible and the texts of the first century that narrate and confess Jesus Christ. This style of interpretation coheres with the view of Christianity being a religion of and for the community at large. A variable aspect is the broader or narrower scope of the rule. For instance, in Irenaeus's explicit appeals to the rule of faith in *Against Heresies* (1.9.5, 1.10, 3.1–5) the scope is narrow. Focally, it concerns the identification of the creator with God almighty, and the identification of Jesus of Nazareth, as the one narrated in the Gospels, and confessed in Paul, as the Redeemer. The Spirit is mentioned, but not expressly articulated, while it obviously implies a principle of reading necessary for linking the Father-creator with Jesus Christ–redeemer. By contrast, in *On the Apostolic Preaching*, Irenaeus offers a more expansive articulation of the rule of faith in which the content extends beyond the two identifications central in *Against Heresies* and includes as a focus the creation of human being and its fall that sets the stage for the coming of Jesus Christ.[87]

Considered complexly as both a set of summary theological conclusions and principles for reading scripture, the rule of faith at once clearly schematizes a narrative and presents something like a narrative creed.[88] In doing so, it offers a grammar of biblical narrative and/or a grammar for the interpretation of the biblical rendering of the enactment of that reality that Irenaeus refers to in his doxology at the end of the *On the Apostolic Preaching* as the "All Holy Trinity and One Divinity: Father, Son and all-provident Holy Spirit" (101). This narrative grammar and/or grammar of reading in turn supposes or demands a biblical canon, specifically a linkage between Hebrew scriptures and the belated texts produced in the Christian communities, a link made by appeal to the Spirit. In its most expanded form, then, the rule of faith in effect offers the following grammar of biblical narrative, conceived both as summary conclusions and the principles for the right reading of scripture, which shows itself to be nothing more or less than the trinitarian history of salvation: (1) Divine perfection consists exclusively of Father, Son, and Holy Spirit. (2) The Father is the almighty and good creator of all that is, not excluding human beings. (3) The fall of human being consists in disobedience with respect to a God of rule who is not only almighty but also caring. (4) Jesus Christ is the incarnation of the Word, the redeemer who suffers, dies, and is resurrected. (5) All are included in Jesus Christ's saving activity, Jew and gentile, with salvation being conditioned by faith in Jesus Christ, the performance of good works, and hope in the resurrection.

If the rule of faith represents a biblical narrative grammar, then Irenaeus's counterproposal to Gnostic theological conclusions and Gnostic principles of reading represents an exemplary instance of this grammar. As an exemplary instance of this grammar, that is, as a theological product that obeys the rules for articulating biblical narrative, it should not be confused with biblical narrative grammar. To the extent to which in his proud profession of unoriginality Irenaeus tends toward identifying his own production with this grammar, which is open to multiple interpretations, he misunderstands both himself and the rule of faith. The counterproposal to Gnosticism and Gnostic hermeneutics of scripture articulated in *Against Heresies* offers a rendition of biblical narrative grammar that is more ample than that articulated in the rule of faith and offers an interpretation of scripture and what it renders in accordance with the principles of or for reading scripture that yet bears Irenaeus's own personal stamp.

As Irenaeus presents his rendition of biblical narrative grammar, he is variously reserved and expansive, theologically indeterminate and superdeterminate. For example, Irenaeus is reserved with respect to the divine Trinity, outside of activity in salvation history (1). He does insist that together Father, Son, and Spirit exhaust divine perfection (2.1, 2.4, 3.8–9, 4.1) and that in their activities they function as identifiably determinate entities. In addition, in all the events in which they are involved they function exclusively in agential fashion by contrast with the pathos that haunts the personifications that articulate Valentinian perfection. None of this amount to making explicit the distinction between the Trinity *in se* and the trinitarian missions that will become de rigeur from Nicaea on, although I should point out that the determinacy of attribution and the agential emphasis aids rather than hinders the distinction. Again, from a post-Nicene perspective Irenaeus is relatively indeterminate, or underdetermined, with respect to the relations that hold between Father, Son, and Spirit. He satisfies himself by expostulating on the relations as they are disclosed in the economy. And what he does say by way of addressing the issue at a relatively more structural level, namely, what is summed up in his image of the Son and the Spirit as the two hands of the Father, is from the post-Nicene vantage point determinate in the wrong way because it is subordinationist in its implications. At the very least, Irenaeus's articulation of the Trinity is just one of many possible articulations and by no means the most sophisticated at that. Thus, it requires supplementation. In the theological tradition this supplementation comes in many forms, for example, in the form of the Cappadocians, Augustine, Aquinas, Bonaventure, Barth, Rahner, and Balthasar.

By contrast, in his depiction of the creator and his creation (2), Irenaeus is both determinate and expansive. This creator, who can legitimately utter the words "I am who am" (3.8.3), creates out of nothing. *Creatio ex nihilo* underscores divine sovereignty and power (3.8.3, 4.11) while suggesting the gratuity of all that is, human being as well as the cosmos (2.1, 3.8.2). As Irenaeus's articulation of human being as the image of God (Gen. 1.26) indicates, support of creation from nothing is not incompatible with conferring dignity on human being. But it does mean that the analogy between a creature and creator is undergirded by an even greater disanalogy. Although this interpretation of the creator and the creation will become in time the dominant one and is articulated in different ways in Augustine, Gregory of Nyssa, Aquinas, and Luther, it is important to point out that it is an interpretation. As such, it puts under severe pressure rather than absolutely defeats views that to various extents tend to work more nearly with a prime matter option. An interpretation of the biblical creator and creation conducted in conversation with the template of demiurgic activity in the *Timaeus* would not necessarily constitute an infraction of biblical narrative grammar. When Augustine entertains a prime matter reading of Genesis in the *Confessions* (Bk. 13), if only finally to prefer a creation from nothing view, when Milton in his vast extrapolations on biblical narrative in *Paradise Lost* adopts the prime matter view,[89] and when Barth tempers his creation from nothing view in the *Church Dogmatics* with his strange reflections on *Das Nichtige*, they are disagreeing with Irenaeus's highly determinate reading, and articulating a minority opinion, but one not expressly forbidden by biblical narrative grammar as such.

In addition, Irenaeus has a view of the Adamic condition as childlike that is not demanded by biblical narrative grammar. In fact, he offers an interpretation of the dynamic-teleological movement from image to likeness that Augustine and the bulk of the Western tradition will reject.[90] Irenaeus's expansiveness with respect to creation is, perhaps, best shown in his treatment of the angels and their role in the economy. Whereas for obvious reasons in his dispute with the Gnostics in *Against Heresies* Irenaeus is silent with respect to the creation of the angels,[91] in the *On the Apostolic Preaching* (9–10) he narratively and iconically extends the act or activity of creation by making the creation of the cosmos and human being as image follow that of the creation of the angels. If the purpose of such following is primarily to establish the identity of the serpent that tempts Adam (16), Irenaeus makes a move that he feels is not ruled out by biblical narrative grammar. If the Gnostics or Valentinians extrapolate wildly and without constraint, Irenaeus does not rule out narrative and iconic expansion of scripture as long as these preserve among other things the sovereignty and goodness of God the creator. Biblical narrative grammar is not unpermissive with respect to narrative and iconic expansion. Later Augustine and Milton, the latter dependent proximally on the articulation of the former in the *City of God* (Bk. 11, 9–15, 32–34, Bk. 12, 1–9), will take advantage of this permission and be empowered by the template already laid down by Irenaeus to break the Bible's silence on the angels. Milton, of course, goes much further than Augustine. Indeed, in *Paradise Lost* he offers with Dante's *Divine Comedy* one of the most comprehensive narrative and iconic extensions of biblical narrative in the Western Christian tradition.[92] And arguably Milton's narrative and iconic extension stretches but does not break with a biblical narrative grammar, since it does not break the rules for narrative and iconic extension that are implied by a biblical narrative grammar.[93] I will discuss this point in my volume on Romanticism in which I disengage Milton from his Romantic assimilation, and in particular from his coupling with Blake, whom I argue is a quintessential Valentinian who breaks the rules of narrative and iconic extension.

With respect to the fall of human being (3), although Irenaeus is not especially reserved, his account is from a theological point of view relatively indeterminate, or perhaps better stated, relatively underdetermined. Against the speculative Valentinian alternative, he supports what he takes to be both the literal and community reading of Genesis 1.3 to offer a reliable guide with respect to the damaged existence of human being. *Sin* is the fundamental category insofar as it points to human being as the origin of the damage and parses the damage in terms of the withdrawal of the goods that properly belong to human being in right relationship with God. *Disobedience* is the fundamental character of sin and involves repressing the fact that God's rule is not for God alone but provides the measure for creaturely being. Disobedience also involves an illegitimate elevation of human autonomy to the level of the divine. Not surprisingly, then, an interpreter sympathetic to the Valentinians rather than Irenaeus such as Elaine Pagels,[94] correlates the support of heteronomy, first with authority and second with authoritarianism. Nevertheless, outside what it excludes, Irenaeus's position on sin is relatively undeveloped. He does not attempt to correlate *disobedience* with all the biblical namings for sin, for example, *rebellion, offense, swerve, rejection, idolatry*, or the *flesh*. Nor does he probe in the way an Augustine does the motivational structure of sin, in which the categories of *self-love* and *pride* loom large. Nor does he explore the issue as to what makes disobedience so serious, specifically whether the seriousness is predicated on the attitude of the offender or the dignity of the offended party. Between Augustine and Anselm, and Anselm and Luther, these and other questions raised by the biblical text that Irenaeus reliefs, but does not deeply explore, will be plumbed. Irenaeus's account of the origin and nature of sin will find both complements and supplements within the theological tradition that works within the coordinates set by biblical narrative grammar.

More in keeping with his articulation of the creator-created or creator-creature relation (2), than with his articulation of what biblical narrative grammar allows with respect to the perfection of the divine Trinity (1) and his account of the fall (3), Irenaeus is determinate with respect to his figuration of Christ (4). Obviously, his biblical orientation makes his figuration soteriological rather than ontological, although his insistence that the salvific activity of Christ supposes that Christ is both human and divine (3.12.15) provides the necessary basis for all later ontological analyses of the person of Christ. Moreover, the symbol of kenosis serves an important role in this soteriological analysis. Irenaeus insists both on the reality of kenosis and its exclusively christological horizon as he focuses on Philippians 2.6–11 and 2 Corinthians 12.9. Ruled out is anything like a principle of divine self-emptying. If Irenaeus's Adam-Christ typology was even a commonplace in his own day, in his symbol of *anakephalaiōsis* he offers an interpretation of Romans 5.12–21 that is individual (3.12.16, 3.18.6–7, 3.21.9–10, 3.22).[95] In Irenaeus's depiction of the overcoming of sin by Christ, the emphasis falls more nearly on overcoming the major consequence of the loss of perfection, that is, mortality, than on the healing of the dispositional dynamics, which is the emphasis of Augustine and a significant part of the Western tradition (3.18–19). In addition, Irenaeus's model of the atonement of Christ for human sins proceeds without appeal to the juridical categories that are popular in the West in Tertullian in the second century and that receive a rationalist expression in Anselm's *Cur Deus Homo*.[96] Irenaeus's own christological position, then, is just one position among many that satisfy biblical narrative grammar. Other positions, both soteriological and ontological, both operating with his dramatic atonement model and those that follow the juridical path of Tertullian, complement and supplement his.

Finally, Irenaeus's views of salvation and who qualifies (5), while extraordinarily broad, does not lack the kind of determinacy that constitutes it an interpretation. Salvation essentially consists of the redeeming offer of Christ in the Cross vouchsafed in the resurrection that overcomes the sin of Adam and its historical manifestations as recorded in Hebrew scriptures. With regard to the issue of who qualifies for salvation, other than denying that some are constituted by nature to be saved, Irenaeus leaves a great deal open. Both grace and free will are asserted, but no clarity is brought to their relationship. Clarity is absent because fundamentally there is no problematization. This problematization awaits the later Augustine, to be retrieved by the Reformers and, arguably, by the Jansenists in Catholicism. Also evident is a tension between the universality of salvation that is suggested in the symbol of Christ as *anakephalaiōsis*, and his acceptance of the possibility, maybe even the actuality, that some will refuse the offer of salvation in Jesus Christ. But again this tension is hardly explored in the way it can be, as witnessed in the efforts of modern theologians such as Barth, Rahner, and Balthasar. Here, as in the case of all previous elements of biblical narrative grammar, Irenaeus offers an interpretation that is important, but by no means exhaustive. It allows, even requires, complementarity and supplementarity.

In bringing this section to a close, in interpreting Irenaeus's rule of faith as essentially amounting to a biblical narrative grammar, I wish to give credit to Irenaeus for a profound insight that is sometimes obscured by his confounding his own articulation with the rule of faith and most important his reading of the rule of faith as if it consisted of a set of ineluctable propositions that escaped the circle of interpretation. The Irenaean blind spot is overcome, I suggest, by consistently holding to a grammatical view of biblical narrative that has as a correlative recognition that all articulation of biblical narrative is an interpretation. Removing Irenaeus's blind spot means refiguring him. In this refiguration Irenaeus is both less and more than he was: less in that aspects of him are rejected; more in that one of the basic tendencies of his work is amplified and refined to do genealogical work. The refigured Irenaeus supports the plurality of interpretation of biblical narrative and can do so by appeal to biblical narrative grammar. What is opposed to Valentinian narrative grammar with its obvious plurality, therefore, cannot be a biblical *Urnarrative*. The battle, therefore, is a battle between grammars, but this battle takes place always in the form of specific renditions of these grammars. Moreover, it takes place always in historically specific forms of these grammars. And if finally it is possible to see the grammars of biblical and Valentinian narrative as not confined to their classical instances, it is possible to see that the narrative grammaromachia need not be confined to Irenaeus's time or the Hellenistic world in general. It is possible that the battle of narrative grammars is also a phenomenon evident in modern discourse.

4.2. Valentinianism's Relation to Other Narrative Discourses

I turn now to the second of the two foci of this crucially important, yet essentially transitional, chapter on Valentinian narrative grammar. The subject is no longer the general prospects of a narrative grammar construal of Valentinianism and what assistance is available from the tradition of interpretation toward vouchsafing the validity of the enterprise. The subject is rather the hospitality of classical Valentinian narrative texts to other narrative discourses, particularly those of Neoplatonism and apocalyptic. More specifically, the subject is whether the hospitality shown by classical Valentinian narrative texts toward other non-Valentinian narrative discourses is itself a feature of Valentinian narrative grammar, such that were Valentinian narrative to be operative in the modern period, then we might expect this hospitality to non-Valentinian narrative discourses to be in evidence and possibly even extended beyond Neoplatonism and apocalyptic.

I begin with the vexed issue of the relation between Neoplatonism and Gnosticism. For the major figures involved in hypothesizing a Gnostic return in modernity, determining the relation between Neoplatonism and Gnosticism, and especially Valentinianism, has been a conceptual need. The results have not been especially happy. As indicated in part 1, both Baur and Staudenmaier blur their boundaries. Even that genealogist *malgré lui*, Blumenberg, manages to read these discourses as so neighborly that their otherness, which forces the issue of relation in the first case, tends to be forgotten. Admittedly, at one important point in *Die christliche Gnosis* (417–459) Baur does point to the alterity of these discourses by recalling Plotinus's famous denunciation in the *Enneads* (1.8, 2.9) of Gnosticizing interpretations of Plato's classic texts. The support for Plotinus's act of discrimination turns out to be provisional, however, because Baur goes on to suggest that Gnosticism and Neoplatonism are joined by a deeper relation, which it turns out, after Hegel, is a relation on the infrastructural level of narrative (449–457).[97] I return in due course to this conflation of Neoplatonism and Gnosticism in genealogical discourse, which, as Jonas among others recognizes, fails to appreciate adequately the fundamental rightness of Plotinus's classic act of discrimination. But to put the relation on the right genealogical footing, addressing its historical and textual aspects is necessary.

Few scholars of the history of Platonism in the Hellenistic period have doubted the veracity of Plotinus's report of the presence of Gnostics in the Platonic schools. And several scholars have drawn parallels between the kinds of Gnostic positions condemned and the pronounced dualism of a Middle Platonist such as Numenius.[98] Nag Hammadi has revived the historical question of relation by making scholars wonder whether *Allogenes*, for instance, really is the text referred to by Plotinus,[99] in much the same way as scholars speculate whether the Nag Hammadi *Gospel of Truth* is the text to which

Irenaeus refers by the same name (*Against Heresies*, Bk. 3). On purely internal textual grounds there is evidence of significant overlap in vocabulary and even substance between non-Valentinian texts such as *Marsanes*, *Zostrianos*, and, of course, *Allogenes* and second- and third-century reflection on Plato in the Platonic schools.[100] Scholars invoke even texts such as the *Apocryphon of John* and the *Origin of the World*, which appear to be more seriously engaged with the Genesis creation story than with the Platonic conundrum of the relation between the demiurge and the absolute One or Good.[101] The evidence for Gnostic contact with Platonic modes of discourse is more rather than less compelling in the case of Valentinianism. Texts such as the *Gospel* and the *Tractate* are replete with Platonic symbolism and avail themselves of Platonic conceptualities to present their metaleptic versions of the biblical narrative. While the symbols belong to a Hellenistic cornucopia, these texts employ the symbolic pairs of knowledge and ignorance, sleep and wakefulness, error and truth, purity and impurity in oppositional ways that recall Platonic texts such as the *Phaedo* and the *Phaedrus*. More important are the conceptual adaptations. Here I focus on those elements of adaptation in the *Gospel* and the *Tractate* that push Valentinianism in a direction different from that of *PSY*.

In their reduction of personification and their attempt to reduce contingency and eventness in narrative episodes, Valentinian texts such as the *Gospel* and *Tractate* evince an attraction for a philosophical regime that is at once hospitable to and critical of mythic discourse. This philosophical regime is determinate: It is basically Platonic rather than Stoic.[102] We see this, for example, from the way the texts appeal to the Timaean "God is not jealous" trope to suggest a more positive estimate of the creator, act of creation, and the resulting world than that found in *PSY*. We see this too in the way these two texts evoke the construct of providence, which will play such a prominent role in Plotinus (*Enneads* 3.2.2) and Proclus. Several other conceptual borrowings seem equally evident. The *Gospel*'s and *Tractate*'s reflection on the Son and aeons as forms of consciousness or self-consciousness reflect attempts in the Platonic schools to find a mediation between the One, which is beyond Being, but plausibly also beyond self-consciousness in any determinate sense,[103] and a demiurge made problematic by a universe characterized more by the shapelessness of chaos than the form of cosmos, and ignorance rather than knowledge.

I find, however, that the Platonic borrowings modify, but do not fundamentally transform, both the event character of Gnostic myth and the basic story of the tragic fall and recovery of the divine. The trope "God is not jealous" (*Enneads* 6.8) and the construct of providence, neither singly nor together, replace the straightforward negative evaluation of the act of creation and the result, evident for instance in *PSY*, by an equally straightforward positive evaluation. What they do effect is a second-order affirmation: Maintaining the first-order negation, they suggest that fault may turn out to be happy.

The difference between what is effected by these Platonic elements in Gnostic and Neoplatonic contexts is illustrated by Plotinus in the *Enneads*. Having the Sophia myth directly in mind, Plotinus offers a paradigm in his reflection on *tolma* of what such a first-order substitution would look like (*Enneads* 6.9).[104] In this new regime of discourse in which philosophical principles replace aeons, audaciousness (*tolma*) with respect to knowledge of the transcendent no longer has transgressive force. Audaciousness is, indeed, the eros for knowledge, but this eros is nothing more nor less than the legitimate responsiveness of Nous to the diffusive love of the One.[105] In the *Tractate*, by contrast, what remains basic is that the eros of or for knowledge is transgressive. Evil is only legitimated on a second-order level by being seen to be elicited by the transcendent Father, who like Plotinus's One is beyond predication and yet the ultimate ontological root.[106] Similarly, in Plotinus the world over which providence rules is a world that has a basically mimetic structure, even if at its limit it is bereft of features that mimic the divine intelligible world. Although the *Tractate* does not renege altogether on suggesting a mimetic relation between the physical and the aeonic world, the fundamental structure of the physical world is that of antitype. The antitype may break down and ultimately reveal shards of intelligibility, perhaps even a general pattern of mimesis, but the rule of providence is as dialectical as the relation between the first-level countermimesis and second-level mimesis or supermimesis.

Thus we cannot erase particular narrative features of the type best instanced in *PSY*. More important, we cannot erase general narrative features. Although the *Gospel* and the *Tractate* try to carry through as comprehensively and rigorously as possible the Platonic view of the communication of divine perfection, they do not support the unbroken continuum view of communication that Plotinus and Proclus think is a necessary feature of absolute reality as expressive.[107] Events remain discernible in these Valentinian paradigms, but so also does discontinuity, tear, or gap in divine expression. Again, continuity is affirmed as a reality on a different level:

continuity in communication of divine perfection takes place *across* discontinuity, *despite* tear and gap that signify a refusal of divine communication, a kind of expressive excommunication. One can similarly see in the *Tractate* in particular a way in which the Platonic communication model of perfection fails to master implications in the myth of the erring aeon of fragility, and thus lack at the level of divine perfection. Indeed, such implications are exacerbated. What results is an erotic view of perfection that would be no more accepted by Middle Platonists criticized by Plotinus than by Plotinus himself.

The very continuity in the movement of perfection introduced by the model of divine communication aids the retrogressive hints of imperfection at the base of the pleroma. These hints suggest that the very movement of the divine and not simply the movement of time or human being, which is classically the case in the *Symposium*, is a movement of the overcoming of lack by fullness, *penia* by *poros*.[108] In short, perfection is developmental and indeed pedagogic in a way Plotinus refuses. His exit-return narrative does not make distinctions between the perfection of the One from which one comes and the perfection of the One to which one goes. Plotinus can talk of the Nous filling itself (*peplerkos heauto*) (*Enneads* 6. 4. 2) and being filled by contemplation. But neither he nor his Middle Platonic precursors even hint that perfection could be a matter of *plērōsis*, which would affect all the binary oppositions in a narrative, for example, seeing-not seeing, light-dark, life-death, reality-nothing, pure-impure, etheriality-massiveness. *Plērōsis* is indicated when the second term becomes a means to the full realization of the first. This, of course, means that the binary oppositions are overcome. The positive first becomes an even more positive third. Thus, the full patterns are now seeing-not seeing-seeing, light-dark-light, life-death-life, reality-nothing-reality, pure-impure-pure, and etheriality-massiveness-etheriality. In short, in Plotinus, as in his Middle Platonist precursors, we find no evidence of the narrativizing pressure evinced at least in the *Tractate*, and that I argue in the next chapter is an obtrusive mark of many, if not all, modern instances of Valentinian narrative grammar.

It is time to return to Plotinus's resistance to the Gnostics in the *Enneads* (1.8, 2.9) with a view to understanding more its systematic than historical importance. He famously rehearses Gnosticism's lack of strict philosophical rigor, its hermeneutic irresponsibility shown in the great deviance from Plato's texts and the tradition of interpretation of Plato, its un-Platonic antipathy to the demiurge, and its un-Greek hatred of the physical universe. He answers the Gnostics positively and is constructive in the articulation of his own system founded on the One beyond being (*epekeinai tēs ousias*). Here an uninterrupted giving of perfection reaches into the cosmos. It finds a limit only in matter, which has to be regarded as the exhaustion of perfection rather than the antithesis. Even if Plotinus's intervention from a historical point of view makes the issues between Gnosticism and Platonism more stark than they were in the century preceding him,[109] arguably the tradition of interpretation of Plato as a whole supports his reading, and justifies his line in the sand.

In this context it is more important to recall the kinds of texts rather than the actual identity of the texts to which he was referring, whether non-Valentinian or Valentinian. Plotinus objects to mixed discourses of Platonism and Gnostic myth. At a minimum, he thinks such mixtures compromise Platonic discourse, and at a maximum, he thinks that such mixtures totally vitiate Platonism because Gnosticism then becomes hegemonic. Plotinus does not specify further the means by which Gnosticism achieves hegemony. But if our reading of the *Gospel* and the *Tractate* as classical genres of Valentinian narrative grammar is correct, the way in which Gnosticism achieves hegemony is clear enough: however Platonic their look, Gnosticism of whatever variety declares itself by continuing to regard the base narrative to be a mythic conjugation of dramatic divine fall and recovery. Topologically represented, if Platonism is present in the *Gospel* and the *Tractate*, then it belongs to the secondary narrative stratum rather than the primary narrative stratum that is occupied by Gnosticism.

I do not wish to emphasize exclusively, however, the distinct narrative levels within these Valentinian texts. It is possible to be too influenced by Plotinus's profound prophylaxis. And this turns out to be a genealogical straightjacket. I want, for the sake of conceptual determinacy, to do two things. First, I want to push, as far as possible, for decisions whether particular narrative ontotheological discourses in modernity, or indeed a band of these discourses that evidences both Valentinian and Neoplatonic properties, are Valentinian or Neoplatonic. I allow, of course, that one can rule out beforehand neither undecidability nor complex ascription. With regard to this genealogical task, both Plotinian criteria and the narrative stratigraphy to which I referred are useful tools for reaching decisions. Second, I want to acknowledge and determine respects in which Valentinian narrative grammar remains open to Platonism and Neoplatonism. Such openness may easily be exacerbated under certain conditions in modernity. Modern paradigms or genres of Valentinian narrative grammar may show even greater instances of Platonic or Neoplatonic presence and modification. Once more, however, we may be prepared to see greater instances of what is, in effect, discourse cooption or enlisting. I reflect further on this facet of Valentinian narrative grammar in the third section of chapter 5 after I have discussed the conditions in modernity, or its threshold, of a non-mechanical repetition, an innovative repetition as it were (in the second section).

At this juncture, however, broaching a question implied by the openness of Valentinianism to Platonic and Neoplatonic modes of thought is necessary. Valentinianism is not simply a Gnostic discourse; it is metaleptic Christian discourse that bears complex relations to other narrative discourses within the biblical text that are possessed of a certain imaginative brazenness and claim to revelation. I bring the relation between Gnosticism and apocalyptic into view, and this is not without some scholarly sanction.[110] What I attempt now is to sort out the relation between Valentinianism and apocalyptic within the Hellenistic field, which will allow me later to draw the genealogical consequences from this clarification.

Justification of the ascription of *apocalypse* to Valentinian narrative grammar as a whole does not lie in the use of the Greek word *apokalypsis* or its Coptic equivalent in Valentinian texts. It lies rather in the double role played by revelation or disclosure: Revelation is an event *in* the narrative in which the savior-figure, associated with Christ, brings enlightenment. At the same time revelation is an event of knowing that has the entire ontotheological narrative of whence and whither of a divine self as its object. The fact that Valentinian narratives are rendered in registers as different as the dogmatic-mythological and the epistemological implies that Valentinian apocalypse admits of a variety of forms. *PSY*, for instance, would never justify David Dawson's felicitous designation of the *Gospel* as an apocalypse of mind.[111] The question arises, however, whether anything new has been added to Valentinianism by the addition of the descriptor apocalypse, especially in the absence of the kind of conceptual determinacy provided by relating paradigmatic forms of Valentinianism to paradigmatic forms of apocalyptic such as Daniel, *Enoch*, and, of course, above all, Revelation.

This comparative route is both valid and valuable in determining the specificity of Valentinian apocalypse. Nevertheless, some scholars suggest that we should base the conceptual determinacy of Gnostic apocalypse exclusively on differences between its paradigms and the paradigms of apocalyptic.[112] While I agree that differences are essential for the definition of Gnosticism, and especially for Valentinianism, which is a relative latecomer to apocalypse ascription, two dangers attend the emphasis on difference. First, the emphasis may serve to repress both actual recalls of literary features of biblical apocalyptic in Valentinian texts, and Valentinian hospitality to apocalyptic on the level of theological substance. Second, to define Valentinianism in a totally oppositional way to apocalyptic has invidious genealogical consequences. For the logic of exclusion deprives the interpreter of a way to account for features in a band of narrative or metanarrative discourses in modernity that recall both Valentinian and apocalyptic paradigms. As determined in part I, most if not all of the discourses in the Baurian line of narrative ontotheologies evidence the presence of both. It is possible, however, both rigorously to maintain differences and to construe the relations between Valentinianism and apocalyptic in their classical expressions in such a way to avoid these distinct kinds of danger.

Where scholars draw an absolute line of demarcation between apocalyptic and Gnostic texts, they proceed along fairly typical lines. On the level of literary surface they recur to the absence in Gnostic texts of the familiar apocalyptic signatures of cataclysmic signs ushering in the eschaton, and to the absence of the journey, physical or imaginative, of a privileged seer, who moves from nonvision to vision. On the level of theological substance, they suggest, as an absolute discrimen between Gnosticism and apocalyptic, the centrality of history in the latter, and specifically the agon between good and evil as history's basic structuring force, the expectation of a radical interruption in which history is transcended and its meaning revealed, and God's providential guidance of history toward an end that reflects gloriously on God. Ironically, these criteria of discrimination distinguish too little as well as too much. On the level of theological substance especially, the criteria fail to cut deeply enough. Attention needs to be drawn to the fact that no less in Revelation than in Baruch and Daniel, the sovereign Lord of history corresponds to the biblical God of justice and mercy that both non-Valentinian and Valentinian Gnosticism condemn. In apocalyptic, creation is not cast as fall, as it is in the Valentinian paradigms we examined. And in Revelation, the apocalyptic figuration of Christ as the lamb most certainly involves a judgment that classical Valentinian texts repudiate, namely, that Christ's suffering and death functions salvifically with respect to human beings in general, or at least a particular group, that is, the elect.

Crucially, for our present purposes, the criteria of discrimination also distinguish too much. The literary signs, supposed decisively to define apocalyptic, insufficiently mark it off from Valentinian apocalypse. If scholars show that destructive signs marking the eschaton are found in non-Valentinian Gnosticism,[113] such signs are also apparent in the Valentinian paradigms we exegeted. In *PSY*, as we have seen, the eschaton is a reality accompanied by the apocalyptic sign of fire consuming the earth. The *Tractate* too thinks of the destruction of the physical world as necessary, and evokes wrath as an agent in the process of cleansing in which the true Church comes into being as the Bride (94.135–8). As we might expect in a text in which narrative features of any type are played down, the *Gospel* does not focus on the theatrical accompaniments to the eschaton. Nonetheless, crucial symbols of Revelation such as the "book of life" (19.35–37) and salvation as constituting an "inscription" (21.5–6) are recalled. Also (although this brings us on to the level of theological substance), we find the connection between these symbols and Christ's "death for many" (20.10–15) and the theme of election. Similarly with the other literary feature used to discriminate between apocalyptic and Gnosticism: in apocalyptic the movement toward vision is not always accompanied by a visionary journey,[114] and, contrariwise, numerous texts in Nag Hammadi, (especially *Allogenes*, *Zostrianos*, and *Marsanes*), feature ecstatic journeys through the various levels of the divine world. Moreover, these visionary journeys are complemented in the Nag Hammadi Library by recountings of angelic revelation to particular emblematic figures such as Seth and Melchizedek, features that once again are supposed to be unique to apocalyptic.[115]

The would-be criteria of distinction also fail to function decisively on the level of theological substance. First, one can exaggerate both ways the focus on time and history that marks a deep difference between Gnostic, and specifically Valentinian, forms of apocalypse and the classical forms of apocalyptic. That is, one can fail to note in apocalyptic the sometimes extensive description of the transhistorical world in both its originary and eschatological dimensions, and also fail to record sufficiently the tension of fact and value between eternity and time in which the reality of time is that of a parenthesis between two modalities of eternity. Correlatively, one can fail to note in general that time is provided some kind of value in non-Valentinian Gnostic texts through the kind of periodization of history discernible there,[116] and in particular ignore the fact that Valentinian texts such as the *Tractate* lie against time in a much more modest way than Bloom, after Puech,[117] thinks characteristic of Valentinianism in general.

Second, and relatedly, the providentialism that is one of the defining features of apocalyptic is not necessarily unique to this form of apocalypse discourse. It is not absent in such non-Valentinian Gnostic texts as the *Apocalypse of Adam*, the *Gospel of the Egyptians*, the *Trimorphic Protennoia*, and even the *Apocryphon of John*.[118] More important, our uncovering of tensions in *PSY* and the *Gospel* indicated possible traces of providentialism. In the *Tractate* such providentialism is patent. Moreover, in the *Tractate* providence is connected with a divine not so pure and transcendent as to be uninvolved in the creation of the cosmos.

Third, and finally, absolute discrimination between the two forms of apocalypse fails to take into account that as the chronic dualistic perspective, which achieves its crescendo in the eschaton, tends in apocalyptic toward ontologizing distinctions between human beings, in Valentinian texts the discourse of ontological distinction between human beings shows that they can be modified not only by the discourse of election (*Gospel*), but also by the discourse of freedom (*Tractate*).

To controvert a scholarly view of some substance and authority, I have focused most of my criticism against drawing too great a distinction between Gnosticism and apocalyptic, and more specifically between Valentinian Gnosticism and apocalyptic. But this is neither to claim that attention to distinguishing features is unimportant, nor to deny the necessity of amplifying the distinctions adduced by serious proponents of the difference between Gnosticism and apocalyptic. Despite the commendable attempts of such a reputable scholar as Schmithals to dissolve the difference between Gnosticism and apocalyptic under a generic apocalypse rubric, differences of the sort already mentioned ensure their irreducibility. The real issue is not whether there are real and deep differences, but whether these differences function as relative or absolute criteria of discrimination and thus definition. In addition, it is important to get at the full extent and depth of differences, especially at the narrative level, if the boundaries between Valentinian paradigms and apocalyptic are to be stable as well as clear.

I think we must both relativize differences and amplify and deepen them if Valentinian apocalypse is to have genealogical use. Both tasks are a sine qua non. For one of the ways in which post-Hellenistic ontotheological narratives might instance Valentinian narrative grammar while going beyond its classical genres or paradigms is to expand on and deepen the negative capability toward apocalyptic that is a feature of Valentinianism in the Hellenistic field. Nevertheless because this potential expansion and deepening would not occur at the cost of basic differences between Valentinian and apocalyptic forms of apocalypse, the assimilation of apocalyptic into a narrative, whose basic ontotheological structure remains an instance of Valentinian grammar, would not necessarily compromise its integrity and certainly not challenge its hegemony. Later I discuss the relation between Valentinian apocalypse and apocalyptic in post-Hellenistic discourses when I begin to deploy the constructs of *apocalyptic inscription* and *apocalyptic distention* introduced in chapter 2.

This discussion of the nature of Valentinian narratives demonstrates that they are irreducible while not disdaining relationship with the non-Valentinian narrative discourses of Neoplatonism and apocalyptic. The weaker way of talking about the relationship is to say that Valentinian discourses are hospitable to these non-Valentinian narrative discourses. The stronger way of talking is to say that Valentinian narrative is able to enlist these narrative discourses, where the phenomenon of enlisting is at least negatively indicated in the preservation of the integrity of Valentinian narrative. I will pick up on this stronger way of talking in the next chapter. But more important for present purposes is the claim that such hospitality is a general feature of classical Valentinian texts and thus can be genuinely regarded as a feature of Valentinian narrative grammar. As a feature of Valentinian narrative grammar, one could expect that such a phenomenon would characterize modern narrative ontotheologies to the extent to which they exemplify a Valentinian narrative grammar, albeit under specifically modern conditions. In the next chapter I demonstrate that this is in fact the case, with these particular narratives showing even greater hospitality and greater power of enlistability.

CHAPTER 5

~

Genealogical Capability of Valentinian
Narrative Grammar

In this final chapter, I attempt to develop genealogically on the concept of Valentinian narrative grammar that was generated in and through an analysis of classical Valentinian discourses (chaps. 3 and 4). I argue now categorically what in part 1 I argued hypothetically. Specifically, I argue (1) that ontotheological narratives in the Baurian line are instances or paradigms of a Valentinian narrative grammar that bears a metaleptic relation to Christian narrative grammar; (2) that ontotheological narratives in the Baurian line deviate considerably from the classical Valentinian paradigms presented in chapter 3, or, in our more technical language, that they represent deformations of classical Valentinian paradigms; and (3) that the deformations of classical Valentinian paradigms, enacted in and by narrative ontotheologies in the Baurian field, represent rule-governed deformations of the classical Valentinian genres in that (a) the deformations follow an identifiable pattern that do not issue in a subversion of Valentinian narrative grammar, and (b) these subversions are preindicated in classical Valentinian genres themselves.

Obviously, in light of historicist and especially Blumenbergian objections, much of this chapter reflects on the types of deformations and the specific deformations within the types. As deformation by ontotheological narratives in the Baurian field can be specified broadly as a radicalization of recessed features in the classical Valentinian paradigms, the types of deformation can be specified as pertaining to narrative register and narrative form. I suggest that in narrative ontotheologies in the Baurian manifold a tendency exists to radicalize the gnoseological rather than mythological register of Valentinian narrative. Most important, I argue as a matter of fact and not simply as a matter of speculation that in

179

narratives of the loss and regaining of divine perfection in the Baurian line, the circular and nonincremental form dominant in classical Valentinian narratives is replaced by an incremental or developmental form of narrative in which divine perfection is in fact realized through loss. I further suggest that the ground for such a replacement can be found within the classical paradigms themselves, where a tension exists between the nondevelopmental narrative surface and the developmental narrative depth. Two major points are made about what can be called the *theogonic deformation* of classical Valentinian genres. First, this deformation is itself a feature of Valentinian narrative grammar in that narrativity radicalization enacted in the Baurian field belongs to the range of possible Valentinian narrative conjugations. Second, the theogonic deformation is inclusive of a number of less general transformations. Listing only the most basic, these include: the subversion of the priority of the archeological divine perfection and the consequent valorization of the divine perfection that succeeds the interruption and abandonment of perfection; explicit championing of an ontotheological version of felix culpa in which the divine fall is a means to the realization of divine perfection; radicalization of a view of kenosis, present though not dominant in classical Valentinianism, in which kenosis, far from suggesting the sacrifice of perfection, suggests its acquisition; and finally, the radicalization of the narrative codes that provide the basic symbolism in classical Valentinian accounts of the movement from divine perfection through loss to its reinstatement.

Elucidating these deformations and providing examples of their operation in the narrative discourses of the Baurian field is the main tasks of the chapter and is prosecuted in the second section. By contrast with my treatment in part 1, however, the elucidation here no longer takes for granted the identification of the Baurian line of narrative discourses with Protestantism. The validity claim of such an identification now needs to be examined. This examination has both negative and positive dimensions. I proceed negatively by raising the issue of whether excluding Catholic discourses from the Baurian field of narrative discourses, and thus from Gnostic return, is legitimate. Bringing in a verdict that Catholic discourses also should be included would undermine the Protestant identification of the Baurian line and determine that at best the Protestant designation is relatively adequate. I do not bring in any such verdict, however, and point to conditions in Catholicism that are inhospitable to Gnostic return. Positively, I support the Protestant identification of the Baurian line by presenting the general conditions in the post-Reformation and post-Enlightenment Protestant fields that encourage Gnostic return. Presenting the validity claims for Protestant identification of the Baurian line of narrative discourses is the topic of the first section.

This final chapter has as its third focus the issue of the narrative complexity of ontotheologies in the Baurian line, which is discussed in the third section. The specific issue is whether the presence of apocalyptic, Neoplatonic, and Kabbalistic narrative strands within complex modern narrative discourses within the Baurian line imply the impossibility of a *Valentinian* ascription. On the basis of our hypothetical account of the phenomenon of Valentinian enlisting of these narrative strands in part 1, noting the hospitality in classical Valentinian paradigms for Neoplatonic and apocalyptic narrative elements (chap. 3) and the grammatical generalization of this hospitality (chap. 4), I attempt to justify the categorical reality of Valentinian enlisting of these three other narrative discourses in the Baurian field.

5.1. Justifying the Protestant Identification of the Baurian Line

I begin not with the two major foci of the chapter, that is, how ontotheological narratives in the Baurian line deviate from classical Valentinian norms and how they enlist non-Valentinian narrative discourses for Valentinian purposes; rather I begin with a more procedural issue, specifically the issue of entitlement regarding the Protestant identification of the Baurian line of discourses as the putative site of Gnostic return in modernity. In all our extension, correction, and rehabilitation of Baur's view as presented in *Die christliche Gnosis* we left fundamentally unquestioned his Protestant identification of Gnostic return, and I now subject this identification to critical scrutiny. Baur's own framing of the issue encourages coming at the issue of identification from several angles. Baur regarded as demonstrated that Catholicism excludes Gnosis in the pre-Reformation period and suggests at the very least that Catholicism is constitutionally incapable of illustrating such return. Because this negatively buttresses the case for a Protestant identification of Gnostic return, we need to examine Baur's position. I sustain Baur's position that pre-Reformation Catholicism does not evidence Gnostic return. But I supplement him by pointing to constitutive features in Catholic discourse, and not simply its authority system, that discourage Gnostic return. I also approach the issue of Protestant identification head-on. With Baur of *Die christliche Gnosis* more as a stimulus than a guide, I suggest reasons why in the post-Reformation and post-Enlightenment Protestant field ideational conditions pertain that foster, although they do not make necessary, Valentinian deformation of the biblical narrative.

In what amounts to an ex post facto justification of the operative synonymity of Baurian line of narrative ontotheologies and Protestantism of the third line, I should say in advance that my argument proceeds on a fairly general and abstract level. In significant part the abstractness is a function of the separation of this methodological introduction from actual execution of the genealogy. Both the negative and positive sides of the case made in favor of the identification would be more persuasive if the level of detail were more significant. Still the discussion of examples of rule-governed deformation of classical Valentinian genres in the modern field (section 5.2) and the discussion of the phenomenon of Valentinian enlisting of non-Valentinian discourses (section 5.3) help to give some direct support to the case for Protestant identification. One will have to wait for execution of the genealogy itself for discussion of Catholic test cases that challenge the Protestant identification. Such test cases include the convert to Catholicism, Novalis,[119] whose divagations on dark and light, death and life, and the masculine and feminine, make him with Blake a Romantic candidate for Gnostic or Valentinian ascription, and nineteenth-century Catholic religious thinkers such as Franz von Baader (1765–1841) and Anton Günther (1783–1863), whose narrative discourses are so influenced by Schelling and Hegel, respectively.[120]

Both formal and material conditions must be satisfied if Valentinian narrative grammar is to be exercised beyond the Hellenistic field. The formal conditions to be satisfied are as follows: (1) Stated negatively, Valentinian narrative grammar is not understood as exhausted by its classic Hellenistic paradigms. Stated positively, Valentinian narrative grammar is open to new and later lexical instances. (2) Valentinian narrative grammar is understood to be rich enough not only to permit new and later lexical instances, but also a wide variety of newer and later lexical instances. (3) Ontotheological narratives in modernity understood to be new lexical instances of Valentinian narrative grammar, thus new genres or paradigms, recall one or more of the classical Valentinian genres or paradigms.

(4) Despite recalling one or more of classical Valentinian paradigms, ontotheological narratives, understood to be lexical instances of Valentinian narrative grammar, show sufficient differences from these classical paradigms to be regarded as deformations. These deformations are rule governed, however, in that (a) the differences are not such as to indicate a different narrative grammar than that evident in the classical Valentinian genres, and (b) in the sense that one can specify the main lines of deformation on the level of narrative itself and its fundamental register.

This brings us to the material conditions to be satisfied. Here material conditions mean ideological or ideational conditions. I do not mean by *material* what the word implies in the context of a Marxist and/or social-historical methodology. The word does not refer to the economic, social, political, or other factors that condition the basic drifts of discourses, nor the reflexive effect of these discourses on their conditions. Clearly, as shown by Sartre's 2,000-page book on Flaubert,[121] which represents an experiment in the application of a historical methodology descriptively thick enough to be explanatory, our explanatory ambitions necessarily have to be more humble given the number of discourses that come in for examination and their wide separation in time, culture, nationality, and language. Still, granting that these material-ideational conditions bear complex relations to economic, social, and political realities and their governing discourses, it is these material-ideational conditions that bear most immediately on the way in which the biblical narrative gets read in a thoroughgoing metaleptic way.

The following six material conditions are the crucially important ones: (1) A sense prevails not only that Christian orthodoxies are moribund, but also that they are mistaken in how they envisage the divine, how the divine relates to the world in creation and redemption, and how they conceive the nature and value of human beings. This sense translates into a willingness to contest a more or less exclusive emphasis on the divine as transcendent creator, sovereign in his freedom and impeccable in his justice, to contest a view of the cosmos as indifferent to divine manifestation, and to contest a view of human beings as ontologically mean and noetically incapacitated, a systemic anthropological structure deepened by the fall. (2) Despite the presumption of mistakenness, there is a refusal simply to give up on Christianity and the Bible. Rather we see the determination to revision Christianity and its basic text. (3) Revisioning the Bible requires fundamental shifts in the practice and context of interpretation. More specifically, modes of exegesis shift from the literal to the pneumatic and from community to individual contexts of reading. In these shifts the authority ratio between biblical text and interpretive scheme changes radically. So does the perception of the fit between scripture and tradition. The Bible may continue formally to enjoy incommensurability status, but interpretation brings so many supplements that its authority is displaced. In a sense the Bible is descriptured, while the revisioning, whether it be in literary, religious, or philosophical mode, is accorded something akin to scriptural status.

(4) The revisioning of Christianity as a system of belief is global rather than piecemeal, radical rather than superficial. It centrally involves proposing a metanarrative as authentically disclosive of reality that includes all elements of the Christian narrative but changes their community and traditionally based meaning. (5) A deep sense of dissatisfaction with the Christian tradition's handling of the question of evil prevails. The tradition is seen to avoid or short-circuit the issue of theodicy or to provide answers that impugn either the divine goodness or human freedom. This dissatisfaction leads to a theodicy that, going beyond ratiocination, also goes beyond its cul-de-sacs. The alternative offered focuses on a description of the narrative development of the divine that absolves the divine from blame by making narrative development self-legitimating. (6) Pneumatic privilege and distinction are established. These occur despite extraordinarily high views about humanity's general participation in divinity, views that make conceiving of distinctions that make a difference difficult. Nevertheless, even though human beings are no longer regarded as ontologically mean, epistemically opaque, and existentially miserable, the Orwellian law that "all are equal, but some are more equal than others" tends to prevail.

Now if following Baur one suggests that these conditions apply in the case of Romantic and Idealist discourses, and by extension their precursor and successor discourses, this can only be, as I suggested in part 1, a matter of contingent fact and not a matter of historical necessity. These conditions are specific to related but distinct contexts in the unfolding of Protestant thought.

First and primitively, a post-Reformation but pre-Enlightenment discourse emerges that radicalizes the Reformation dissatisfaction with the theological tradition of the Catholic period, yet subjects to critical scrutiny central tenets of the Reformation itself. In fact in the case of Jacob Boehme and his sixteenth-century precursors in speculative alchemy such as Paracelsus (1490–1543) and Valentin Weigel (1533–1588), all six of the material conditions of the exercise of Valentinian narrative grammar outside the Hellenistic period apply in significant measure. Boehme and his precursors are persuaded that the Lutheran tradition holds many untenable positions. Its support of an absolutely sovereign God fails adequately to see the world as manifesting the divine, just as its prioritization of divine justice over mercy does not correspond to the vision of God given in the redemption wrought by Jesus Christ.[122] Nevertheless, Christianity remains ineluctable, even if its conventional forms call for revision, and the Bible remains basic even if one has to worry about what constitutes an adequate mode of interpretation. With respect to biblical interpretation, Boehme and his precursors call for a lifting of the prohibition against mystical or anagogic modes of interpretation and a removal of the devaluation of the charism of individual insight and discernment. The revisioning of Christianity and commitment to pneumatic interpretation meet in Boehme and his precursors in a metanarrative that includes the entire biblical narrative, but changes the meaning of each of its elements as they are understood, for instance, by Luther, Melanchton, and their followers.[123] Boehme's absolutely inclusive metanarrative of a self-developing divine changes the meaning of the inner Trinity, creation, incarnation, redemption, the cross, the church, and the eschaton. A guiding concern in the disfiguring and refiguring of the biblical narrative is to justify the divine in the face of suffering and evil by pointing out the necessities for divine development. Such necessities include divine self-exile and the attendant pain that is gestured to in the symbol of the cross. Finally, although Boehme and his precursors articulate a high anthropology that stresses freedom and the possibility of vision, nonetheless, vision in the strict sense, that is, the truly speculative sense, is the prerogative of the few.

Each one of these aspects of a complex swerve from and revision of standard Lutheran confessional discourse could do with exemplification and amplification. But as I said in my introduction, examples in this programmatic text are probative and anticipatory. In the next volume I make up for the lack of detailed illustration herein, offering what amounts to a demonstration of Boehme's fulfilling the material conditions for Gnostic return.

Second, a post-Enlightenment form of discourse emerges that, without abrogating its Enlightenment assumptions about the impossibility of orthodoxy, advocates a critical retrieval of Christianity in which the biblical narrative is reconfigured. The post-Enlightenment situation is undoubtedly new insofar as this recommendation takes place in an environment in which narrative or myth has tended to be marginalized, and in which scripture has lost its authority.[124] Again, as in the case of post-Reformation discourse such as Boehme's, the material conditions that we mentioned apply. Let us take Blake and Hegel as two examples.

I take it as uncontroversial that Hegel agreed with Enlightenment estimates about the debits of confessional Christianity both from a cultural and a theoretical point of view. A creedal Christianity was neither relevant culturally, nor could it sustain its claims to truth. Nonetheless, as the *Lectures on the Philosophy of Religion* in particular shows,[125] Hegel was not prepared to say that scripture was without meaning. The meaning of scripture, however, was a matter of contestation, and Hegel presumed it was a wax nose that admitted quite different interpretations.[126] He was persuaded, however, that the interpretations of orthodoxy that were tied to the literal sense had proved inadequate, and he saw himself in the pneumatic tradition of interpretation of the biblical text, which he believed was legitimated by the Reformation. Moreover, he felt that the speculative spiritual wing of Protestant thought had shown the priority of narrative over doctrine.[127] Thus, after Kant of *Religion within the Limits of Reason Alone*, Hegel advocated narrative as an advance on the Enlightenment disposition toward atomism. At the same time, the narrative that provides a frame of meaning and meaningfulness absent in the Enlightenment is considered to disclose the truth of reality. This truth of narrative is the truth of the divine, which concerns the development of the divine that is intrinsically tied to a world, interpreted as fall and evil. Thus the development of the divine involves pain (*Schmerz*) and disintegration as realities to be transcended yet preserved. As integrating evil and pain, the narrative of the divine, reframing the biblical narrative and articulating Christianity truly, is already incipiently a new kind of theodicy.[128]

All that is lacking is the conceptual means of translation, such that the truth of narrative can be justified and theodicy verified. But conceptual justification in Hegel, by contrast with Kant, is fully theological in two related respects: It concerns the divine, specifically the development of the divine in and through the finite, and at the same time concept is a form of divine knowledge. Moreover, as I showed in *The Heterodox Hegel*, in the unfolding of this narrative each and every element of the biblical narrative, whether the intratrinitarian milieu, creation, fall of human being, incarnation, redemption, church, and eschaton is interpreted in a way that is not only different than, but fundamentally at odds with, how it is rendered in the Lutheran tradition. Through the elevation of this metanarrative into the domain of concept, which is the proper realm of discourse or the realm of discourse proper, the metaleptic operation performed on biblical narrative is clearly justified and protected from criticism. The attack on the authority of the biblical text, which includes emphasizing its interpretive malleability, making revelation extratextual, and denying the privilege of a salvation-history model of revelation that concludes with Jesus of Nazareth, in effect descriptures the biblical text. *Descripturing*, however, does not go all the way down. For going hand in hand with the attack against the authority of scripture is the claim that the system is the scene of unsurpassable disclosure. No more than in the Bible can one change dot or tittle of the System's categorial unfolding. The bleeding of the authority of the biblical text is accompanied, therefore, by an act of *rescripturing*. Hegel, then, provides an example in the Baurian line of rescripturing as the other side of descripturing.

In his discussion of Hegel in *Die christliche Gnosis* Baur clearly has a grip on Hegel's dissatisfaction with orthodox Christianity, his pneumatic orientation, and his predilection for a narrative reformulation of Christianity. And if we take his other works into account, especially his great work on the Trinity,[129] Baur is aware that the mode of scriptural interpretation advocated by Hegel is just the opposite of the community sense of scripture. But as I mentioned in part 1, a major lacuna in Baur's reading of Hegel and his precursors is his lack of focus on the transgressive hermeneutic practice, in which the meaning of every single episode of the biblical narrative as communally interpreted is changed. In short, Baur does not understand that to continue the Gnostic line is to continue a metaleptic practice of interpretation. Part of the reason why he does not understand this is that he fails to distinguish adequately between Gnosticism and Neoplatonism, and thus between two fundamentally different modes of interpretation. Here Bloom gets it right when, following Irenaeus's lead, he points to the transgressive and metaleptic nature of Gnostic hermeneutics as marking it off completely from the conservatism of Neoplatonic hermeneutics.[130]

This brings me to Blake. Once again, I will be brazenly schematic, leaving for a future volume demonstration of the claim that at least in Blake, Romanticism realizes all the material conditions of Gnostic return. Blake is horrified at the effects wrought on Christianity by rationalism and moralism, and inveighs against Christianity as a religion of rational demonstration and evidences. Averring that a recovery of true Christianity, that is, biblical Christianity, is not only possible, but also absolutely necessary for modern culture, he suggests that an inspired mode of interpretation can gain access to the truth of reality, which it turns out is a narrative truth. Inspired interpretation is just the opposite of conventional interpretation. It is transgressive interpretation, with the object of its transgression being the community reading of the biblical narrative. Against the Enlightenment's disregard for narrative and, despite its assertions to the contrary, its ultimately low sense of the possibilities of human knowledge, Blake insists on the meaning, value, and truth of his visionary retelling of the biblical narrative, prosecuted in different ways in *The Book of Urizen, Milton*, and *Jerusalem*.[131] This retelling both displaces the biblical account by a plurality of literary accounts of a divine fall and reintegration while siphoning off scriptural authority to vest it in his visionary poems. Of special interest in what is essentially an operation of rescripturing is the way in which these narratives justify the fall and pain of the divine-human as a necessity of the realization of an authentic form of eternity.

To claim that in the Romantic field Blake satisfies the material conditions for Gnostic return is not to claim that other Romantics do so because we cannot decide beforehand that Blake is typical; he might well constitute the extreme. The latter is in fact the position that I will adopt in the volume on Romanticism, where I suggest Blake represents the limit of Romanticism in the sense of limen. Blake is at once inside and outside Romanticism. Thus, Gnosticism, or Valentinianism, represents the limit rather than the definition of Romanticism. As suggested in part 1, however, clearing Romanticism of the charge of Gnosticism or Valentinianism by no means implies that Romanticism does not represent a deformation of biblical narrative. It simply means that deformation is not metaleptic in the strict sense; that is, deformation does not involve a comprehensive refiguration as well as disfiguration of biblical narrative.

To summarize, the specificity of the post-Reformation and post-Enlightenment contexts amplifies the temporal distance between the Hellenistic and modern periods. Baur himself senses a Catholic hiatus, one that underwrites understanding post-Hellenistic ontotheological narratives as deformations of classical Valentinian genres. He thinks that the post-Reformation and post-Enlightenment forms of *Gnosis* are somehow more theogonic than the forms found in the Hellenistic field, and that this specifies enough difference to legitimate talk of development. As I said in part 1, however, Baur's discussion of development is insufficient, and his recognition of difference is not carried through. For him, all forms of *Gnosis* imply some form of theogonic narrative. By contrast, I want to highlight difference and underscore the deviance of the post-Reformation and post-Enlightenment theogonic narratives from the classical Valentinian genres. At the same time, I suggest that the modes of deviance from and/or deformation by these post-Reformation and post-Enlightenment narrative ontotheologies of classical Valentinian genres is ruled governed.

I will shortly be making thematic the two systemic features of the modern deformation of the ancient Valentinian genres. That is, I reflect explicitly on the theogonic bias of narrative ontotheologies in the third line of Protestant discourses and their radical epistemic framing of inclusive metaleptic narrative. I argue that these deformations are rule governed. I remind the reader of a basic point of my discussion of rule-governed deformation in chapter 2. A formal but constitutive aspect of the rule governedness of deformation is that whatever differences exist between post-Reformation and post-Enlightenment discourses, which bear a metaleptic relation to the biblical narrative, and classical Valentinian genres, both kinds of narrative obey the same rules of formation. Otherwise put, both kinds of narrative are determined by the same narrative grammar. We can see in both cases a six-stage narrative, or a triadic synoptic version, of movement from divine perfection to its recovery through the hiatus of its loss, which bears a metaleptic relation to the biblical narrative. The theogonic turn in the third line of Protestant thought constitutes a more material specification of Valentinian narrative grammar—although *theogony* itself is a cover term for a number of more specific narrative features that include a substitution of a process interpretation of divine perfection for a static one, a radicalization of the ontotheological felix culpa that is bourgeoning in classical Valentinianism, and a deepening of classical Valentinianism's latent commitment to deipassionism.

As I argued in chapter 3, the dominant tendency in classical Valentinian paradigms is not theogonic. Now if there were no trace of such tendency, then modern narratives in the Baurian field would deviate from classical Valentinian paradigms in such a way that it would raise the question whether one is dealing with an entirely different narrative grammar. But an important result of our analysis was the claim that a theogonic tendency existed in classical Valentinianism, even if it was relatively recessive. This means that the deformation by the explicitly theogonic modern narratives of the classical Valentinian paradigms is rule governed insofar as such deformation is a radicalization of a preexistent tendency in the classical paradigms themselves. A similar point can be made with respect to the epistemological register of modern metaleptic narratives when compared with the classical genres. That this register is much more developed in narratives in the Baurian line goes without saying. Again, however, no absolute deformation of classical Valentinianism occurs, since this register is present in the classical Valentinian paradigms, most patently in the *Gospel* and the *Tractate*.

We need not accept in an unnuanced form Baur's verdict on the Catholic hiatus, which functions to establish two distinct, if not heterogeneous, horizons of Gnostic expression. In fact he does not argue for this in *Die christliche Gnosis*, which rests squarely and comfortably on a Hegelian recapitulation of Reformation assumptions about Catholicism being a spurious interregnum between two authentic modes of Christianity.[132] In Baur's case, as in Hegel's, the apostolic age appealed to in the Reformation becomes a variable that can be filled with quite nonapostolic content. Both Hegel and Baur fill it with the kind of speculative content that other early nineteenth-century evangelical theologians suggest represents the corruption of the apostolic age.[133] In addition, in *Die christliche Gnosis* Baur sees no reason why the formal symmetry between the originary Christianity and post-Reformation Christianity cannot be upset in favor of the latter rather than the former.[134] Here Baur seems to be following Hegel in overturning the repristinative aspect of the Reformation and the thought that devolves from it. It is evident from the *Lectures on the Philosophy of History* that Hegel thinks of the Reformation as a novum in the history of Christianity,[135] in fact a reality that has more right to be called revolutionary than the French Revolution. The fullest expression of Hegel's view is to be found in *Lectures on the Philosophy of Religion*, a text Baur cites frequently in *Die christliche Gnosis*. Consistently in the lecture series of 1821, 1824, 1827, and 1830, Hegel distinguishes between Christian origin, development, and realization.[136] Christianity is fully realized only in the Reformation. But the Reformation from Hegel's point of view has yet to be realized, since the values of freedom and reason and their pertinence to the communal and social world have yet to be universalized. In this sense, the Enlightenment is, on the one hand, the extension of the Reformation and, on the other, a deformation that can be corrected by appeal to the values of the Reformation where freedom and reason have a more than secular foundation.[137]

Elsewhere, Baur says more than that Catholicism is a matrix that represents the absence of *Gnosis*; he says something specifically about the features of Catholicism that function to block Gnostic return. Not unexpectedly in the wake of Enlightenment and Hegelian

critiques of Catholicism, authoritarianism and dogmatism are conspicuous.[138] Granting the Protestant bias of Baur's reading of the
Catholic period, and its monolithic nature, still arguing that the
material conditions for Gnostic return do not apply to the post-
Hellenistic Catholic period is not difficult. There are a number of
reasons why this is the case.

First, in general terms, although significant challenges to orthodoxy are found throughout the Christian period, challenges increasingly in evidence in the medieval period with the Cathars and
the so-called heresy of the Free Spirit, one cannot say that there is
chronic unhappiness with orthodoxy. Certainly, in Baur and his
Catholic contemporaries, we see a tendency to reduce the plurality
and tensions within Catholicism, although for quite different reasons. The Catholics stress the uniform nature of the tradition over
Protestant splitting and sectarianism. Protestants point to the lack
of theological vitality that is a consequence of Catholic authoritarianism. Of course, neither side is above drawing attention on an ad
hoc basis to modes of heterodox thought that anticipate the Reformation. Baur points to Meister Eckhart.[139] Staudenmaier, licensing
a long-standing practice within the Protestant tradition,[140] points to
Joachim de Fiore and what came to be known as the heresy of the
Free Spirit.

Second, Catholicism neither calls for a revision of the Christian
narrative, nor suggests how the Christian narrative can be saved yet
surpassed by a more encompassing metanarrative that changes the
meaning of all the narrative elements. I grant that this may seem to
underestimate the kind of challenge to the orthodox reading of the
biblical narrative presented, for instance, by the Cathars. One could
argue that the classic text of the Cathars, *The Book of Two Principles*,[141] for example, proposes an important revision of biblical
narrative in that it legitimates a view of the physical world as intrinsically evil, nothing less in fact than the offspring of an evil
demon, associated with the God of the Old Testament. This revisioning leads to sustained reflection on the nature of the redeemer, who
is the good God, and to sustained questioning of the media of redemption, specifically whether the Church and sacraments are authentic, even viable, media of redemption. Of course, the answer to
this latter question is a firm no. Nevertheless, although *The Book of
Two Principles* revises the community reading of the biblical narrative in important respects, in the final analysis it does not revise it
in a way that is fundamentally Valentinian. Or otherwise put, it
does not revise it in a way that is metaleptic in the strict sense.

Although the bad creator is distinguished from the good God, who is the redeemer, the focus is not on the etiology of the bad creator God. Furthermore, description of this evil god and evil creation is not inserted into a unified comprehensive narrative that also tells about their overcoming. Rather the narrative focus is the redeemer and the means of redemption outside the network of priestly mediation. Depiction of the evil God serves as a kind of backdrop to the account of redemption and its means. Thus the revision of the community rendition of the biblical narrative is not fully comprehensive. This is not to say, however, that the Cathar account of an evil creation and evil creator does not have effect on other aspects of orthodox faith; for example, from the demonization of the physical and biological universe a docetic Christology will follow. And, for *The Book of Two Principles*, the evil of a material creation rules out the free will that the orthodox, on the authority of Augustine, regard as axiomatic for Christian faith. As is well known, *The Book of Two Principles*, on the very same authority of Augustine, argues precisely the opposite conclusion. The revision of the community rendition of the biblical narrative is then extensive and deep, but not comprehensive and deep in the way typical of Valentinianism.

But what then is the best category for the kind of revision enacted? Looked at from the point of view of the historical influence on the Cathars of the Bogomils,[142] scholars have argued that Catharism can be classed as a form of Manichaeism.[143] There is some merit to this designation, even if proving the influence of the Bogomils on the Cathars and prior groups on the Bogomils, does not clinch the issue. It will be necessary after all to sustain the argument that these precursor groups are themselves Manichaean. This in itself is not easy given the apparent exhaustion of Manichaeism in the sixth century. In any event, with an interest of not multiplying categories, I would like to recall the distinction I made in part 1 between Marcionism and Valentinianism, and whose trace at least is found in Irenaeus, as demonstrated in chapter 4, ironically at the point in which Irenaeus seems to go out of his way to deny it. In bringing Hans Blumenberg to task in chapter 2, I argued that the constitutive difference between a Marcionite and a Valentinian revisioning of the biblical narrative, or its community reading, is that in the former the revisioning is neither radical nor comprehensive. This is so because the interest is not in explaining the whence as well as whither of evil, but in pointing to its overcoming and our grounds for confidence that this is and will be the case. A Marcionite revisioning revises the biblical image of a good creator and a good creation with the interest of describing the condition from which human beings have to be saved.

From a typological point of view, therefore, Catharism represents not a Valentinian challenge to orthodoxy but a Marcionite challenge. Relative to Valentinianism, its narrative focus is extraordinarily contracted. It highlights redemption to such an extent that, in Gestalt terms, the evil God and evil creation is but ground to redemption as figure. In addition, while the Cathars argue their theological case and oppose their hermeneutic of scripture to that of the orthodox, consistent with Marcionism rather than Valentinianism, Catharism does not attempt argumentative closure. It does not assume that its position is invulnerable to contestation or has risen to the level of a self-justifying discourse.

I can be briefer with respect to the lack of the other conditions for Gnostic return in pre-Reformation Catholicism. In general Catholicism not only does not suggest the principled transcendence of a community reading of scripture, it disbars it. The community reading is defined by the traditional reading, which is to say the reading that is regarded as having the widest contemporary spread and greatest historical depth. The reading of scripture occurs either with this self-consciously in mind or with the view that individual interpretations that seem novel will survive the test of time and become part of the sedimented tradition. Again, despite its endorsement of anagogic or mystical exegesis, as Henri de Lubac has influentially pointed out,[144] Catholicism does not separate the mystical sense from the moral or literal-historical senses. In general, the mystical sense meshes with the other senses even if it is not actually anchored in them. Nor does Catholicism, in any systematic way, turn scripture into an agent of subversion vis-à-vis the theological tradition, although Eckhart and Joachim de Fiore among others stress the theological tradition mightily with their interpretations of scripture.[145] Nor, finally, despite a high sense of human participation in the divine life, especially the divine life of the Trinity, does Catholicism support, either in the case of humanity in general, those with special charisms or those who engage in the mystical life, a view that would lessen the incommensurable distance between the divine and the human, the creator and the created. For instance, with the possible exception of Meister Eckhart, who focuses on the uncreated ground of the human soul and the indistinction between human beings as sons and the divine Logos,[146] one would be hard pressed to name a single mystical theologian in the Catholic tradition who fails to assert that grace is the condition of human being's participation in the life of the Trinity. The ontological gap between uncreated and created remains intact, as does the ontological gap between creator and creation. The Victorines (twelfth century), William of St. Thierry (twelfth century), Bonaventure (thirteenth century), and Ruysbroeck (fourteenth century) all provide examples. But even in the Dionysian tradition in general, not excepting Scotus Eriugena, who was an influence on Eckhart, participation in the divine life supposes that participating human being is created.[147]

Obviously, I do not believe that I have demonstrated conclusively that the material conditions for Gnostic return are lacking in pre-Reformation Catholicism. I do think that I have shown that there are some reasons for thinking that Baur's intuition that Catholicism is not a hospitable breeding ground for the return of Gnosticism is sound, even when we put in parenthesis Catholic zeal in recognizing the return of ancient heresies and Catholic determination to root them out. Indeed, to the extent to which Catholicism in the post-Reformation period remains faithful to its pre-Reformation constitution, it discourages modes of thought that depart significantly from given views about scripture, narrative, and authority. Given its renegade status in post-Tridentine Catholic figuration, Protestantism can be associated with every heresy that preceded it. In the nineteenth century, both Möhler and Staudenmaier, Catholic contemporaries of Baur, are not shy about associating Protestantism with Gnosticism of the first centuries. As I pointed out in chapter 1, they variously emphasize the existential deformations of the pride and vanity taken in idiosyncratic construction,[148] and the substitution of the biblical narrative by another narrative form. For Staudenmaier, for example, Protestant thought, particularly in its speculative aspect, which is now taken to define it, recalls ancient Gnosis precisely by articulating narrative ontotheologies of a theogonic kind.

From a logical point of view, one cannot rule out the possibility that Catholicism's encounter with the Enlightenment and subsequent encounters with post-Enlightenment discourses might not change it in ways that make it too an environment in which Gnostic return could occur. Certainly, Catholicism's encounter with the secular world in the twentieth century, its adoption of methods of biblical criticism generated within Protestantism, and its greater openness to Protestantism and other varieties of Christian and non-Christian thought have brought about significant changes in perspective. And cumulatively these changes challenge the sedimented tradition. But however we assess these changes, they do not appear as yet to allow for Gnostic return. One would be hard pressed to come up with a single instance of

Gnostic return in contemporary Catholic theology,[149] although somewhat ironically one of the Catholic thinkers who is sometimes accused of Gnosis, sometimes, although not always, on grounds of his dependence on Hegel, is none other than Balthasar, who plays something like the role of an Irenaeus redivivus throughout our Gnostic return project.[150] This raises the question whether Baur's determination of Catholicism as a hiatus between two forms of Gnosticism points beyond itself to something like a systemic hiatus between the Gnostic return possibilities within the Catholic and Protestant fields.[151]

Let us return once again to the conditions of repetition. A supplement is in order. In addition to the formal and material conditions previously specified, one further condition is necessary if an ontotheological narrative in the extended Baurian field is to be regarded as a lexical instance of Valentinian narrative grammar. This condition, which is neither properly formal nor material, although sharing features of both, is stipulative: It insists on a *text transmission minimum* if one is finally to count a Christian ontotheological metanarrative of a metaleptic sort in the post-Reformation field as an instance of Valentinian narrative grammar. Without ruling out a considerable unconscious element in Valentinian repetition, either some direct engagement with Valentinian sources, or at least some indirect engagement with Valentinian sources via engagement with one or more thinkers familiar with Valentinian sources, is required. Given that none of the figures to be discussed in future volumes, with the possible exception of Altizer and his postmodern successors, are familiar with Nag Hammadi, this means that in terms of textual history at least, *PSY* enjoys a certain privilege. And as I will demonstrate in two subsequent volumes, this particular classical paradigm is deeply and directly engaged by both Boehme and Blake. At the same time, however, this engagement with a particular paradigm is engagement with a grammar.

The basic thrust of this somewhat preliminary section was to provide some reasons why Protestantism, and not Catholicism, evinces favorable conditions for Gnostic return. However, I would like to make two additional points. As I indicated in my rehabilitation of Irenaeus's notion of deposit in the last chapter (4.1), the Christian narrative that is the object of metaleptic attack is itself a grammar open to numerous community and/or confessional representations. The grammar is, of course, not open merely synchronically, but also diachronically. A metaleptic attack on biblical narrative grammar will, of course, necessarily proceed through an attack on a particular community rendition or interpretation of this narrative. So, for example, Boehme's narrative ontotheology represents a metalepsis of Luther's theology of the cross narrative. Similarly, the narrative ontotheologies of Hegel and Schelling represent such a metalepsis, although the metalepsis is complicated by both the post-Enlightenment situation of discourse in which narrative is fundamentally questioned and the history of effects of Luther's narrative though Lutheran orthodoxy, Pietism, and late-eighteenth-century rational theology. Again, keeping in mind the complications of Moltmann's ecclesial identity, that is, the Reformed tradition, as well as his dependence on earlier metalepticists such as Hegel and Schelling, Moltmann's narrative performs a similar disfiguration-refiguration of the biblical narrative as rendered by Luther and Calvin.

The final point I want to make concerns the theoretical range of my justification of *Protestant* ascription of the Baurian line of Protestant ontotheologies. Even allowing for further discussion in this chapter of Protestant discourses that seem to illustrate Gnostic return, and even counting the demonstrating in the multivolume genealogy that follows that such is the case, the theoretical range of my justification of *Protestant* ascription is clearly restricted. Ruling out Catholicism, both specifically and generally, as a site of Gnostic return, does help the case for *Protestant* ascription. But the case arguably can only be fully secured if, and only if, one can similarly rule out the candidacy of Eastern orthodoxy. Nevertheless, although I recognize the limitation, particularly in mind of figures associated with the Eastern orthodox tradition such as Soloviev, Berdyaev, Florenski, and Bulgakov, I risk this theoretical underdetermination. I do so partly because I am trying to obey Goethe's maxim of "dare to be finite," partly because my major interest as well as competence is Western Christianity, but also partly because a great deal of work has to be done sorting through the relative dependence of these thinkers on Western narrative forms of thought, especially the dependence of figures in the Baurian line such as Boehme, Hegel, and Schelling, and, as well, work remains in examining the formal and material possibilities in Eastern orthodoxy for Valentinian deformation.

5.2. Baurian Line and Rule-Governed Deformation of Classical Valentinian Genres

The central thrust of this section is showing in a general way how narrative ontotheologies in the Baurian line can now more securely and legitimately be classed as instances of Valentinian narrative grammar despite obvious deviations from classical Valentinian paradigms. Rule-governed deformation of classical Valentinian genres is a concept generated in part I to account for the discontinuities between ancient and modern forms of Valentinian narrative discourse in the event of sustaining a case for Valentinian narrative grammar. On the supposition that a case for Valentinian narrative grammar now has been successfully made, we can proceed to redeem this concept for categorical use.

As with Hegel and Schelling, and several twentieth-century Christian thinkers, the Valentinian genres or paradigms generated by Boehme and Blake reflect groups of features judged deviant when measured against the stereotypical Valentinian paradigm, *PSY*. Two groups of features are important and underscore the historical shift Baur both suggests and obscures in *Die christliche Gnosis*. These are the narrativity or theogony features that were conspicuously present in the *Tractate*, although arguably latent in the other Valentinian paradigms, and the epistemic and anthropological features of the *Gospel*.

One can expect, then, that the metaleptic ontotheological narratives of the extended Baurian field in both its post-Reformation and post-Enlightenment regions would display in a more radical and consistent form a group of narrativity features that mark the *Tractate* as a Valentinian narrative paradigm, and thus effectively turn a narrative discourse that at least is not explicitly theogonic into a theogonic discourse. In what follows I touch on the radicalization of the narrativity gestures that are clearly evident in the third of our Valentinian paradigms.

(1) While the coordinates of classical Valentinian tensions between divine inexpressivity-expressivity, inexpressibility-expressibility, and the infinitude-finitude of knowledge are repeated, a more reflective commitment to divine erotics leads to an even more decided favoring of the second term of each binary pair. Indeed, in many if not most cases, it leads to argumentative justification. Thus, inexpressivity tends to be read increasingly as a subjunctive or a notional possibility. Apophasis is increasingly read as either trumped by or inscribable within kataphasis. And the aporetics of representation tends to be read as deemphasizing epistemic humility and the need for doxological response. Religious thinkers in the Baurian manifold, or thinkers who articulate the third line of Protestant thought identical with neither theological orthodoxy nor liberal theology, suggest the necessity of finite representation for the knowability of the infinite, incapable of being comprehended in an infinite act of intellection.[152]

Hegel in fact explicitly provides the interpretive contours for such a revisioning of the classical genres of Valentinianism in *Lectures on the History of Philosophy*.[153] He reads the relation between the nonexpressive Propater and the expressive Nous of *PSY* as suggesting that the real, as opposed to apparent, thrust of the text is to valorize the expressivity, expression, and self-reflection of the latter. This Hegel applauds as anticipatory of his own metanarrative construction that charts the dynamics of divine becoming. At the very least classical Gnosticism encapsulates values that his own trinitarian narrative displays and justifies. For Hegel thinks that the Unknown God is an anti-Christian construction too often recurred to throughout the Christian tradition and especially in post-Kantian thought.[154] It represents an impoverishment of the notion of God from both the ontological and epistemological points of view. As immanifest the divine is not fully real. Insisting on the unknowability of divine amounts to suggesting that knowing is itself an accidental feature of the divine. For Hegel, in fact, the knowing by finite being of the divine is ultimately the divine knowing not only of finite being but also of itself, thus divine self-knowing.[155] But this means that divine self-knowledge proceeds through the detour of representation, that is, knowledge of a subject-object sort.

Jacob Boehme does not go as far as Hegel. In his texts he relativizes rather than absolutely negates the dimension of divine reality beyond expressivity, expression, and self-knowledge, which is summed up in his symbol of the Unground.[156] He does so by defining the Unground as always on the way to manifestation, as finding itself in the ground of the Son, and of being self-reflected, initially in Wisdom, but thereafter in the realization of knowledge and freedom that depends on the interruption of darkness and wrath in God. If the split into subject-object, accomplished in Wisdom, is a condition of the possibility of divine knowledge, as *Mysterium Magnum* and other texts indicate,[157] full divine self-knowledge supposes more than separation (*Schiedlichkeit*): it supposes actual contradiction.[158] No more than *PSY*, however, does Boehme totally renege on the immanifest aspect of the divine transcendent with respect to narration. One does not observe as thoroughgoing an erasure of inexpressivity and apophasis as is apparent, for instance, in Hegel.

(2) The complex judgments on the creation and cosmos and human beings, which is enacted in classical Valentinian paradigms and summed up in the figure of felix culpa, are also repeated in the Baurian line. Comparatively greater stress, however, falls on the *felix* aspect of the figure. This affirmation of creation, cosmos,

human being, and even fall, which even in the most wildly enthusiastic cases in the Baurian field does not erase the originary negative sign, reflects itself also in the greater attention given to time, history, and its vicissitudes. If the *Tractate* suggests that unilateral declarations about Valentinianism's "lying against time" might be something of a shibboleth, still it is a long way from the *Tractate*'s hesitant withdrawal of absolutely negative status to time and history to the kind of positive avowal that Boehme and Blake make to be followed by others in the Baurian line.

The case of Blake, who reflects Boehme's judgment and looks forward to Altizer, is especially interesting. As Bloom points out,[159] the commitment not only to passion, energy, but also time, history, and social transformation mark off Blake from classical versions of Gnosticism. This judgment, which is supported in Altizer's explicitly theological reading of Blake,[160] is right as far as it goes. Nevertheless, it does not justify determining Blake as either a non-Gnostic or anti-Gnostic thinker. What fails to get noticed in Bloom's final refusal of Gnostic attribution to Blake, and Altizer's consistent anti-Gnostic interpretation, is that the affirmation of time and history is dialectical. Like matter, time and history as such represent the refusal of imaginative knowing. Blake wishes to say, however, that such resistance can be and is overcome. In the sphere of resistance overcome, it becomes possible

> To see a World in a Grain of Sand
> And a Heaven in a Wild Flower
> Hold Infinity in the Palm of your Hand
> And Eternity in an Hour.[161]

(3) The agonic constitution of Christ central to Valentinian genres such as the *Gospel* and the *Tractate* is repeated in the narrative ontotheologies that articulate Protestant thought in its third line. The agonic constitution has paradigmatic and symbolic rather than direct salvific effect on human beings. In narrative ontotheologies from Boehme to Altizer, the accent falls on both the kenotic interpretation of Christ and on the links in a kenotic-erotic chain that reach back through creation into the divine. What is finally suggested is nothing less than a passional interpretation of the divine at odds with the traditional theological view of the principled invulnerability of the divine to suffering.

Jürgen Moltmann supplies the most influential contemporary theological critique of the commitment to divine impassibility, which is one of the hallmarks of Christian theologians such as Irenaeus and Tertullian, the basic thrust of whose work is the resistance to Gnosticism.[162] Moltmann enlists scripture and the work of those theologians whom he views as remaining in the biblical orbit, and he points to the incoherence of the tradition in supporting a view of the divine at odds with the deliverances of its basic text. Problems begin to emerge, however, when Moltmann positively articulates his view of divine passibility. In texts such as *The Crucified God* and *Trinity and the Kingdom*, it is not just scripture or theologians such as Luther and Heschel that are appealed to, but raising the level of discourse to explanation and justification, Moltmann makes appeal to Hegel, Boehme, and Berdyaev, with Hegel being central.[163] On the explanatory level, passibility is a necessary feature of the divine, in that the divine would not be divine without suffering.

Ironically the road to deipassionism is through Valentinianism, whose classical instances are marked by a hyperbolic emphasis on impassibility that is not characteristic of orthodoxy that insists on the reality of Christ's suffering and its saving significance. Indeed, orthodox emphasis on impassibility is a function of a reaction-formation with respect to the deipassionism that is perceived as the ultimate and logical outcome of Valentinian thought. As I showed in chapter 4 (4.1), Irenaeus sees clearly that the hyperbolic assertion of impassibility (or the assertion of a hyperbolic or exaggerated form of impassibility) is dialectically undermined in Valentinianism by an equally hyperbolic commitment to divine passibility (or commitment to a hyperbolic form of divine passibility). Irenaeus has difficulty himself in tying together in a consistent and coherent way the axiom of divine impassibility with an emphasis on the real condescension and kenosis of the divine in salvation history. Yet if tension exists in *Against Heresies*, it is not of the dramatic and dialectical variety that characterizes Valentinianism and Gnosticism in general. In the very assertion of its impassibility, Irenaeus construes the divine of Father, Son, and Spirit to be essentially open to the economy that reveals its true nature.

(4) The distinction noted in the *Tractate* between the different perfection ratios of the divine prior to fall and the divine as having gone through narrative adventure is not only repeated in the Baurian line, but the valorization of an economically defined perfection is also argued for and celebrated. As indicated in part I, Baur thinks that an economically defined perfection defines both ancient and modern forms of Gnosticism with only enough difference between them to announce the modern forms as a development. In contrast, I

wish to underscore the difference. I affirm the presence of theogonic tendency in classical Valentinianism, but do so insisting that it is a recessive rather than dominant tendency. One important way in which narrative ontotheologies in the Baurian field differ then is that the theogonic tendency is dominant.

I agree with Baur, however, in thinking of Hegel as the high point of a championing of a perfection that is result rather than origin. Hegel's role as supreme exemplar of this position is in part verified by the number and the quality of the critiques to which his archeoteleological view of the divine has been subjected to in recent years. Hegel scholars such as Brito have revived the kind of critique of Hegel's theogonic posture made famous by Staudenmaier in the nineteenth century.[164] Less conscious of the history of nineteenth-century critique, William Desmond underscores the erotic nature of Hegel's divine and opposes to it a divine that is originary perfection and gift.[165] John Milbank also belongs within this manifold of Hegelian critique, and his expostulations on the gift echo postmodern reflections—themselves explicitly resisting Hegel—and recalls Neoplatonic horizons of thought in which the perfection of the divine is constitutive of the gift quality of createdness [166]

(5) Anticipatory (*prolepsis*) and recollective (*analepsis*) mechanisms that are aspects of divine narrativity in classical Valentinian paradigms, above all in the *Tractate*, are not only repeated by discourses in the Baurian line, they are also accentuated and justified. Sometimes these mechanisms support or are supported by Neoplatonic tropes such as *the nonenviousness of the divine* and divine providence. At other times they support, or are supported by, the radicalization of the narrative codes I earlier suggested were important in classical Valentinian accounts of the movement from divine perfection, through loss, to its regaining, that is, the ocular, weight, nothing, speech, organic, and gender codes. Seeing is made dependent on blindness, as light is on darkness. The bearable lightness of perfect being is made dependent on the heaviness and massiveness of the antitype.[167] The actuality of being is dependent on the nothing that denies being. Speech is made dependent on the silence that refuses it. Life is made dependent on the death that it overcomes. The general fertility of the divine is evidenced in its power to absorb and digest the nondivine. Finally, the aberrant femaleness that introduces nonbeing and ignorance is made a condition of the realization of perfect being and knowledge. Of course, femaleness need not be at the origin of fault, but it does seem to be so explicitly in Boehme and Blake. In the case of Boehme, for instance, the movement from the immanent

divine sphere to the realm of nature involves a movement from divine wisdom to the degraded and essentially evil form of eternal nature, which bears the closest possible relationship to Acamaoth or Physis of *PSY*. And in Blake's Prophetic Poems, Vala and Enitharmon among others are female figures identifiable with nature. Moreover, if Derrida's powerful interpretation of Hegel in *Glas* is to be trusted,[168] matter, as other than spirit, is defined by a negative femaleness that it is the task of Hegel's Christianity to overcome and his conceptual discourse to complete and justify.

(6) Related directly to (4) and (5), and indirectly to (1), (2), and (3), the *Tractate*'s theodicy strategy is repeated, which shifts the focus from identifying the source of evil to redescribing evil. And the strategy is radicalized on both the axes of ascribing intelligibility to matter, time, and history, and the scope and means of redemption.

With respect to the scope of redemption, not only are determinist and predestination views set aside as in the *Tractate*, but the scope of salvation becomes also more universal. It becomes increasingly difficult to comprehend the refusal of salvation. And at the same time—and possibly as a function of this enlargement of scope—a distinction seems to be drawn between two qualitatively different groups of the saved: those who have speculative grasp of the whole divine process (e.g., Boehme, Hegel) or rise to the level of vision in imagination (e.g., Blake, Schelling, Altizer), and those who do not.

With respect to the means of salvation in the Baurian line of Valentinian narratives, ethos ceases to be the poor cousin of contemplation. While the *Tractate* grants a status to ethics that is surprising given Irenaeus's account of Gnosticism, on the whole ethics clearly does not enjoy the role it enjoys in narrative ontotheologies in the Baurian line. But it is not simply a matter of reinscription. In the case of Boehme and Moltmann, for example, ethics is always more than conventional Christian morality. And in Blake and Altizer the new form of life recommended transgresses conventional morality. The case of Hegel is especially interesting in that although he does not advocate the flouting of morality, he suggests (a) that the deep-seated value system of modern culture (*Sittlichkeit*) may be at odds with morality (*Moralität*),[169] which he takes to be summed up in Kant, and (b) that the philosopher inhabits the divine point of view, which as the *Lectures on the Philosophy of History* underscores, fails to issue any condemnation of the victimizers in history.[170]

(7) Metaleptic ontotheological narratives in the extended Baurian field not only repeat the entire set of radical features, but also

repeat them at a much higher level of integration. This higher level of integration is a function of the exacerbation and radicalization of the theogonic features suggested in a classical Valentinian text such as the *Tractate*. This higher level integration is thus a real possibility of Valentinian narrative grammar.

A sense of what this greater integration looks like can be gleaned from the reading of Hegel prosecuted in *The Heterodox Hegel*. With the *Tractate* explicitly in mind, (1) there I drew attention to Hegel's radically kataphatic stand, his commitment to a divine that is expressive (chap. 1), and his view that the divine self-consciousness requires finite acts of consciousness (chap. 2). I also argued (2) that for Hegel nature and finite spirit were conceived as fallen and evil (chap. 3), with the biblical fall of human being having an essentially felix culpa pattern. I showed (3) that the suffering of Jesus was symbolic of divine pathos, despite or because of the fact that the suffering is predicated of what is other than the divine and that this suffering had no saving significance for human being (chap. 4). Central to my reading of Hegel (4) was the view that the articulation of Spirit implied that perfection cannot be applied to the divine as origin, but only to the divine that has completed its exile in the finite (chap. 6). I also showed (5) how narrative operations such as *prolepsis* and *analepsis* serve to constitute divine development as teleological through and through (chaps. 1.3, 7). If the tendency in Hegel is to expand the scope and means of salvation, I argued (6) that he introduces a distinction between higher and lower modes of salvation, on the one hand, and both valorizes and relativizes *ethos* as a mode of salvation, on the other (chap. 6).

Of course, one need not suppose that differences in the adoption and radicalization of narrativity between the post-Reformation and post-Enlightenment regions of the Baurian field would not exist, nor that the reasons, focal or tacit, used to justify narrativity would be the same in all cases. For instance, one might expect, on the one hand, that in the embracing of narrativity in the post-Reformation field the pull of orthodoxy would continue to be experienced and, on the other, that the reasons offered for a revision of Christian narrative would be more or less exclusively intramural. Of course, orthodoxy itself would be complex and a matter of debate in a situation in which the Bible is given principled precedence over tradition, and regularity of profession remains an issue. Moreover, the biblical text's figuring of a dynamic, active, and living God, just the supposed opposite of the God of the philosophers, offers encouragement and a measure of justification for those who wish to make the move from an active and living divine to a narratively engendered divine. I will argue the case in detail with respect to Jacob Boehme in the next volume, although I will also touch on precursors such as Valentin Weigel and successors in the Pietist tradition such as Oetinger. In contrast, one might expect that in the post-Enlightenment field orthodox constraints are not felt in the same way and that while intramural Christian reasons would continue to be adduced, at the very least they would be supplemented by appeals of a humanist and/or philosophical kind. The Schelling of the *Philosophy of Mythology* and the *Philosophy of Revelation*, so important to Tillich,[171] is a good example. We have good reasons to believe that Schelling is absolutely sincere in his claim that he wants to render the living God of the Bible and in his rehabilitation of the event character of revelation. At the same time, whatever his unhappiness with the logical and immanentist interpretation of revelation in Hegel,[172] he does not wish to reinscribe the transcendent God of traditional theism: This is the God of the dead, not the living, a God who does not move human being toward the future of kingdom. Again, the texts of the later Schelling do not eschew the task of elaborating a dynamic relational ontology that takes account of Hegelian criticisms of the shortcomings of Schelling's own Identity-Philosophy.[173]

Needless to say, this description of trajectory is general and is upset in some cases. It would not be surprising if a twentieth-century post-Enlightenment Valentinian candidate such as Moltmann were to show more orthodox latencies not only than the German Idealists, but also more than a pre-Enlightenment Valentinian candidate such as Jacob Boehme, and if his reasons were to prove by and large no less intramural than the Lutheran mystic. I will be careful throughout to render as well as register the traditional and orthodox elements in the discourses of figures who fundamentally belong to and articulate the third line of Protestant thought.

To summarize this discussion of the radicalization of the narrativity features that mark one of the more significant of the classical Valentinian paradigms, one can say that the radicalization of these features by discourses in the Baurian line issues in a theogonic rendition of Valentinian narrative grammar. A theogonic rendition is necessarily an erotic rendition in which the divine has itself as its own object. At the same time, theogonic rendition is necessarily agonistic, since eros for divine realization proceeds through the tragic loss of an archeological divine perfection. To speak of a theogonic radicalization of Valentinian narrative paradigms is necessarily to speak of a rule-governed deformation. To speak of a theogony as a rule-governed deformation is to imply an erotic and agonistic deformation.

The narrativity features, instanced in the Hellenistic field above all by the *Tractate*, are not the only kinds of features repeated in the ontotheological narratives of the Baurian field. A second group of features, associated with the *Gospel*'s epistemological registering of Valentinianism, are also candidates for repetition and rearticulation. Three features are central.

(1) The *Gospel* shifts the emphasis from an ontotheological narrative in which knowing is one element among others onto the event of knowing itself, which, nevertheless, cannot dispense with ontotheological narrative. This shift is repeated and rearticulated in modern contexts that stress the appropriation of faith (post-Reformation) and presuppose the epistemological turn (post-Enlightenment). In the former case, faith is not so much the antithesis to knowledge as the knowing that is more than knowledge, that is, more than ratiocination. Thus, the fiducial element of the Reformers, and especially of Luther, is taken up into an extraordinary, pneumatic form of knowledge that finds its realization in Boehme, but that is already anticipated in Paracelsus and Weigel. In the latter, the epistemological turn, variously articulated in England and on the continent,[174] creates a backdrop that is inhospitable to narrative discourse while promoting a narrative reaction.

A constant theme in Blake's poetry, for example, is the destruction wrought on the imagination by Lockean epistemology.[175] Locke's empiricism amounts to a materialism. One sees with rather than through the eyes,[176] and the world that is available is the sense world bereft of spirit and mystery. The material world then is nondisclosive and nonsymbolic. Resistance to Locke is in the first instance primarily a defense of symbol. But it is also a defense of narrative that structures symbols because imagination not only captures the symbolic dimension of existence, but also tells the story of imagination's fall and redemption in a metanarrative that has the biblical narrative as its base. Here narratively specified knowledge defeats Lockean knowledge and its systemic atomism that finds correlates both in Newton's scientific method and Hobbes's political theory.

(2) The related anthropological recentering of the *Gospel* is repeated while articulated in contexts in which the criteria for identifying a divine humanity become more fluid than the Hellenistic environment that tended to favor contemplation over modes of existence that were more practical, ethical, and political. Blake and

Moltmann supply examples in the third line of Protestantism of this shift of accent. Blake is not simply a poet of vision, he is also a prophetic poet in the literal sense that his poems embody a protest against dehumanizing social conditions, especially for women, children, and the poor. Even more, his poems in general, but his prophetic poems in particular, embody a critique of the religious and political ideologies that justify this dehumanization. In a quite different context, Moltmann's elaboration of political theology supports the practical and transformative context and force of thought. Despite practical and political accents in the metaleptic discourses of those in the third line of Protestantism, I will argue in later volumes that the contemplative and visionary dimensions of thought regain a certain privilege. Vision articulates the narrative whose function is to account for and justify the evil that, if the antithesis of the divine, is constitutive for divine self-genesis.

(3) Two associated features of the *Gospel*'s focus on knowing, that is, the synoptic simplification of narrative and even more explicit movement of demythologization, are repeated while being brought to new levels of clarity in a post-Reformation context that discourages speculative myth and a post-Enlightenment context in which myth is at once impossible and necessary, as Blumenberg, and Cassirer before him,[177] have shown.

Hegel provides the classic example in the post-Enlightenment field of the operation of synoptic simplification of encompassing metaleptic narrative proceeding in tandem with systematic demythologization. Similar to the *Gospel*, in texts such as the *Phenomenology* and the *Encyclopedia* Hegel attempts a reduction of a complex narrative, which bears metaleptic relation to biblical narrative, to a more simple triadic form.[178] As in the *Gospel*, the becoming of knowledge is both the subject and object of the narrative. In the case of Hegel, if the triadic form of the narrative already indicates that Hegel is putting some distance between himself and the inclusive metaleptic narrative with respect to discursive adequacy, his proposal that the reconfigured biblical narrative needs to be conceptualized suggests that all narrative is a figuration of knowledge, although precisely as prefiguration.[179]

If the narrativity and epistemological declensions of the ontotheological narratives in the Baurian field, which constitute new Valentinian genres, show themselves to be systemic, this would still allow for a wide variety of combinations and permutations of features. For example, discourses could still continue to have a strong mythological base of the *PSY* type, as is the case with Boehme and

Blake, while emphasizing more nearly the theogonic (Boehme) or epistemological emendations (Blake). Alternatively, the mythic base is merely echoed, and different dominant-recessive relations between the theogonic (e.g., Schelling, Moltmann) and epistemological (e.g., Hegel, Altizer) emendations prevail. Again, synoptic simplification of ontotheological narrative could be provided an explicit trinitarian form (e.g., Boehme, Hegel) or avoid it (e.g., Schelling, Tillich). Or synopsis could be emphasized at the expense of demythologization (e.g., Boehme, Schelling) or demythologization over synopsis (e.g., Altizer, Tillich). I discuss trinitarian synopsis in the next section, for this touches on the crucial issue of how the Trinity functions in the third line in Protestant thought. It is now time to explore in detail the important issue of Valentinian enlisting of other narrative discourses in the narrative ontotheologies that constitute the Baurian line.

5.3. Valentinian Enlisting of Non-Valentinian Narrative Discourses

In the last section I argued that the concept of rule-governed deformation of classical Valentinian genres could have categorical and not simply hypothetical use value, for we could see in a general and proleptic way (1) how narrative ontotheologies in the Baurian line deviate from or deform classical Valentinian paradigms by producing Valentinian narratives in both radical theogonic and also epistemological keys, and (2) how these deviations or deformations are insinuated in the classical paradigms themselves and are thus a feature of Valentinian narrative grammar. Modeling our discussion here on chapter 4.2, I now turn to another suggested feature of Valentinian narrative grammar that most likely would be repeated in the Baurian line of narrative discourses. I refer to the phenomenon or operation observable in classical Valentinian genres of the enlisting of non-Valentinian narrative discourses for Valentinian narrative purposes.

Before I begin my discussion, I want to make three preliminary points. First, discourses in the Baurian line are, at least from a narrative vocabulary point of view, even more complex than the classical Valentinian narratives. To the Neoplatonic and apocalyptic narrative strands, one must add the Kabbalah as a third narrative strand. Second, the enlisting might be even more systematic and powerful because of, and not simply despite, the greater presence and effect of the non-Valentinian narrative strands. Third, having in mind both our discussion of the theogonic nature of Valentinian narratives in the Baurian line and how a triadic synopsis of the six-stage metaleptic narrative could have trinitarian effect, I address in a general way about how in and through Valentinian enlisting of the three non-Valentinian discourses, the traditional separation of the Trinity *in se* and the trinitarian missions is undone.

Valentinian Enlisting of Neoplatonism

I begin with the enlisting in Protestant discourses of the third line of Neoplatonic narrative elements for Valentinian narrative purposes. Clearly, that the interpretive stakes are raised when the two nine-teenth-century mainstays of the Gnostic hypothesis (i.e., Baur and Staudenmaier) suggest the possibility that a *Neoplatonic* ascription may be just as adequate as a *Gnostic* ascription for important post-Reformation (e.g., Boehme) and post-Enlightenment (e.g., Hegel, Schelling) narrative discourses, when powerful analyses of the discourses of particular figures (e.g., Blake, Hegel, Schelling) in the extended Baurian field bring in verdicts that the ancestor discourse is Neoplatonism, and when some of these figures (e.g., Blake, Hegel, and Schelling) themselves show little reluctance to accept *Neoplatonic* ascription. If there is a problem for our thesis of Gnostic return, it is not that Platonism and Neoplatonism are not evident in these modern narratives, but rather all too evident. One cannot rule legitimately against a *Neoplatonic* ascription beforehand. Whether it or *Valentinianism* is a more adequate ascriptor has to be demonstrated on a case-by-case basis. But it is important to point out, on the basis of our analysis of the presence of Platonic/Neoplatonic elements in the classical Valentinian paradigms, that even what could be taken to amount to a relative saturation of a modern narrative ontotheology by Neoplatonic elements would not necessarily entail the verdict that the discourse is intrinsically Neoplatonic.

In denying the entailment, I have in mind more than the obvious fact that in these narrative ontotheologies in the Baurian line specifically post-Reformation and/or post-Enlightenment elements are present and thus necessarily must be taken into account. I am in fact referring to the principle, generated by our analysis of the classical Valentinian paradigms, that in complex narrative ontotheologies, showing both Neoplatonic and Valentinian features, Neoplatonism counts ascriptively if and only if it, and not Valentinianism, operates at the narrative depth rather than the narrative surface or effectively abolishes the distinction. Failing this, Neoplatonism would have to be seen as a supplement to or modifier of Valentinian discourse no matter how exigent the presence of the "God is not jealous" trope or the construct of providence, and no matter how determined the attempt to establish an uninterrupted continuum of divine communication or expression.

The supplemental or modifier status of Neoplatonism with respect to narrative ontotheologies in the Baurian field is shown if, as in the case of the classical paradigms, it becomes evident that the scope of the "God is not jealous" trope is limited to revising a negative view of the physical world and its creator, not rescinding it, and if it becomes evident that the workings of providence's rule is similarly indirect and dialectical. That is, intelligibility is not directly or immediately present in a universe that is countermimetic rather than mimetic of the divine intelligibility, but is indirect and mediate in that intelligibility imposes itself against the grain of unintelligibility that is more than intelligibility's mere privation, indeed is intelligibility's aggressive other. Supplemental or modifier status also becomes evident if the continuity of divine communication is established only across discontinuity, despite the tear or gap of noncommunication or excommunication. A final indicator of the irreducible modifier status of Neoplatonism occurs when the overall drive of the narrative is erotic and developmental, when the communicating of perfection is the same time, and more fundamentally, the process of its achievement. Divine perfection is economic in that its giving or communication realizes surplus value. The hypothesis that subsequent volumes hope to verify is that with respect to ontotheological narratives in the Baurian field Neoplatonism systemically functions in this modifying or supplemental way. Boehme, Blake, Hegel, Schelling, and even Tillich, Altizer, and Moltmann will be adduced as examples.

But one can go much further than this. The relatively more exigent presence of the Timaean trope of "God is not envious," the notion of providence, and the commitment to continuity in divine communication of a presumed agapaic kind, would function to make a Valentinian narrative more rather than less erotic. First, all of these features would teleologize the narrative. Second, they would provide second-order justifications for narratives proceeding in a dialectical way. In addition, and again for the same reasons, by helping to remove the accidental character of pathos from the narrative of divine self-communication, Neoplatonism would contribute paradoxically to the ascription of pathos to the divine, which it vociferously denies throughout its historical instantiations in the classical, medieval Christian, and Renaissance periods.

There is a certain abstractness in speaking this way about the cooption or enlisting of Neoplatonism by a different narrative grammar and not simply for the reason that as yet I have provided no extensive evidence for the existence of such a phenomenon in modern narrative ontotheological discourses. Until now I have not mentioned the relationship between Neoplatonism and Christianity in the Baurian field, specifically the issue of whether Neoplatonism's historical relationship to Christianity is changed as it is enlisted by a new grammar. I grant, of course, that from the beginning tensions existed in Christianity between the faith that was formed by the biblical narrative and Neoplatonism as an explanatory discourse. This is the limited truth of Harnack's famous hellenization of Christianity hypothesis. Yet in the numerous transactions between biblical faith and philosophy as an explanatory discourse that occurred in the patristic (e.g., Cappadocians, Augustine, Maximus), medieval (e.g., Aquinas, Bonaventure), and even early Renaissance periods (e.g., Cusa), Neoplatonism showed that it could function as a faithful ancillary of biblical narrative and could translate it into a conceptually defensible idiom. In the context of the Baurian manifold, however, Neoplatonism's enlisting by Valentinian narrative grammar means that it too comes to function metaleptically with respect to the biblical narrative. It contributes to metalepsis by helping to form an ontotheological felix culpa that is radically different from the anthropological felix culpa of Gregory of Nyssa, where the emphasis falls on the stability of perfection made possible by pedagogy, on the one hand, or what one might call the doxological felix culpa of Augustine, on the other, where the fortunate element of fall is that God gets to display his justice and mercy for which human beings should be grateful in that they come to have experiential knowledge of God.[180] In the Baurian field, by contrast, felix culpa functions not anthropologically but theologically, not doxologically but ontologically. Neoplatonism, then, contributes to metalepsis by supporting a divine erotics in which the divine's reality is constituted by the very story in which it is the major protagonist. The enlisting of Neoplatonism further contributes to metalepsis by aiding the view of divine agonistics that, nevertheless, rules out the possibility that Christ's suffering is salvific. The enlisting of Neoplatonism also contributes to metalepsis insofar as in a context where seeing is no longer intrinsically connected to ascetic practice and faith, knowledge is deprived of both the ethos that legitimates it in

Christian Neoplatonic circles and its role of explicator of faith, whether that of belief or trust.

In the genealogical volume that follows this programmatic text I will show how Boehme's narrative discourse provides an emblematic form—and the emblematic form in the post-Reformation and pre-Enlightenment field—of the enlisting of Neoplatonism for ends that it did not serve in any of the three periods (i.e., patristic, medieval, Renaissance) in which Neoplatonism had general currency. The ontological generosity so central to Neoplatonism is translated in this narrative environment into the ungrounded will to manifestation that has erotic momentum. The dramatic agon between the divine and antidivine is undergirded by telos, such that continuity redresses the rupture of manifestation brought about by the emergence of the antidivine. Indeed, the teleological graphing justifies rupture of communication of the divine and the emergence of the antidivine.

Such enlisting is equally evident in the case of Blake and the later Schelling. In Blake the antithetical realm of matter and time from a higher order point of view contributes to the manifestation of the divine. And the movement from unity to unity through fragmentation is interpreted as a movement toward perfection rather than back to it. And not without some justification have scholars of Schelling commented on the extent of the influence of classical Neoplatonism in his texts.[181] Moreover, while acknowledging the difference between a text such as *Bruno*, which belongs to his Identity-Philosophy phase, and texts such as the *Essay on Human Freedom* and *The Ages of the World*, on the one hand, and the *Philosophy of Mythology* and the *Philosophy of Revelation*, on the other, scholars have argued more or less successfully for the presence of Neoplatonic tropes and narrative structures in Schelling's post-Idealist phase. In the former pair of texts, for instance, the dramatic nature of the manifestation of the infinite in and through eternal nature, which is the aggressive denial of manifestation, is teleological: the rupture with manifestation is a function of continuity of manifestation. The dramatic route manifestation follows is the route that issues in the personhood of the divine that is not there from the beginning.

If the enlisting of Neoplatonic narrative elements aids the fashioning of a theogonic and erotic revision of classical Valentinianism, it also aids a general shift in narrative register toward the gnoseological and away from the mythological. For the dominant register in the historical forms of Neoplatonism is gnoseological. Even if the narrative of exit-return has more than subjective status in the classical Neoplatonism of Plotinus and Proclus, nevertheless, some critical distance is taken from the underlying narrative. If the Christian Neoplatonism of Pseudo-Dionysius and Eriugena does not surrender the objectivity of the narrative of emanation and return, there exists, as more than one scholar has argued, a shift to the subjective or knowledge pole.[182] And in the late Renaissance form of Neoplatonism represented by Cusanus, one could argue à la Blumenberg, but also others,[183] that the narrative of manifestation is even more subjectivized. Enlisting of any one, or more than one, of these historical forms of Neoplatonism does not hinder and, I argue, facilitates a gnoseological exacerbation of Valentinian narrative in which the movement that is the object of narration is at the same time the movement of mind.

As I have suggested, the two discourses in the Baurian field that most successfully accomplish this kind of Neoplatonic enlisting are the discourses of Hegel and Blake. It will be the burden of the volumes on Romanticism and Hegel respectively to demonstrate not only the self-conscious appropriation of various historically specific forms of the Neoplatonic narrative of exit-return, but also the assimilation of their gnoseological register that helps translates the modern theogonic renditions of Valentinian narrative grammar into an agonistics of mind. Although the point has to be demonstrated in each case, importantly, in neither case is the assimilation of Neoplatonism and its register independent of the assistance such assimilation plays in the construction of a narrative alternative to the biblical narrative. Or, otherwise put, assimilation in both cases aids metalepsis.

Associated with the enlisting of the gnoseological thrust of Neoplatonism in both Blake and Hegel is the repetition of a phenomenon evident in the most gnoseologically acute of the classical Valentinian paradigms, that is, the *Gospel*. I am speaking here of the displaced identity of the narrative subject. In the case of the *Gospel* this displaced identity is indicated in collapse of the transcendent divine into the divine that introduces fault and the collapse of this divine into the demiurge. In the case of the modern instances of Valentinian narrative grammar this displacement is further radicalized into a displacement from the divine into the incarnate Christ and from Christ into the human. One of the major contributions of the scholarship of Altizer is to have so consistently recognized this point and registered it in different idioms. Blake's major poems, he argues, relentlessly present a narrative subject that is neither divine nor human. In addition, in his classic account of revealed religion in the *Phenomenology*, Hegel determines that the Son, identified with the human community, is at an equally distant remove from the pure or abstract divine and from the all too human, beset by frailty, weakness, and death.[184] Supporting Altizer's insight, I suggest not only that the basic pattern for this is established in classical Valentinian paradigms and aided by the recessive erotic thrust, but also that in the narratives in the Baurian line this anthropological displacement can be supported by Neoplatonism's emphasis on divine self-expression or communication.

Undoubtedly, all of these metaleptic assists given by Neoplatonism to Protestant discourses of the third line are extrapolatable from what we have learned about the enlisting of Neoplatonism in classical Valentinian narrative genres. What I want to discuss now is not so automatically deducible; it is the way in which in its cooption Neoplatonism behaves very differently toward the biblical narrative in the patristic and early and late medieval periods. In these periods, Neoplatonism serves in Christian theology to extend trinitarianly the biblical narrative at both ends and provides conceptual support for the distinction between the Trinity as such and its activities. One hardly needs to point out that this process took considerable time and that a second-century orthodox theologian such as Irenaeus, no less than the authors of the *Gospel* and the *Tractate*, did not have a trinitarian discourse that could pass the Nicene test. In any event, in post-Nicene adaptation in both the West (e.g., Augustine) and the East (e.g., Gregory of Nyssa, Gregory of Nazianzus) Neoplatonism eventually came to support distinctions between the divine as such and the divine in the economy or missions that were thought to be essential to Christian faith. The God who created, redeemed, and sanctified is a God who is fully sufficient, and without need of a supplement, not to mention a supplement that is constitutive of divine identity, thus no supplement at all.

If only through a glass darkly, Baur, and to a much greater extent, Staudenmaier, suggest that ontotheological narratives in the post-Reformation and post-Enlightenment contexts deconstruct the distinction between the trinitarian divine as such and the trinitarian divine in its acts or missions, or what from the nineteenth century on has been called the distinction-relation between the immanent and the economic Trinity. Ironically, Neoplatonism becomes an agent in the deconstruction of a distinction that traditionally it helped foster. It is now enlisted to support narrativity, and thus an erotics of divine, which makes the economy not simply an expression of divinity, but the indispensable means by which the divine becomes divine. The trinitarian divine, therefore, is economic in almost a literal sense: It reaps dividends on a giving of itself that is anything but expenditure without reserve,[185] to evoke Bataille.

Valentinian Enlisting of Apocalyptic

As with the relation between Valentinianism and Neoplatonism, the relation between Valentinianism and apocalyptic becomes more rather than less urgent in the context of the ontotheological narratives of the Baurian field. As I pointed out in chapter 2, a Valentinian reading of such major figures in this field as Boehme, Blake, Hegel, Schelling, Altizer, and even Moltmann finds itself challenged by powerful readings of these thinkers as belonging either to the primary apocalyptic tradition, that is, the tradition defined by biblical apocalyptic texts,[186] and especially Revelation, or the secondary apocalyptic tradition, that is, a tradition that in modernity is defined by Joachim of Fiore's interpretation of Revelation or, better, its effective history.[187] Thinkers whose proximity to the primary apocalyptic tradition is underscored include Boehme and Blake. Thinkers who are thought more nearly to belong to the secondary tradition of Joachim include Hegel, Schelling, and Altizer. Moreover, a number of thinkers within the Baurian field of ontotheological narrative invoke *apocalyptic* as a self-ascription. Such is the case with Moltmann, who does this almost from the beginning of his career. His early *Theology of Hope*, which is influenced by Bloch's endorsement of apocalyptic's visionary and interruptive qualities, adopts apocalyptic as the counter to Christian discourses that valorize the present or conceive the future as a teleological extrapolation. One thing that other- and self-ascription of *apocalyptic* makes clear is that the incidence of apocalyptic elements in general, and especially the openness to time and history and its agon in particular, is considerably higher in the post-Reformation and post-Enlightenment narrative ontotheologies of the Baurian field than it is in Valentinian paradigms of the Hellenistic period. But again the issue is whether in these complex narrative ontotheological discourses affirming a high incidence of apocalyptic is incompatible with regarding these narrative ontotheologies as lexical instances of Valentinian narrative grammar, although, as I have suggested, rule-governed deformations of classical Valentinian genres.

Our analysis of the presence of apocalyptic elements in the classical paradigms of Valentinianism (4.2), although it does not demand a negative answer to the previous question, nevertheless, strongly suggests one. In classical Valentinian paradigms apocalyptic elements modify a more basic narrative ontotheology by dampening the hostility to time and insinuating the presence of providence in history. Importantly, the hegemony of Valentinian narrative is left intact insofar as creation, time, and history still continue to have negative status on the first-order level, and providence does not bespeak the presence of the biblical God who creates and judges. The increased presence of apocalyptic in the narrative ontotheologies in the Baurian field could possibly alter the infrastructural Valentinian commitments. Yet it could also be the case that these modern Valentinian narrative ontotheologies would accommodate a much heavier apocalyptic load than classical Valentinian paradigms without detriment to narrative base, and thus without detriment to their status as belated instances of Valentinian narrative grammar. The latter is essentially the proposal being made here, and one that I hope to demonstrate in the genealogy that follows.

In his analysis of Boehme's and Hegel's trinitarian ontotheology in *Die christliche Gnosis*, Baur hints at the direction conceptual formulation might take by describing the theology of history of a Joachimite type being enfolded in ontotheological narratives that admit of being called *theogonic*. Extrapolating, therefore, from what is evident in the classical Valentinian genres and what is hinted at by Baur, one can suggest that, as long as the meaning of the apocalyptic elements is regulated in the final analysis by an apocalypse form with distinct narrative, visionary, and hermeneutic disposition, then one can talk about *apocalyptic inscription* by and, correlatively, *apocalyptic distention* of a more encompassing apocalypse form identified as Valentinian. What would be radically different in the post-Reformation and post-Enlightenment context, by contrast with the Hellenistic, is the extent and intent of inscription and distention. This could reach such levels that it might tempt an alternative ascription. It is precisely these new levels of inscription and distention that encourage good readers of Boehme, Hegel, and Schelling (e.g., Altizer and de Lubac) and good readers of Blake (e.g., Bloom and Erdmann) to bring in apocalyptic verdicts.

To avoid repeating what I have said about apocalyptic inscription and distention, it is best to refer the reader to our discussion of these concepts generated in chapter 2 to meet a conceptual need. What I suggested there hypothetically about the discourses such as those of Boehme, Hegel, Blake, and even Altizer, I wish now to assert categorically, given our eneucleation of a Valentinian narrative grammar in chapters 3 and 4. No more here than in chapter 2, however, is it possible to be demonstrative. That burden is shifted onto the genealogy that begins with a volume on Boehme. It is worth repeating, however, that *inscription* and *distention* are spatial metaphors that point to the most important aspect of Valentinian enlisting of biblical apocalyptic. The metaleptic Valentinian narrative, which plays the role of host, encompasses the apocalyptic narrative and avails of its agonistic christological and its salvation-history commitment to fashion its theogonic deformation of classical Valentinian genres.

The two other aspects of Valentinian enlisting of apocalyptic are also important. For example, further dominance of apocalyptic by Valentinian apocalypse, one might say further conscription, occurs when the post-Reformation and post-Enlightenment ontotheologies of the Baurian field either recapitulate, or in some cases expand on, the kind of epistemological or gnoseological thrust evident in the *Gospel* paradigm. In narratives in the Baurian line, the exteriority of revelation may be effaced and the narrative mechanisms for its realization may become recessed when the focus is placed on knowing as transconceptual knowing, as event, if not advent. Blake and Schelling provide just two of the many examples. In the case of Blake revelation becomes focused in imagination, which surpasses and even transgresses conceptual forms of knowledge. Posited as a capacity, imagination is at the same time posited as event: actual vision is the event of the imagination. A feature that unites the early and the later Schelling is the conviction that a power of knowing exists that transcends the limitations set by Kant. In the earlier part of Schelling's career he calls it intellectual intuition or productive imagination. Later, with a greater grasp that the premodern religious and philosophical traditions consistently distinguish between conceptual and supraconceptual forms of knowing, Schelling is content with speaking of nonconceptual knowledge or vision. And as in the case of Blake, vision supposes that reality is both given to knowledge and constituted by it.

In addition to encompassing a dramatic eschatological narrative in a metaleptic narrative of absolutely encompassing range, and interiorizing and securing vision's authority, ontotheological narratives in the Baurian field, as belated exempla of Valentinian narrative grammar, also enlist an apocalyptic hermeneutics. In the next volume, which deals with Jacob Boehme, I will outline in some detail how the inscribing apocalypse form transcends the already quite immodest claims to knowledge made within the apocalyptic framework by suggesting revelation of reality that is not only total, but also fully adequate. At the same time, however, I will note the ways in which the mastered form of apocalyptic sometimes exerts pressure by modifying the claim to totality and epistemic adequacy that defines the pansophistic opus of Boehme and his sixteenth-century precursors, Paracelsus and Weigel. This reflexive influence by the enlisted narrative form on the enlisting Valentinian narrative is a specific manifestation of *apocalyptic distention*. The primary manifestation of apocalyptic distention, as I pointed out in part 1 (2.1), is that the inscribed apocalyptic narrative both extends and valorizes the temporal-historical line in Valentinian narrative. One of the claims made in the Boehme volume is that the level of apocalyptic distention is greatly in excess of that evident in the classical Valentinian genres and that this excess of apocalyptic extension is exemplary for the Baurian field as a whole.

The increased incidence of Neoplatonic or apocalyptic elements does not imply that Neoplatonism or apocalyptic achieve a status other than that of a modifier of a particular expression of a Valentinian narrative grammar that remains basic. In this respect, therefore, the belated instances of Valentinian narrative grammar continue the pattern observed in the case of the classical paradigms. Arguably, however, a new possibility of real difference emerges, if one supposes that some of the narrative ontotheologies of the Baurian field, for example, Boehme and Blake, Hegel and Schelling, show increased incidence of both Neoplatonic and apocalyptic elements. On the one hand, their combination would result in overlapping stresses on the goodness of creation, divine providence, and the goodness of the creator inseparable from absolute reality; on the other hand, their way of supplementing each other—for instance apocalyptic supplying a dramatic focus to history and a dramatic interpretation of Christ, and Neoplatonism underwriting divine goodness—might be sufficiently powerful to undo the Valentinian narrative hegemony. This possibility will occupy us throughout the texts that follow this programmatic volume. But if this possibility proves unsupported—and I am convinced that it will prove unsupported—then all the changes of meaning wrought by the underlying narrative on the introduced Neoplatonic and apocalyptic elements discussed heretofore would continue to apply. The physical world would be affirmable only on a second level, as would the goodness of the divine of which creation is an expression. Christ's suffering and death would continue to have no direct salvific effect with respect to human beings, either in general or with respect to a privileged group. Again if the possibility of these two non-Valentinian discourses combining to upset Valentinian hegemony is unsupported, this would mean that these new forms of Valentinian narrative grammar are powerful enough in their erotic dynamics to enlist simultaneously the diffusion metaphysics of Neoplatonism and the apocalyptic dramatics of history and eschatology.

On this basis one could predict that if any of the new Valentinian paradigms that assimilate significant apocalyptic and Neoplatonic elements were given express trinitarian form, the trinitarian articulation would continue to dismantle the immanent-economic distinction that Neoplatonism helped articulate and will continue to fail to acknowledge the merely economic or missional status of Joachim's three kingdoms. The Trinity would now cover a single field of divine becoming, in which at best the immanent aspect serves as a kind of trinitarian prologue to the economic that is constitutive of the narrative identity of the divine. In speaking of Boehme and Hegel in particular as offering new narrativized and historical forms of Sabellianism, Staudenmaier was groping toward a registering of this subversion.[188] But he also pointed to another feature of what he thought was a new trinitarian phenomenon. The chronic erotics not only dehypostatized the Trinity at the level of the preworldly Trinity and introduced subordination—thus the relation, although not without difference, between ancient and belated forms of Sabellianism—but dehypostatizing was also a phenomenon observable throughout the activities of the divine in creation and history that were constitutive of an identity that was finally a single and not a trinitarian identity.[189] Of course, this trinitarian suggestion here can function merely proleptically; it will have to be demonstrated through an analysis of major figures in the Baurian trajectory, beginning immediately with Boehme in the next volume. One of the major theological contributions of the genealogy prosecuted in this multivolume series is that it will enable an understanding of much of trinitarian theology from Boehme to Hegel and from Hegel to the present day.

One should note, however, that, without the benefit of a fully articulated model of Gnostic return, my *The Heterodox Hegel* went down this interpretive road when it suggested that Hegelian Trinity, in both its narrower immanent extension and its fully inclusive extension could be thought of as a species of dynamic narrative modalism already visible in Boehme.[190] The necessarily modalistic and/or Sabellian nature of trinitarian thought in the context of an erotic, kenotic, and agonistic total narrative is stipulated by Altizer, who in general regards the Trinity as the bastion of what is theologically reactionary and sectarian (*GG*, 108). There are, according to him, only two viable options, antitrinitarianism or the kind of trinitarianism for which Hegel provides the template. This is specified by Altizer as a "deeply modern Sabellian Trinitarianism, and precisely so in refusing all ultimate or final distinctions within the absolute spirit who is the Godhead" (*GG*, 108).[191]

Interestingly, this framing of an either-or between a dynamic modalistic Trinity and the hypostatic orthodox variety is made also by Blumenberg who, like Altizer, champions the heterodox variety. Uncoupling this alternative dynamic modalistic Trinitarianism from classical Sabellianism, Blumenberg thinks that it can be associated with the Gnostics, at least if Gnosticism is read deeply rather than superficially. Superficially read Gnosticism favors unity over multiplicity, stasis over kinesis, and apophasis over kataphasis. Probably influenced by the late Jonas, Blumenberg thinks that Gnosticism ultimately favors multiplicity, kinesis, and kataphasis, and does so because it is committed to telling the story of the divine. And a divine that is one, static, and mysterious is a reality about which no story can be told.[192] Within the Gnostic horizon of thought, the storying or theogonic element is to the fore whenever a trinitarian conspectus makes an appearance. By contrast, the orthodox Christian tradition is caught in the dilemma that it represents a break from monism into pure narration of the divine and simultaneously a purging of narration. In *Work on Myth*, Blumenberg writes: "The Trinitarian hypostases remain processes of pure inwardness, and an account of the identical nature of the three Persons—that is, their equal eternity—no story can be told, either, of what led to this generation and spiration. Dogma having awakened a need for myth, immediately summons it back to *raison* [reason]" (260). By contrast, to the extent to which Valentinianism invokes or evokes the Trinity, it neither freezes nor abolishes narration. This is evident in classical Valentinianism in the *Tractate* and is even more evident in the absolute myth of Hegel. Yet the combination of Trinity and the developmental ontotheological conditions of narration in exemplary thinkers such as Boehme and Hegel in the Baurian line necessarily subverts the classical Trinity and presents a dynamic modalistic or Sabellian simulacrum.

Proceeding on the basis of the enlisting relations within the Hellenistic field between Valentinian and Neoplatonic discourses on the one hand, and between Valentinian and apocalyptic discourses on the other, inferences were drawn as to what relations might hold between these discourses in the complex narratives of the Baurian manifold that satisfy the requirement of these complex narrative discourses being genres of Valentinian narrative grammar, albeit rule-governed deformations of classical Valentinian genres. The relation of enlisting of apocalyptic and Neoplatonism by Valentinianism we determined would be not only be repeated in the Baurian field, but repeated on a higher level of intensity and integration. Moreover, through this enlisting, the potential displayed in classical Valentinianism for a fully erotic, kenotic, and agonistic rendition is actualized.

Valentinian Enlisting of the Kabbalah

Conspicuously absent from our discussion up until now has been the Kabbalah, whose importance for understanding discourses in the Baurian line I underscored in part 1. The reason for the absence is obvious: the Kabbalah is itself a belated discourse and evolves centuries after the demise of classical Gnosticism and/or Valentinianism. Certainly the Kabbalah is a belated discourse if one adopts the convention that the *Book of Creation [Sefer Yetzirah]* or *Book of Formation [Sefer ha Bahir]* marks the emergence of Kabbalah in the strict sense because one is talking about a discourse that comes into being in the twelfth or early thirteenth century.[193] The relation of the Kabbalah to putative Gnostic or Valentinian narrative elements in the modern field is different, therefore, from that of the relation of Neoplatonism and apocalyptic to Valentinianism in the sense that no inferences can be drawn from relations between narrative discourses within the Hellenistic field.

Of course, much debate has occurred about the origins of Kabbalah and its constitutive elements, and in this context, scholars have proposed both Gnosticism and Neoplatonism as explanatory factors.[194] The issue of origins is a tangled one, and it is certainly the case that strong analogies exist between Kabbalah and Neoplatonism on the one hand, and Kabbalah and Gnosticism on the other. Yet finally, it is perhaps best, taking account of genetic factors and formal and material elements, to regard the Kabbalah as more or less sui generis and possessed of a determinate identity. In any event, in the post-Renaissance and post-Reformation contexts in which Christian thinkers appropriate Kabbalah, the Kabbalah functions as something of speculative religious *Ersatz* in which it has nothing to do with Torah, in which in fact it is a discourse that is anti-Torah. If Reuchlin is an important influence on the Renaissance appropriation-expropriation of Kabbalah in Florence, he also represents the ultimate origin of Kabbalah in post-Reformation Germany as it plays out in Paracelsus in the sixteenth century, Boehme in the seventeenth century, and Oetinger in the eighteenth century.[195] In any event, the particular German expropriation of the Kabbalah is relevantly similar and dissimilar to the Florentine expropriation. It is similar in that the Kabbalah becomes exclusively a theogonic discourse in which the secrets of Christ and/or the Trinity are spelled out. It is dissimilar in that the problem of evil is more urgent, and theogony has a more agonic cast.[196]

The Kabbalah then constitutes the third non-Valentinian narrative strand of the complex narrative weave of discourses in the Baurian manifold. In the Protestant discourses that articulate the Baurian line, it so overlaps with the other narrative strands, particularly Neoplatonism and Valentinianism, that unraveling it is sometimes difficult. At the same time, like apocalyptic that is inscribed in Valentinian narrative and Neoplatonism that is included in it, the Kabbalah too is regulated by Valentinianism, which supplies the rules for theogonic formation, rules that are part of its grammar but not enacted within the classical sphere. In the context of the Kabbalah's regulation by another narrative discourse one may recall Jonas's well-known remark about Gnosticism being a form of metaphysical anti-Semitism,[197] a provocation that is redeemable in part at least in the context of Nag Hammadi by reference to the biblical God as cosmic bungler, legalist, resentment figure, and violator. Allowing that it is preferable to speak of anti-Judaism rather than anti-Semitism, Jonas's remark tends to focus an important issue, namely how the Kabbalah, when included in a metaleptic Christian narrative, contributes to a Valentinian agenda, a central component of which is its attack against the God of the Hebrew Bible.

One could say that in narratives of the Baurian field, one witnesses a phenomenon that goes beyond common garden varieties of Christian supercessionism and even beyond the more exacerbated forms of supercession in evidence where Christianity tends toward a Marcionite appraisal. That is, as a strand in complex metaleptic narrative discourses, the Kabbalah is a discourse set in opposition to the creator God, the God of justice, who represents the dark side of God that must be overcome if God is to be God. The next volume on Boehme will offer a classic example of this interpretive move in operation. But its operation is also transparent in Blake and Hegel. In Blake's *Jerusalem*, for example, the God of Hebrew scriptures is excoriated. The God of law and rule is a God of repression and oppression, a God jealous of liberated and knowledgeable human being, a

God so transcendent as to be without reality. To this spurious divine is opposed a God with a definite shape that integrates divine qualities, including qualities that are variously masculine and feminine. This God of definite shape, the divine human, is associated with the Kabbalistic Adam Kadmon.[198]

In Hegel, the God of Abraham is the God of the nomad, the one who is sovereignly transcendent and who thereby evacuates the natural world, but especially human being, of meaning and value. The introjection of this essentially Judaic view into Christianity, Hegel judges, functions virally, and incapacitates it. Specifically, it encourages Christians to forget what essentially constitutes it, that is, its core belief that God is a God known (or to be known) as defined by relation to nature and finite spirit. This view laid down early in Hegel's career is the view that continues to have force in his reflections on the unhappy consciousness in the *Phenomenology*, and that persists, although not without some emendation, in the published and unpublished texts of Hegel's mature period.[199] Yet, ironically, of the religious discourses known to Hegel, the Kabbalah is relatively privileged: it is a discourse of divine self-presencing, thus a discourse that avows real knowledge, that is, speculative knowledge of the divine. Moreover, Kabbalistic narrative discourse is dramatic since one of its basic urges is to explain contradiction or evil in the light of the self-development of the divine. For Hegel, then, in a structural sense the Kabbalah is a Christian narrative discourse superior to orthodox renderings of the biblical narrative.[200] As such, it represents a privileged site of narrative resistance within Christianity to the hegemony of the Judaic narrative of the transcendent and sovereign divine that accompanies the career of Christianity and emasculates it. Important for Hegel, as well as Blake, is the figure of Adam Kadmon, who sums up the displacement from transcendence to immanence and the displacement from an apophatic regime of divine beyond being into a radically kataphatic arena in which the divine is both a figure and object of knowledge. Paradoxically, then, Adam Kadmon is a figure who articulates Christianity as a religion of revelation, that is, a religion in which the divine is unveiled. Yet this unveiling continually needs to be asserted against a persistent recidivist tendency in Christianity to regress into Judaism from which Christianity emerged precisely as its overcoming.

But if regulated finally by Valentinian rules of narrative formation that are only enacted in the modern period, the Kabbalistic narrative strand, again like apocalyptic and Neoplatonism, is not without reflexive force on the Valentinianism of the inclusive metaleptic narratives in the Baurian line. This enables us to speak about how the Kabbalah contributes to the overall Valentinian thrust of complex narrative formations while introducing a more positive twist to a view of creation as divine expression and tempering the erotic interpretation of divine process by suggesting that the divine who becomes in the process is paradoxically always already more.

In introducing a more positive twist to creation, conceived as antithetical divine expression, the Kabbalistic narrative strand reinforces the reflexive force exerted by apocalyptic and Neoplatonic narrative strands in discourses in the Baurian line. Doing so helps release the theogonic potential of Valentinian narrative grammar that was merely latent in the classical Valentinian genres, for creation now is an instrument of divine becoming. I judged that this effect operates at some level in all the narratives that belong to and articulate the Baurian field, but perhaps most clearly so in Boehme, his immediate precursors such as Paracelsus and Weigel, and successors such as Hegel, Blake, and Schelling. The tempering of the erotic thrust of the narrative divine is, by contrast, a more restricted phenomenon. On the one hand, religious thinkers in the Baurian line such as Hegel and Altizer will enter no caveats with respect to the ontological status of the divine presupposed: it is unequivocally that of privation rather than fullness, nothingness rather than being. On the other hand, while Boehme and Schelling overall elaborate a theogonic and erotic view of the divine, just enough superlative attributions are made of the archeological divine to suggest the possibility at least that its further manifestation can be interpreted as gift rather than the economy of need or necessity. I will, of course, determine in the analyses of specific kinds of discourses in the post-Reformation and post-Enlightenment Baurian field that the gift interpretation ultimately cannot be sustained. Unlike the exemplars of Neoplatonism such as Plotinus, Pseudo-Dionysius, and even Nicholas of Cusa, and unlike postmoderns such as Desmond, Marion, and Milbank, the agapaic quality of gift merely functions on the surface. It is interfered with and effectively enlisted by an erotic mechanism that abolishes the gratuity and sacrifice of giving.

The Kabbalah enacts two other stretchings of classical Valentinianism, although this does not amount to an infraction of Valentinian narrative grammar. First, the Adam Kadmon figure contributes to the blurring of the boundaries between theogony and anthropogony that is so evident in the narrative discourses of Blake, Hegel, and Schelling. Second, the Kabbalah helps significantly toward articulating a more than purely epistemological account of divine attributes, as well as offering something like a template for how Christians might lessen the gap between natural and revealed theology by articulating a particular view of the relation between sequences of divine attributes that parse the kind of modalistic Trinity that Altizer, as we have seen, celebrates.

Without explicitly invoking the Kabbalah in *The Heterodox Hegel*, I paid considerable attention to the way in which the relation between trinitarian articulation and the sequence of divine attributes parses the relation between revealed and natural theology. Hegel's surprisingly high estimate of the Kabbalah's articulation of divine names suggests the prospect that the Kabbalah is at least an element of Hegel's constructive view of attributes as an articulation of divine life. Oetinger serves as the exemplary eighteenth-century Pietist in his adoption of the Kabbalah as a speculative resource for Protestant thought. In his complex work the focus is on an elaboration of divine names that goes beyond that of rationalism and rationalist orthodoxy and that at the same time interconnects with a vitalist rehabilitation of the Trinity. But in the Protestant tradition the adoption of the Kabbalah goes back to Boehme, as does also the conjugation of a Kabbalistic understanding of divine names as dynamic powers and a vitalistic Trinity. Importantly, however, while the Kabbalah can be enlisted for a trinitarian purpose—and as a theologian I am particularly interested in this purpose—this need not be so. The enlisting of the Kabbalah, however, contributes in every case to the general theogonic dynamic of the divine. This is so in Blake, for instance, in whose prophetic poems the aboriginal divine sphere is more nearly quaternarian than trinitarian.[201]

In any event, like Neoplatonism and apocalyptic, the Kabbalah is a discursive presence in the Baurian line of modern narrative ontotheologies. As such, it is a narrative discourse that is enlistable, indeed actually enlisted by the Valentinian narrative grammar that gets enacted in these discourses. Needless to say, it is a more exigent presence in some of these discourses than others. In the next volume I will examine the discourse in the third line of Protestant thought where the Kabbalah's influence and effect is greatest, that is, the narrative discourse of Boehme. But this discourse is a presence also in the complex narrative ontotheologies of Schelling and Hegel, Moltmann and Altizer, and Blake. Of course, it is not the only non-Valentinian narrative strand, but one strand in a complex weave of non-Valentinian narrative discourses that are regulated by Valentinian narrative grammar. Singly and together these regulated narrative strands have effect on the regulating Valentinian discourse, and in fact assist in the constitution of gnoseologically exacerbated and theogonically focused forms of Valentinianism that are distinct from Valentinian productions in the Hellenistic field. Otherwise put, these non-Valentinian narrative strands assist in the formation and consolidation of a line of discourse that represent rule-governed deformations of classical Valentinian genres.

Summary

This chapter has two major foci. The first of these is the determination (5.2) that narrative ontotheologies in the Baurian field were legitimate expressions of Valentinian narrative grammar, but only as rule-governed deformations of classical Valentinian genres. That is, these narrative ontotheologies were regarded as legitimate Valentinian expressions only to the extent to which shifts in narrative emphasis from static to dynamic and from mythological to gnoseological register are understood to be radicalization of features that exist in a preformed stage in the classical Valentinian paradigms themselves, from which Valentinian narrative grammar is extracted. This chapter confirmed then what was hypothetically maintained in part 1 concerning the differences between modern and ancient forms. This chapter, however, not only brought in categorical verdicts about continuity and change in Valentinian narrative formation, it also deepened reflection on theogonic and gnoseological shift by specifying the general and particular elements of the former and by showing clearly how the shift of register from the explicitly mythological to the gnoseological does not abolish the underlying narrative ontotheological, or ontotheological narrative, commitment.

The second major focus of the chapter (5.3) concerned the perdurance, development, and exacerbation in narrative ontotheologies in the Baurian line of the kind of enlisting evident in classical Valentinian paradigms of non-Valentinian narrative discourses. As perdurance in the Baurian line was indicated by the enlisting of apocalyptic and Neoplatonic narrative discourses, both of which I showed in chapters 3 and 4 were enlisted in classical Valentinian genres, development was indicated by the enlisting of the post-Hellenistic discourse of the Kabbalah. And exacerbation was indicated by the intent and extent of enlisting. Exacerbation was the central concern because I continued to pursue the issue raised in part 1 about what distinguishes the modern genres of Valentinian narrative grammar from the ancient genres. I suggest that

Valentinian narrative masters each of these three narrative discourses as well as their weave, and confirms, and to some extent assists in the production of new, more theogonic, more erotic, and more agonistic forms of Valentinian narrative grammar.

Prefacing the two main foci was the attempt to provide warrants for the identification of the Baurian line as Protestant (5.1) that in part 1 functioned as an assumption. Taking off from Baur's judgment that unlike Reformation and post-Reformation Protestant thought, pre-Reformation Catholic thought shows no evidence of Gnostic return, I speculated as to what ideational conditions might be absent in Catholicism that are present in Protestantism for a metaleptic figuration of biblical narrative. I accepted the explanatory limits of the proposal, first by begging off accounting for the complex interrelation between ideational conditions and social, political, and economic conditions, and second, by excluding Eastern orthodox thought from consideration more on procedural than substantive grounds.

An important leitmotif in the chapter was the way the classical view of the Trinity, and not simply the biblical narrative, was affected by the modern genres of Valentinian narrative grammar. Herein I conclude that the theogonic erotic drift of these modern forms of Valentinianism subverted the classical distinction between the Trinity *in se* and its missions and that the subversion was attended by the affirmation of divine suffering that is repressed rather than excluded in the classical Valentinian paradigms. A new uniquely theogonic and agonistic version of Sabellianism is the upshot of this subversion. I also suggested that the general shift in Valentinian register affected trinitarian discourse that supports biblical narrative, since the agential reality and interdependence of divine persons is replaced by a Trinity that is little more than the triadic synopsis of an inclusive, and discursively complex, metaleptic narrative. This shift in turn supported the general Sabellian shift. And finally, I marked how the complex enlisting of non-Valentinian narrative discourses aided in the deformation of the classical view of the Trinity and the construction of a theogonic Sabellian *Ersatz*.

Conclusion

This book describes a movement from a defense of the principled intelligibility of Gnostic return and a presentation of the basic contours of a viable model (part I) to the assertion of its actuality and a categorical, as opposed to a merely hypothetical, deployment of the concepts of the model (part II). There is, then, in part II both a retracing of part I and a moving forward with respect to the selection of Baur as the best starting point for a Gnostic genealogy of modern discourses. It retraces part I in that it presupposes the narrative criterion of Gnosticism that was one of the hallmarks of Baur's analysis in *Die christliche Gnosis*, keeps in view Baur's own list of essentially Protestant modern suspects while extending and emending the list, and puts into critical play the concepts that were generated in conversation with Baur. It crucially moves forward, however, by indicating the nonnotional status of Valentinian narrative grammar, which it excavates from Valentinian narratives of the Hellenistic period. Availing of *PSY*, the *Gospel*, and the *Tractate* as three very different but equally comprehensive examples of widely varied Valentinian narrative production, Valentinian narrative grammar seemed justified as an explanatory construct that accounts for the diversity as well as the unity of Valentinian narratives within the Hellenistic field. If in part I I pointed to the theoretical difficulties of supposing a Valentinian *Urnarrative*, exegesis of classical Valentinian narratives drawn from Nag Hammadi and Irenaeus show the wrongheadedness of such an approach. But exegesis also confirms that despair over unity is not the responsible course. In and through the great differences between the three Valentinian narratives explicated, one could see that they obeyed the same rules of narrative construction. Each articulated in different ways a six-staged encompassing narrative that subverts each episode of the biblical narrative, and they cumulatively subvert the general meaning and function of biblical narrative. Each narrative was capable of triadic synopsis. Significant variety, however, was possible with respect to the details of the subversion of the biblical narrative, just as significant variation was possible with respect to whether the encompassing narrative is understood in a teleological (*Tractate*) or nonteleological way (*Gospel*), and presented in a mythological (*PSY*) or epistemological register (*Gospel*).

Of course, the excavation of Valentinian narrative grammar from Hellenistic texts also has genealogical pertinence, since there is no reason to limit the domain of the exercise of this narrative grammar to the Hellenistic field. On the basis of this nonnotional status of Valentinian narrative grammar, I argued to the reality of its modern instances. It is important, however, that we avoid thinking that Hellenistic Valentinian narratives simply represent a ladder to Valentinian narrative grammar that can be kicked away once the grammar is reached. Having the status of classic Valentinian genres, *PSY*, the *Gospel*, and the *Tractate* are genealogically relevant, serving as they do to set both general and specific baselines for assessing discontinuity and continuity between Valentinian paradigms of the Baurian and the Hellenistic field.

Categorical redemption of the primary concept of Valentinian narrative grammar (chaps. 3 and 4) in part II grounds the categorical redemption of most, if not all, of the other concepts deployed in part I. Only on the basis of the categorical redemption of the former is the categorical redemption of rule-governed deformation of classical Valentinian genres possible (5.2). Specifically, salient modes of deviance from classical Valentinian narratives by discourses in the Baurian field such as theogonic, erotic, and agonistic complexion in the narrative, and a general demythologizing tendency, are not regarded as constituting infractions of Valentinian narrative grammar (chap. 5.3). Indeed, these changes from, or wrought on, classical Valentinian narratives are preindicated in the classical genres themselves, since theogonic thrust, erotic development, and agonism, on the one hand, and demythologization, on the other, operate at a recessed level in these classical Valentinian genres themselves. Categorical redemption of rule-governed deformation of classical Valentinian genres is a necessity if we are to underscore, in a way Baur does not, the specificity and modernity of narratives in the Baurian line and their relative discontinuity as well as continuity with Valentinian narratives of the Hellenistic period.

Categorical redemption of the primary concept of Valentinian narrative grammar also enables a categorical redemption of the notion of enlisting non-Valentinian narrative discourses for Valentinian purposes. The subject was broached in part I as a way to affirm Baur's insight about the Gnostic character of a line of modern narrative discourses while paying respect to the discursive complexity of these narratives and the palpable presence of non-Valentinian narrative elements. For it is evident (chap. 3, and esp. chap. 4.2) that enlisting of non-Valentinian narrative discourses is a feature of Valentinian narrative grammar. I argued more specifically that, to the two narrative discourses typically enlisted by the classical Valentinian genres (i.e., apocalyptic and Neoplatonism), modern Valentinian genres add the narrative discourse of the Kabbalah. I argued also that the enlisting in the modern Baurian field of non-Valentinian narrative discourses was not only more complex because of the number of non-Valentinian narrative discourses enlisted, but also because of the extent and intent of the enlisting. All three non-Valentinian narrative discourses are more rather than less present than Neoplatonism and apocalyptic were in classical Valentinian genres, so that mastering all three suggests the greater integrating power of Valentinianism in the narrative ontotheologies in the Baurian field. At the same time, I showed that this greater integrating power is purchased at the price of systemic modifications of the regulating Valentinian narrative that, arguably, assists in the (self-)differentiation of modern forms of Valentinianism. As it helps toward accepting a nonnotional view of enlisting in general, categorical redemption of Valentinian narrative grammar specifically helps categorically to redeem *apocalyptic inscription* and *apocalyptic distention*, concepts introduced in part I as possible ways to account for the presence of apocalyptic elements in the complex narratives in the Baurian line that we considered candidates for *Valentinian* ascription, but that tempted the likes of Altizer to assert an *apocalyptic* ascription.

The categorical redemption of metalepsis closely attends the categorical redemption of Valentinian narrative grammar. In part I, metalepsis functioned merely hypothetically with respect to a particular band of modern narrative ontotheologies, a fundamental characteristic of which is a comprehensive disfiguration-refiguration of biblical narrative. Seeing how metalepsis is a feature of all three basic Valentinian paradigms (chap. 3) enables us to conclude that it is a basic element of Valentinian narrative grammar (chap. 4.1). Thus, no matter how disguised, metalepsis is a feature of narrative ontotheologies in the Baurian line that we regard as instances of Valentinian narrative grammar and, at the same time, rule-governed deformations of classical Valentinian genres. And in part II I bring out, in a way I do not in part I, that the metalepsis of biblical narrative, enacted in and by narrative ontotheologies in the Baurian line, is at once a metalepsis of a particular rendition of biblical narrative and a disfiguration-refiguration of biblical narrative grammar, the latter because the former (chap. 5.2).

A discussion on metalepsis provides the primary context for an appropriation and correction of Irenaeus with the aim of fashioning a figural Irenaeus. Irenaeus is the Christian thinker who has the clearest conceptual grasp of metalepsis as essentially consisting of a disfiguration-refiguration of biblical narrative. Moreover, in an interpretive move whose genius can be fully appreciated in light of the Nag Hammadi texts, Irenaeus indicates how disfiguration-refiguration of narrative has surface and depth narrative dimensions: On the surface the biblical narrative is disfigured and refigured by an inclusive narrative that moves from an archeological divine perfection to its reconstitution after the contingent mishap of a divine fall that brings the antidivine and/or the otherness of nature into existence. On the depth level, the biblical narrative is disfigured and refigured by an inclusive narrative where the divine perfection of omega is regarded as qualitatively superior to the divine perfection of alpha, and when it is understood teleologically to rehabilitate the accidental nature of fall and teleologically integrate the suffering attendant on the fall, thereby justifying both. A figural Irenaeus not only appreciates the doubleness of the Valentinian challenge, but also recognizes that in the modern period the challenge of the teleological rendition of inclusive metaleptic narrative will be much more to the fore.

Irenaeus is also the Christian thinker who first points to the aesthetic and fundamentally literary character of Valentinian production, the former in its emphasis in creative supermimesis, the latter in its wide, if not wild, improvisation on common themes. In suggesting the plural and varied nature of Gnostic and specifically Valentinian production, Irenaeus points toward a grammatical construal of Valentinian narrative. Unfortunately, Irenaeus is not quite as helpful on the biblical narrative front. Arguably overdetermined by his opposition to the perceived plurality and fertility of Valentinian production, Irenaeus is tempted to repress the dynamic and historical implications of the rule of faith to which he makes constant appeal and ignore his own act of interpretation.

The rule of faith thereby becomes a group of axiomatic theological presuppositions that articulates, more or less synoptically, the biblical narrative, or, rather a complex interaction between theological conclusions that set basic parameters, and principles for reading scripture and the salvation history story it narrates. However comprehensible Irenaeus's affirmation of an invariant biblical narrative is as a reaction-formation to Gnostic and Valentinian improvisation, it represents a blind spot that must be overcome if Irenaeus is to be of genealogical use. This essentially involves drawing out the dynamic and historical features latent in the rule of faith and conceiving of the rule of faith as setting forth essentially broad parameters for right belief and relatively permissive principles for interpreting the biblical narrative.

We can sum up this revisioning of Irenaeus by saying that we grammatically emend Irenaeus's view. Thus, we speak now not of an invariant biblical narrative, but of a biblical narrative grammar, not of an invariant interpretation of the biblical narrative but of a grammar of interpretation. Among its many benefits, a grammatical emendation of Irenaeus allows us to see that the challenge represented by Valentinianism in his day is the challenge presented by a different narrative grammar, indeed, an antigrammar that is both inside and outside and that his response ultimately is the assertion of a biblical narrative grammar. In addition, a grammatical emendation or refiguration of Irenaeus also allows us to understand that the battle between Valentinian and biblical narrative is always concrete and historically specific: The battle between grammars is always the battle between historically specific forms of both Valentinian and biblical narrative. This realization is of immense genealogical value because it reminds us that grammatical understanding of Valentinian and biblical narrative is respectful of the historical specificity of both the forms of Valentinian and biblical narrative and consequently of their agon.

The truly important issue as to what this biblical narrative grammar looks like is not dodged in my rehabilitation of Irenaeus's rule of faith (chap. 4.1). I give determinacy to the notion of biblical narrative grammar by speaking of it as a five-stage narrative that, if it sets constraints to parsing, does not compel any particular one. Irenaeus himself provides just one of the many permissible interpretations, even if his rendition has a certain classic status, as *PSY*, the *Gospel*, and the *Tractate* have with respect to Valentinian narrative grammar. Relative to my articulation of Valentinian narrative grammar my treatment of biblical narrative grammar is relatively cursory. In a sense, it serves as a kind of placeholder, something just good enough to make the point that symmetry applies between the case of Valentinianism and biblical Christianity, that if the former is a grammar, indeed a grammar of transformation, this implies that the biblical narrative transformed is also a grammar.

This refigured or figural Irenaeus can also say something to an attendant feature in Valentinian metalepsis of biblical narrative, that is, the deconstitution of the classical conception of the Trinity. Obviously, in *Against Heresies*, in his articulation of divine perfection as consisting exclusively of Father, Son, and Spirit, Irenaeus neither formulated a definite defense of the classical doctrine of the Trinity, nor critiqued Valentinianism for explicitly deforming it. Nicea is in the relatively distant future. Nevertheless, to the degree to which Irenaeus supports the purely agential character of Father, Son, and Spirit, and correlatively refutes the passivity of divine perfection that is an implicate at least of Valentinian depiction, even he, the most economic of trinitarians, proleptically supports a distinction between the Trinity *in se* and the trinitarian economy. The pressure to take this stance is his sense that, if not overtly, then covertly, Gnosticism in general, Valentinianism in particular, suggests that the hypostases and aeons that articulate divine perfection are subject to fall, fault, degradation, and suffering. What the historical Irenaeus asserts proleptically and vaguely as a general feature of Valentinianism, in a refigured or figural Irenaeus is asserted retrospectively and specifically. Against the backdrop of the classical Trinity, and its various renditions in the Christian tradition, and focusing on the narratives in the Baurian line, the figural Irenaean position is that the deconstitution of the classical Trinity is a general feature of Valentinian narrative grammar.

But, as I indicated more than once, I am in essential agreement with Altizer when he suggests that trinitarianism in the Baurian line is not only economic and agonistic, but kenotic (erotic) and modalistic. Again, while the historical Irenaeus does not make these accusations outright against Valentinian discourses, taking as both cue and clue Irenaeus's insight of the split level of Valentinian discourse, I suggested in my analysis of Valentinian narratives of the Hellenistic field that the multiplication of hypostases, and especially their nominalization and thus their essential substitutability effectively bleeds Father, Son, and Spirit of hypostatic density (chap. 3). In addition, the erotic and kenotic subtext of the relation between all hypostases in general, not excepting Father, Son, and Spirit, leaves room only for forms of divine identity that would exclude the tripersonality of the divine. What an analysis of the classical Valentinian texts suggests is possible trinitarianly is an kenotic and agonistic modalism or Sabellianism. What functions inchoately and preemptively in classical Valentinian genres with respect to the classical hypostatic understanding of the Trinity, functions explicitly in the narratives of the Baurian field that represent belated genres of Valentinian narrative grammar. The modernity of this variety of nonorthodox trinitarianism has to be granted. Indeed, granting that the modernity of this form of trinitarianism is one of the functions of a refigured Irenaeus or refigured Irenaeanism, nevertheless, its modernity is not a Blumenbergian novelty, but a repetition of a position virtually advanced in Irenaeus's encounters with second-century Valentinianism.

Assisting in the deconstitution of the classical Trinity in the modern instances of Valentinian narrative grammar is the enlisting of non-Valentinian discourses for Valentinian purposes. As I indicated in chapter 5, all three discourses enlisted serve the erotic, kenotic, and agonistic thrust of Valentinian narratives in the Baurian line. Thus, when the essentially Valentinian narrative is trinitarianly framed and landscaped, as it is in Boehme, Hegel, and Moltmann, these discourses do not protect a classical understanding of the Trinity, but subvert it. Perhaps of the three enlisted discourses, the behavior of Neoplatonism stands out. In classical forms of Christian Neoplatonism, whether Augustine or Gregory of Nyssa, Pseudo-Dionysius or Maximus the Confessor, St. Thomas or Bonaventure, the understanding that agape is the origin and end of all reality, and the understandings of providence as God's solicitude protect the Trinity *in se* from reduction to the economy. Enlisted, however, Neoplatonic agape subserves the eros of a Valentinian narrative of divine self-constitution, and providence ceases to be pure solicitude and becomes a means of such self-constitution. Nothing comparable in terms of actual effects of enlisting on trinitarian formulation is to be found in classical Valentinian genres. Differentiation then exists between the two fields of Valentinian paradigms and, therefore, something specifically modern about the role enlisting plays in the deconstitution of the classical Trinity. Still, I do want to underscore that classical Valentinian genres preclude, if they not exclude, the classical view of the Trinity and that the non-Valentinian discourses enlisted there, covertly at least, subserve a theogonic program that makes any formulation of a distinction between a Trinity *in se* and trinitarian economy unsuitable if not impossible. There is not so much a tripersonal divine origin and end, but rather a grammatical divine subject that in the narrative process becomes a real subject, that is, a complex, self-differentiated subject.

Part II circles back to part I and moves forward in another way when it submits to interrogation the Protestant identification of modern Valentinian discourses (chap. 5.1), which, on the authority of Baur, functioned more or less as an assumption throughout part I. Baur's fundamental insight that Gnostic return is a Protestant rather than Catholic phenomenon is sustained, but it is bolstered with arguments about the ideational conditions that promote Gnostic return or hinder it. I underscore, however, the very general nature of my account of ideational conditions—although these will be greatly supplemented when I discuss in detail in later volumes particular Valentinian discourses in the Baurian line. I further restrict the explanatory claims of my Gnostic return model when I limit its scope to Western forms of Christianity. At the same time, while judging that Catholicism in the post-Reformation and post-Enlightenment periods, as in the pre-Reformation period, precludes Gnostic return in a way that Protestantism does not, I do not necessarily rule out that these conditions might obtain in the future.

It is more a function of the genius of Baur's insights than the cogency of his arguments that I label *Baurian* the model of Gnostic return articulated first in its hypothetical (part I) and then in its categorical phase (part II). Construction of a viable model of Gnostic return has to return to Baur, the first genealogist of modern Gnosticism, if it is to have a possible future. The position of *Die christliche Gnosis*, however, must be submitted to considerable amplification and correction. The conceptual center of correction lies in a narrative grammar revisioning of Valentinianism, that (1) respects the differences between the classical Valentinian accounts as well as the differences between Valentinianism and Neoplatonism, on the one hand, and Valentinianism and Marcionism, on the other, and (2) allows for greater emphasis on the difference between modern Valentinian narratives and those of the Hellenistic period. An Irenaean emphasis on the metaleptic character of Valentinianism, specifically, the metaleptic character of Valentinian narrative grammar, supplements the grammatical reformulation of Baur's Gnostic return thesis, and provides evaluative edge to my analysis. This Irenaean edge became more evident in the movement from part I to part II. On the basis of chapters 4 and 5 I think it unproblematic to declare categorically that the model of Gnostic return proposed here is Baurian with an Irenaean twist.

The value of a conceptual scheme is proportionate to the interpretive work that it does. This introductory volume, however ambitious, is limited in its goals. Even in the more categorical part II, the Valentinian narrative grammar model cannot justify itself. And it cannot do so because it does not enter sufficiently deeply into the world of texts and assumptions of discourses in the Baurian line to persuade that the analysis is valid. This means that a significant amount of the argumentative burden is shifted onto the individual volumes of the genealogy that are intended to demonstrate, and not simply illustrate, the grammatical model of Gnostic return in the case of particular figures and specific kinds of narrative discourse. This is not an alibi for shirking the truly difficult work. The programmatic volume has significant burdens of its own, and these burderns are not simply methodological, although these indeed have been to the forefront. In chapter 2 in a preliminary way, and focally in chapter 5, I indicated the ways in which particular figures and discourses, which together constitute the third line of Protestant thought, exemplify Gnostic return in modernity. These indications were not only broad, they also were probative and anticipatory. They looked forward to their interpretive redemption in the more expansive environment of a multivolume genealogy in which claims of Gnostic return could be demonstrated.

My discussion of figures and forms of discourse as Gnostic or Valentinian was therefore both less than and more than illustrative. My discussion was less than illustrative, since in the absence of detailed exegesis one cannot be convinced that any discourse represents an instance of Valentinian narrative grammar. My discussion of figures and regions of discourse was more than illustrative in that it looked forward to full-scale treatment in which the Gnostic or Valentinian character of a particular discourse in the Baurian field is demonstrated. This demonstration must account for manifest differences between these post-Reformation and post-Enlightenment discourses and the classical Valentinian paradigms, and show the taxonomic and genealogical superiority of Valentinianism over rival taxonomic and genealogical accounts of narratives in modernity, especially of apocalyptic, Neoplatonism, and Kabbalah.

In the introduction I said much about the interests the Gnostic return project subserves. In chapter 4, in my discussion of Irenaeus in particular (chap. 4.1), I confessed to the evaluative tendency in my analysis. This book and the genealogy this methodological volume supports, and in turn is supported by, is much more than an exercise in the history of ideas. I wish to identify a line of narrative discourses in modernity of extraordinary power and attractiveness, proximally and approximately identified by Baur, with a view to breaking their spell. The enterprise is apotropaic through and through. The spell is broken in significant part by identifying the metaleptic inner workings of these discourses, by pointing to the haunting in their complex narrative confines of biblical narrative grammar by another and different grammar, a grammar of imitation, a metamorphic grammar.

I see this modern line of discourse as a fabulous catastrophe in a double sense. The catastrophe is fabulous in one sense in that the narrations are magnificent in their speculative adventurousness, in their aesthetic appeal that runs counter to the narrative contraction that goes hand in hand with Luther's theology of the cross and the narrative eclipse that is authorized by the Enlightenment; fabulous also in the way in which narrative discourses in the Baurian line function as alternative to both the dead letter of Christianity in the post-Reformation period and the death of Christianity in the post-Enlightenment period. But the catastrophe is fabulous in a second sense in that it is a catastrophe of fabula or narrative in which the biblical narrative is recalled for whatever lingering authority or aura it possesses, but its narrative is systematically disfigured and refigured into an encompassing narrative that makes a claim not only to truth but to its self-authentication. Interestingly, when Lyotard attacks metanarratives and sets the stage for Mark C. Taylor by linking Hegelian with biblical narrative,[202] it is this self-referring legitimating, or metalinguistic property rather than narrative scope, that ultimately defines what is wrong with the Western tradition. But if we are right, then it is Hegel and his precursors and successors in the Baurian line, and not the biblical narrative and its historical interpreters, who illustrate this metalinguistic property. This property belongs to Valentinian narrative grammar, and especially to those narrative discourses in the Baurian line that we are suggesting represent rule-governed deformations of classical Valentinian genres. It is this grammar that calls for correction and transcendence. Relative to these discourses, exemplars of biblical narrative grammar are always postmodern, always in another mode to the dissimulating narrative discourse whose discursive imprisoning and misprisoning is matched only by the legitimation of violence transacted in the narratives themselves.

Notes

Introduction

1. The rise of the history of religions school at the beginning of the twentieth century put the study of the texts of the first centuries of the common era on an entirely new level. The texts of the early Christian period were examined with much greater attention to detail both on the specifically historical and philological levels. In addition, definite identities of religious trends relevant to the study of the New Testament were marked out. Bultmann and even Harnack show an ability, simply unapproached by Baur, to distinguish between Hellenistic discourses. With respect to method and approach, then, Baur definitely belongs to an older and surpassed dispensation. The surge of interest in Gnosticism in the 1920s further left the Baurian dispensation behind, as Valentinianism was distinguished from Manichaeism and Mandaism, although for certain purposes (i.e., existential purposes) all of these discourses could be grouped together. This was certainly true of Bultmann's work on the Gospel of John, as it was true of the work of the early Hans Jonas. See his *Gnosis und spätantiker Geist*, vol. 1, *Die mythologische Gnosis* (Göttingen, Germany: Vandenhoeck and Ruprecht, 1934); vol. 2, *Von der Mythologie zur mystischen Philosophie* (Göttingen, Germany: Vandenhoeck and Ruprecht, 1954). Of course, in the wake of the Nag Hammadi discovery and the further leap in historical and philological finesse that encourages more microscopic analyses of texts and their historical and linguistic situations, not only do the specifics of Baur's views seem wrongheaded, but also the kind of grand genealogical enterprise represented by his work.

2. For a partial translation of *Die protestantische Theologie im 19. Jahrhundert*, see *From Rousseau to Ritschl* (London: SCM Press, 1959).

3. For a synoptic account of what Harnack calls a "critical reduction" of Christianity, see his *What Is Christianity?*, trans. Thomas Bailey Saunders, introd. Rudolph Bultmann (Philadelphia: Fortress Press, 1986), pp. 268–301.

4. Ferdinand Christian Baur, *Die christliche Gnosis: Oder, Die christliche Religions-philosophie in ihrer geschictlichen Entwiklung* (Tübingen, Germany: Osiander, 1835). One should note, however, that in Baur's later *The Church History of the First Three Centuries*, trans. Allan Menzies, 2 vols.; 3rd ed (London: Williams and Norgate, 1878–1879), Baur is treated as a historical phenomenon with no genealogical purchase.

5. Hans Frei, *The Eclipse of Biblical Narrative: A Study in Eighteenth and Nineteenth Century Hermeneutics* (New Haven, Conn.: Yale University Press, 1974).

6. See Frei, *The Eclipse of Biblical Narrative*, pp. 17–50. See also Frei, " 'Narrative' in Christian and Modern Reading," in *Theology in Dialogue: Essays in Conversation with George Lindbeck*, ed. Bruce D. Marshal (Notre Dame, Ind.: Notre Dame University Press, 1990), pp. 149–63.

7. The metaphor of "absorbing the world" to describe the power of scripture to interpret all of reality is coined by George Lindbeck rather than Hans Frei. It is, however, coined by him in a context in which there is significant dependence on Frei's account of how scripture functioned in the premodern period. See his *The Nature of Doctrine: Religion and Theology in a Postliberal Age* (Philadelphia: Westminster, 1984), p. 118. For an essay on this metaphor that supports the priority of the application of the biblical text and the necessity of resistance to the modern consensus that the biblical text must submit to independent criteria of meaning, meaningfulness, and truth, see Bruce D. Marshall, "Absorbing the World: Christianity and the Universe of Truth," in *Theology in Dialogue*, pp. 69–102.

8. See Thomas Altizer, *Genesis and Apocalypse: A Theological Voyage toward Authentic Christianity* (Louisville, Ky.: Westminster/John Knox, 1990; hereafter cited in text as *GA*), and *The Genesis of God: A Theological Genealogy* (Louisville, Ky.: Westminster/John Knox Press, 1993; hereafter cited in text as *GG*).

9. See Altizer, *Genesis and Apocalypse*, p. 108–9.

10. See Baur, *Die christliche Gnosis*, pp. 555 ff.

11. Richard Smith is a scholar of Gnosticism who has pointed to the elasticity of application of Gnostic to discourses of all types in the modern field with more than a little alarm. *Gnostic* attribution is made to the work of Blake, Hesse, even Melville, Jung, Hegel, and Marx, Enlightenment and anti-Enlightenment discourses, discourses within and without Protestantism. See Smith's Afterword, "The Modern Relevance of Gnosticism," in *The Nag Hammadi Library in English*, ed. James M. Robinson, rev. ed. (San Francisco, Calif.: Harper and Row, 1988), pp. 532–49. The list continues to grow. Thomas Pynchon is one of the latest additions. See Dwight Eddins, *The Gnostic Pynchon* (Bloomington, Ind.: Indiana University Press, 1990). A useful survey of some of the more reputable modern uses, including refer-

ences to Hesse and Jung, but without Smith's alarm, can be found in Giovanni Filoramo, *A History of Gnosticism*, trans. Anthony Alcock (Oxford, England: Blackwell, 1991), xiii–xviii.

12. Ioan P. Culianu, "The Gnostic Revenge: Gnosticism and Romantic Literature," in *Religionstheorie und Politische Theologie*, band 2, *Gnosis und Politik* (Munich, Germany: Wilhelm Fink/Ferdinand Schöningh, 1984), pp. 290–306, esp. p. 290. See also Culianu's *The Tree of Gnosis: Gnostic Mythology from Early Christianity to Modern Nihilism*, trans. Hilary Suzanne Wiesner and I. P. Culianu (San Francisco, Calif.: HarperSanFrancisco, 1992).

13. The elevation of impossibility is asserted in the context of Kierkegaard's reading of Abraham as the knight of faith in *Fear and Trembling* (Princeton, N.J.: Princeton University Press, 1941).

14. For Althusser's notion of *intervention*, see, in particular, *Lenin and Philosophy, and Other Essays*, trans. Ben Brewster (London: NLB, 1971), pp. 61, 105.

15. Michael Allen Williams is just one of the scholars of Gnosticism who complains about the general vagueness of definition. See his *Rethinking "Gnosticism": An Argument for Dismantling a Dubious Category* (Princeton, N.J.: Princeton University Press, 1996), pp. 1–3.

16. The deviance of these thinkers from Eastern orthodox thought is well established, although obviously the amount and kind of deviance is a variable. Bulgakov is clearly the least heterodox of these thinkers despite his commitment to a radical form of kenosis that challenges the patristic axiom of divine impassibility. Deviance from a confessional tradition, however, is hardly a sufficient condition for *Gnostic* attribution. But Soloviev and Berdyaev show significant dependence on Boehme, German Idealism, and/or Schelling. This dependence raises the question, therefore, in the event of a Gnostic judgment being rendered with respect to all three German discourses, whether it might not be rendered with respect to these Russian discourses.

17. See Czeslaw Milosz's fascinating account of Polish literature from the mid-nineteenth century in *The Land of Ulro*, trans. Louis Iribarne (New York: Farrar, Straus, Giroux, 1981). As the evocation of Blake's mythological counter for the chaotic material world indicates, Milosz is especially interested in poetry of a speculative and/or mythological vintage. Milosz finds the influence of the Kabbalah, Emanuel Swendenborg (1688–1772), Jacob Boehme (1575–1624), and his eighteenth-century French follower, Louis Claude de Saint-Martin (1743–1803), to run deep in this literature. Importantly, however, he denies that these esoteric influences justify a Gnostic labeling. Rather these influences dictate poetic articulations that are profoundly anti-Gnostic. Of course, the premise is that the Kabbalah as it

functions outside Judaism, the thought of Jacob Boehme and Swendenborg, and the thought of Blake, are themselves anti-Gnostic. One of the most interesting aspects of this book (see esp. Milosz, *The Land of Ulro*, pp. 155–82) is Milosz's spirited counterproposal to the view that "Blake was at heart a Valentinian Gnostic," attributed to an unnamed U.S. scholar who did not offer this judgment in print (Harold Bloom?); see p. 160.

18. A good representative of Genette's contribution to narratology is *Narrative Discourse: An Essay in Method*, trans. Jane E. Lewin (Ithaca, N.Y.: Cornell University Press, 1980).

19. See Harold Bloom, *The Flight to Lucifer: A Gnostic Fantasy* (New York: Farrar, Straus, Giroux, 1979); "Lying against Time: Gnosis, Poetry, Criticism," in *The Rediscovery of Gnosticism*, vol. 1, *The School of Valentinus*, ed. Bentley Layton (Leiden, The Netherlands: Brill, 1980), pp. 57–72; and *Agon: Towards a Theory of Revisionism* (London: Oxford University Press, 1975).

20. The Kant passage to which I am referring is, of course, the famous one in the introduction to *The Critique of Pure Reason* where, speaking of the a priori categories of understanding and the forms of intuition (space and time) as the coconditions of knowledge, Kant says that understanding without intuition is empty, intuition without understanding is blind.

21. See Jean-Paul Sartre, *Search for a Method*, trans. and introd. Hazel E. Barnes (New York: Knopf, 1963). I should point out, however, that "search" is not present in the French title, "Question de Méthode" (the prefatory essay in Sartre's *Critique de la raison dialectique*). Nonetheless, Sartre's synthetic-regressive method is a method that has to be sought because within history one seeks by regression in a holistic manner the conditions of unique events and unique subjects, that is, unique freedoms.

22. What is foremost in *Search for a Method* is a critique of scholastic Marxism with its economic reductionism and determinism. At the same time, *Search for a Method* espouses a view of method that is far from Husserl's "philosophy as a rigorous science," and Descartes's view of science as having an indubitable basis. Sartre is also taking his leave of an exclusive subjectivity orientation that haunts the existentialist phase of his work, which was crowned by *Being and Nothingness*.

23. See Jean-Paul Sartre, *Critique of Dialectical Reason: Theory of Practical Ensembles*, trans. Alan Sheridan-Smith, ed. Jonathan Rée (London: NLB, 1976), and *The Family Idiot: Gustave Flaubert, 1821–1857*, trans. Carol Cosman, 5 vols. (Chicago: University of Chicago Press, 1981–1993). *Search for a Method* is the prefatory essay for *Critique of Dialectical Reason*, and Sartre understands *The Family Idiot* to represent an illustration of the regressive synthetic method elaborated in *Search for a Method*.

24. The dependence of Comte de Lautréamont (Isidore Lucien Ducasse, 1846–1870), Georges Bataille, and Jean Genet on de Sade is well established. The text that definitively establishes the de Sade-Lautréamont relation is Maurice Blanchot's *Lautréamont et Sade* (Paris: Éditions de Minuit, 1963). The importance of de Sade for Bataille can be established on internal as well as external grounds. The relationship between evil and eros is the theme of almost all Bataille's novels. Moreover, Bataille explicitly reflects on de Sade's contribution to the thematics of evil in *Literature and Evil*, trans. Alastair Hamilton (New York: Marion Boyars, 1985), pp. 103–29. The very same thematic also defines the work of Genet. The case for the relation between Genet and de Sade has been made with unparalleled force by Philip Thody. See his *Jean Genet: A Study of His Novels and Plays* (New York: Stein and Day, 1969), pp. 25–44. Of course, this dependence on de Sade matters little from the point of view of Gnostic attribution unless a case can be made that de Sade's own work shows Gnostic allegiances. This is, indeed, precisely what is claimed by the great commentator on de Sade, Pierre Klossowski. See his *Sade, mon prochain* (Paris: du Seuil, 1947). See also his "Nature as Destructive Principle," which serves as one of the two introductions to *The 120 Days of Sodom and Other Writings*, trans. Austryn Wainhouse and Robert Seaver (New York: Grove Press, 1966), pp. 65–86. Needless to say, I am not claiming either that a case has been made that this represents a Gnostic line of thought or that a case can be made.

25. A Gnostic reading of a line of philosophical discourse from Descartes to Husserl would obviously depend upon highlighting the dualism between consciousness and bodiliness and making this anthropological-ontological split the criterion for ascribing the label of *Gnosticism*. On this criterion Sartre's account of the relation of consciousness to physical reality in *Being and Nothingness* could also be classed as providing evidence of Gnostic allegiance. Whether anything like such a criterion is adequate is discussed in part I.

26. Johann L. Mosheim offers a good example of this. See his *Institutionem historiae ecclesiasticae* (Helmstedt, Germany: C. F. Weygand, 1755). In fact Mosheim was preceded by Gottfried Arnold in drawing attention to heresiological thought. See his *Unparteiische Kirchen-und Ketzerhistorie* (Hildesheim, Germany: Olms, 1967). This text was originally published in 1697.

27. See Irenaeus, Against Heresies in *The Anti-Nicene Fathers*, vol. 9, ed. Allan Menzies (New York: Christian Literature, 1896). Irenaeus announces in the Preface of Book 2 that his aim is the detection (*detectionis*; Greek = *elenchos*) of Gnosis. But this is connected with the "overthrow" (*eversionis*; Greek = *anatropē*). If ultimately the overthrow consists in a positive articulation of the basics of Christian faith, already in a provisional way in the presentation of the Gnostic tradition that is the subject of Book 1, the overthrow is under way because the disguise of certain forms of

pseudo-Christian discourse is being removed. See especially, Irenaeus, *Against Heresies,* 1.11.1.

28. After his detection in Book 1, which suggests a huge variety of mythological material that bears on the salvation of selves and its increasing proliferation, Irenaus will recommend the safety of apostolic authority and the continuity of the rule of faith, which is at once the principle of tradition and the principle for the hermeneutics of biblical texts. See part II, chapter 4.1 following.

29. See Hans Urs von Balthasar, in particular, *The Glory of the Lord: A Theological Aesthetics*, vol. 1, *Seeing the Form*, trans. Erasmo Leiva-Merikakis, ed. Joseph Fessio and John Riches (San Francisco, Calif.: Ignatius Press, 1982).

30. According to Balthasar, Hegel is arguably the supreme example of a "metaphysics of spirit" in which the proper view of God, Christ, and their relation to human being is eclipsed. See Hans Urs von Balthasar, *The Glory of the Lord: A Theological Aesthetics*, vol. 5, *The Realm of Metaphysics in the Modern Age*, trans. Oliver Davies et al., ed. Brian McNeil and John Riches (San Francisco, Calif.: Ignatius Press, 1991), pp. 451–610; esp. pp. 572–90. Hegel is an even more important object of attack in *Theo-Drama*. Indeed, Hegel is Balthasar's major modern philosophical interlocutor in *Theo-Drama*, as Heidegger was in *The Glory of the Lord*. Balthasar's critique in volume 1 of Hegel's famous thesis about the death of art sets the stage for the later four volumes. See Hans Urs von Balthasar, *Theo-Drama: Theological Dramatic Theory*, vol. 1, *Prolegomena*, trans. Graham Harrison (San Francisco, Calif.: Ignatius Press, 1983), pp. 54–70.

31. See Marc C. Taylor, *Erring: A Postmodern A/theology* (Chicago: University of Chicago Press, 1984).

32. In the *Orator*, for example, Cicero distinguishes between low style (*genera tenue*), middle style (*genera medium*), and high style (*genera grande*), and recommends the middle style as the best and most persuasive. Augustine's *De doctrina christiana* is deeply indebted to this tradition of differentiation of styles as well as preference. For a good account of the importance of the distinction of styles, see George Alexander Kennedy, *Classical Rhetoric and Its Christian and Secular Tradition from Ancient to Modern Times* (Chapel Hill: University of North Carolina Press, 1980).

33. I speak in chapter 1 of Hegel's approval of the Gnosticism that he was aware of through its mediation in his contemporary, August Neander. Peter Hodgson notes this dependence in the English translation of volume 3 of the *Lectures in the Philosophy of Religion*, ed. Peter Hodgson, trans. R. F. Brown, P. C. Hodgson, and J. M. Steward (Berkeley: University of California Press, 1985), p. 84, note 71.

34. See, for example, Michel Foucault, *Power/Knowledge: Selected Interviews and Other Writings, 1972–1977* (New York: Routledge, Chap, and Hall, 1988). See also Michel Foucault, "The Subject and Power," in *Michel Foucault: Beyond Structuralism and Hermeneutics*, ed. Hubert L. Dreyfus and Paul Rabinow (Chicago: University of Chicago Press, 1982). For good discussions on Foucault's treatment of power in general and its relation to truth in particular, see Romand Coles, *Self/Power/Other: Political Theory and Dialogical Ethics* (Ithaca, N.Y.: Cornell University Press, 1992). For a good account of Foucault's mode of genealogy, see Michael Mahon, *Foucault's Nietzschean Genealogy: Truth, Power, and the Subject* (Albany: SUNY Press, 1992).

35. See especially Michel Foucault, *The Order of Things: An Archaeology of the Human Sciences* (New York: Random House, 1970).

36. In addition to G. A. Kennedy, *Classical Rhetoric and Its Christian and Secular Tradition from Ancient to Modern Times*, pp. 146–60, see Adolf Primmer, "The Function of the *genera dicendi* in *De doctrina christiana*," in *De doctrina christiana: A Classic of Western Culture*, ed. Duane W. W. Arnold and Pamela Bright (Notre Dame, Ind.: University of Notre Dame Press, 1995).

37. In Book 1 of *Against Heresies*, but especially 1.11.1, Irenaeus speaks of "adapting" (*metharmasas*) of Gnostic principles by the Christian school of Valentinus, seems to suggest something like a pre-Christian Gnosis. For a full account of what Irenaeus means and the plausibility of such a hypothesis, see Anne Marie McGuire, "Valentinus and the Gnostikē Haeresis: An Investigation of Valentinus's Position in the History of Gnosticism" (Ph.D. diss., Yale University, 1983).

38. See John Milbank, *Theology and Social Theory: Beyond Secular Reason* (Oxford, England: Blackwell, 1990), pp. 147–76, 189, 302, 311.

39. See Cyril O'Regan, *The Heterodox Hegel* (Albany: SUNY Press, 1994).

40. See O'Regan, *The Heterodox Hegel*, esp. pp. 60, 70, 93–94, 129–33, 138–39, 180–87, 222–31.

41. I address entitlements in chapter 1 when I ask whether an experiential or existential model for ascribing the term *gnostic* is methodologically sound.

Part I

1. The main text of Ferdinand Christian Baur in which the Gnostic return thesis is articulated is *Die christliche Gnosis*. Of supplementary importance is Baur's *Die christliche Lehre von der Dreieinigkeit und Menchwerdung Gottes in*

ihrer geschichtlichen Entwicklung, vol. 3, *Die neuere Geschichte des Dogma, von der Reformation bis in der neueste Zeit* (Tübingen, Germany: Osiander, 1843).

2. Among the many works in which Derrida attacks metanarratives, especially of the potent Hegelian vintage, see "Violence and Metaphysics: An Essay on the Thought of Emmanuel Levinas" and "From Restricted to General Economy: A Hegelianism without Reserve," in *Writing and Difference*, trans. and introd. Alan Bass (Chicago: University of Chicago Press, 1978), pp. 79–153, 251–77; "Différance," "The Pit and the Pyramid: Introduction to Hegel's Semiology," and "White Mythology: Metaphor in the Text of Philosophy," in *Margins of Philosophy*, trans. Alan Bass (Chicago: University of Chicago Press, 1982), pp. 1–27, 69–108, 207–71; *Glas*, trans. John P. Leavey and Richard Rand (Lincoln: University of Nebraska Press, 1986). For Jean François Lyotard, see *The Postmodern Condition: A Report on Knowledge*, trans. Geoff Bennington and Brian Massumi (Minneapolis: University of Minnesota Press, 1984), especially pp. 27–37; *The Postmodern Explained*, trans. ed. Julian Pefanis and Morgan Thomas, trans. Don Barry et al. (Minneapolis: University of Minnesota Press, 1993), esp. 17–37. As Bill Readings underscores in his chapter "Postmodernity and Narrative" (chap. 2), in *Introducing Lyotard: Art and Politics* (London: Routledge, 1991), pp. 53–85, what Lyotard is especially interested in contesting is the claim in metanarratives to put an end to the process of narration or narrative formation, thus its metalinguistic claim and/or its claim to be a form of knowledge or discourse that is in principle comprehensive, adequate, and thus irrefutable. Taylor's classic statement on the overcoming of the narrative or the book is still *Erring*, which combines Lyotardian *epochalism* with Derrida's view of the radical semiosis of texts.

3. The word *chaosmos* is a neologism coined by Umberto Eco to register the polyvalence and endless semiotic reference of modernist literary works, exemplary representatives of which are provided by Joyce, who ironically harks back to medieval aesthetic models, only to hollow out their implications. See his *The Aesthetics of Chaosmos: The Middle Ages of James Joyce* (Cambridge, Mass.: Harvard University Press, 1982). Nevertheless, Eco does not think that semiosis excludes in a binary fashion strands of narrative coherence in discourse.

4. *"Wegmarken"* supplies the title to one of the volumes (vol. 9) of Heidegger's *Gesamtausgabe* (Frankfurt, Germany: Vittorio Klostermann, 1975).

5. For examples of gnostic appelation in Voegelin's huge corpus see, among other texts, *Science, Politics, and Gnosticism: Two Essays* (Chicago: Regnery, 1968), pp. 40–44, 67–70; *New Science of Politics: An Introduction* (Baton Rouge: Louisiana State University Press, 1982), pp. 112–13, 124; *From Enlightenment to Revolution*, ed. John H. Hallowell (Durham, N.C.: Duke University Press, 1975), pp. 240–302; *Order and History*, vol. 4, *The Ecumenic Age* (Baton Rouge: Louisiana State University Press, 1974),

pp. 121–22; *Order and History*, vol. 5, *In Search of Order* (Baton Rouge: Louisiana State University Press, 1987), pp. 48–70; also *Published Essays, 1966–1985*, ed. with introd. Ellis Sandoz (Baton Rouge: Louisiana State University Press, 1990), pp. 293–303, 333–34; and *What Is History? And Other Late Unpublished Writings*, ed. with introd. Thomas A. Hollweck and Paul Caringella (Baton Rouge: Louisiana State University Press, 1990), pp. 143–44. Interestingly, Voegelin does appeal to the authority of Baur in a number of places. See, for example, *Order and History*, vol. 5, p. 53; "Response to Professor Altizer's 'A New History and a New but Ancient God,'" in *Published Essays*, pp. 292–303, esp. 296. Voegelin's discourse is self-consciously pathological. In texts in which it is suggested that Hegel is a Gnostic, Voegelin appeals explicitly to the language of pathology. See, for example, "The Eclipse of Reality," in *What Is History? And Other Late Unpublished Writings*, pp. 11–162, esp. 137–38, 158–62, where Hegel is accused of being schizoid and as having a pneumpathological ailment. From Voegelin's point of view, pathological characterization of thinkers is not an *argumentum ad hominen*, or if it is, it is an element of philosophical discipline. In a rich analysis of Plato's dialogues in *Order and History*, vol. 3, *Plato and Aristotle* (Baton Rouge: Louisiana State University Press, 1957), especially of the *Republic* and the *Gorgias*, Voegelin shows that Socrates is not simply rebutting the arguments of the Sophists but protesting against the state of their souls. Voegelin proves fairly persuasively that rhetorically the texts are structured in such a way to indicate that the real issue is existence rather than argument. Voegelin has been something of a lightning rod in political science and philosophy, and approbrium has been visited on his work from both quarters, as scholars have questioned his interpretation of Liberalism, Hegel and Marx, and Heidegger among others. But Voegelin is perhaps also the thinker who has most annoyed the specialists in Gnosticism, for he is often cited for illegitimate extension of the concept *Gnosticism* beyond the Hellenistic field.

6. *Demonologist* is the attribution provided Voegelin by Thomas Altizer in "The Theological Conflict between Strauss and Voegelin," in *Faith and Political Philosophy: The Correspondence between Leo Strauss and Eric Voegelin, 1934–1964*, trans. and ed. Peter Emberley and Barry Cooper (University Park, Pa.: Pennsylvania University Press, 1993), pp. 267–77, esp. p. 272. Altizer denies Gnostic attribution to modernity, and especially to Hegel, whom he agrees with Voegelin is the representative modern thinker. Altizer believes that not only is Voegelin wrong, but absolutely idiosyncratic in thinking of Hegel in this way. Altizer's judgment here is itself odd, given that Baur's nineteenth-century ascription is not a well-kept secret, even if Baur's texts have ceased to be read.

7. See Jacques Derrida, "Of an Apocalyptic Tone Newly Adopted in Philosophy," trans. John P. Leavey, in *Derrida and Negative Theology*, ed. Harold Coward and Toby Foshay (Albany: SUNY Press, 1992), pp. 25–71. The Kant text, which Derrida understands himself to be creatively repeating, is of

course Kant's broadside on enthusiasts such as Jacobi who believe that faith (*Glauben*) does not need to be regulated by knowledge (*Wissen*), that is, *Vom einem neuerdings erhobenen vornehmen Ton in der Philosophie*, in volume 8 of *Kant's gesammelte Schriften*, ed. Königlich Preussischen Akademie der Wissenschaften (Berlin: de Gruyter, 1923), pp. 387–406. For an English translation of this text, see "On a Newly Raised Superior Tone in Philosophy," trans. Peter Fenves, in *Raising the Tone of Philosophy: Late Essays by Immanuel Kant, Transformative Critique by Jacques Derrida*, ed. Peter Fenves (Baltimore, Md.: Johns Hopkins University Press, 1993).

8. Baur's later judgment of Gnosticism was somewhat more critical. Now Gnosticism is not regarded so much as the theological road less traveled so much as constituting a danger that Christianity should avoid just as much as overinstitutionalization. Authentic Christianity steers between pneumatic and institutional extremes. See especially *Das Christenthum und die christliche Kirche der drei ersten Jahrhunderte* (Tübingen, Germany: L. F. Fues, 1853), pp. 178–83, 185–88. For a good discussion of this and related points, see Peter C. Hodgson, *The Formation of Historical Theology: A Study of Ferdinand Christian Baur* (New York: Harper and Row, 1966), pp. 66–70. This shift in judgment toward Gnosticism went hand in hand with a cooling toward Hegelian-style historiography and a disenchantment with Hegel's view of God in history. Hegel's historiography was not sufficiently empirical and scientific, just as his view of the intimate relation between God and history tended to compromise both the independence of the divine and the human, but perhaps much more seriously the latter. For an indispensable discussion of all of these points, see Hodgson, *The Formation of Historical Theology*, pp. 37–38, 54–70, 131–41.

9. Arguably, there are two criteria for inclusion in the Gnostic return line operative in *Die christliche Gnosis*. The first and most obvious one—and this is the one agreed on by most critics—can be called the pneumatic or philosophy of religion criterion. Baur effectively points to a trajectory in modern Protestant thought that is pneumatic rather than institutional in orientation, and that whatever its express statements on the matter it remains open to philosophical influence, and thus represents a continuation of an ancient tradition in which religion and philosophy intersected rather than being contraries. When this criterion is in use, then including Luther and Schleiermacher with Boehme, Hegel, and Schelling makes sense. The second and narrower criterion is the narrative criterion. This means that what will ultimately define a specific trajectory in Protestant thought is its repetition of a dramatic narrative ontotheology that is the fruit of the theology-philosophy intersection. It is the narrower and more specific criterion, which is definitely called on less by Baur, that is truly genealogically useful.

10. Möhler's reading of Gnosticism antedates Baur's famous text that appeared in 1835. See his 1825 text, *Unity in the Church or the Principle of Catholicism: Presented in the Spirit of the Church Fathers of the First Three*

Centuries, ed. with trans. and introd. Peter C. Erb (Washington, D.C.: Catholic University of America Press, 1996). Heresy in general seems to be identified with Gnosticism of the first centuries on the grounds that Gnosticism is archetypal heresy (p. 288). Heresy and Gnosticism are fundamentally characterized by egotism (pp. 161, 164). Although Möhler scrupulously tends to avoid going beyond an anatomy of heresy, he does make a point that will be capitalized on later by Staudenmaier that the medieval heresy of the free spirit could be classed as a Gnostic survival or revival (pp. 152, 288). In the context of the definition and protection of orthodoxy that, from Möhler's point of view, involves the protection of the community basis and regulation of Christianity, Irenaeus is the truly central Church Father. It is he who distinguishes between true and false gnosis and who suggests what is psychically wrong with the Gnostic. The Gnostic is an egotist who is self-isolating and self-aggrandizing. In the same year in which *Die Einheit und der Kirche* was published, Möhler wrote a review essay on August Neander's "Antignostikos: Geist des Tertullians und Einleitung in dessen Schriften, mit archäologischen und dogmen-historischen Untersuchungen," in *Theologische Quartalschrift* 7 (1825): 646–64. This essay, as might be expected from *Unity in the Church*, was much more critical of Gnosticism and more in favor of the heresiologists than Neander, who, it happens, is Hegel's main source for Gnosticism and someone with whom Baur has to deal in his *Die christliche Gnosis* (1835). This was not the end of Möhler's engagement with Gnosticism. Six years later a short essay on the origins of Gnosticism appears. See "Versuch über den Ursprung des Gnosticismus," first published in *Beglückwünschung Dr. Gottlieb Jacob Plank* (Tübingen, Germany: 1831), reprinted in *Gesammelte Schriften und Aufsätze* ed. J. J. I. Döllinger, 2 vols. (Regensberg, Germany: Manz, 1839–1840), Vol. 1, pp. 403–35. Although more historical than systematic, Möhler does not repeal his essentially Irenaean judgment about the lack of community and ecclesial spirit in Gnosticism.

11. For Staudenmaier, see esp. his *Zum religiösen Frieden der Zukunft, mit Rücksicht auf die religiös-politische Aufgabe der Gegenwart*, 3 vols. (Tübingen, Germany: Minerva, 1846–1851). Volume 3 has "Gnosticism" in the title: *Die Grundfragen der Gegenwart, mit einer Entwicklungsgeschichte der antichristlichen Principien in intellectueller, religiöser, sittlicher und socialer Hinsicht, von den Zeiten den Gnosticismus an bis auf uns herab*. From a retrospective point of view we find both Baurian and Voegelinian elements of analysis. The Baurian features most apparent are the reading of the trajectory of modern Protestant thought being largely Gnostic (pp. 109–74), a theogonic characterization of this mode of thought (pp. 109–16), and the centrality of Hegel (pp. 360–67). The Voegelin feature most transparent is the preoccupation with the social consequences of thought, of Reformation and Hegelian thought indirectly, the former insofar as it gives way to the thought of the Enlightenment, which will a have major effect in the French Revolution, the latter insofar as it gives way to the Hegelian left wing with its call to praxis and social transformation whose issue is the revolution of

1848 in Germany. Irenaeus is called forth as an emblematic figure in resisting comprehensive accounts of reality (p. 415). The divine dimensions of reality are deeply mysterious and unnarratable (*innarabilis*) in the sense of an account that claims to be knowledge. Arguably Staudenmaier's Irenaean retrieval here presents a precedent for, although not the actual basis of, Voegelin's claim that a distinguishing feature of a Gnostic thinker such as Hegel is the manufacturing of a narrative or myth of a totalizing kind that functions as if it were irrefutable. See Voegelin, *Order and History*, vol. 5, pp. 50, 69; Voegelin, *Science, Politics, and Gnosticism*, pp. 41–42, 68; Voegelin, "On Hegel: A Study in Sorcery," in *Published Essays*, pp. 213–53, esp. pp. 216–18, 225–27; also Voegelin, "The Gospel and Culture," in *Published Essays*, pp. 172–212, esp. pp. 176–77; Voegelin, "Wisdom and the Magic of the Extreme," in *Published Essays*, pp. 315–75, esp. pp. 348, 370.

12. Scholars generally agree that not only in *Die christliche Gnosis* (1835), but also *Die christliche Lehre von der Versohnung* (1838) and *Die christliche Lehre von der Dreieinigkeit* (1841–1843), Baur was heavily influenced by Hegel. This is especially the case with *Die christliche Gnosis*. It is not simply that Hegel's work, above all this *Lectures in Philosophy of Religion*, is a subject of analysis in this early Baur work; it seems also to be the case that Hegel's *Lectures on the History of Philosophy* provide a genealogical template. For a succinct account of Hegel's early influence on Baur, see Hodgson, *The Formation of Historical Theology*, pp. 20–28.

13. For Hegel's reflection on Gnosticism and Neoplatonism, see *Lectures on the History of Philosophy*, vol. 2, trans. E. S. Haldane and Frances H. Simson (London: K. Paul, Trench, Trübner, 1892–1896; Lincoln: University of Nebraska Press, 1995), pp. 374–453. For Boehme, see *Lectures on History of Philosophy*, vol. 3, trans. E. S. Haldane and Frances H. Simson (London: K. Paul, Trench, Trübner, 1892–1896; Lincoln: University of Nebraska Press, 1995), pp. 188–216.

14. For Blumenberg, see esp. *The Legitimacy of the Modern Age*, trans. Robert M. Wallace (Cambridge, Mass.: MIT Press, 1983).

15. For instance, in *New Science of Politics*, Gnosticism is a category so broad that it includes the Puritans (pp. 136 ff). Again Voegelin offers insightful remarks into the dangers of Puritan thought, but the problem is whether the dangers of feeling chosen, with its colossal sense of entitlement and responsibility, amounts to Gnosticism.

16. This acknowledgment is, however, more implicit than explicit. As I have pointed out, in his *Lectures on the History of Philosophy* Hegel is extraordinarily positive about both Gnosticism and Boehme. In addition, throughout *Lectures on the Philosophy of Religion* in particular, the Gnostics and Boehme have a value that orthodox Christian forms of thought do not have. I have commented in detail on Hegel's allegiance to these forms of thought in *The Heterodox Hegel*.

17. Not only Lyotard and Derrida (see note 2), but also Adorno challenge Hegel on this point. See Theodor Adorno, *Negative Dialectics*, trans. E. B. Ashton (New York: Seabury Press, 1973). We find considerable overlap between Voegelin and these other critics of Hegel on this point. See note 5 for Voegelin.

18. Baur makes specific mention of Neander's *Genetische Entwickelung der vornehmsten gnostischen Systems* (Berlin: Dümmler, 1818). See Baur, *Die christliche Gnosis*, pp. 3–6.

19. Of course, as I have indicated (see note 9), this is not the only drift in *Die christliche Gnosis*. The other drift is a much broader drift of identifying *Gnosis* with pneumatic religion, which is open to both nonnarrative and narrative illustrations. It is the narrative drift in Baur or, otherwise put, his use of a narrative criterion for *Gnosis* and thus *Gnostic return* that I believe has genealogical pertinence. And it has such pertinence for the simple reason that narrative criterion is determinate in a way that the pneumatic and/or existential criterion is not.

20. For Staudenmaier's recapitulation of Baur's thesis, see *Zum religiösen Frieden der Zukunft*, pp. 109–74; for Balthasar's, see *Theo-Drama: Theological Dramatic Theory*, vol. 2, *The Dramatis Personae: Man in God*, trans. Graham Harrison (San Francisco, Calif.: Ignatius Press, 1990), pp. 409–23; also *Theo-Drama: Theological Dramatic Theory*, vol. 3, *Dramatis Personae: The Person in Christ*, trans. Graham Harrison (San Francisco, Calif.: Ignatius Press, 1992), p. 317.

21. See especially his essay "Delimitation of the Gnostic Phenomenon—Typological and Historical," in *The Origins of Gnosticism*, ed. U. Bianchi (Leiden, Germany: Brill, 1967), pp. 90–108.

22. These three interests often overlap in Bloom's multivalent texts. For instance, Bloom can offer an anatomy of certain discourses of the literary tradition (e.g., Romanticism) that involves description of interpretive practice and inference with respect to state of mind. And again, focusing on issues of interpretive practice, Bloom can speak to Gnostic state of mind and provide examples from the literary tradition where this is in evidence. An example of the latter is his essay, "Lying against Time: Gnosis, Poetry, Criticism," in *The Rediscovery of Gnosticism*, vol. 1, *The School of Valentinus*, pp. 57–72. Nevertheless, texts can be roughly categorized according to these interests. The clearest instance of (1) is undoubtedly *The Flight of Lucifer: A Gnostic Fantasy*. Examples of (2) include *Kabbalah and Criticism* (New York: Seabury Press, 1975), *Agon: Towards a Theory of Revisionism*, and *Ruin the Sacred Truths: Poetry and Belief from the Bible to the Present* (Cambridge, Mass.: Harvard University Press, 1989). Examples of (3) include *The American Religion: The Emergence of the Post-Christian Nation* (New York: Simon and Schuster, 1992); and *Omens of the Millennium* (New York: Riverhead, 1996).

23. The most important text in Jung's corpus from the point of view of a Gnostic return hypothesis is *Aion*, which explicitly explores Gnostic texts and remarks on their dreamlike clarity and power. See *The Collected Works of C. G. Jung*, ed. Herbert Read, Michael Fordham, and Gerhard Adler, vol. 9 (London: Routledge, Kegan Paul, 1957). Other texts that are important because they amplify various thematic elements such as the feminine and the negative, transformation (*enantiodromia*), and integration touched on in *Aion*, are *Mysterium Coniunctionis* and *Symbols of Transformation*, volumes 14 and 5, respectively, of *The Collected Works*. Perhaps the clearest statement of the value of Gnosticism and Jung's support for it is to be found in volume 6 of *The Collected Works*: "In Gnosticism we see man's unconscious psychology in full flower, almost perverse in its luxuriance; it contained the very thing that most strongly resisted the *regulae fidei*; that Promethean and creative spirit which will bow only to the individual soul and to no collective ruling. Although in crude form, we find in Gnosticism what was lacking in the centuries that followed: a belief in the efficacy of individual revelation and individual knowledge" (241–42). Also important, because they open up the question touched on by Voegelin, namely, the issue of the relationship between ancient Gnostic texts and the texts of the Renaissance magus tradition, are the volumes on Alchemy. See *Psychology and Alchemy* and *Alchemical Studies*, volumes 12 and 13 respectively of *The Collected Works*. The importance of Jung for the possibility of comprehending Gnosticism has been recognized by scholars of Gnosticism such as Gilles Quispel and Gerard Hanratty. See Quispel's "Jung und die Gnosis," in *Eranos Jahrbuch* 37 (1968): 277–98; also "Gnosis and Psychology," in *The Rediscovery of Gnosticism*, vol. 1, pp. 17–31. See also Gerard Hanratty, "The Gnostic Psychology of C. G Jung," in *Studies in Gnosticism and the Philosophy of Religion* (Dublin, Ireland: Four Courts Press, 1997), pp. 128–42; Dan Merkur, *Gnosis: An Esoteric Tradition of Mystical Visions and Unions* (Albany, N.Y.: SUNY Press, 1993), esp. pp. 49–54; June Singer, *Seeing through the Visible World: Jung, Gnosis, and Chaotic Systems* (San Francisco, Calif.: Harper and Row, 1990); and Robert A. Segal, "Jung and Gnosticism," in *Religion* 17 (1987): 301–36; and *The Gnostic Jung: Selected and Introduced*, ed. Robert A. Segal (Princeton, N.J.: Princeton University Press, 1992).

24. For Voegelin and the trope of *libido dominandi*, see among other texts, "On Hegel: A Study in Sorcery," in *Published Essays*, pp. 316, 318; and *Order and History*, vol. 4, pp. 260–66, where will to power is related in a Möhlerian way to egotism. Specifically, Voegelin speaks of the basic Gnostic tendency as being an "egophany."

25. See, among other texts, Voegelin, *Published Essays*, pp. 176–77, 216–18, 225–27, 348, 370; Voegelin, *The Collected Works of Eric Voegelin*, p. 156; Voegelin, *Order and History*, vol. 5, p. 64.

26. See Johann A. Möhler, *Unity in the Church*, pp. 161, 164.

27. To be fair to Voegelin, however, often he does much more than this. He analyzes symbols and makes arguments against the validity of totalizing discourses on grounds of coherence and ethics. These elements of Voegelin's thought are brought out by a follower of Voegelin such as David Walsh. See his *After Ideology: Recovering the Spiritual Foundations of Freedom* (San Francisco, Calif.: Harper and Row, 1990).

28. See Hans Urs von Balthasar, *Die Apokalypse der deutschen Seele: Studien zu einer Lehre von letzten Haltungen*, 3 vols. (Salzburg, Austria: Pustet, 1937–1939).

29. See Hans Urs von Balthasar, *The Glory of the Lord: A Theological Aesthetics*, vol. 2, *Studies in Theological Style: Clerical Styles*, trans. Andrew Louth, Francis McDonagh, and Brian McNeil; ed. John Riches (San Francisco, Calif.: Ignatius Press, 1984), pp. 31–94. See esp. pp. 38–39 where Hegel is associated with the Gnostics with whom Irenaeus does battle.

30. See Balthasar, *The Glory of the Lord*, vol. 1, pp. 49, 195. Arguably, in the second part of the trilogy, that is, *Theo-Drama* Balthasar is clearer about the Gnostic connection. In *The Glory of the Lord*, vol. 1, whether the Boehme-Hegel line represented the return of Neoplatonism or Gnosticism was not clear. See Balthasar, *Theo-Drama*, vol. 2, pp. 419–23; also Balthasar, *Theo-Drama*, vol. 3, p. 317.

31. See Balthasar, *Theo-Drama*, vol. 2, pp. 34–35, 255–64.

32. Gilles Quispel, *Die Gnosis als Weltreligion* (Zurich, Switzerland: Origo, 1951).

33. See Milbank, *Theology and Social Theory*, pp. 160, 170–72; David Walsh, *The Mysticism of Innerworldly Fulfillment: A Study of Jacob Boehme* (Gainsville: University Presses of Florida, 1983), pp. 63, 99 for explicit tie-ins with Hegel that are treated in extenso in Walsh's "The Esoteric Origins of Modern Ideological Thought" (Ph.D diss., University of Virginia, 1978); also "The Historical Dialectic of Spirit: Jacob Boehme's Influence on Hegel," in *History and System: Hegel's Philosophy of History*, ed. Robert L. Perkins (Albany: SUNY Press, 1984), pp. 15–35; O'Regan, *The Heterodox Hegel*, esp. pp. 151–56, 180–87, 221–31, 308–19.

34. In the case of Walsh, the sociopolitical emphasis is clearer in his *After Ideology* than it is in the Boehme book. But Baur's *Die christliche Gnosis* is acknowledged as a source for all attempts to think of discourses in the modern period being Gnostic. See *After Ideology*, p. 135, note 44. See also Gregor Sebba, "History, Modernity and Gnosticism," in *The Philosophy of Order: Essays on History, Consciousness and Politics*, ed. Peter J. Opitz and Gregor Sebba (Stuttgart, Germany: Klett-Cottal, 1981), pp. 190–241, esp. pp. 190–96.

35. Whether Baur is justified in associating Schleiermacher with Schelling and Hegel in a stronger sense is debatable, especially in light of

Baur's narrative criterion, and will be discussed in the Hegel volume in the genealogy.

36. Balthasar, *The Glory of the Lord*, vol. 1, 79–83, 87, 194; also *The Glory of the Lord*, vol. 5; for Schiller, see pp. 513–46, esp. pp. 515, 527, 542; for Hölderlin, see pp. 298–338.

37. The full title of this work is *Darstellung und Kritik des Hegelschen Systems: Aus dem Standpunkte der christlichen Philosophie* (Mainz, Germany: Kupferberg, 1844).

38. We will be treating this topic in extenso in a future volume. The Romantics most consistently labeled *Gnostic* are Blake and Shelley. In the case of the former, the label has been around since the beginning of the nineteenth century, but the issue has gained new prominence in the Bloom era of literary criticism.

39. I suggest that at this stage of his career Baur tends to accept Hegel's own view of his discourse as completing both philosophical and Christian thought. A transcending of Hegel's discourse, at least on its own terms, is not thought to be possible. In fact, this is a view that tends to be shared by both Hegel's supporters and detractors alike, with the supporters making appeal to Hegel's authority and the detractors suggesting new nonspeculative vistas to be explored in both theology and philosophy.

40. See Berdyaev's introductory essay, "Unground and Freedom," to the translation of Boehme's *Six Theosophic Points, and Other Writings*, trans. John R. Earle (New York: Knopf, 1920), v–xxxvii. Other texts of Berydaev of special importance because of their systematic character and their indebtedness to Boehme and Schelling, and to a somewhat lesser extent Hegel, are *Freedom and the Spirit*, trans. O. F. Clark (London: Bles, 1935); *Spirit and Reality*, trans. George Reavey (London: Bles, 1939); and *The Beginning and the End*, trans. R. M. French (London: Bles, 1952).

41. See Walter Kasper, *Das Absolute in der Geschichte: Philosophie und Theologie der Geschichte in der Spätphilosophie Schellings* (Mainz, Germany: Grünewald, 1965); Wolfhart Pannenberg, *Metaphysics and the Idea of God*, trans. Philip Clayton (Grand Rapids, Mich.: W. B. Eerdmans, 1990).

42. See, for instance, *Trinity and the Kingdom: The Doctrine of God*, trans. Margaret Kohl (San Francisco, Calif.: Harper and Row, 1981), pp. 203–22. Joachim is also a major presence in *History and the Triune God: Contributions to Trinitarian Theology*, trans. John Bowden (New York: Crossroad, 1992).

43. Henri de Lubac, *La postérité spirituelle de Joachim de Flore. 1: De Joachim à Schelling* (Paris: Lethielleux, 1979).

44. Both Voegelin and Staudenmaier tend to think of Hegel as both the end of a filiation of the apocalyptic of Joachim of Fiori and as the beginning of its practical political translation. For Staudenmaier, see *Zum religiösen Frieden der Zukunft*; for Voegelin, see *From Enlightenment to Revolution*, ed. John H. Hallowell (Durham, N.C.: Duke University Press, 1975), esp. pp. 240–320, where the Marx-Hegel relation is discussed; *Order and History*, vol. 4, p. 260; *Order and History*, vol. 5, p. 63; also "Wisdom and the Magic of the Extreme," in *Published Essays*, pp. 318–19, 370. For his followers, see Gregor Sebba, "History, Modernity and Gnosticism," in *The Philosophy of Order*, pp. 190–242, esp. 232; Hanratty, *Studies in Gnosticism and the Philosophy of Religion*, pp. 47–54; and Walsh, *After Ideology*, pp. 194, 108.

45. In *La postérité spirituelle de Joachim de Fiore*, vol. 2, de Lubac ranges wide and includes Fourier, Marx, and Compte in Joachim's trajectory. It is possible that here the value of de Lubac's analysis is less than it was in volume 1. Other scholars of Joachim such as Bernard McGinn would suggest that because the criteria for inclusion has become so general, de Lubac would be advised to change the adjective from *Joachimite* to *Joachite*.

46. Werner Beierwaltes, *Denken des Einen. Studien zur neuplatonischen Philosophie und ihrer Wirkungsgeschichte* (Frankfurt, Germany: Klostermann, 1985); and *Identität und Differenz* (Frankfurt, Germany: Klostermann, 1980).

47. Creuzer was the major disseminator of the classical Neoplatonism of Plotinus and Proclus at the end of the eighteenth century and beginning of the nineteenth. He was involved in conversation with Hegel and Schelling throughout his career, and his *Symbolik und Mythologie der alten Völker, besonders der Griechen* (Leipzig, Germany: Heyer und Leske, 1819–1823) was an important starting point for Schelling's *Philosophie der Mythologie* (1842).

48. See George Mills Harper, *The Neoplatonism of William Blake* (Chapel Hill: University of North Carolina Press, 1961); Kathleen Raine, *Blake and Tradition* (Princeton, N.J.: Princeton University Press, 1968); also her *Blake and the New Age* (London: Allen and Unwin, 1979).

49. Baur, *Die christliche Lehre von der Dreieinigkeit und Menchwerdung Gottes in ihrer geschichtlichen Entwicklung*, vol. 3.

50. Staudenmaier, *Die Philosophie des Christenthums, oder Metaphysik der heiligen Schrift als Lehre von den göttlichen Ideen und ihrer Entwicklung in Natur, Geist und Geschichte, Band 1: Lehre von der Idee* (Giessen: Minerva, 1840). Hegel (pp. 228–42, 798–810) and Schelling (pp. 176–226) represent the culmination of a movement in Platonism. Staudenmaier pays special attention to Philo as the thinker who blended together Platonism and scripture (pp. 361–439).

51. Speaking of Boehme, von Baader, and Hegel, Balthasar links the Kabbalah and Gnosticism as if they were the same thing: "In the context of Gnostic or Cabbalistic cosmogenesis and anthropogenesis of this kind, antiquity's 'reserve" in the face of the *theion* is lost, and the natural awareness of the *analogia entis* is weakened or entirely extinguished" (*Theo-Drama*, vol. 2, p. 420). For Milbank, see *Theology and Social Theory*, pp. 302.

52. See, among other texts, *Kabbalah and Criticism*; *The Breaking of the Vessels* (Chicago: University of Chicago Press, 1982); also *Gershom Scholem*, ed. with introd. Harold Bloom (New York: Chelsea House Publishers, 1987).

53. See *Lectures on the History of Philosophy*, vol. 2, pp. 394–96. For an account of how the Kabbalah functions in Hegel's own discourse, see Cyril O'Regan, "Hegel and Anti-Judaism: Narrative and the Inner Circulation of the Kabbalah," in *The Owl of Minerva* 28 (1997): 141–82, esp. 156–72, 178–82.

54. Ernst Benz, *The Mystical Sources of German Romantic Philosophy*, trans. Blair R. Reynolds and Eunice M. Paul (Allison Park, Pa: Pickwick Publications, 1983).

55. For Balthasar's reflections on the Kabbalah, see *Theo-Drama*, vol. 2, pp. 262–66. Interestingly, Balthasar also seems to confound Gnosticism and Kabbalah; see p. 420.

56. Johann Gottfried Herder, *God: Some Conversations*, trans. Frederick H. Burkhardt (New York: Veritas Press, 1940).

57. For Moltmann, see *Trinity and the Kingdom*, pp. 108–10; also *God in Creation: An Ecological Doctrine of Creation* (London: SCM Press, 1985), pp. 86–87.

58. In *Order and History*, vol. 4, Voegelin acknowledges the difficulty of associating *The Gospel of Truth* with Hegel and recognizes the symbolic and content discontinuities. What these are, however, is left unspecified. At the same time, Voegelin does not give up on continuity altogether, which is apparent in the following quotation that distinguishes the essential from the contingent elements of Gnosticism. He writes: "The essential core is the enterprise of returning the pneuma in man from the state of alienation in the cosmos to the divine pneuma of the Beyond through action based on knowledge" (p. 20). Again in his recall of Baur in *Order and History*, vol. 4, Voegelin suggests differences between classical Gnosticism and deviant forms of modern thought (p. 53), although here also he does not deny continuity. Similarly, in his engagement with Baur in his essay on Altizer, invoking "Gnosticism" as a category does not issue in a procrustean form of interpretation in which modern forms of thought are reduced to the narratives of the second and third centuries. Voegelin is aware of the post-

Enlightenment historical context and the actual influence of Neoplatonism and apocalyptic in the discourses of German Idealism. In his important essay, "History, Modernity, and Gnosticism," Gregor Sebba has argued that, unlike Baur, Voegelin did acknowledge discontinuity and argues for his superiority over Baur on this count. Indeed, in a real sense, Sebba argues, Voegelin does not offer a Gnostic genealogy, but an account of deformation in modern discourses for which apocalypticism is probably the most adequate concept. The connection between ancient Gnosticism and deviant forms of modern thought are at best analogical. Pheme Perkins argues a similar position in her essay "Gnosis and the Life of the Spirit: The Price of Pneumatic Order," in *Voegelin and the Theologian. Ten Studies in Interpretation*, ed. John Kirby and William M. Thompson (Lewiston, N.Y.: Mellen, 1983), pp. 222–39.

59. Of course, even in the case of Baur one might argue that his commitment to the post-Reformation trajectory in Christianity represents a commitment to a pneumatic and thus experiential form of Christianity.

60. This is not to say, however, with respect to Voegelin, that there is no emphasis on narrative structure. Especially when examining Hegel, Voegelin tends to emphasize that one of the major identifiers of Hegelian discourse is its repetition of a circular metanarrative that is typical of Hellenistic discourses such as Neoplatonism and Hermeticism.

61. By *apocalyptic* here I mean the second-order kind offered that devolves from Joachim de Fiore. Before de Lubac, Staudenmaier came to the conclusion that one of the ways in which Hegelian and post-Hegelian thought could be understood was as an extension and/or improvisation of Joachim. See Staudenmaier, *Zum Religiösen Frieden der Zukunft*, esp. vol. 3, pp. 116–37.

62. Jonas argues this position is his essay "The Gnostic Phenomenon." In *Glory of the Lord*, vol. 2, Balthasar suggests that the genius of Irenaeus's reading of the Gnostics is that he does not take their ontotheological commitments to be static and supportive of divine immutability and impassibility. The implications of their narratives go in a process direction in which one can more nearly talk of divine fullness or the pleroma being an eschatological rather than an archeological reality; see esp. pp. 38–39, 41, 58–60.

63. See Hegel, *Lectures on the History of Philosophy*, vol. 2, pp. 396–99.

64. In philosophy, the concept of *grammar* has been made popular by Wittgenstein and has been picked up by philosophers, social scientists (Peter Winch), and theologians. See *Philosophical Investigations*, trans. G. E. M. Anscome, 3rd ed. (New York: Harper and Row, 1969). Ferdinand de Saussure is at the source of another trajectory for the notion of grammar in his view of *langue*. See his *Course in General Linguistics*, ed. Charles Bally and Albert Sechehaye, trans. Wade Baskins (New York: Philosophical Library, 1959). In theology the notion of grammar has been especially fecund.

See in particular, George A. Lindbeck, *The Nature of Doctrine*, and Kathryn Tanner, "Theology and the Plain Sense," in *Scriptural Authority and Narrative Interpretation*, ed. Garrett Green (Oxford, England: Basil Blackwell, 1987), pp. 59–78.

65. See Paul Ricoeur, *Time and Narrative*, trans. Kathleen McLaughlin and David Pellauer, 3 vols. (Chicago: University of Chicago Press, 1984–1986), vol. 1, pp. 69–70.

66. We discuss this point in some detail in chapter 4.1 where Irenaeus's role in constructing a viable model of Gnostic return is our central topic.

67. Albert Franze provides the most comprehensive treatment of Staudenmaier's relation to Hegel, which was for the most part negative. See his *Glauben und Denken. Franz von Staudenmaiers Hegelkritik als Anfrage an das Selbstvertändnis heutiger Theologie* (Regensburg, Germany: Verlag Friedrich Pustet, 1983). The text that arguably most specifically links Hegel and Gnosticism is *Zum Religiösen Frieden der Zukunft*; see esp. vol. 3, pp. 45–174.

68. The achievements of *Time and Narrative* are manifold. For instance, in volume 1, part 2, and in volume 2, Ricoeur attempts to mediate a historiography committed to providing causal accounts of singularities and historiography of a narrativist bent. Sustaining the ambitions of neither exclusively, he suggests that narrativist historiography is of value, but it must beware its constructive tendency, be committed to the value of description of singularities, and scrupulously avoid making absolute claims to truth.

69. By *radical historicism* I mean forms of epistemology or historiography that deny continuity in history and question the truth-value of narrations, especially large-scale narrations of periods and the move from one period to another. Radical historicists attempt to be adequate to the contingent and the particular on what Mikael Bakthin calls the event quality of history. *Nonradical* here means not only being prepared to talk about larger patterns of discourse—as Blumenberg seems immensely comfortable in doing—but also being prepared to qualify in some way the discursive independence of the modern age.

70. David Walsh raises this question in his *After Ideology*. He suggests that the major achievement of *The Legitimacy of the Modern Age* is to forestall any monolithic applications of the secularization thesis. He thinks that Blumenberg goes too far in suggesting that no material relations whatsoever exist between modern positions such as progressivism and prior Christian construals such as eschatology (pp. 103–5).

71. Nicholas of Cusa is the other major figure in *The Legitimacy of the Modern Age*; see esp. pp. 457–547. Boehme is introduced into Blumenberg's genealogical discussion in *Work on Myth*, trans. Robert M. Wallace (Cam-

bridge, Mass.: MIT Press, 1985), pp. 529, 533, and 542, in the context of specific reflection on narrative discourses in modernity.

72. It is strange to say that Gnosticism "reoccupies" Neoplatonism because the classical Neoplatonism of Plotinus is a response to the presence of Gnosticism in the larger network of Platonic schools. One can, of course, speak of Gnosticism "reoccupying" Platonism because the Middle Platonism of Plutarch and Numenius among others shows similarities to Gnosticism, and Plotinus himself speaks about Gnosticizing interpretations of Plato. Moreover, given the prominence of the *Timaeus* in Middle Platonic and Gnostic discourses, both non-Valentinian and Valentinian, why cannot one talk about more than reoccupation, in fact about actual deformation? Similar criticisms are made of Blumenberg in Elizabeth Brient's dissertation "The Immanence of the Infinite: A Response to Blumenberg's Reading of Modernity" (Ph.D. diss., Yale University, 1995), pp. 32–33. In his *Neuplatonische und gnostische Weltablehnung in der Schule Plotins* (Berlin: de Gruyter, 1975), Elsas focuses on Plotinu's resistance to Gnostics whose beliefs and attitudes are similar to those of Numenius.

73. This criticism is also made by Brient, "The Immanence of the Infinite," pp. 43–44.

74. See Hans Jonas, *The Gnostic Religion: The Message of the Alien God and the Beginnings of Christianity*, rev. ed. (Boston: Beacon Press, 1963), p. 323.

75. I am speaking here of the later Jonas, with special reference to his essay "Delimitation of the Gnostic Phenomenon."

76. See "The Marriage of Heaven and Hell," in *Blake's Poetry and Designs*, ed. Mary Lynn Johnson and John E. Grant (New York: Norton, 1979), pp. 84–102, esp. p. 101.

77. See Karl Löwith, *From Hegel to Nietzsche: The Revolution in Nineteenth Century Thought*, trans. David E. Green (Garden City, N.Y.: Doubleday, 1967).

78. For the connection between Goethe and Boehme, see Blumenberg, *Work on Myth*, pp. 533–35.

79. For Blumenberg's interpretation of Schelling, see *Work on Myth*, pp. 554–56.

80. Here I am thinking of Hans Frei; see *The Eclipse of Biblical Narrative*.

81. See Eric Voegelin, *Anamnesis* (Notre Dame, Ind.: University of Notre Dame Press, 1978), p. 108. Voegelin is referring to Aristotle's discussion of metalepsis in the *Metaphysics*, 1072 b 20.

82. See, among other texts, Harold Bloom, *A Map of Misreading* (New York: Oxford University Press, 1975), pp. 102–3. Bloom's source is the rhetorician Quintilian rather than Aristotle, for whom metalepsis or *transumptio* means the taking of a figure from one place to another by means of an intermediary. I capitalize here on Quintilian's and Bloom's focus on transition. In my use of *metalepsis*, however, there is something actually carried across that ground: the haunting of a later discourse by an earlier.

83. For an English translation of this text, see *Attempt at a Critique of All Revelation*, trans. and introd. Garrett Green (Cambridge, England: Cambridge University Press, 1978).

84. In the interpretation of Schelling a number of periodization schemes have been employed, some quite complex. Here, I am simply distinguishing between the transcendental Idealist and/or Identity-Philosophie Schelling and the later Schelling who has taken a mythological and speculative realist turn. The text that marks the difference is the *Essay on Human Freedom* (1809), which is concerned with the becoming of the divine (theogony) and human being (anthropogony). I treat the essentially theogonic refiguring of the Christian narrative by Boehme in *Gnostic Apocalypse: Jacob Boehme's Haunted Narrative*. I plan to treat this topic in Schelling in extenso in a later volume in the series.

85. Commentators who suggest that this is the case for Boehme include Robert F. Brown and David Walsh. See Brown, *The Later Philosophy of Schelling: The Influence of Boehme on the Works of 1809–1815* (Lewisburg, Pa.: Bucknell University Press, 1977); Walsh, *The Mysticism of Innerworldly Fulfillment: A Study of Jacob Boehme*.

86. This is especially to the fore in *Philosophie der Offenbarung*, in which Schelling tries to show that although God is a God who becomes, the becoming of God involves no deficiency. We will address whether Schelling's aim to reconcile becoming with a divine freedom that is a plenitude while still being indeterminate is possible in a later volume.

87. Obviously, this definition takes seriously the Irenaean criterion about the closure or potential closure of the texts of revelation as being a condition of the assignation of scripture. This is, undoubtedly, a more restrictive and normative reading of scripture than would be embraced by some scholars. For a more inclusive and more sociologically inspired reading of what constitutes scripture, and what thus would legitimate the locution Gnostic scriptures, see Bentley Layton, *The Gnostic Scriptures* (New York: Doubleday, 1987). Layton writes: " '*Scripture*' ('writing')—in the general sense of the word—means a body of written religious literature that members of religion or group consider authoritative in matters such as belief, conduct, rhetoric, or the running of practical affairs. Scripture often contains a system of symbols within which readers can orient themselves, and make sense of their relationships to the world, the divine, and other people.

Such a system is sometimes expressed in story form and is then technically called *myth*" (p. xvii).

88. For an alternative view of Gnosticism as a nonmetaleptic discourse, see Michael Allen Williams, *Rethinking Gnosticism*, chap. 3, "Protest Exegesis: On Hermeneutical Problem Solving," pp. 54–78.

89. Harold Bloom, "Lying against Time," in *The Rediscovery of Gnosticism*, vol. 1, *The School of Valentinus*, ed. Bentley Layton (Leiden, Germany: 1980), pp. 57 ff. The fragment is fragment C, which I discuss in chapter 3 when I analyze the *Gospel of Truth*.

90. Here I am speaking especially of Irenaeus's suggestion that what the Gnostics do is alter the portrait of the divine, transforming that of the king into that of dog. The figure for such alteration is *metharmottein*. For a good account of this figure, which is somewhat static and plastic, see the dissertation of Anne McGuire, "Valentinus and the Gnostikē Haeresis," pp. 16–18. See also Rowan A. Greer, "The Dog and the Mushroom: Irenaeus's View of the Valentinians Assessed," in *The Rediscovery of Gnosticism*, vol. 1, pp. 146–75; and David Dawson's discussion of Valentinian hermeneutics in *Allegorical Readers and Cultural Revision in Ancient Alexandria* (Berkeley: University of California Press, 1992), pp. 127–82.

91. Blumenberg is clearly aware of Jonas's *Gnosis und spätantiker Geist*; see *The Legitimacy of the Modern Age*, p. 626, note 21.

92. This criticism is also made by Brient. See "The Immanence of the Infinite," pp. 34–35. At one point Blumenberg says interestingly that Marcion is not yet a Gnostic for he does not provide a total myth in which the God of Law and the creation is demonized (pp. 194–95). If there is a long heresiological history of linking Marcion and Valentinus (see *Against Heresies*, 2.31.1), there is also a tradition of separating them. See, for example, Harnack's *History of Dogma*, vol. 1, trans. Neil Buchanan (London: Williams and Norgate, 1905), pp. 223–86; also E. C. Blackman, *Marcion and His Influence* (London: SPCK, 1948), pp. 71, 82–87.

93. For a convenient English translation, see *Religion within the Limits of Reason Alone*, trans. Theodore M. Greene and Hoyt H. Hudson (New York: Harper and Row, 1960).

94. See Harnack, *History of Dogma*, vol. 1, pp. 267–86. The positive judgment about Marcion's evangelical probity, which distinguishes him from both Gnosticism and emerging orthodoxy as twin forms of the "hellenization of Christianity," is to the fore also in Harnack's famous text on Marcion, that is, *Marcion: Das Evangelium vom fremden Gott*. For a convenient English translation, see *Marcion: The Gospel of the Alien God*, trans. John E. Steely and Lyle D. Bierma (Durham, N.C.: Labyrinth Press, 1989).

95. See Baur, *Die christliche Gnosis*, pp. 626–68.

96. Friedrich Schleiermacher, *The Christian Faith*, trans. H. R. Mackintosh and J. S. Stewart (Philadelphia: Fortress Press, 1928). For Schleiermacher's reflections on creation, see part 1, pp. 131–256.

97. It is open to Blumenberg to claim, as in fact he does in *Work on Myth* (p. 130), that total myth functions to stop questioning rather than answer a conundrum. But here there seems, on the one hand, to be tension between what Blumenberg says with respect to the total myth within the Hellenistic environment and what he says about total myths in modernity. He seems prepared to accept that the modern forms have theodicy valence in a way Hellenistic total myth does not. But here Blumenberg has two problems. The first is that it is not clear whether Marcionism is made to stand proxy for Hellenistic total myth, which it is not in a position to do because as Blumenberg points out, Valentinian myth is more total than Marcionite myth. Second, it would seem to be the case that all total myths will foreclose questions peremptorily. It is the very nature of myth to offer a total narrative that is taken to be a total explanation, which total explanation can survive only in an environment of noncriticism. Blumenberg poses then a false either-or, that is, either preempting further questioning or offering a complete explanation. Rightly understood, myths offer total explanations while preempting criticism and forestalling alternatives.

98. For this point, see, for example, Balthasar, *Mysterium Paschale: The Mystery of Easter*, trans. and introd. Aidan Nichols (Edinburgh: T and T Clark, 1990), pp. 62–63. Balthasar is not perfectly consistent in his thinking. Sometimes he thinks that discourses of modernity such as Romanticism and Idealism show Valentinian traits—this is particularly so in the case of Hegel. On other occasions, he seems to suggest that Marcionism's uncoupling of the New Covenant from the Old Covenant provides a general mark of Gnosticism in the modern period.

99. Cited in Introduction note 8.

100. See Thomas Altizer, *The New Apocalypse: The Radical Christian Vision of William Blake* (East Lansing: Michigan State University Press, 1967).

101. In *GA* Altizer argues that Gnosticism is born with Christianity and represents not so much the latter's deformation as its self-caricature (pp. 82–83).

102. See Blumenberg, *The Legitimacy of the Modern Age*, p. 30.

103. The Hegelian and process theology evocations are unmistakable in this passage.

104. The latter, of course, was one of the major burdens of Altizer's book on Blake, *The New Apocalypse*; see esp. pp. 17–24.

105. See also Altizer, *GG*, p. 108.

106. I do not mean to deny that very different emphases cannot be found in the canonic tradition. One pole is defined by Augustine who takes the point of view of God, since he is interested in his justification. The other is defined by the fourth-century Greek father Gregory of Nyssa, whose point of view is human being and the opportunity the fall gives to growth in virtue and knowing.

107. See *GG*, pp. 64, 70, 108–9; *GA*, pp. 17, 19, 87–88.

108. See *GG*, pp. 111, 165–67, 173–74.

109. For recall of Joachim, see *GG*, p. 108.

110. These points have been made by a number of scholars of Joachim. See esp. Bernard McGinn, *The Calabrian Abbot: Joachim of Fiore in the History of Western Thought* (New York: Macmillan, 1985), pp. 161–203; also Winfried H. J. Schachten, *Ordo Salutis: Das Gesetz als Weise der Heilsvermittlung: Zur Kritik des hl. Thomas von Aquin an Joachim von Fiore* (Münster, Germany: Aschendorff, 1980), pp. 26–28; also *Trinitas et Tempora: Trinitätslehre und Geschichtsdenken Joachim von Fiore* (Freiburg, Switzerland: 1975).

111. *Distentio* translates the Greek *diastēma* or *diastasis*. For an emblematic expression, see *Enneads*, 3.7.

112. See Maurice Blanchot, *The Writing of the Disaster*, trans. Ann Smock (Lincoln: University of Nebraska Press, 1986). Playing with the Latin word for star, *aster*, Blanchot talks about and recommends a discourse that will swerve from the star as a point of orientation, thus a discourse that will not have a stable point of reference, especially narrative reference. The writing of disaster is a writing in excess of realistic narrative, a writing that is the very antithesis to the epic, especially as this epic form of narration is realized in the precincts of the philosophy of Hegel. As with other French thinkers such as Levinas and Derrida, the thinker to be dealt with is Hegel. For a good account of the relation between Blanchot and the narrative traditions with their commitment to a totality that from Blanchot's point of view must be breached, see Mark C. Taylor, *Altarity* (Chicago: University of Chicago Press, 1987), pp. 219–53.

113. See O'Regan, *The Heterodox Hegel*, 6.2, "The Genre of Hegelian Apocalypse," pp. 298–310.

114. See de Lubac, *La postérité spirituelle de Joachim de Flore*, vol. 1, p. 219.

115. I treat Boehme's apocalyptic commitment in particular detail in chapter 6 of *Gnostic Apocalypse: Jacob Boehme's Haunted Narrative* to be published in 2001 by SUNY Press, Albany, N.Y.

116. Joachim's commitment to symbols has been underscored by important scholars such as Marjorie Reeves and Bernard McGinn who reflect explicitly on his use of figure (*figurae*). For McGinn, see *The Calabrian Abbot*, chap. 3, "Joachim the Symbolist," pp. 101–22. A scholar who capitalizes on this point to show the difference as well as relation between Joachim and Hegel is Paul S. Miklowitz. See his *Metaphysics to Metafictions: Hegel, Nietzsche and the End of Philosophy* (Albany: SUNY Press, 1998), pp. 87–103. In calling Joachim's apocalyptic a form of *Gnosis*, arguably, Miklowitz does not distinguish sufficiently Joachim's form of thought from that of Valentinus (p. 88).

117. See Hans Urs von Balthasar, *Theo-Drama: Dramatic Theological Theory*, vol. 4, *The Action*, trans. Graham Harrison (San Francisco, Calif.: Ignatius Press, 1994), p. 458, note 2. For other places where Balthasar comments on the presence of Joachim in thinkers within the Baurian line, see *Theo-Drama*, vol. 4, pp. 425, 446; also *Theo-Drama*, vol. 3, pp. 400, 512. Interestingly, volume 4 is introduced by a section titled "Under the Sign of the Apocalypse."

118. See *Theo-Drama*, vol. 1, p. 119; *Theo-Drama*, vol. 2, pp. 419–23. Also on more specific points, see *Theo-Drama*, vol. 2, pp. 79, 83–88 (on Gnosticism's overcoming event and historicity); pp. 83, 119, 419 (priority of knowledge over faith); pp. 256–57, 261 (need in the divine); pp. 34–35, 53–57, 445, 452 (deformation of Christian discourse).

119. See also Blumenberg, *The Legitimacy of the Modern Age*, p. 130.

120. The comparison here is with Middle Platonists such as Albinus and Iamblichus. The definitive text on Middle Platonism still remains John Dillon's *The Middle Platonists: 80 B.C. to A.D. 220* (Ithaca, N.Y.: Cornell University Press, 1977).

121. Harold Bloom, "Lying against Time," p. 65; also *Kabbalah and Criticism*, pp. 62, 87.

122. Plotinus writes in *Enneads*, 2.9.6 about the Gnostics reading of Plato: ". . . where they differ, they are at full liberty to speak their minds, but not to procure assent for their own theories by flaying and flouting the Greeks: where they have a divergent theory to maintain they must establish it by its own merits, declaring their own opinions with courtesy and with philosophical method and stating the controverted opinion fairly; they must point their minds towards the truth and not haunt fame by insult, reviling and seeking in their own persons to replace men honoured by the fine intelligences of past ages" (Mckenna's translation, p. 138).

123. See Blumenberg, *The Legitimacy of the Modern Age*, pp. 76–81.

124. See *Timaeus*, 29E–30A.

125. Johannes Scotus Eriugena, *De divisione naturae*, ed. and trans. Sheldon Williams (Dublin: Institute of Advanced Studies, 1972).

126. This is, of course, the view that Blumenberg puts forward in *The Legitimacy of the Modern Age*. In an odd way this view is supported by the Idealists who are Blumenberg's express enemies at least on the historiographical front.

127. In his work on Eriugena that preceded *Die christliche Gnosis* (1835) by one year, Staudenmaier thinks of German Idealism as being more or less continuous with Eriugena. Though Staudenmaier has reservations about German Idealism at this point, they are nothing like they will be later, that is, in the post-1840 period. See his *Johannes Scotus Erigena und die Wissenschaft seiner Zeit* (Frankfurt, Germany: Andreäischen Buchhandlung, 1834), esp. pp. 38–39, 491. In his later *Die Philosophie des Christenthums* (1840), Staudenmaier thinks that, although the line between Eriugena and Hegel can be charted, Eriugena's *De divisione dei* can be read as a profoundly imaginative theological narrative that provides critical leverage with respect to modern theogonies that have their consummation in Hegel.

128. See Werner Beierwaltes, *Denken des Einen: Studien zur neuplatonishen Philosophie und ihrer Wirkungsgeschichte* (Frankfurt, Germany: Klostermann, 1985); *Identität und Differenz* (Frankfurt, Germany: Klostermann, 1980). See especially, "The Revaluation of John Scotus Eriugena in German Idealism," in *The Mind of Eriugena*, ed. John J. O'Meara and Ludwig Beiler (Dublin, Ireland: Irish University Press, 1973), pp. 190–98. For a scholar in the Beierwaltes line who elaborates at length on the relationship between Eriugena and German Idealism, see Dermot Moran, *The Philosophy of John Scotus Eriugena: A Study of Idealism in the Middle Ages* (Cambridge, England: Cambridge University Press, 1989).

129. See O'Regan, *The Heterodox Hegel*, pp. 101–6, 133–34, 174–80.

130. Hegel consistently underscores the trope of *Bonum diffusium sui* as a structural feature of Neoplatonic metaphysics. This means that the divine is defined as the thrust to communication and manifestation. See references to Hegel's support of this trope in *The Heterodox Hegel*, pp. 121, 124, 175, 217. By contrast, Hegel believes that Gnosticism on the surface at least is less committed to the self-manifesting and self-communicating nature of the divine. See Hegel, *Lectures on the Philosophy of Religion*, vol. 3 (1821 lectures), pp. 23–24. See O'Regan, *The Heterodox Hegel*, pp. 134–35.

131. See O'Regan, *The Heterodox Hegel*, pp. 319–27.

132. This was one of the most important points made in *The Heterodox Hegel*; see especially pp. 288–98.

133. For the concept of *overdetermination*, see Louis Althusser, *For Marx*, trans. Ben Brewster (London: Penguin Press, 1969), pp. 87–128.

134. The historiographic debate between the older school of Kabbalistic studies, represented by Scholem, and the newer school that has Moshe Idel as the most distinguished exponent, cannot simply be reduced to the conflict of interpretation between an extramural philosophical understanding that tends to reduce Kabbalah to its speculative content and a position that understands Kabbalah as a specifically Jewish discourse even in its more speculative moments wedded to Torah, liturgy, and the prayer life of the Jewish community. Scholem has important things to say about Jewish liturgy, and a central line in his thought is his elaboration of the mystical significance of the Torah. For the former, see esp. *Major Trends in Jewish Mysticism*, trans. Ralph Mannheim (New York: Schocken Books, 1969), pp. 118–57; for the latter, see pp. 32–86. Nevertheless, to some extent in his interpretation, Scholem tends to suggest that Torah and liturgy become something other than they are in the Jewish community as a whole. In particular, he underscores the distinction between the Torah and the mystical Torah, which is a purely speculative reality. This pneumatic, if not antinomian, tendency is brought out by both David Biale's and Harold Bloom's reading of Scholem's *Ten Unhistorical Aphorisms*. See David Biale, "Gershom Scholem's Ten Unhistorical Aphorisms on Kabbalah: Text and Commentary," in *Modern Critical Views: Gershom Scholem*, ed. and introd. Harold Bloom (New York: Chelsea House Publishers, 1987), pp. 199–223; also Bloom, "Scholem: Unhistorical or Jewish Gnosticism," pp. 207–20. Apart from calling for the historical specificity of Kabbalistic texts, Idel is concerned not to allow the kind of gap that he senses is present in Scholem to open up between Kabbalah and exoteric Judaism. For his most succinct expression of methodology, see *Kabbalah: New Perspectives* (New Haven, Conn.: Yale University Press, 1988), pp. 4 ff. In his introduction to the translation of Reuchlin's *De Arte Cabalistica*, although not making the point explicit, he tends to associate speculative reductions from whatever quarter with Christian adaptation of the Kabbalah. See *De Arte Cabalistica: On the Art of the Kabbalah*, trans. Martin and Sarah Goodman (Lincoln: University of Nebraska Press, 1983), v–xxlx.

135. See O'Regan, "Hegel and Anti-Judaism," pp. 156–64.

136. One might speculate that one of the reasons why Bloom can move so easily from a Valentinian to a Kabbalistic hermeneutic model is that in his view the Kabbalah repeats Gnosticism's metaleptic posture toward the biblical canon. But this is already to presuppose as normative what in effect is its discursive expropriation in Christian circles.

137. Aside altogether from the close relation of Neoplatonism and Kabbalah in the Christian Kabbalah of Florence, there is enough affinity between the classical Kabbalah of the *Zohar* for the question to arise whether

Kabbalah represents a species of Neoplatonism. From Scholem to Idel the answer has tended to be no, with the former emphasizing differences in the structure of emanation, which is their greatest commonality, and the latter pointing to the exegetical and biblical background of the Kabbalah. The relation between Kabbalah and Gnosticism has been just as burning an issue with the issue having genetic and systematic aspect. On the genetic side Scholem was the first to raise the question whether *Merkabah* mysticism, which lasted from the second century to the tenth century, with its high point between the sixth and seventh centuries, is not a proto-Gnosticism and thus a courier into the period of the *Sefer Yetzihar (Book of Creation)* and the somewhat later *Sefer ha-Bahir (Book of lights)*. See *Major Trends in Jewish Mysticism*, pp. 40–79; also *Jewish Gnosticism, Merkabah Mysticism, and Talmudic Tradition* (New York: Jewish Theological Seminary of America, 1960).

138. Scholars such as Scholem have commented on the similarities between the Kabbalah and Neoplatonism. Of course, even greater similarities are evident between Neoplatonism and the Christian Kabbalah. This should not be a surprise because during the Renaissance, Christian adaptation of Kabbalah took place by means of an essentially Neoplatonic modality of thought. Such is emblematically the case in Pico della Mirandola.

139. Bloom, "Lying against Time," p. 66.

Part II

1. The argument that Christian narrative grammar may be as generous grammatically as Valentinian narrative grammar does not mean that it is so for the same reasons. A license for improvisation is granted in Valentinianism that is not granted within mainline Christian communities of faith. Nonetheless, possibly because of its longevity and the sheer number of minds that the biblical narrative is refracted through, there is an astonishing variety of second-order renditions of the biblical narrative.

2. This charge of gnosis against Balthasar's work has been made by a theologian of the stature of Karl Rahner. By it Rahner does not intend to suggest that Balthasar's work is continuous with Gnosticism of the first centuries, but rather that his project is in line with that of Moltmann's depiction of a tragic God that ultimately harkens back to Hegel. Balthasar rejects the charge as early as 1966. See his *Cordula oder der Ernstfall* (Einsiedeln, Germany: Verlag, 1966). This charge continues to provoke Balthasar. See the introductory note to *Theo-Drama: Theological Dramatic Theory*, vol. 5, *The Last Act*, trans. Graham Harrison (San Francisco, Calif.: Ignatius Press, 1998), p. 13. The German text, *Theodramatik*, Vierter Band: *Die Endspiel*, was published in 1983. Another critic who moves close to calling

Balthasar a gnostic on the grounds of his association with Hegel is Ben Quash. See his " 'Between the Brutely Given, and the Brutally, Banally Free': Von Balthasar's Theology of Drama in Dialogue with Hegel," in *Modern Theology* 13 (1997): 293–318. See also Quash, "Drama at the Ends of Modernity," in *Balthasar at the End of Modernity*, ed. Lucy Gardiner, David Moss, Ben Quash, and Graham Ward (Edinburgh: T and T Clark, 1999), pp. 139–71.

3. See Hegel, *Lectures on the History of Philosophy*, vol. 2, pp. 394–96; and August Neander, *Genetische Entwickelung der vornehmsten gnostischen Systems*.

4. In introducing the category of Sethian Gnosticism as distinct from Valentinian Gnosticism, I am taking no stand with respect to genetic relation. I am not claiming for instance that Sethian Gnosticism is identical to the so-called Gnostics whom Irenaeus suggests are the precursors of Valentinians such as Ptolemaeus, although Irenaeus may be more reliable on these matter than his critics give him credit for. By *Sethian* I mean those texts in the Nag Hammadi Library that feature Seth as a figure of knowledge. These texts include *The Hypostasis of the Archons*, *Origin of the World*, *The Apocryphon of John*, *Trimorphic Protennoia*, and *The Three Steles of Seth*. Scholars of Gnosticism are divided on whether Sethianism constitutes a unitary literary phenomenon and thus is a distinct form of Gnosticism. Frederick Wisse takes a negative view, whereas Hans-Martin Schenke and Michel Tardieu take a positive view. See Wisse, "Stalking Those Elusive Sethians," in *The Rediscovery of Gnosticism: Proceedings from the International Conference on Gnosticism at Yale*, ed. Bentley Layton, 2 vols. (Leiden, Germany: Brill, 1981), vol. 2, pp. 563–76; Schenke, "The Phenomenon and Significance of Gnostic Sethianism," in *The Rediscovery of Gnosticism*, vol. 2, pp. 577 ff.; and Tardieu, "Les livres mis sous le nom de Seth et les Sethiens de l'hérésiologie," in *Gnosis and Gnosticism: Papers Read at the Seventh International Conference on Patristic Studies*, ed. Martin Krause (Leiden, Germany: Brill, 1977), pp. 204–10.

5. The contrast here is between a typological and a genetic version of Irenaeus's claim. For an exhaustive analysis of the claim made in *Against Heresies*, 1.11.1, see McGuire, "Valentinus and the Gnostikē Haeresis: An Investigation of Valentinus's Position in the History of Gnosticism" (Ph.D. diss., Yale University, 1983).

6. These contemporary commentators include Bentley Layton, Anne McGuire, and Kurt Rudolph. See Layton's Introduction to *The Gnostic Scriptures* (New York: Doubleday, 1987); McGuire, "Valentinus and the Gnostikē Hairesis"; and Rudolph, *Gnosis: The Nature and History of Gnosticism*, trans. Robert McLachlan Wilson (San Francisco, Calif.: Harper and Row, 1983).

7. Contemporary narrative theorists who have grasped this point well include Gérard Genette, Paul Ricoeur, and Hayden White. See Genette,

Narrative Discourse: An Essay in Method, trans. Jane E. Lewin (Ithaca, N.Y.: Cornell University Press, 1980); Ricoeur, *Time and Narrative*, trans. Kathleen McLaughlin and David Pellauer, 3 vols. (Chicago: University of Chicago Press, 1984); and White, "The Value of Narrativity in the Representation of Reality," in *On Narrative*, ed. W. J. T. Mitchell (Chicago: University of Chicago Press, 1981), pp. 1–28.

8. Balthasar makes this point in his essay on Irenaeus in *Glory of the Lord*, vol. 2. Jonas makes essentially the same point in his essay, "Delimitation of the Gnostic Phenomenon: Typological and Historical."

9. For an English translation, see Layton, *The Gnostic Scriptures*, pp. 281–302.

10. Examples include *The Hypostasis of the Archons*, *The Apocryphon of John*, and *The Origin of the World*.

11. This is the position, for instance, of Gilles Quispel, as it also seems to be the position reflected in the organization of Layton's *The Gnostic Scriptures*.

12. The hypothesis that has gained increasing acceptance is that Sethian Gnosticism, that is, those texts of Nag Hammadi in which the figure of Seth is prominent, seems determined by its anti-Jewish polemic. Scholars continue to disagree, however, about whether Sethian texts emerge from a group of heterodox Jews or a former Jewish group or from a non-Jewish group antagonistic toward Jewish religion in general. Gilles Quispel was perhaps the first major scholar who in the light of the Nag Hammadi discovery pointed to the Jewish context of non-Christian Gnosticism. See his "Der gnostische Anthropos und die jüdische Tradition," in *Eranos Jahrbuch* 22 (1953): 195–234, reprinted in *Gnostic Studies*, vol. 1 (Instanbul: Nederlands Historisch-Archaeologisch Instituut, 1974), pp. 172–95. Quispel has been adopted and modified by reputable scholars such as Alexander Böhlig, Nils A. Dahl, George McRae, and Birger A. Pearson. To a certain extent these scholars have revived a hypothesis that had considerable currency in the nineteenth century. See especially in this respect, Heinrich Hirsch Graetz, *Gnosticismus und Judenthum* (Krotoschin, Germany: Monasch und Sohn, 1846; reprinted Farnborough: Gregg International, 1971); also M. Friedländer, *Der vorchristliche jüdische Gnosticismus* (Göttigen, Germany: Vanderhoeck and Ruprecht, 1898; reprinted Farnborough: Gregg International, 1972).

13. Here *PSY*, arguably, is indicating an overdetermination of Gnostic, Platonic, and Christian influences and interests.

14. Although the author in passing evokes myriad New Testament passages and does not exclude either the Synoptics or Paul, it is John who is to

the forefront. 1.8.5, for instance, represents an extended commentary on the Johannine Prologue.

15. Here I am focusing on the curiosity of Eve that in the Hellenistic environment might well function in tandem with the myth of Pandora.

16. See Irenaeus, *Against Heresies*, 1.2.2, 1.2.5, 1.3.5, and 1.4.1.

17. Ptolemy's account is rigorously docetic. He elaborates an extrinsicist Christology in which the earthly Jesus and the divine Christ are two different realities (*Against Heresies*, 1.7.2). Only the former and not the latter can suffer. For a general discussion on doceticism in Valentinianism, see Simone Pétrement, *A Separate God: The Christian Origins of Gnosticism*, trans. Carol Harrison (San Francisco, Calif.: HarperSanFrancisco, 1990), pp. 144–56. Pétrement is of the opinion that the situation in Valentinianism is complicated with Valentinianism being neither univocally docetic nor nondocetic. Unfortunately, Pétrement does not make clear whether the undecidability arises because different texts take different positions or because the situation is complicated in all Valentinian texts.

18. There are different ways of dividing up the narrative. Bentley Layton in *The Gnostic Scriptures* (p. 13) thinks of the Valentinian narrative as consisting of four acts: (1) Expansion of solitary first principle into a divine spiritual realm; (2) creation of material universe; (3) creation of human being, and (4) history of the human race. Anne McGuire has a somewhat more complex narrative structure that takes into account the appearance of the Savior (Jesus Christ) and the eschatological event of the salvation of the human race. I am indebted in my own account to McGuire's narrative model in "Valentinus and the Gnostikē Hairesis."

19. Biblical narrative is always a function of interpretation, so in and of itself it does not provide a final court of appeal in a situation of conflict of interpretations. One can make a distinction, however, between first-order and second-order interpretation, where first-order interpretation adopts a fundamentally positive relation to Hebrew scriptures and its depiction of God, both his being and his rule, and accepts our dependent and our relatively lower situation—and not simply in light of some primal fall—and assimilates this in the light of the good news of redemption. Of course, this too is interpretation, indeed, one with a certain level of circularity, since the scripture, which is to norm theological practice, is already constituted as canon by interpretation. There is no way, then, of deciding neutrally between positions. The issues are whether Christianity is relatively continuous with Judaism, whether interpretation is more a community than an individual affair, and the degree of free play in interpretation. Irenaeus and Valentinus, and one will want to say Luther and Boehme, Bengel and Oetinger, Coleridge and Blake, Hamann and Hegel, Kierkegaard and Schelling, and Altizer and Balthasar divide in complex ways on these issues that later volumes on Gnostic return in modernity will unfold.

20. See Rowan Greer, "The Dog and the Mushrooms: Irenaeus's View of Gnosticism Assessed," in *The Rediscovery of Gnosticism*, vol. 1, pp. 146–73.

21. See Hegel's interpretation of Gnosticism in *Lectures on the History of Philosophy*, vol. 2, pp. 394–96, for a reading in which he announces that, correctly understood or translated, Gnosticism is less about mystery than manifestation, more about speech than silence.

22. I have nothing eccentric in mind. I simply mean to point out that one of the registers is that of *life*. Life will prove important in our genealogical investigations in subsequent volumes, especially in our studies of Boehme and Romanticism.

23. Here I touch upon a conundrum in Gnosticism that is echoed also in Neoplatonism and, as far as a thinker such as Rodolphe Gasché is concerned, is central in German Idealism. For the importance of this issue in a thinker such as Plotinus, see J. M. Rist, *Plotinus: The Road to Reality* (Cambridge: Cambridge University Press, 1967), pp. 38–64. For German Idealism, see Gasché, *The Tain of the Mirror: Derrida and the Philosophy of Reflection* (Cambridge, Mass.: Harvard University Press, 1986), esp. pp. 13–59. As we shall see in the first of the genealogical volumes, this is the case with Boehme also. One very interesting connection between Gnostic texts and Boehme and German Idealism is the role mirroring and reflection play in the articulation of the epistemological problem. It should be said, however, that the role of mirroring and reflection is greater in non-Valentinian Gnostic or Sethian texts than it is in Valentinian texts. See Francisco García Bazán, "The 'Second God'" in Gnosticism and Plotinus's Anti-Gnostic Polemic," trans. Winifrid T. Slater, in *Neoplatonism and Gnosticism*, ed. Richard T. Wallis and Jay Bregman (Albany, N.Y.: SUNY Press, 1992), pp. 55–83, esp. 72–75.

24. Blumenberg, *Work on Myth*, pp. 259–61.

25. See especially Kendrick Grobel, *The Gospel of Truth: A Valentinian Meditation on the Gospel* (New York: Abingdon Press, 1960); and Benoit Standaert, "L'Évangile de vérité: Critique et lecture," in *New Testament Studies* 22 (1975): 243–75.

26. See Standaert, "L'Évangile de vérité," p. 260. This point is also made by David Dawson in his chapter on Valentinus in *Allegorical Readers and Cultural Revision in Ancient Alexandria* (Berkeley: University of California Press, 1992), pp. 127–70.

27. This point is underscored by Grobel in particular. But see also Harold Attridge, "The Gospel of Truth as an Exoteric Text," in *Nag Hammadi, Gnosticism, and Early Christianity*, ed. Charles W. Hedrick and Robert Hodgson, Jr. (Peabody, Mass.: Hendrickson, 1986), pp. 239–55.

28. See William R. Schoedel, "Gnostic Monism and the Gospel of Truth," in *The Rediscovery of Gnosticism*, vol. 1, pp. 379–90; and "Typological Theology and Some Monistic Tendencies in Gnosticism," in *Essays on the Nag Hammadi Texts in Honour of Alexander Böhlig*, ed. Martin Krause (Leiden, Germany: Brill, 1972), pp. 88–108.

29. See Grobel, *The Gospel of Truth*, pp. 35, 55; also commentary by Harold W. Attridge and George McRae in *Nag Hammadi Codex I (The Jung Codex)*, 2 vols. (Leiden, Germany: Brill, 1985), vol. 2, pp. 39–135, esp. pp. 40, 53.

30. This point is made with particular force by Attridge and McRae in *Nag Hammadi Codex I*, vol. 2, p. 62.

31. That the philosophical frame of the *Gospel* is Platonic is agreed on by a significant number of commentators. Grobel, Schoedel, and Standaert, for example, all agree on this point, although different shades of opinion exist with respect to the issue of whether the frame behaves, or does not behave, in a determinative way. A comprehensive analysis of the Platonic horizon of the *Gospel* is provided by Cullen Story, *The Nature of Truth in the 'Gospel of Truth' and in the Writings of Justin Martyr* (Leiden, Germany: Brill, 1970), pp. 43–49.

32. Story, Schoedel, and Standaert are all in agreement here.

33. The work of Schoedel has been to the forefront here, but that there is a monistic bias in the *Gospel* represents something like a consensus view.

34. Attridge and McRae still espy in the *Gospel* the mythological tragic element of *PSY* that is presented in *Against Heresies*, 1.1.1–8. See *Nag Hammadi Codex I*, vol. 2, pp. 41–45. Attridge offers a similar reading in his essay, "The Gospel of Truth as an Exoteric Text," pp. 251 ff.

35. See especially Attridge and McRae, *Nag Hammadi Codex I*, vol. 2, p. 83; Grobel, *The Gospel of Truth*, p. 115; and J. E. Ménard, *L'Évangile de vérité* (Leiden, Germany: Brill, 1972), p. 134.

36. Attridge and McRae are emphatic on this point in *Nag Hammadi Codex I*.

37. The nondocetic nature of the *Gospel*'s christological reflection has been underscored by Attridge and McRae in *Nag Hammadi Codex I*, vol. 2, p. 60, and Ménard in *L'Évangile de vérité*, pp. 94 ff. This is also the opinion of S. Arai, who to date has written the most substantial account of the Christology of the *Gospel*. See *Die Christologie des Evangelium veritatis: Eine religionsgeschichtliche Untersuchung* (Leiden, Germany: Brill, 1964).

38. For this point, see Pheme Perkins, *The Gnostic Dialogue: The Early Church and the Crisis of Gnosticism* (New York: Paulist Press, 1980), pp. 177–90, esp. p. 187.

39. Layton offers convenient translation of fragment F in *The Gnostic Scriptures*, p. 239. Dawson makes much use of this passage for his interpretation of Valentinianism in his important *Allegorical Readers and Cultural Revision in Ancient Alexandria*.

40. See *Gospel*, 26.36, 27.4, 30.17.

41. The mystical thrust of the *Gospel* is underscored by Grobel and Story in particular.

42. At certain points, especially 25.6 and 25.19, the *Gospel* suggests that whoever has a revelation, and thus becomes enlightened, is proleptically integrated into the pleroma. Other Gnostic texts, however, seem to suggest that knowledge and liberation are possible only in the postmortem state.

43. More clearly than in *PSY* the gnostic does not simply have the hypostases of *Son* and *Church* as objects; the gnostic articulates them, especially the latter.

44. I am here recalling Dawson's interesting ascription of the *Gospel* in *Allegorical Readers and Cultural Revision in Ancient Alexandria*, chap. 3, pp. 127–70.

45. I am here availing of Layton's translation. See Layton, *The Gnostic Scriptures*, p. 235.

46. Again I depend on Layton's translation. See Layton, *The Gnostic Scriptures*, p. 237.

47. As is well known, *supermimesis* is a construct in Ricoeur's *Time and Narrative* to indicate the creativity of narrative discourse that fulfills its vocation to truth precisely in its surpassing of mimesis.

48. For a very interesting reading of the Son as speech from a Lacanian perspective, see Joel Fineman, "Gnosis and the Piety of Metaphor: The Gospel of Truth," in *The Rediscovery of Gnosticism*, vol. 1, pp. 289–318.

49. Even in texts in which the philosophical frame tends to be Platonic, one should not be surprised by the presence of Stoic vocabulary and ideas. In the early centuries of the common era, one cannot talk about a pure form of Platonism that rigorously excludes other philosophical species. Vocabularies and conceptualities are highly permeable. Stoic vocabulary is found in *PSY*. See *Against Heresies*, 1.8.5. See also *Against Heresies*, 1.14.2, where Irenaeus thinks of Marcus as having a seminal view of the aeons.

50. Perhaps the best account of the Platonism of the *Tractate* is provided by Peter Kenney. See his "The Platonism of the Tripartite Tractate," in *Neoplatonism and Gnosticism*, pp. 187–206.

51. For this point see the commentary on the *Tractate* by Harold Attridge and Elaine Pagels, in *Nag Hammadi Codex 1*, vol. 2, pp. 217–497, esp. p. 238.

52. Kenney and Attridge and Pagels have underscored this point. See especially Attridge and Pagels, *Nag Hammadi Codex I*, vol. 2, p. 236.

53. The raison d'être of the *Tractate*'s use of *unbegotten* is ready at hand. Obviously, in the world of assumption within which the text is written, *begotten* and *created* function as synonymous terms: thus to deny the attribution of the latter to the Son is to deny the former. This lack of distinction would tend to rule out a fourth-century dating of the text and place it decisively within the third century.

54. See Christopher G. Stead, "The Valentinian Myth of Sophia," in *Journal of Theological Studies* 20 (1969): 75–104.

55. See Attridge and Pagels, *Nag Hammadi Codex I*, vol. 2, p. 340.

56. The reference to *Jesus* at 117.12 constitutes an exception to the rule. In contrast, *Jesus* is a name widely used in the *Gospel*.

57. Here the *Tractate* corresponds to the *Gospel* (20.28–30). Both assume that the body and soul of the Savior figure are human and neither support *PSY*'s view of a psychic body.

58. The kenotic nature of the Christology is emphasized by Attridge and Pagels in their commentary; see *Nag Hammadi Codex I*, vol. 2, p. 436.

59. As Attridge and Pagels point out, reconciling the view articulated in the *Tractate* with the saved by nature view of Valentinian soteriology reported by the heresiologists is difficult; see *Nag Hammadi Codex I*, vol. 2, p. 446. Pagels also contests the view that the saved by nature view represents an accurate reflection of Valentinianism in *The Johannine Gospel in Gnostic Exegesis: Heracleon's Commentary on John* (Nashville, Tenn.: Abingdon Press, 1973), pp. 100, 110. See also Pétrement, *A Separate God*, pp. 189–200, for a questioning of the saved by nature view.

60. The free-will view is associated with Clement of Alexandria and Origen. Clement is especially important because his advocacy of free will seems to be directed against Gnostic groups. For good secondary material on Clement's anti-Gnosticism, see Elizabeth A. Clark, *Clement's Use of Aristotle: The Aristotelian Contribution to Clement of Alexandria's Refutation of Gnosticism* (New York: Mellen Press, 1977); William E. G. Floyd, *Clement of Alexandria's Treatment of the Problem of Evil* (London: Oxford University Press, 1971), pp. 281 ff; and Salvatore R. Lilla, *Clement of Alexandria: A Study in Christian Platonism and Gnosticism* (London: Oxford University Press, 1971).

61. "Noetics of space" recalls the French philosopher of science and symbol, Gaston Bachelard's, famous analysis of the poetics of space, that is, the way in which space is metaphorized outside the context of scientific discourse. See Gaston Bachelard, *The Poetics of Space*, trans. Maria Jolas (Boston: Beacon Press, 1969). Extrapolating from Bachelard's work, which primarily dealt with literature, one can say that in Gnostic systems soteriological estate tends to be spatialized on an up-and-down, or vertical, axis. Interestingly, the *Gospel* sometimes resists the dominant vertical axis in its perspectival rendering of salvation. In this respect it is very close to suggestions made by Plotinus about unity with the One, despite his articulation of a metaphysical hierarchy.

62. See especially *On the Making of Man*, in *Nicene and Post-Nicene Fathers*, vol. 5, *Gregory of Nyssa*, trans. William Moore and Henry Austin Wilson (Grand Rapids, Mich.: Eerdmans, 1892), pp. 387–427, esp. 411–14.

63. For a discussion of these narrative operations, see O'Regan, *The Heterodox Hegel*, pp. 9–11. *Prolepsis* and *analepsis* are constructs to the fore in the narrative theory of Gérard Genette. See especially *Narrative Discourse*, pp. 33–79.

64. It is important to point out that Jonas, who in "The Gnostic Phenomenon" supports a developmental interpretation of Valentinianism, even or especially taking into account the Nag Hammadi corpus, does not deny the functional importance of a distinction between two planes of reality, one characterized by stasis, the other by kinesis. For a splendid account of the function of this distinction, see Michael Williams, *The Immovable Race: A Gnostic Designation of the Theme of Stability in Late Antiquity* (Leiden, Germany: Brill, 1985). From Williams's point of view, to affirm the importance of this distinction is also to affirm the importance of the connection between Gnosticism and Platonism.

65. For Hegel, see *Lectures on History of Philosophy*, vol. 2, pp. 396–99, where the abyss of Basilides is regarded as more notional than real. Despite itself, the emphasis in Gnosticism seems to fall on the dynamic of manifestation rather than mystery understood in some entitative way. Here Blumenberg seems to support, after his own fashion, the Hegelian and Baurian reading. In *Work on Myth*, for example, on a number of occasions Blumenberg suggests a nonobvious pro-manifestation interpretation of Gnosticism. The break-up of the simplicity of the One by the not-One, he maintains, is inscribed in the One of Gnosticism from the beginning (p. 22). Perhaps even more interesting in the light of the high degree of *apophasis* present in Gnostic texts in general, and abundantly evident in the *Gospel* and the *Tractate*, is his suggestion that silence is systematically trumped by speech (pp. 199–201). Having particularly in mind the *Apocryphon of John*, Blumenberg generalizes that "from the nameless one there explodes a cataract of names, and from silence, a superabundance of loquacity" (p. 201). This

covert prioritization of manifestation and *kataphasis* over mystery and *apophasis* is also to the fore, he thinks, in Basilides's depiction of the movement from the One to the Trinity, for with this movement a story can be told, and what is at issue in the end is whether a story can be told or not (p. 260).

66. See Violet McDermot, "The Concept of 'Pleroma' in Gnosticism," in *Gnosis and Gnosticism: Papers Read at the Seventh International Conference on Patristic Studies*, ed. Martin Krause (Leiden, Germany: 1977), pp. 79–86.

67. Although she does not address the *Tractate* specifically, McDermot is anxious to underscore that this dynamic view of filling is expressed in Gnostic texts. Setting the precedent for David Dawson, she cites the *Gospel* as a particularly conspicuous example. See "The Concept of 'Pleroma' in Gnosticism," p. 79.

68. I realize the appearance of circularity here. Outright affirmation of the canon and thus biblical narrative is a result of contestation in the second century. To that extent the canon is, as Pagels would suggest, constructed. Yet even as constructed, there is a sense of the canon's traditionality and the narrative of salvation history functioning at least as an implicit norm.

69. Rowan Greer is the commentator who has paid most attention to the role the complaint of mushrooming plays in *Against Heresies*. See his "The Dog and the Mushrooms." In Greer's important article the emphasis falls on the prodigality of production and the temporary nature of what is produced. But, of course, symbolically, the symbol is overdetermined. Mushrooms also thrive in miasmal conditions and are essentially parasitic. It is the latter feature that establishes a line of connection between *mushroom* and *dog* as the inversion of *God*. A condition of the possibility of inversion is that Gnostic discourse is parasitic on a host biblical discourse.

70. Commentators on the *Gospel* with as different takes on the text such as Fineman, Grobel, Schoedel, Standaert, and Cullen Story have all pointed to the nonrealist epistemology that operates throughout.

71. See Blumenberg, *Work on Myth*, p. 260.

72. Although Balthasar spends considerable time critiquing Hegel as offering the quintessential form of modern Gnosticism, he realizes that Hegel is an advocate of the revealed or revelatory rather than the unknown God. For him, this simply means that there can be modes of Gnosticism, even Valentinianism, that are nonapophatic. However, he also thinks that there are forms of modern apophatic thought, which are speculative in nature such as that of Boehme and his successors, that are Gnostic or Valentinian in their basic drive. To the degree to which a discrimen for Valentinianism is suggested, theogony is to the fore. Admittedly, a discrimen is not always forthcoming, and thus Gnosticism and apophaticism are linked together without justification.

73. For a good account of the variety of allegorization, see Dawson's *Allegorical Readers and Cultural Revision in Ancient Alexandria*. Dawson shows superbly the differences between the allegorical modes of exegesis of Philo, Clement of Alexandria, and Valentinus.

74. To do justice to Voegelin, however, it is important to point out that when he analyzes modern varieties of thought that he deems to be Gnostic, he, despite his essentially psychological or pneumatological mode of analysis, does in fact engage in something like a narrative analysis. For instance, in his analysis of the French Encyclopedia he suggests that Gnosticism might help interpret it, for Gnosticism is committed to a narrative in much the same way as the Encyclopedia. See "Response to Professor Altizer's 'A New History and a New but Ancient God,' " in *Published Essays, 1966–1985*, ed. with intro. Ellis Sandoz (Baton Rouge: Louisiana University Press, 1987), pp. 296 ff. Similarly, when he discusses Hegel's version of the Encyclopedia—and Hegel is the consummate modern Gnostic—as in the case with the French Encyclopedia, the Hegelian Encyclopedia represents a teleological process of knowing. More, in its movement, Hegel's Encyclopedia renders a process in which the divine comes to full self-knowledge through the detour of human knowing. See Eric Voegelin, "The Gospel and Culture," pp. 154 ff.

75. Marcionite renditions of Christianity in the modern period, whether Romantic, Idealist, Liberal Protestant, or existentialist, simplify Christianity by determining that essential or authentic Christianity consists in the message of redemption as communicated by or about the founder of Christianity. Resistance here involves the refusal to separate the New Testament from the Hebrew Bible toward which it, obviously, bears an intratextual relation. Correlatively, it involves asserting that the God of Hebrew scriptures is the God of Jesus Christ. Resistance also involves refusing the tendency in the different species of modern thought toward the collapse of creation into redemption. By contrast, modern Valentinian renditions of Christianity insist upon the connection between the New Testament and Hebrew Scriptures, and thus insist on explaining the relationship between the God of Hebrew scriptures and both Jesus Christ and the God of Jesus Christ. Resisting Valentinian versions of Christianity in modernity involves denying the urge toward total explanatory adequacy that makes a theodicy of narrative, and a refusal to accept that Jesus Christ is the contrary to the Hebrew God who creates, judges, and institutes the law, and that the God of Jesus Christ is a God whose perfection greatly surpasses that of the God of Hebrew scriptures characterized by deficiency, ignorance, anxiety, and significant doses of jealousy and malice.

76. Kendrick Grobel in *The Gospel of Truth* suggests that, given the *Gospel* and especially Ptolemy's *Letter to Flora*, Irenaeus cannot be taken to be a reliable presenter of Valentinian thought; see esp. pp. 14–22.

77. As indicated in part 1, section 2, however, Blumenberg equivocates on this point. See esp. *Work on Myth*, pp. 76–81, 361, 365.

78. By foregrounding the Gospel of John I do not wish to suggest that Irenaeus neglects either Paul or the Synoptics. Given Irenaeus's view of the canon, it only makes sense that both play a prominent role. If the Gospel of John has any priority, it is because of its crucial role in establishing the relation of the Word and Christ to Father as the God depicted in Hebrew Scripture and the saving significance of Christ's death. Discussion of Irenaeus's citation of Paul, as well as the multiple ways in which Paul is assimilated into Irenaeus's biblical theology, have been constants in scholarship on Irenaeus since the mid-twentieth century. See John Lawson, *The Biblical Theology of Saint Irenaeus* (London: Epworth Press, 1948). By contrast, Irenaeus's use of the Synoptics, and the dependence of his theology upon it, has not been as widely recognized nor as widely commented on. Gustaf Wingren was one of the first scholars to point to the importance of the Synoptics. See his *Man and the Incarnation: A Study in the Biblical Theology of Irenaeus*, trans. Ross Mackenzie (Philadelphia: Muhlenberg Press, 1959), pp. xx–xxii. Much work has been done in this area over the last decade or so. The most significant monograph yet to appear is, arguably, D. Jeffrey Bingham's *Irenaeus' Use of Matthew's Gospel in Adversus Haereses* (Louvain: Peeters, 1998).

79. Even in a period of scholarship marked by greater acknowledgment of Irenaeus's general intellectual competence, very few commentators confuse Irenaeus with Plotinus. In accordance with his primary training, the mode of Irenaeus's refutation of Gnosticism is primarily rhetorical rather than philosophical in the strict sense. Irenaeus's dependence upon Hellenistic rhetorical traditions, and the kinds of rhetorical strategies he typically favors have been objects of discussion in the secondary material. See William R. Schoedel, "Philosophy and Rhetoric in the *Against Heresies* in Irenaeus," in *Vigiliae Christianae* 13 (1959): 22–32; also Pheme Perkins, "Irenaeus and the Gnostics: Rhetoric and Composition in *Against Heresies* Book One," in *Vigiliae Christianae* 30 (1976): 193–200. See also Gérard Vallée, *A Study in Anti-Gnostic Polemics: Irenaeus, Hippolytus, and Epiphanius* (Waterloo, Ontario: Wilfrid Laurier Press, 1981). Vallée's book provides a systematic first-order account of Irenaeus's rhetorical strategies. He does not trace these strategies back to Hellenistic rhetoric, anxious as he is to underscore how Irenaeus provides a template for later heresiological discourse. Vallée's book is also interesting in that it emphasizes the social interests that inform Irenaeus's rhetoric that issue in his support of a church with a strong central authority (pp. 23–30).

80. It is clear from *Against Heresies* that Irenaeus regards Valentinian aesthetics as pure artifice. If his support of the canon encourages a distinction between scripture and literature, his insistence that human beings are not the prime creators-preservers of the biblical canon solidifies the distinc-

tion. Although this suggests a nonliterary ethos for genuine Christians, Irenaeus is not prepared to confine Christians to the realm of the unaesthetic. For him, the biblical narrative renders a triune God who is comprehensively and radically aesthetic. This triune God creates, shapes, and moves a world toward its christological fulfillment. Irenaeus, then, opposes a properly Christian aesthetic to that offered by the Gnostics, and asserts the superiority of the former. Balthasar makes much of Irenaeus's aesthetic orientation and the structural opposition between Gnostic and properly Christian aesthetics. In *The Glory of the Lord*, vol. 2, he argues that Irenaeus provides an unsurpassable instance of a "theological aesthetics" by contrast with an "aesthetic theology," that is, a theology that subverts the properly christological and trinitarian center of Christianity.

81. That one of the fundamental issues revolves around the nature and limits of knowledge is indicated in the subtitle of Irenaeus's text, that is, "A Refutation and Subversion of Knowledge Falsely So-Called." Throughout, Irenaeus points to the incoherence (1.31.3), lack of reason (2.26.1), and absurdity (2.29.1–6) of Gnosticism. The problem lies with the illegitimate extensions of knowledge beyond its sphere. Knowledge is knowledge of and by a creature, which is always finite (2.28). Moreover, even as for creaturely knowledge, a fundamental difference exists between the knowledge possible eschatologically and the knowledge possible in the preeschatological state. Only in the former case is knowledge even relatively adequate.

82. Arguably, the most comprehensive reflection on the trinitarian thought of Irenaeus is offered by Jacques Fantino. See his *La théologie d'Irenée: lecture des Écritures en réponse a l'exégèse gnostique: une approache trinitaire* (Paris: Cerf, 1994).

83. See part I, note 64, where I refer to the work of George Lindbeck and Kathryn Tanner. In contrast to Lindbeck, Tanner would not necessarily see either Schleiermacher or Tillich as problematic from a grammatical point of view. She understands grammar in a less restrictive way than does Lindbeck and gives less priority to the sedimented tradition. There appears to be a move in Tanner's latest work to abandon the notion of a Christian theological and/or narrative grammar.

84. My way of framing the contrast here is in continuity with the way the contrast was framed by theologians of the nineteenth-century Catholic Tübingen School as they sought a third position. Although great differences exist between Möhler (see part I, note 10) and Johann Sebastian Drey, both desire a version of orthodoxy that is more plural and more dynamic historically than the rigid version of orthodoxy that is usually opposed to heresy. While Möhler, as is well known, becomes more conservative over time, his first major text, *Unity in the Church*, advocates this more plural and dynamic view of orthodoxy, even as it recalls the early church's defense of Christian faith against the corrosive of Gnosticism. For Drey, see his *Brief*

Introduction to the Study of Theology: With Reference to the Scientific Stand-point of the Catholic System, trans. Michael Himes (Notre Dame, Ind.: University of Notre Dame Press, 1994), #240, #256–60; pp. 11, 116–19. For a good discussion of Drey's rejection of the binary opposition of static orthodoxy and heterodoxy and his attempt to articulate a third option, see John E. Theil, *Imagination and Authority: Theological Authorship in the Modern Tradition* (Minneapolis, Minn.: Fortress Press, 1991), pp. 63–94.

85. I am thinking in particular of Elaine Pagels. See her "One God, One Bishop: The Politics of Monotheism," chap. 2, in *The Gnostic Gospels* (New York: Random, 1979), pp. 33–56.

86. Here I am in essential agreement with the reading of the rule of faith advanced by Mary Ann Donovan. See her *One Right Reading?: A Guide to Irenaeus* (Collegeville, Minn.: Liturgical Press, 1997), esp. pp. 11–20. A considerable amount of good work has been done on Irenaeus and the rule of faith. See among others, William R. Farmer, "Galatians and the Second Century Development of the *Regula Fidei*," in *Second Century* 4 (1984): 143–70; P. Hefner, "Theological Methodology and St. Irenaeus," in *Journal of Religion* 44 (1964): 294–308; and William Schoedel, "Theological Method in Irenaeus," in *Journal of Theological Studies* 35 (1984): 31–49.

87. See *On the Apostolic Preaching*, trans. and introd. John Behr (Crestwood, N.Y.: St. Vladimir's Seminary Press, 1997), #11 ff., pp. 46 ff.

88. See Donovan, *One Right Reading?*, pp. 11–14.

89. See *Paradise Lost* Bk. 1, Preface: Bk. 2, Preface, 150, 890; Bk. 3, 16 ff., 708 ff, in *Works of John Milton*, vol 11, ed. Frank Allen Patterson (New York: Columbia University Press, 1931). See also *On Christian Doctrine*, in *Works of John Milton*, vol 14, trans. Charles R. Sumner, ed. James Holly Hanford and Waldo Hilary Dunn (New York: Columbia University Press, 1933), 1.7.

90. Of course, it will not be rejected to the same extent in the Greek East. Gregory of Nyssa in the latter half of the fourth century will articulate a similar view and with a similar commitment to divine pedagogy. *On the Creation of Man* represents Gregory's classic expression of the increment involved in moving from the protological to the eschatological paradise. Obviously, the excess of eschatological paradise over the protological paradise suggests that fall is in a fundamental respect a felix culpa.

91. Clearly it does not serve Irenaeus's purpose in *Against Heresies* to intercallate angels or archons between the demiurge and the world and human beings. For this gives Gnostic speculators an opening to talk about the role the angels play in the creation of the world. This role will, of course, turn out to be mischievous.

92. One could say with a great deal of justification that *Paradise Lost* and the *Divine Comedy* provide the most significant and comprehensive narrative and iconic extension of the protological and the eschatological dimensions of the biblical narrative respectively.

93. A treatment of the rules of narrative and iconic extension that provides the full lists and offers a justification for their operative reality in both *Paradise Lost* and *Paradise Regained* must await my volume on Romanticism and Gnostic return. These rules will be described in detail especially in the context of my treatment of the difference between Milton and Blake. But I can at least mention the following as applying: (1) Figuration of the divine that goes beyond that given explicitly in the biblical text should be emphatic about divine goodness. (2) Any figuration of creation, whether of angels or human beings, should recognize creation's aboriginal goodness. (3) All figuration of creation should recognize the ontological difference between creator and creature. (4) In any figuration of creaturehood, the dominant notes should be filial obedience, gratitude, and praise.

94. See note 85.

95. Although scholars recognize that Irenaeus based his symbol of *anakephalaiōsis* on a well-established typological connection, they also suggest that his privileging of this type-antitype is a creative act. This is the opinion of Lawson in his *The Biblical Theology of Saint Irenaeus*, as well as Balthasar in *Glory of the Lord*, vol. 2, pp. 51–53.

96. For an emphatic commitment to the theme of Christ as dramatic victor, see *Against Heresies*, 3.18–19. In my comparisons between Irenaeus and Tertullian, on the one hand, and Irenaeus and Anselm, on the other, I am obviously evoking Gustav Aulén's famous text, *Christus Victor: An Historical Study of the Three Main Types of the Idea of Atonement*, trans. A. G. Hebert, introd. Jaroslav Pelikan (New York: Macmillan, 1969). I recall these contrasts more for their pragmatic than theoretical value and believe that the lines in most cases cannot be as clearly drawn as Aulén suggests. For instance, Luther, who is supposed to represent the dramatic or mythological view, borrows heavily from the two juridical traditions. In addition, Balthasar, who in his fight against what he takes to be modern Gnosticism, reprises Irenaeus, and elaborates a theology of paschal mystery that owes an obvious debt to Irenaeus, nevertheless feels that he can equally call on Anselm to help him construct a viable soteriology. See *Theo-Drama: Theological Dramatic Theory*, vol. 4, *The Action*, trans. Graham Harrison (San Francisco, Calif.: Ignatius Press, 1994), pp. 231–423.

97. In making this connection, Baur has in mind the precedent of Hegel in *Lectures on the History of Philosophy*, vol. 2, pp. 374–453, where he puts the classical Neoplatonism of Plotinus and Proclus and Gnosticism under a general umbrella of *Neoplatonism*. Neoplatonism comes to function as a rubric for different forms of thought, from different historical periods—

Hegel also includes the Kabbalah—that have in common a narrative of divine development.

98. In addition to Elsas's work, cited in part 1, note 72, see H. C. Puech, *En quête de la gnose*, 2 vols. (Paris: Gallimard, 1978), vol. 1, pp. 25–54; also Richard T. Wallace, "The Soul and the Nous in Plotinus, Numenius, and Gnosticism," in *Neoplatonism and Gnosticism*, pp. 461–82.

99. For this point, see among others A. H. Armstrong, "Dualism: Platonic, Gnostic, and Christian," in *Neoplatonism and Gnosticism*, pp. 33–52.

100. For a good account of the relation between these texts and Platonism of the second century, see John D. Turner, "Gnosticism and Platonism: The Platonizing Sethian Texts from Nag Hammadi in their Relation to Later Platonic Literature," in *Neoplatonism and Gnosticism*, pp. 425–59.

101. See especially John Dillon, "The Descent of the Soul in Middle Platonism and Gnostic Theory," in *The Rediscovery of Gnosticism*, vol. 1, pp. 357–64; and Bazán, "The 'Second God' in Gnosticism and Plotinus's Anti-Gnostic Polemic," in *Neoplatonism and Gnosticism*, pp. 55–83.

102. This is not to say, however, that no Stoic elements are present in Valentinian texts. We have seen in the *Gospel* and the *Tractate* that the idea of *logos spermatikos* plays a significant role. John Dillon makes note of this borrowing in "Pleroma and Noetic Cosmos: A Comparative Study," in *Neoplatonism and Gnosticism*, pp. 99–110, esp. pp. 100–102. Also, it is important to observe that second-century Middle Platonism is far from pure and has incorporated a number of Stoic features. Dillon underscores this point in his magesterial *The Middle Platonists: 80 B.C. to A.D. 220* (Ithaca, N.Y.: Cornell University Press, 1977).

103. For the issue of the status of knowledge in the Plotinian One, see esp. *Enneads*, 3.9.9, 5.4.1, and 5.4.2. In these texts Plotinus denies knowledge insofar as it points to a subject-object bifurcation, a distinction between the act of thinking and what is thought. It is the hypostasis of the Nous that bears the burden of this form of knowledge, and Nous is ontologically posterior to the One. Nevertheless, having denied knowledge of this kind to the One, Plotinus feels obliged to speculate whether the One has a special form of self-knowing, and speaks of the One having a perception (*synaisthesis*) of itself, and forms of knowing that are other than the subject-object type, thus a *katanoesis*, and higher than that of the subject-object type, thus a *hypernoesis*. For a fine discussion of this problem in Plotinus, see John Rist, *Plotinus: The Road to Reality*, pp. 38–64.

104. For a discussion of *tolma*, see Arthur Hilary Armstrong, "Dualism: Platonic, Gnostic, and Christian," p. 45; also Bazán, "The 'Second God' in Gnosticism and Plotinus's Anti-Gnostic Polemic," p. 62.

105. See, for example, *Enneads*, 5.2.4 where the One is said to be without need.

106. For this point, see Kenney, "The Platonism of the Tripartite Tractate," p. 196.

107. The continuity motif is even more conspicuous in Proclus than it is in Plotinus and is calibrated by the principles of remaining, procession, and reversion. See *The Elements of Theology*, trans. E. R. Dodds, 2nd ed. (London: Faber and Faber, 1969). For a good reflection on Proclus's articulation of procession-return, see Stephen Gersh, *From Iamblichus to Eriugena: An Investigation of the Prehistory and Evolution of the Pseudo-Dionysian Tradition* (Leiden, Germany: Brill, 1978).

108. Of course, in the *Symposium*, *eros* is defined as the coincidence of *penia* and *poros*, or lack and fullness, the latter in so far as fullness is aimed at, the former in so far as *eros* signifies that one is not in possession of what is desired.

109. As we have pointed out on more than one occasion, Plotinus's definition of Platonism is clearly a prophylactic against various kinds of combination of Platonic philosophy and philosophical myth of which Numenius, perhaps, supplies the best but not necessarily the only example. See part I, notes 72, 122; part II, notes 98–101.

110. See in particular, George McRae, "Apocalyptic Eschatology in Gnosticism," in *Apocalypticism in the Mediterranean World and the Near East*, ed. David Hellholm (Tübingen, Germany: Mohr, 1983), pp. 317–29; Henri I. Marrou, "La théologie de l'histoire dans la gnose valentinienne," in *The Origins of Gnosticism*, ed. U. Bianchi (Leiden, Germany: Brill, 1967), pp. 215–26; also Walter Schmithals, *The Apocalyptic Movement: Introduction and Interpretation*, trans. John E. Steely (Nashville, Tenn.: Abingdon Press, 1975), pp. 89–110. Of course, earlier scholars of Gnosticism such as Jonas also saw a connection between apocalyptic and Gnosticism. See Jonas, *Gnosis und spätantiker Geist*, vol. 1, pp. 5–7.

111. See Dawson, *Allegorical Readers and Cultural Revision in Ancient Alexandria*, pp. 127–70.

112. Henri Charles Puech is the classic example of a scholar who makes an antithesis of apocalyptic and Gnosticism. The case was first made in his famous essay, "Le Gnose et le temps," in *Eranos-Jahrbuch* 20 (1951): 57–113. Puech's position is a major influence in Bloom's "Lying against Time," in *The Rediscovery of Gnosticism*, vol. 1, pp. 57–72.

113. See McRae, "Apocalyptic Eschatology in Gnosticism," p. 319, where McRae examines *The Origin of the World* (12.6) and the *Trimorphic Protennoia* (62) as well as *PSY* for eschatological signs.

114. Ithamar Gruenwald is one scholar who makes this point quite strongly. See his *Apocalyptic and Merkavah Mysticism* (Leiden, Germany: Brill, 1980).

115. This uniqueness was brought seriously into question by McRae and Schmithals in particular. See McRae, "Apocalyptic Eschatology in Gnosticism," p. 323; and Schmithals, *The Apocalyptic Movement*, pp. 95, 102.

116. This theology of history centers around the seed of Seth as constituting a sacred line.

117. As indicated in note 112, Puech's 'Le Gnose et le temps" is a major source for Bloom's view of the Gnostic sense of time in "Lying against Time." Puech might also be an interpretive influence in Bloom's drawing of the important distinction between radical Gnostic and nonradical Neoplatonic interpretive strategies. See his "Plotin et les Gnostiques," in *Les Sources de Plotin* (Geneva: Fondation Hardt, 1960).

118. Schmithals picks out the *Apocalypse of Adam* for particular mention. See *The Apocalyptic Movement*, p. 102.

119. I will pay particular attention to Novalis's *Hymns to Night*, as well as his reading in the theosophic tradition and particularly of Boehme.

120. For a brief but lucid account of the interplay between von Baader's and Schelling's thought, see Thomas F. O'Meara, *Romantic Idealism and Roman Catholicism: Schelling and the Theologians* (Notre Dame, Ind.: University of Notre Dame Press, 1982), pp. 77–89. As O'Meara shows well, influence is at least two way, with von Baader influencing Schelling just as much as Schelling influences von Baader. Indeed, von Baader plays a role in making Boehme an important figure for the work of the later Schelling. We will articulate this relationship in detail in our volume on Schelling in this genealogy. The work of Anton Günther shows the most persistent (more than 35 years) and most comprehensive positive influence of Hegel in Catholic theological thought in the nineteenth century. The influence of Hegel on Staudenmaier is just about as great, although for the second part of his career (1840–1856), Staudenmaier is involved in one of the most comprehensive and vitriolic critiques of Hegel by a religious thinker in the nineteenth century. For an excellent account of the dependence of Günther on Hegel, see Christoph Kronable, *Die Aufhebung der Begriffsphilosophie: Anton Günther und der Pantheismus* (Freiburg, Switzerland: Verlag Karl Alber, 1989).

121. See Jean-Paul Sartre, *The Family Idiot: Gustave Flaubert, 1821–1857*.

122. These are only two of the more conspicuous of the many inadequacies of the orthodox position. The full gamut of perceived inadequacies

are discussed at length in my *Gnostic Apocalypse: Jacob Boehme's Haunted Narrative*. Here I mention, however, that Boehme and his precursors are reacting also against the lack of explanatory capability in mainline Reformation thought, particularly Lutheran thought. For them, comprehension of the divine-world, divine-human relations are a sine qua non. The origin and nature of evil in particular have to be explained. It turns out that, as in the case of classical Gnosticism, this explanation or theory takes the form of a second-order or reflective myth.

123. As I point out in *Gnostic Apocalypse*, whereas Boehme has many sixteenth-century precursors with respect to a pneumatic and apocalyptic exacerbation of Reformation thought, he has relatively few precursors with regard to the comprehensive metalepsis enacted in and by his speculative system. Andrew Weeks has plotted the general ideational conditions for Boehme's thought in his *Boehme: An Intellectual Biography of the Seventeenth-Century Philosopher and Mystic* (Albany: SUNY Press, 1991). My own interest, however, is in plotting the ways in which Boehme continues and develops the metaleptic line of thought begun in Paracelsus and continued through Valentin Weigel.

124. I am here in essential agreement with Frei's *The Eclipse of Biblical Narrative*.

125. The *Lectures on the Philosophy of Religion* represent Hegel's most extended and discursive engagement with Protestant thought. While Hegel suggests that scripture cannot justify doctrine, but rather doctrine must justify it, there is copious citation of scripture, and extended discussion of biblical themes such as sin, the passion and death of Christ and the kingdom of God. Needless to say, the rehabilitation of doctrine is not an end in itself. Hegel thinks not only that many doctrines are found wanting even given their own communal and traditional standards, but also that all doctrines, those that concern the Trinity as well as those that concern Christ and creation, have to be brought up to intellectual code. This involves what Emil Fackenheim has called the speculative transfiguration of representation (*Vorstellung*). See Fackenheim, *The Religious Dimension of Hegel's Thought* (Bloomington: Indiana University Press, 1967), pp. 160–215. See also O'Regan, *The Heterodox Hegel*, pp. 327–70, esp. 454–64. For a development and modification of the view elaborated in *The Heterodox Hegel*, see Cyril O'Regan, "Hegel and the Folds of Discourse," in *International Philosophical Quarterly*, 39 (1999): 173–93.

126. Hegel uses this particular expression to point to the fact of conflict of interpretations, but also their inevitability, in *Lectures on the Philosophy of Religion*, vol. 1 (1824 lectures), p. 123. This colorful expression, however, is not his own. Hegel borrows it proximally from Lessing and, as Hodgson points out in his note (30) to the translation, the expression dates back to the twelfth-century theologian, Alain de Lille.

127. This speculative spiritual wing had its origin but not its term in Jacob Boehme. Among others, David Walsh has brought out the historical links as well as symbolic connections between Hegel and Boehme. My own *The Heterodox Hegel* attempted to bring out the systematic links that are based on narrative. Nevertheless, as important as the historical Boehme is, equally important is a Swabian line of discourse continued into the eighteenth century by Oetinger. Although one cannot be sure whether Hegel read Oetinger or, if so, how much he read, Oetinger's retrieval of Boehme and his attempt to use a speculative theology to critique rationalist philosophy and a theology based on the letter represented a kind of template for Hegel's own enterprise. I will have much more to say about Oetinger in *Gnostic Apocalypse* and also the volume on Hegel.

128. See, for example, *Lectures on the Philosophy of Religion*, vol. 1 (1824 Lectures), p. 147. See also my discussion of Hegelian theodicy in *The Heterodox Hegel*, pp. 310–26.

129. The agenda of the genealogy of *Die christliche Gnosis*, which is to trace synoptically an alternative line of thought to orthodoxy, essentially prohibits discussion as to how deviant this line of discourse is relative to orthodoxy. In principle, this is not the case in *Die christliche Lehre von der Dreieinigkeit* because, as a work in the history of dogma, it is impossible to avoid portraying, and even commenting on, the difference between what has been taken to be orthodox and excluded as heterodox.

130. See Bloom's "Lying against Time," p. 257 ff.

131. In the fourth volume in the Gnostic return project, titled *Deranging Narrative: Romanticism and its Gnostic Limit*, out of the welter of Blake's Prophetic Poems that includes *America, Asia*, and *The Four Zoas*, I will focus on these three poems to make my case that in Blake, as in no other Romantic writer, the relatively common subversion of key elements of the Christian narrative becomes systematic, thus metaleptic in the strict sense.

132. The Reformation view of Catholicism as a fall in or of Christianity is assimilated, even if tonally modified, in texts such as *Lectures on the Philosophy of History* and *Lectures on the Philosophy of Religion*. Hegel thinks of Catholic Christianity as a deformation of the essence of Christianity. He, and later Baur, however, go beyond the Reformation view in thinking that this essence is only a promise in the apostolic period, a promise that is only fully realized in the Reformation.

133. Arguably, August Tholuck was the most famous of these evangelical theologians who saw the doctrine of the Trinity as at best a decoration of evangelical faith and at worst a pure deformation brought about by an illicit borrowing of the resources of philosophy, especially Hellenistic philosophy. The former view is expressed in his *Die Lehre von der Sünde und vom Versöhner*, 2nd ed. (Hamburg, Germany: Perthes, 1825). The latter is ex-

pressed in his *Die speculative Trinitätslehre des späteren Orients* (Berlin: Dümmler, 1826). As Peter Hodgson points out, Tholuck is one of the theologians whose position on the Trinity Hegel contests. See Hodgson's note in *Lectures on the Philosophy of Religion*, vol. 1 (1827 Lectures), p. 157.

134. For a full discussion of Hegel's view of the excess of end over origin and its priority with respect to defining the essence of Christianity, see O'Regan, *The Heterodox Hegel*, pp. 245–49.

135. For a treatment of the Reformation as being for Hegel the originary and founding event of modernity, and not the Enlightenment, nor the French Revolution, see Cyril O'Regan, "The Religious and Theological Relevance of the French Revolution," in *Hegel on the Modern World*, ed. Ardis B. Collins (Albany: SUNY Press, 1995), pp. 29–52, esp. pp. 41–47.

136. See O'Regan, *The Heterodox Hegel*, pp. 245–49.

137. See O'Regan, "The Religious and Theological Relevance of the French Revolution," pp. 39–48.

138. See Ferdinand Christian Baur, *The Church History of the First Three Centuries*, trans. Allan Menzies, 2 vols., 3rd ed. (London: Williams and Northgate, 1878–1879). In volume 2, Gnosticism is characterized as being vigorous and energetic with an abundance of creative power (pp. 1–4). By contrast, emerging orthodoxy, especially on its Latin side (Tertullian and Irenaeus), is regarded as dogmatic and ultimately hierarchical. Interestingly this characterization differs very little from the one provided by Elaine Pagels among other champions of Gnosticism in recent years.

139. See Ferdinand Christian Baur, *Die christliche Lehre von der Dreieinigkeit und Menchwerdung Gottes in ihrer geschichtlichen Entwicklung*, vol. 3, *Die neuere Geschichte des Dogma, von der Reformation bis in der neueste Zeit* (Tübingen, Germany: Osiander, 1843), pp. 881–897.

140. For Staudenmaier, see esp. his *Zum religiösen Frieden der Zukunft, mit Rücksicht auf die religiös-politische Aufgabe der Gegenwart*, 3 vols. (Tübingen, Germany, Minerva, 1846–1851), vol. 3, pp. 116–37. The Reformation appropriation of Joachim has been covered well in the secondary literature by among others Marjorie Reeves and de Lubac. For Reeves, see *Joachim of Fiore and the Prophetic Future* (London: SPCK, 1977). A very important text by Robin Barnes, which emphasizes the connection between Joachim and the Reformation while tracing the general continuity of apocalyptic thought in Lutheranism throughout the latter half of the sixteenth century, is *Prophecy and Gnosis: Apocalypticism in the Wake of the Lutheran Reformation* (Stanford, Calif.: Stanford University Press, 1988).

141. For *The Book of Two Principles*, or *Liber duobus principiis*, dating from the thirteenth century, see *Écritures Cathares*, ed. René Nelli (Paris:

Éditions Planète, 1968). Much good work has been done on Cathar theology in general, *The Book of Two Principles* in particular.

142. This lack of metalepsis essentially disqualifies Catharism from Gnostic attribution, if by Gnostic one means something as determinate as the Valentinian or Sethian systems. Hans Söderberg is a scholar who has braved a Gnostic attribution, but without tying it exclusively to a particular Gnostic system. See his *La religion des cathares: Étude sur le gnosticisme de la basse antiquité et du moyen âge* (Uppsala, Sweden: Almqvist and Wiksells, 1949). Steven Runciman also suggests that Catharism and its historical precursors in Eastern Europe might be regarded as Gnostic, a judgment all the more surprising because it is prosecuted in a book whose thesis is that Catharism, which is fed by the Bogomils ideology of Rumania, is neo-Manichaean. See Runciman, *The Medieval Manichee: A Study of the Christian Dualist Heresy* (Cambridge, England: Cambridge University Press, 1947), p. 22.

143. In addition to Runciman's classic *The Medieval Manichee*, see Dimitri Obolensky and Milan Loos, both of whom avail of the categories of Manichaean or neo-Manichaean in their connecting of the Cathars with the Bogomils. For Obolensky, see *The Bogomils: A Study in Balkan Neo-Manichaeism* (Cambridge, England: Cambridge University Press, 1948). For Loos, see *Dualistic Heresy in the Middle Ages* (Prague: Academia, 1974).

144. See *Exégèse médiévale: Les quatre sens de l'écriture*, 4 vols. (Paris: Aubier, 1959–1964).

145. In his own day Baur's position was contested by Catholic theologians. Möhler contested both Baur's reading of the early church and his favoring of the Gnostics over the emergent institutional church, and his favoring of the Protestant principle over the institutional and doctrinal orientation of Catholicism. In his great work *Symbolik* (1834), Möhler argued that the Protestant principle leads to sectarianism and ultimately secularization because a fragmented church is a church in dissolution. As we have seen in part I, Staudenmaier seems to accept the basic lines of Baur's narrative of Gnostic return only to change the value in every instance.

146. For a discussion of Eckhart and the perceived problems of this thought from a theological point of view, see Cyril O'Regan, "Balthasar and Eckhart: Theological Principles and Catholicity," in *Thomist* 60 (1996): 203–39.

147. In *De divisione naturae*, for example, Eriugena is anxious to underscore the distinction between the uncreated and created, even if at times the distinction seems to hug very close to the Platonic distinction between the immutable and the mutable.

148. The relevant information for Möhler and Staudenmaier is contained in part I, notes 10 and 11.

149. It is important to underscore theology here. Were I to enlarge the canvas and include Catholic literature, then matters might get more complicated. In part I, I mentioned how Milosc raises the Gnosticism question with respect to Eastern European Catholic authors of the nineteenth and twentieth centuries.

150. In a later volume I will not only exonerate Balthasar from the Gnostic charge, but argue that, if any contemporary theologian justifies the label of *Irenaeus redivivus*, it is he.

151. But *systemic* does not mean absolutely actual here. For Catholicism is still in development, and one cannot rule out that in the future Catholicism might itself show signs of Gnostic return. If such happened, one hypothesizes that the sedimented languages of the Baurian line would play a significant role.

152. See *Summa Theologiae* 1 a Q 14, arts. 4, 12.

153. See Hegel, *Lectures on the History of Philosophy*, vol. 2, pp. 394–96.

154. For a discussion of this point, see O'Regan, *The Heterodox Hegel*, pp. 31–44.

155. In making this assessment Hegel not only represents an Idealist development of Kant, but also links up with forms of thought as different as those of Spinoza and the Christian mystical tradition. For instance, the notion of the intellectual love of God, which figures so prominently in Book 5 of Spinoza's *Ethics*, is clearly pertinent, as is the mystical thought of Eckhart. For a treatment of the relation between Hegel and Eckhart, see Cyril O'Regan, "Hegelian Philosophy of Religion and Eckhartian Mysticism," in *New Perspectives on Hegel's Philosophy of Religion*, ed. David Kolb (Albany: SUNY Press, 1992), pp. 109–29.

156. For a full account of the Unground as origin, see chapter 1 of *Gnostic Apocalypse: Jacob Boehme's Haunted Narrative*. Almost all Boehme scholars agree on the pivotal role this symbol plays in his thought. These scholars include Nicholas Berdyaev and Alexandre Koyré. For Berdyaev, see "Unground and Freedom," in *Six Theosophic Points*, trans. John Rolleston Earle (Ann Arbor: University of Michigan Press, 1958), v–xxxvii. For Koyré, see *La philosophie de Jacob Boehme* (Paris: Vrin, 1929).

157. *Mysterium Magnum* is Boehme's two-volume interpretation of Genesis written in 1622. As is typical of most of Boehme's works of the period from 1620 to his death in 1624, this text contains copious reflection on the Unground, and how the quiescent Unground moves toward definition,

determination, and life. Other major texts that feature prominently the Unground include *De Signatura Rerum* (1621) and *De electione gratiae* (1623).

158. The philosopher Michel Henry has been particularly struck by this point and thinks that it separates Boehme from Eckhart because it joins him to Hegel. See *The Essence of Manifestation*, trans. Girard Etzkorn (The Hague: Nijhoff, 1973), pp. 108 ff.

159. See Harold Bloom, *The Visionary Company.: A Reading of English Romantic Poetry* (Ithaca, N.Y.: Cornell University Press, 1961), pp. 7–123; David V. Erdman, *Blake: Prophet Against Empire* (New York: Doubleday, 1969), and *The New Apocalypse: The Radical Christian View of William Blake* (East Lansing: Michigan State University Press, 1967); Northrop Frye, *A Study of William Blake* (Princeton, N.J.: Princeton University Press, 1969), pp. 30–56. The most concentrated treatment of the relation of Blake to biblical apocalyptic is provided by Joseph Anthony Wittreich, Jr. See his *Angel of Apocalypse: Blake's Idea of Milton* (Madison: University of Wisconsin Press, 1975).

160. Altizer believes that it is the theological reading that in and of itself differentiates his *The New Apocalypse: The Radical Christian Vision of William Blake* (East Lansing: Michigan State University Press, 1967) from all other works on Blake. (See *GA*, p. 108). In fact, however, it is more nearly the *type* of theological reading that distinguishes Altizer. Other kinds of theological interpretation have been proffered. Indeed, however counterintuitive, Blake has been read as a quintessentially orthodox thinker. See, for example, J. G. Davies, *The Theology of William Blake* (Oxford, England: Clarendon Press, 1948).

161. These are the famous first four lines of *Auguries of Innocence*. See *Blake's Poetry and Designs*, ed. Mary Lynn Johnson and John E. Grant (New York: Norton, 1979), p. 209.

162. Moltmann's critique of impassibility, as indicating a Hellenistic cooption of the biblical message, is to the fore in *The Crucified God* and *The Trinity and the Kingdom*.

163. Hegel is the common thread between *The Crucified God* and *Trinity and the Kingdom* despite the fact that one of the purposes of the latter text is to correct Hegel's impersonal trinitarianism.

164. See Emilio Brito, *La christologie de Hegel: Verbum Crucis* (Paris: Beauchesne, 1983). For a quite differently expressed, but similar view, see Iwan Iljin, *Die Philosophie Hegels als kontemplative Gotteslehre* (Berne, Switzerland: Franke, 1946).

165. The contrast between *agape* and *eros* in pivotal in the thought of William Desmond, one of whose concerns is to construct an alternative to an erotic metaphysics, that is, a metaphysics that suggests that reality is a

movement of self-realization that depends on an initial lack that is gradually overcome. Contrasted with this view is the view that the origin is not indigent, but superabundantly full, and that the going forth is the excess or generosity of the origin that is without need. Reality does not become. A corollary is that if philosophy is to think God, God does not become. The most mature statement of Desmond's position is to be found in *Being and the Between* (Albany: SUNY Press, 1995), pp. 63, 157, 160, 246–49, 260. For Desmond, Hegel represents the apogee of erotic metaphysics. Resistance has to be especially emphatic here.

166. See John Milbank, "Can a Gift be Given," in *Modern Theology* 11 (1995): 119–61.

167. I am here evoking Milan Kundera's *The Unbearable Lightness of Being*, trans. Michael Henry Heim (New York: Harper and Row, 1984).

168. See part I, note 2.

169. Texts of Hegel in which *Sittlichkeit* is important include *The System of Ethical Life* (1802–1803), the *Phenomenology* (#444–83), the *Encyclopedia* (#513–52), *The Philosophy of Right* (#142–360), and *Lectures on the Philosophy of Religion*, vol. 3 (1827) E 252, 341–42. For a lucid account of *Sittlichkeit* and its contrast with *Moralität*, see Charles Taylor, *Hegel* (Cambridge: Cambridge University Press, 1975), pp. 365–88. For the two most developed accounts, see Robert R. Williams, *Hegel's Ethics of Recognition* (Berkeley: University of California Press, 1997), and Allen W. Wood, *Hegel's Ethical Thought* (Cambridge, England: Cambridge University Press, 1990).

170. For a discussion of Hegel's view of history as theodicy and its critique, see O'Regan, *The Heterodox Hegel*, pp. 310–26.

171. These texts of the late and so-called positive philosophy of Schelling will be treated in detail in a later volume in the series. These texts, which eventually provoked the ire of Kierkegaard, have fared much better in theology than in philosophy. The works of the late Schelling continue to be read by German theologians in their attempt to forge a theology-philosophy rapprochement. Tillich gave them currency in Protestant thought at the beginning of the twentieth century by writing two dissertations on Schelling that featured these texts. See *Mysticism and Guilt-Consciousness in Schelling's Philosophical Development*, trans. and introd. Victor Nuovo (Lewisburg, Pa.: Bucknell University Press, 1974), and *The Construction of the History of Religion in Schelling's Positive Philosophy*, trans. Victor Nuovo (Lewisburg, Pa.: Bucknell University Press, 1974).

172. This unhappiness is at the root of the vitalist, mythic turn taken as early as 1809 and represented by the essay *On Human Freedom*. This text and texts from the same period such as the *Stuttgart Lectures* (1811) and *The Ages of the World* (1815) break decisively with Hegel, though it is

arguably only in the work of the 1840s that Schelling finally settles on a logical immanentist interpretation of Hegel. The clearest account of what divides Schelling from Hegel is provided by Schelling himself. See his critique of Hegel's philosophy as negative and epistemological rather than truly positive and ontological in *On the History of Modern Philosophy*, trans. and introd. Andrew Bowie (Cambridge, England: Cambridge University Press, 1994), pp. 134–63, also introd., pp. 23–35. We will have a great deal more to say about this vitalist, mythic turn in a later volume, which we hope will show a mastery of the voluminous secondary literature on the post-transcendental Idealist Schelling. An important ingredient of this account is the relation between Schelling and Jacob Boehme. The classic study still remains Robert F. Brown, *The Later Philosophy of Schelling: The Influence of Boehme on the Works of 1809–1815* (Lewisburg, Pa.: Bucknell University Press, 1977).

173. This point, for instance, is central in the work of Alan White and Walter Schulz. See Alan White, *Schelling: An Introduction to the System of Freedom* (New Haven, Conn.: Yale University Press, 1983), and *Absolute Knowledge: Hegel and the Problem of Metaphysics* (Athens: Ohio University Press, 1983); Walter Schulz, *Vollendung des deutschen Idealismus in der Spätphilosophie Schellings*, 2ⁿᵈ ed. (Pfullingen, Germany: Neske, 1975).

174. The epistemological turn in England can be dated from Locke's *An Essay Concerning Human Understanding* at the end of the seventeenth century. The conflict about what is known leads Locke to reflect upon the apparatus of knowing and what can be known with certitude, probability, or not at all. Many of the more important topics about which human beings constantly fight—for example, those of politics and religion—do not admit certitude. Locke, of course, resists the skeptical conclusion that Hume will later draw. By contrast, the epistemological turn in Germany occurs in the latter part of the eighteenth century and can be dated from the first appearance of Kant's *The Critique of Pure Reason*, which represents Kant's response to Hume.

175. Blake made no secret that Lockean epistemology was both cause and symptom of what was wrong, socially, politically, and artistically, at the end of the eighteenth and beginning of the nineteenth century. By reducing human knowing to the senses, Lockean epistemology denied a power of knowing recognized by both the religious and the philosophical traditions. This transdiscursive power, associated in Blake with imagination, was the condition of the elevation of human being to the divine. For as knowledge goes, so does being. A particularly strong expression of Blake's hostility to Locke is to be found in Blake's great epic, *Jerusalem*. See Book 1.15, 11–6; Book 2.30, 40; Book 3.54, 16–17. Although Blake has been submitted to widely variant interpretations, almost every scholar of Blake from S. Foster Damon and Northrop Frye through Harold Bloom, David V. Erdman,

Morton D. Paley, Donald Ault, and Thomas Altizer to contemporary students of Blake emphasize this ideological resistance.

176. See *The Everlasting Gospel* 4.104.

177. See Blumenberg, *Work on Myth*; Ernst Cassirer, *The Myth of the State* (New Haven, Conn.: Yale University Press, 1946).

178. See O'Regan, *The Heterodox Hegel*, chap. 6, pp. 287–326.

179. See O'Regan, *The Heterodox Hegel*, chap. 7, pp. 327–70. See also O'Regan, "Hegel and the Folds of Discourse."

180. This position is suggested in *The City of God*, Book 22.1.

181. Obviously, in a text such as *Bruno* (1802), the Neoplatonic elements are conspicuous because the last of the great Renaissance Neoplatonists, Giordano Bruno, is recalled as offering a metaphysics that is superior to that found in Fichte. Although a major upheaval in Schelling's thought did occur at the end of the decade in which *Bruno* was written, and on the face of it, the voluntarist turn in Schelling's thought takes him far from the intellectualist paradigm of Neoplatonism, Beierwaltes and others have maintained that it continues to persist even within the later phases of Schelling's thought in his recall of the Indifference Point and in his appeal to the authority of Plotinus and Proclus. Throughout the period from 1815 to 1840, Schelling remained enthusiastic about the thought of Plotinus and Proclus, as Beierwaltes in particular has underscored. See his *Platonismus und Idealismus*, pp. 103 ff.

182. See especially Gersh, *From Iamblichus to Eriugena*. This is also the view of Werner Beierwaltes.

183. Blumenberg, *The Legitimacy of the Modern Age*, pp. 485–548. The position is also supported by Louis Dupré. See his *Passage to Modernity: An Essay in the Hermeneutics of Nature and Culture* (New Haven, Conn.: Yale University Press, 1993), pp. 59–62, 186–202.

184. See O'Regan, *The Heterodox Hegel*, pp. 191–201.

185. See Georges Bataille, *Theory of Religion*, trans. Robert Hurley (New York: Zone Books, 1989), pp. 43–61. See also his *Inner Experience*, trans. and introd. Leslie Anne Boldt (Albany: SUNY Press, 1988), pp. 51–61, 101–11. In the latter text, *sacrifice* has been made into an epistemological principle and, as nonknowledge, competes with, and plays the role of an obstacle to, Hegelian knowledge.

186. By *biblical* I mean to include not only such texts as Daniel and Revelation, but also texts such as *Fourth Ezra* and *First Enoch*, which never came to be regarded as canonical within mainline Christian confessions. These latter biblical apocalyptic forms not only throw light on the *eidos* of

biblical apocalyptic, but have had considerable influence in the apocalyptic tradition.

187. It should be noted that if some scholars accept an apocalyptic designation of the work of Joachim, others do not. Bernard McGinn, for example, has no difficulty speaking of Joachim's work itself as a form of apocalyptic. This is reflected in his inclusion of texts from Joachim in his volume titled *Apocalyptic Spirituality* (New York: Paulist Press, 1979). McGinn provides an *apocalyptic* ascription in full knowledge of the secondary and interpretive character of Joachim's work. His *The Calabrian Abbot: Joachim of Fiore in the History of Western Thought* (New York: Macmillan, 1985) makes this point well. On the other side, the great Joachim scholar Marjorie Reeves demurs, thinking that the secondary and hermeneutical character of Joachim's work makes him a philosopher of history rather than a bona fide apocalyptic thinker. See her *The Influence of Prophecy in the Later Middle Ages: A Study in Joachimism* (Oxford, England: Clarendon Press, 1969), and *Joachim of Fiore and the Prophetic Future*.

188. See especially, Staudenmaier, *Zum religiösen Frieden der Zukunft*, vol. 3, pp. 109–74; also *Darstellung und Kritik des Hegelschen Systems*; *Die Philosophe des Christenthums*, pp. 798–810.

189. Staudenmaier intended to formulate a more traditional trinitarian alternative in his dogmatic theology. For a good discussion of his own counterproposal, see Karl Reith, *Die Gotteslehre bei Franz Anton Staudenmaier* (Berne, Switzerland: Lang, 1974), pp. 98–140, 162–89.

190. See O'Regan, *The Heterodox Hegel*, pp. 132–40.

191. Interestingly, in his discussion of Sabellian trinitarianism, Altizer seems to collapse Joachim of Fiore with Hegel, thereby ignoring the Augustinian trinitarian background of Joachim and failing to note that Joachim has an immanent Trinity/economic Trinity distinction that is not found in Hegel. But then with Barth, Augustine's trinitarianism is, for Altizer, a bête noire.

192. With regard to Gnosticism Blumenberg writes in *Work on Myth*: "A ceremonious conceptual iconoclasm is carried out, immediately after which the overthrow and prohibition are extensively disregarded. In addition, the pluralism of powers must be restored, which sets in motion the telling of a story. In dogma, the One is offered as the Ultimate; but stories cannot be told about it, unless were a story about how it ceased to be the One. The dilemma of the history of Christian dogma lies in its having to define a Trinitarian God from the plurality of which no licence [*sic*] for myth is allowed to follow" (p. 260).

193. Scholars from the time of Scholem on have accepted that these are watermark texts. There has been some disagreement about dating, with *Sefer ha-Bahir* being variously dated as twelfth or thirteenth century. There is no dispute that the *Sefer Yetzirah* is somewhat earlier.

194. Neoplatonism becomes possible only as an explanatory factor with respect to classical Kabbalah, and indeed there are resemblances to Neoplatonism with respect to a dynamic movement from the divine that looks quite Neoplatonic, as does the succession of worlds that differentially reflect the divine. And, of course, significant overlaps exist in terms of images of the divine as light and what constitutes union with this divine.

195. I will chart the trajectory in some detail in my next volume on Gnostic return, *Gnostic Apocalypse*. A brief account of this trajectory is offered in O'Regan, "Hegel and Anti-Judaism: Narrative and the Inner Circulation of the Kabbalah," in *The Owl of Minerva* 28 (1997): 141–82, esp. pp. 168–69.

196. One could suggest that by comparison with the Christian Kabbalah of Florence, the Christian Kabbalah in its German trajectory shows considerable more impact by the Lurianic Kabbalah. I argue this case in the volumes on Boehme and Hegel that follow this programmatic essay.

197. See Hans Jonas, *The Gnostic Religion*, p. 323.

198. See especially the introduction to Book 2 of *Jerusalem*, which is entitled "Against the Jews." What is attacked here is the sovereign lawgiver of the Bible, who is shown to be capricious, jealous, and unethical in his absolute yet vague transcendence. What is proposed instead is a God who is neither absolutely transcendent nor sovereign. This God, who is not separable from human being, is at once definite and immanent. In stressing the latter, Blake seems to suggest a connection between the "human form divine" and Adam Kadmon. I will have much more to say on this issue in the volume on Romanticism and Gnostic return. But it should be said in passing that Blake's use of the Adam Kadmon trope to upset a biblical misinterpretation (Jewish) is not confined to *Jerusalem*. It can also be clearly seen in *Milton*. See *Milton* 2.3–4 where the divine-human imagination has the contour of the human body, indeed, the perfect body associated with the name of Jesus. Here one can see not Christian cooption of the Adam Kadmon symbol, but its explicit enlisting against Torah Judaism.

199. Hegel's most virulent critique of Judaism as a religion that validates the transcendent and juridical God at the expense of human beings and their spiritual potential is to be found in his earliest, unpublished work. See his "The Spirit of Christianity and its Fate," in *Early Theological Writings*, trans. T. M. Knox (Chicago: University of Chicago Press, 1948), pp. 181–301. As both Peter Hodgson and Eric van der Luft have correctly pointed out, Hegel does later qualify his critique. See Hodgson, "The

Metamorphosis of Judaism in Hegel's Philosophy of Religion," in *The Owl of Minerva* 19 (1987): 41–52; van der Luft, "Hegel and Judaism: A Reassessment," in *Clio* 18 (1989): 361–78. See also O'Regan, "Hegel and Anti-Judaism."

200. For Hegel's express treatment of the Kabbalah, see *Lectures on the History of Philosophy*, vol. 2, pp. 394–96. The connection between Hegel and the Kabbalah goes deeper than this surprising recall, which may have something to do with the established conventions in the history of philosophy of the time. As I argue in "Hegel and Anti-Judaism," Kabbalistic modes of thought appear to be enlisted against forms of religious thought, Judaism and modern species of Christianity above all, that commit themselves to a sovereign, transcendent God.

201. After Ezekiel's vision of the chariot or throne, for Blake there are four living creatures or *Zoas*. In his personal mythology, which draws upon a variety of esoteric sources, they are given the names of Luvah, Urizen, Tharmas, and Urthona. These four *Zoas* constitute the realm of divine perfection as neither simple nor trinitarian, but quaternarian, a point that Jung, for instance, took pleasure in pointing out. The scholar who has made most of this point is S. Foster Damon. See his *William Blake: His Philosophy and Symbols* (Boston: Houghton Mifflin, 1924).

202. In *Erring: A Postmodern A/theology* (Chicago: University of Chicago Press, 1984), for instance, Mark C. Taylor thinks of the Bible as *the* book, where the book renders the ultimate plot. In one sense, Taylor's interpretation corresponds fairly closely to Irenaeus's view of the Bible as canon that plots the history of God's salvific acts. Taylor distinguishes himself from Irenaeus, however, in thinking that the plot rendered is self-legitimated. But, for Irenaeus, legitimation is only for a community of faith that trusts in the Bible as God's word. The authority of the text is predicated on this trust. Irenaeus distrusts discourses that are self-legitimating. But the discourse that has this property is Gnostic or Valentinian.

Index